ASIAN STUDIES ASSOCIATION OF AUSTRALIA
Southeast Asia Publications Series

No. 21
Business and Politics in Indonesia

D0140920

BUSINESS AND POLITICS IN INDONESIA

ANDREW MACINTYRE

Asian Studies Association of Australia
in association with
ALLEN & UNWIN

First published in 1991
Second impression 1992
Allen & Unwin Pty Ltd
8 Napier Street, North Sydney, NSW 2059 Australia

National Library of Australia
Cataloguing-in-publication entry:

MacIntyre, Andrew, 1960–   .
  Business & politics in Indonesia.

  Bibliography.
  ISBN 0 04 442330 6.

  1. Business and politics—Indonesia. 2. Indonesia—Politics
and government—1966–   . 3. Indonesia—Economic conditions
—1945–   . I. Asian Studies Association of Australia. II. Title.
(Series: Southeast Asian publications series; no. 21).

322.309598

Typeset by Vera-Reyes Inc, Manila

Printed in Singapore by Chong Moh Offset Printing Pte Ltd

Contents

v

For all the J.s

Preface

This is a study of politics and political change in contemporary Indonesia. It has two basic aims: first, to cast light on some of the processes and mechanisms of government in Indonesia, and second, to argue that changes underway in Indonesia raise questions concerning the validity of generally accepted ideas about the Indonesian political system. A widely shared view holds that political life in Indonesia is overwhelmingly dominated by the state, with policy-making processes being subject to tight control. The basic argument of this book is that this simple image is becoming steadily less satisfactory as sections of society come to demand—and attain—greater input to the formation of policy. Two decades of rapid economic development have had a major political impact on Indonesian society, and new political 'winners' and 'losers' have been created. The focus of this study is on the way in which some elements of the business sector have developed new political capabilities which have enabled them to project their demands with much greater effectiveness.

Much of the research for this book was carried out in Indonesia during 1986–1987. Inevitably, I have incurred a large number of debts. My initial research in Indonesia was sponsored by the Indonesian Institute of Sciences (LIPI), and the Centre for Strategic and International Studies in Jakarta was generous in making its facilities available to me as well as offering much encouragement. Numerous individual Indonesians were very generous with their time, advice and friendship. Special mention must be given to (alphabetically) Kusnanto Anggoro, Soedjati Djiwandono, Derry Habir, Dorodjatun Kuntjoro-Jakti, Mohammed Sadli, Sjahrir, Hadi Soesastro and Thee Kian Wie. Beyond this, countless people in government, business, and press circles—many of whom would prefer anonymity here—were very patient in assisting me to gain an insight into the dynamics of political and business life in Indonesia.

I have also benefited greatly from the views and comments of a number of colleagues based mostly in Australia and the United States. Among these are Colin Brown, Rick Doner, Bob Elson, Don Emmerson, Jim Fox, Hal Hill, John Ingleson, Dan Lev, Bill Liddle, David McKendrick, Ruth McVey, Bill O'Malley, David Reeve and Dick Robison. More generally, I have gained much from the enormously stimulating intellectual environments provided by the Australian National University and, now, Griffith University. Finally, I am particularly indebted to Jamie Mackie and Harold Crouch, both for their insight into Indonesian politics and for their support and encouragement over the years.

Some of the material which appears in Chapter 3 has been published in an article entitled, 'Rethinking State-Society Relations in "New Order" Indonesia: Challenges from the Business Sector' in, Arief Budiman (ed.), *State and Civil Society in Indonesia*, Centre for Southeast Asian Studies, Monash University, Melbourne, (forthcoming) 1990; and small sections of Chapter 7 have appeared in 'Corporatism, Control and Political Change in "New Order" Indonesia' in, R.J. May and W.J. O'Malley (eds.), *Observing Change in Asia: Essays in Honour of J.A.C. Mackie*, Crawford House Press, Bathurst, 1989. In both cases I am grateful to the publishers for permission to use this material.

ANDREW MACINTYRE
May, 1990.

Tables

Figures

Glossary and Abbreviations

ABRI   *Angkatan Bersenjata Republik Indonesia* (the Armed Forces).

API   *Asosiasi Pertekstilan Indonesia* (the Indonesian Textile Association).

APSYFI   *Asosiasi Produsen Synthetic Fibre Indonesia* (the Indonesian Synthetic Fibre Makers' Association).

ASPI   *Asosiasi Industri Pemintalan Indonesia* (the Indonesian Spinners' Association).

ASPINDO   *Asosiasi Pertenunan Indonesia* (the Indonesian Weavers' Association).

BAMUNAS   *Badan Musyawarah Pengusaha Nasional Swasta* (the National Business Council).

BMAI   *Badan Musyawarah Asosiasi-Asosiasi Industri* (the Federation of Industry Associations).

BULOG   *Badan Urusan Logistik* (the National Logistics Agency).

C-5   The name given to a registration form for pharmaceutical manufacturers setting out the pharmacological and pricing details of a drug.

CBTI   *Cerat Bina Tekstil Indonesia* (the Indonesian Textile Fibre Development company).

DAI   *Dewan Asuransi Indonesia* (the Insurance Council of Indonesia).

DEIP   *Dewan Ekonomi Indonesia Pusat* (the Central
              Economic Council of Indonesia).

DEVI   *Dewan Ekonomi Veteran Indonesia* (the
              Veterans' Business Organisation).

DOEN   *Daftar Obat Esensial Nasional* (the National
              Essential Medicines List).

DOPB   *Daftar Obat Program Bersama* (the Joint
              Program Medicine List) a cooperative project to
              provide cheap medicines.

DPP   *Dewan Perusahaan dan Perniagaan* (the Council
              of Business and Trade).

DPR   *Dewan Perwakilan Rakyat* (the House of
              Representatives).

DPSN   *Dewan Perusahaan Swasta Nasional* (the
              Indonesian Business Council).

F-API   *Federasi Asosiasi Pertekstilan Indonesia* (the
              Federation of Indonesian Textile Associations—a
              precursor to API).

FITI   *Federasi Industri Tekstil Indonesia* (the
              Indonesian Textile Industry Federation).

Forum Swasta   The Private Entrepreneurs Forum.

GATT   The General Agreement of Tariffs and Trade.

GBHN   *Garis-Garis Besar Haluan Negara* (the Broad
              Outlines of State Policy).

GINSI   *Gabungan Importir Seluruh Indonesia* (the
              Indonesian Importers' Association). This is a
              descendant of KINSI.

GOLKAR   *Golongan Karya* (the state political party).

GPF   *Gabungan Pengusaha Farmasi* (the
              Pharmaceutical Association).

GPS   *Gabungan Perusahaan Sejenis* (Federation of
              Homogenous Enterprises).

HIKSI   *Himpunan Industri Kecil Seluruh Indonesia* (the
              All Indonesia Small Business Organisation).

HIPLI   *Himpunan Pengusaha Lemah Indonesia* (the
              Indonesian Weak Business Organisation).

HIPMI	*Himpunan Pengusaha Muda Indonesia* (the Indonesian Young Entrepreneurs Organisation).
HIPPI	*Himpunan Pengusaha Putra Indonesia* (the Indonesian Indigenous Entrepreneurs Organisation).
HMI	*Himpunan Mahasiswa Islam* (the Muslim Students' Association).
IDI	*Ikatan Dokter Indonesia* (the Indonesian Doctors' Association).
IHO	*Informasi Harga Obat* (Drug Price Information) a manual distributed by the Health Department to all doctors.
IMS	Index of Medical Specialties Pty Ltd (A Singapore-based medical consultants firm which produces the only recognised statistics on the pharmaceutical industry in Indonesia).
IPMG	International Pharmaceutical Manufacturers Group, a sub-section of the Indonesian Pharmaceutical Association (GPF).
ISFI	*Ikatan Sarjana Farmasi Indonesia* (the Indonesian Pharmacy Graduates' Association).
KADIN	*Kamar Dagang dan Industri* (Chamber of Trade and Industry).
KADINDA	*Kamar Dagang dan Industri Daerah* (Regional Chamber of Trade and Industry).
KAPNI	*Kesatuan Aksi Pengusaha Nasional Indonesia* (the National Business Action Front).
KENSI	*Kongres Ekonomi Nasional Seluruh Indonesia* (the All Indonesia National Economic Congress).
KINSI	*Kongres Importir Nasional Seluruh Indonesia* (the All Indonesia National Importers' Congress).
KORPRI	*Korps Pegawai Negeri* (Civil Servants' Corps).
KUKMI	*Kerukunan Usahawan Kecil dan Menengah Indonesia* (the Indonesian Small and Medium Business Organisation).
LP3E	*Lembaga Pengkajian Penelitian dan Pengembangan Ekonomi* (Institute for Economic

Studies, Research & Development—KADIN's economic 'think tank').

LP3ES
Lembaga Penelitian, Pendidikan & Penerangan Ekonomi & Sosial (the Institute for Economic & Social Research, Education & Information).

LPEM
Lembaga Penyelidikan Ekonomi dan Masyarakat (the Institute for Economic and Social Research, University of Indonesia).

MPP
Majelis Perusahaan dan Perniagaan (the Assembly of Business and Trade).

MPR
Majelis Permusyawaratan Rakyat (Peoples' Consultative Assembly).

NGO
Non-Governmental Organisation.

Obat Inpres
A program for the supply of cheap medicine via *puskesmas* clinics which was subsidised by special Presidential funding.

OPS
Organisasi Perusahaan Sejenis (Organisation of Homogenous Enterprises).

OTC drugs
Over-the-Counter drugs, available without a doctor's prescription.

Panca Sila
the state ideology (a set of five social and humanitarian ideals).

PDGI
Persatuan Dokter Gigi Indonesia (the Indonesian Dentists' Association).

PDI
Partai Demokrasi Indonesia (Indonesian Democratic Party—an amalgamation of nationalist and Christian parties).

PERTEKSI
Perserikatan Perusahan Tekstil Seluruh Indonesia (All Indonesia Union of Textile Companies).

PIBTI
Persatuan Industri Barang Jadi Tekstil Indonesia (the Indonesian Garment Makers' Association).

PKI
Partai Kommunis Indonesia (the Indonesian Communist Party).

PPKPHO
Panitia Pengkajian Kerasionalan Penggunaan dan Harga Obat (the Committee of Inquiry into Rational Drug Usage and Prices).

PPP   *Partai Persatuan Pembangunan* (United
                 Development Party—an amalgamation of Muslim
                 parties).

Puskesmas   *Pusat Kesehatan Masyarakat* (local-level public
                 health clinics).

REPELITA   *Rencana Pembangunan Lima Tahun* (Five Year
                 Development Plan).

SEKBERTAL   *Sekretariat Bersama Industri Pemintalan* (the
                 Joint Secretariat of the Spinning Industry). The
                 acronym later came to stand for *Sektoral
                 Kebersamaan Permintalan* [the Joint Spinning
                 Sector (Association)].

SEKBERPAK   *Secretariat Bersama Pakaian Jadi* (the Joint
                 Secretariat of Garment Manufacturers).

SPMI   *Serikat Pedagang Menengah Indonesia* (the
                 Indonesian Union of Medium Traders).

Tata niaga   The label for the restrictive trade regime
                 developed especially in the early 1980s which
                 centred around upstream import monopolies.

Textile Club   An informal group formed in the early 1970s of
                 large spinning and weaving companies, many of
                 which were Japanese joint ventures.

WALHI   *Wahana Lingkunan Hidup Indonesia* (the
                 Indonesian Environmental Association).

WDP   *Wajib Daftar Perusahaan* (a legal requirement for
                 all businesses to obtain a licence by registering
                 with the Department of Trade).

WHO   World Health Organisation.

YLK   *Yayasan Lembaga Konsumen* (the Consumers'
                 Association).

1

Introduction

The transition from authoritarian rule to more democratic regimes in various parts of the world has been one of the most remarkable developments of the 1980s and early 1990s. In both Asia and Latin America strong pro-democracy movements succeeded in forcing changes which enabled greater levels of effective political participation. More recently, quite extraordinary political change has also taken place in Eastern Europe and the Soviet Union. In some cases, such as the Philippines, South Korea, Argentina and East Germany the changes have been dramatic; in others, such as Brazil, Thailand and Taiwan, change has been more gradual. However, not all movements for democratic reform have been so fortunate, as the harsh military backlashes that have taken place in Burma and China show.

Indonesia presents an interesting and curious case. In Indonesia—a country which has for many years had a military-based government—political change is now underway as well. The tight grip the government has held over political life generally, and the policy-making process in particular, is now showing signs of loosening in some areas. But Indonesia does not appear to be following in the paths of these other countries. The signs of change which have emerged so far suggest that while there is movement in the direction of a diffusion of power and greater political input by societal groups, Indonesia is unlikely to move far in the direction of liberal democracy for some time.

Since the late 1950s when the country's first President, Sukarno, suspended democratic government, political life in Indonesia has been marked by a steady centralisation of power. This trend quickened markedly with the establishment of Suharto's 'New Order' government which has ruled Indonesia continuously since 1966.

Under the New Order the political domination of the state over society has been extended enormously. Haunted by the political instability which racked the country at the time they took power, Suharto and his supporters within the armed forces moved firmly and persistently to limit political participation and to concentrate power. In a range of different ways the scope for societal groups to influence the content and direction of public policy was reduced as the government set about a massive restructuring of the country's political landscape. Political parties and interest groups, for example, were tamed and brought within a central corporatist framework of state-dominated political management. As the New Order became more established, societal input was increasingly excluded, with control over policy coming to be monopolised by state officials.

Authoritarian governments are, of course, a common phenomenon, especially in developing countries. Very few, however, have been as long lasting and stable as Suharto's New Order. Two crucial variables have underpinned Suharto's success in sustaining his domination of Indonesian politics for so long: the massive revenue inflow created by oil price rises in the 1970s and early 1980s, and Suharto's ability to retain the firm support of the armed forces. The oil bonanza enabled the government to finance huge investment in domestic economic development. While the benefits of this development have plainly not been uniformly distributed, few sections of society have not had their material circumstances improved in some appreciable way. Material benefits were spread—however unevenly—across most economic and social groups and across all geographical regions. Without this oil-based capacity to finance widespread development, resistance to the government's political restructuring is almost certain to have been far greater. While their economic circumstances were improving, people were less likely to protest their progressive exclusion from political participation. In other words, economic gains went some distance towards compensating people for their political losses.

On occasion, however, the government's economic 'carrot' has proved insufficient compensation for some groups in society and there have been outbreaks of violent protest. These have ranged from large-scale resistance to some aspect of state policy, through to low level localised grievances. In all such cases, however, the government has been able to rely on the armed forces to contain and suppress any unrest. A vital element in the continued armed forces' support for the New Order has been their vested interest in the status quo: key sections of the military have enjoyed wide-ranging political influence and very substantial economic rewards.

The New Order, then, has been a military-based regime with a developmentalist orientation that has been characterised by a high level of state control over politics and policy. As this study will show, however, since the mid-1980s there have been signs emerging which suggest that the state's ability to monopolise influence over some areas of policy has begun to loosen. In making this argument, I will draw evidence from several detailed case-studies which cast much needed light on the dynamics of policy formation in Indonesia. The case-studies centre around examples of industry groups which mobilised themselves politically in pursuit of particular policy objectives. What these three episodes reveal is that some groups outside the state can and do make a direct difference to policy outcomes.

Were this argument to be made in relation to an industrialised democracy it would generate no controversy. As will be seen, however, in the case of Indonesia the prevailing view among academic observers is that the state's domination of political life is so far-reaching that the scope for extra-state groups to influence policy in any direct way is minimal. This is generally seen to be the case even for business organisations. In addition to the system-wide obstacles to organised policy input by extra-state groups, business in Indonesia has been politically hamstrung by the fact that the business class is dominated by Chinese Indonesians (as opposed to *pribumi*, or indigenous Indonesians). As in other parts of Southeast Asia, the Chinese in Indonesia remain an unpopular ethnic minority group. The uncertain social position of the Chinese has generally been seen as depriving the business community of the capacity to project collective political interests in any direct or organised manner. Along with other segments of society, it has been regarded as effectively excluded from political participation by the state.

A central argument of this book is that important changes underway in Indonesia since the mid-1980s necessitate a reappraisal of the situation and a redirection of analytical attention to overcome what has hitherto been an unremitting concentration on the state at the expense of society-based political action. The period since the mid-1980s has been a crucial time in Indonesia. In particular, changes associated with the sharp economic downturn and collapse in oil prices have contributed to a situation in which business has come to develop new and independent political capabilities. Sections of the business class have begun to challenge and transform the restrictive network of corporatist representative associations which overlays the Indonesian political landscape and which has been crucial to the New Order's system of political containment. This study shows that policy-making patterns have become more complex and more dependent on coalition building both inside and outside the state.

An important reason for focusing on the business sector is that there is a newly emerging current of 'post-statist' literature dealing with the nature of relations between business and the state and its broader significance in terms of economic development in relation to other parts of Asia.[1] Running through this recent work is the idea that the heavy analytical emphasis on the state in so much of the political science writing on Asia over the last twenty years, has blinded us to the political significance of organised business as a variable in explaining policy outcomes. Business groups in Japan, and more recently Thailand and South Korea, enjoy considerably more political influence than business in Indonesia.[2] And yet the evidence suggests that though a substantial gap still separates the political matrix of Indonesia from that of Thailand or South Korea—not to mention Japan—there are signs of change in Indonesia as segments of the business class become more assertive.

The structure of this study is relatively straightforward. Chapter 2 examines the prevailing ideas about the nature of relations between state and society in Indonesia. From this it will be seen that there is, indeed, generally little recognition of the possibility that extra-state groups can play a significant role in the shaping of public policy in Indonesia. This rough consensus in the academic literature marks what is, in effect, the point of departure for this study. Chapter 3 introduces the reader to the political setting of contemporary Indonesia. It highlights some of the institutional, ideological and economic variables which bear upon the pattern of interest representation. After a general discussion, special attention is given to the structure and dynamics of business representation in Indonesia. Then follows the heart of the book, three case-studies which show, in considerable detail, ways in which policy is shaped through bargaining and coalition building among contending sets of interests—located both inside *and* outside the state. One of the biggest problems faced by observers of Indonesian politics is an acute shortage of detailed information about the processes of government at the executive level. As a result, policy-making is often regarded as something of an impenetrable 'black box'. One of the purposes of the three case-studies presented here is to go some distance towards illuminating at least a few of the corners of that box. The first of the stories provides an example of policy conflict in the textile sector, in which we see a remarkable campaign by a section of the spinning industry to overturn a set of decisions by the Department of Trade concerning a monopoly restriction on raw material imports. The second case concerns the persistent attempts of the pharmaceutical industry to resist the introduction of price limitation measures by the Health Department, while the third centres on the efforts of the insurance industry to persuade the

Department of Finance to introduce a comprehensive legislative framework for that industry. The final section of the book draws the various threads running through the preceding chapters together in order to argue that the prevailing fixation with the state has prevented us from seeing that there is considerably more to Indonesia's political life than has generally been recognised. It is argued that there appears to be a slow sea change emerging in the structure of interest representation in Indonesia and that, in some policy areas at least, there is a gradual pluralisation and diffusion of power taking place. The book closes by speculating on possible future directions for political change of this sort in Indonesia, and argues that though the current configuration of power seems to preclude anything approaching real democratisation, there is nonetheless reason to expect a continued increase in the scope for societal input into policy as a result of changes emerging in the character of representational structures.

1. See, for example, Anek (1987) and (1989); Ramsay (1986) and (1987); Doner (1988); Doner and Wilson (1988); the forthcoming study of the automotive industry in the Philippines, Thailand, Malaysia and Indonesia by Richard Doner (University of California Press, Berkeley); and the forthcoming political economy study of Thailand's recent economic success by Richard Doner and Ansil Ramsay. On Japan, see in particular Samuels' (1987) important study of Japanese energy markets as well as Ikuo Kume's (1988) study of labour relations.
2. For a comparative analysis of the political position of business in South Korea and Thailand, see MacIntyre (1990) forthcoming.

2

The Theoretical Terrain

Much has been written about politics in Indonesia during the New Order period. Even a quick perusal of this literature will reveal a range of conflicting theoretical images about the nature of the modern Indonesian polity and the relationship between state and society. At least six differing perspectives can be distinguished in the recent literature: an approach which views Indonesian political history as a story of the continued subordination of societal interests to those of the state; an approach which adapts the bureaucratic polity and patrimonialist models; an approach which sees political conflict and plurality within the bureaucracy as a defining characteristic; another which makes use of the bureaucratic authoritarian model developed in relation to Latin America; a structuralist approach; and finally a 'restricted pluralist' perspective. As will be seen, while there is some serious dispute among advocates of the various approaches as to the character of the state itself, there is in fact an underlying consensus that relations between state and society are massively tilted in the direction of the former.

The State-Qua-State

Of the writings on New Order politics, that which places the strongest emphasis on the state is an essay in 1983 by Benedict Anderson.[1] He argued that the policies of the New Order could best be understood in terms of the interests of the state itself. At the heart of his argument is the idea of a fundamental disjunction between the interests of the state and society. He offers a picture of the modern Indonesian state as a self-serving entity, pursuing its perceived self-interest at the expense of other diverse interests in society. He sees the state as greedily consuming the resources and wealth of the nation, while being kept afloat with foreign support and oil revenue. While Anderson is basically concerned with highlighting historical trends, for present purposes the most important element of his analysis is his image of the New Order state as being almost entirely detached from and unresponsive to societal interests. Though the state is at present in the hands of the military, he argues, the basic situation has been essentially unchanged since colonial times. Policy is a reflection of the state's interests, rather than of those of any extra-state class or group, with the partial exception of foreign capital. In this perspective, there is little scope for extra-state participation and little consideration of the issue of interest representation.

Anderson's argument is perhaps most usefully interpreted as a response to instrumentalist Marxist views of the state as a tool of the capitalist class. His argument should not, however, be crudely caricatured as some polar extreme, for rather than focusing solely on the nature of the New Order polity, his principal purpose was to provide a comparative historical framework to enable the identification of continuities in state-society relations with earlier periods.

The Bureaucratic Polity and Patrimonial Cluster

A second approach which stresses the importance of the state revolves around the two related concepts of 'patrimonialism' and 'bureaucratic polity'. The former derives originally from the German sociologist, Max Weber, and was reinterpreted by Roth[2] and Eisenstadt[3] (among others), while the latter stems from Riggs' work[4] on Thailand in the 1950s and 1960s. The two approaches, though distinct, overlap to a very considerable extent. The essence of the patrimonial model is a notion of the head of state operating in a manner comparable to that of traditional rulers in earlier times, preserving his or her position by dispensing material rewards and opportunities to leading members of the elite. The elite is divided into rival cliques which struggle for the patronage and largesse of the ruler. The patrimonial model thus emphasises a pyramid-like network of patron-client relationships, characterised by personal links between individuals of different status, with the client being dependent on the assistance of his or her patron in the position of influence. An additional element of the patrimonial model is the notion that politics is characterised, not by conflict over substantive policy issues, but competition over material rewards and spoils. Those members of the elite nearest to the pinnacle fare the best. The interests of members of society who are not of the elite are simply repressed. In short, the state is not responsive to outside interests or pressures. Slightly less generic than the patrimonial model is Riggs' bureaucratic polity. The gist of this is an argument that the bureaucratic elite is unconstrained by societal interests in the determination of policy. The bureaucratic polity has many patrimonial characteristics, with the political leadership relying largely on the distribution of largesse among elite cliques to maintain its position. Those outside the state elite are effectively excluded from political participation. In this respect, Riggs paid particular attention to the position of what he called 'pariah entrepreneurs'. The business community, largely made up of ethnic Chinese, was no exception to the pattern of political exclusion. The only significant opportunity for influencing political leaders lay in patron-client links.

Thus, with their joint emphasis on political exclusion and patrimonial interpersonal relationships, there is much common ground between these two models. Indeed, for the purposes of viewing Indonesian politics, the two go hand-in-hand. In this light, we can treat them here as loosely constituting one family, or cluster, of thought.

Many writers have sought to interpret Indonesian politics from this perspective, so much so that it is probably fair to think of it as the conventional wisdom or 'mainstream' approach. Although slight differences may be distinguished among these writers, they are largely differences of definition, terminology and emphasis rather than matters of major substance. Apart from being the conventional wisdom among foreign observers, it is also a perspective which enjoys widespread currency in political discourse in Indonesia itself.[5] Karl Jackson was an early analyst to employ these ideas in interpreting New Order politics.[6] He proposed a picture of Indonesian politics in which participation in policy formation is confined almost exclusively to senior members of the state apparatus, military and civilian alike: 'Like islands cut off from the social seas surrounding them, bureaucratic polities are largely impervious to the currents in their society . . .'.[7] In this respect, he is thus not far from Anderson. Jackson seeks merely to distinguish it from other models of governance by the extent to which influence on decision-making processes is confined to the state elite.[8]

The only notable opportunity for participation in national policy formation by interests outside the state elite, according to Jackson, is during the implementation of policy, and mostly minor local-level adjustments.[9] Though he emphasises the inherently exclusionary characteristics of a bureaucratic polity, Jackson, unlike Riggs, does not give much attention to the position of business. The other key element of Jackson's account concerns patrimonial features of the polity. He sees political relationships among the members of the state elite as being characterised by competing cliques which are held together by a network of personalised patron-client links.[10] Harold Crouch is the scholar who probably has done most to develop this approach to Indonesian politics.[11] Writing at the end of the 1970s, he argued that the regime which Suharto had succeeded in establishing bore important resemblances to the traditional patrimonial polities of Javanese antiquity. In seeking to apply the patrimonial model he stressed that intra-elite politics (like that of the sultanistic court) is not primarily concerned with factional competition over substantive policy matters but rather the distribution of material opportunities and the spoils of office. Qualifying this, he also argued that the inherent tensions associated with economic development were likely to result in the gradual regularisation and rationalisation of the political system, causing major policy issues to become increasingly important.[12]

More recently Crouch has sought to address the question of the significance of business as a political force in Indonesian politics. While noting the existence of arguments about an emergent capitalist class in Indonesia, he views this as, at most, an evolutionary development of an uncertain and long term nature, and he therefore remains somewhat sceptical of its political impact.[13] Specifically, in so far as the state is responsive to business interests, according to Crouch it is on a patrimonial basis, with individual senior officials providing particularistic concessions to client business people. A few individual firms, rather than broader segments of the business class receive satisfaction. Following Riggs' notion of a pariah entrepreneur class, Crouch sees racial resentment towards the Chinese-dominated business class in Indonesia as preventing them from achieving political influence. An unpopular ethnic minority like their counterparts in Riggs' Thailand of the 1950s and 1960s, Crouch sees the small Chinese Indonesian population as having little alternative than to rely on informal personal connections (typically graft-based) to patrons within the government for political favours.

Jackson and Crouch have not been the only writers to make use of the intertwined notions of bureaucratic polity and patrimonialism; a number of other writers such as John Girling, Ruth McVey and Jamie Mackie have also sought to interpret Indonesian politics in this fashion.[14] On the central question of state-society relations and the monopolisation of influence over policy formation by senior state officials, their conclusions are similar: there is little scope for those outside the state structure to influence policy, but in so far as this does occur, it is principally on the basis of patrimonial links which are productive of specific and limited benefits (usually material) for individuals, rather than broader social or economic groupings.[15]

The principal difference between the cluster of writers who have viewed Indonesia as a bureaucratic polity and Anderson's state-qua-state approach, is that they do not view the state as a coherent corporate actor, pursuing objective interests of its own. Rather than an *actor*, for these writers, the state is conceived more as an *arena* in which elite cliques compete. Both, however, emphasise the exclusion of societal interests from policy formation processes.

Bureaucratic Pluralism

A third distinguishable theoretical interpretation of Indonesian politics is what Donald Emmerson has labelled 'bureaucratic pluralism'.[16] Emmerson's aim is to provide an alternative approach between what he sees as the two extremes of, on the one hand, the monistic nature of Anderson's account of the state and, on the other, the bureaucratic-policy picture of patrimonial cliques competing merely over the spoils of office.

The crux of the bureaucratic pluralist position is that politics at the national level in Indonesia is both more regularised and more pluralistic than most observers have acknowledged. In order to explore and support this proposition Emmerson has used a case-study involving policy choices over a major industrial development project in Sumatra. His conclusion is that within the parameters of the regime's security concerns, serious debate about policy issues does take place among various agencies within the bureaucracy. He is thus arguing, first, that the state is considerably more pluralistic than Anderson[17] for example, allows, and second, that political competition is not simply about the distribution of personal advantage among client groups (as Jackson in particular suggests), but also, importantly, substantive policy debates.[18]

Emmerson's focus is on the nature and internal characteristics of the state itself. In developing his case for a bureaucratic pluralism approach, he does not claim that there are significant pluralist-like inputs from interests *outside* the state apparatus. In an earlier essay he made it clear that he saw the state as being relatively immune to societal demands and as having gutted representative channels linking state and society.[19] He argued that under the New Order, the bureaucracy has become less of a political arena in which various groups competed and, instead, more a rationalised instrument in the hands of the government. He saw this as having been achieved at the cost of the state becoming much more isolated from and unresponsive to extra-state interests.

The distinctive quality of the bureaucratic pluralist approach is the emphasis it gives to the existence of a plurality not only of interests but also of policy orientations *within* the state. Though he accepts the existence of intra-state competition over largesse, it is bureaucratic competition over substantive policy issues that he is concerned to underscore. Importantly, in common with the two earlier approaches, Emmerson does not see the state as responding to societal pressure or demands. The state (or sections of it) may, by virtue of its own internal diversity, be sympathetic to various extra-state interests, but policy formation is not generally guided by societal demands. In so far as policy decisions may satisfy societal interests, it is because the diversity of actors and interests within it enables some *vicarious* representation to take place. Ultimately then, in this approach too, influence over policy is heavily monopolised by the state.

Bureaucratic-Authoritarianism

Another distinguishable position in the theoretical spectrum is an argument by Dwight King that Indonesia is best understood as a bureaucratic-authoritarian regime.[20] King draws on the earlier work of writers such as Juan Linz on Spain[21] and Guillermo O'Donnell on Latin America.[22] King is not alone in attempting to apply a bureaucratic-authoritarian model, Manuel Kaisiepo in Indonesia has also explored this approach.[23]

The concept of bureaucratic-authoritarianism arises from the experiences of a number of Latin American countries in the 1960s and 1970s, notably Brazil and Argentina, with the collapse of democracy and its replacement by military rule. One of the most striking features about the regimes which emerged was the dramatic shift to political repression and the tight concentration of power in the hands of the military and bureaucratic elites—to the exclusion of societal groups, especially the popular sector. Frequently, a conspicuous factor in the massive reduction in the scope for political participation was the development of a state-controlled corporatist system of interest representation.

A central feature in scholarly arguments about bureaucratic-authoritarianism is the attempt to account for the rise of this authoritarian style of regime which, while clearly military-based, is characterised by a commitment to economic reform and development, with technocratic specialists in the civilian bureaucracy being allowed to steer economic policy. Guillermo O'Donnell has been the most prominent in the development of this model.[24] O'Donnell posed a causal link between this political transformation and the economic shift from import-substitution industrialisation to industrial deepening. While King does not take up this specific link with regard to economic transition, he argues that the bureaucratic authoritarian model is very useful for understanding Indonesian politics. For King, the efforts of Suharto's New Order government to circumscribe political pluralism can be helpfully understood in terms of a corporatist strategy for the management of interest representation. The importance of corporatist structures in Indonesian politics has been a continuing theme in King's work.[25]

Corporatism, it needs to be understood, refers to a particular pattern of interest representation linking segments of society and the state. It is typically contrasted with pluralism as a form of interest intermediation; the former being associated with regularised and state-designated channels for political representation which are differentiated on a functional basis, and the latter with a less structured set of arrangements in which societal groups organise independently of the state and pursue their political interests on a competitive basis. In general terms, corporatism is characterised by the state assuming a much larger role in political life, to the point of specifying the institutions through which the sanctioned political representation of societary interests may take place. As Stepan puts it,[26]

> Corporatism refers to a particular set of policies and institutional arrangements for structuring interest representation. Where such arrangements predominate, the state often charters or even creates interest groups, attempts to regulate their number, and give them the appearance of a quasi-representational monopoly along with special prerogatives.

Governments may thus deliberately seek to employ a corporatist strategy as one means of political management by which they can control demand-making by groups in society. As Malloy has explained,[27] corporatist strategies seek,

> . . . to eliminate spontaneous interest articulation and establish a limited number of authoritatively recognised groups that interact with the government apparatus in defined and regularised ways. Moreover, the recognised groups in this type of regime are organised in vertical functional categories rather than horizontal class categories and are obliged to interact with the state through the designated leaders of authoritatively sanctioned interest associations.

As King and most writers emphasise, it is important not to view a political system as being 'either corporatist or not'. Corporatism, or more usefully, a corporatist strategy, involves institutional arrangements linking state and society that can be developed to a greater or lesser degree across different social sectors. Importantly, the character of corporatist strategies for structuring interest representation can range from the liberal to the authoritarian. The character of corporatist arrangements in, for instance, parts of Western Europe is quite different to that of, say, Latin American countries under bureaucratic-authoritarian regimes.[28] In this respect King follows Philippe Schmitter's[29] distinction between what he calls 'societal' and 'state' variants of corporatism. The societal, or liberal, variant is found in democratic systems and involves a more cooperative arrangement between the state and organised interests in society, with the latter being autonomous from and even penetrating the former to a considerable degree. Under state, or athoritarian, corporatism, the state is in a much stronger position, controlling and penetrating the various dependent interest associations. One is a system of political representation in which the state seeks to include or involve various societal groups in policy-making, while, conversely the other is characterised by political exclusion. State corporatism is thus the variant associated with authoritarian political systems and is quite clearly the form with which King is concerned in his analysis of Indonesia as a bureaucratic-authoritarian regime.

Herein lies the distinctiveness of King's position. King sees many interests in society as wanting to make demands upon the state, but argues that in order to regulate, if not suppress, the flow of these demands, the government has imposed a corporatist network over the top of much of society. He has described many organised interest associations, especially in the business and labour sectors, which are part of this network.[30] He emphasises, though, that he regards the corporatist framework as serving to limit, not facilitate, interest representation.

For present purposes, the significance of King's work lies in his treatment of the political linkages between state and society. In drawing our attention to the corporatist structures which are scattered across Indonesia's political landscape, he takes us beyond the bureaucratic polity and patrimonial cluster and the simple notion that clientelistic relationships are the principal representational interface between state and society. Fundamental to King's view of the New Order as a bureaucratic-authoritarian regime, is the notion that effective political power is very largely concentrated within the state structure. He sees the government's corporatist strategy as serving to exclude societal groups from the shaping of public policy. He is thus very clearly, and self-consciously, working within a state-centred approach to politics, and to this extent shares important ground with other writers.

A Structuralist Approach

The writings of Richard Robison present a challenging and distinctive approach to the problem of interpreting the nature of the Indonesian polity.[31] While he largely accepts the empirical picture that others have painted, Robison believes that the theoretical underpinings of other approaches seriously flaw them.

Robison's work provides something of a taxonomical problem as his approach has evolved significantly in recent years. In 1978 he presented a view of the state which had much in common with that of the bureaucratic polity and patrimonialist cluster.[32] Indeed, he talked explicitly of the 'neopatrimonial nature of the bureaucratic state'.[33] However, while he saw influence over policy as being monopolised by the state (due to a failure in the emergence of a strong indigenous bourgeoisie) and patrimonial links as the norm, he did so in the broader context of a dependency framework in which foreign capital was seen to be an overriding extra-state force.

More recently, Robison's position has shifted—paralleling his identification of an emerging domestic bourgeoisie. In his earlier analysis the major domestic capitalists, the 'bureaucratic capitalists', were seen as mere rentiers, but it is the emergence of a domestic capitalist class which is coming to stand independently of the state that is the centre-piece of his recent argument. He sees bureaucrats who were previously engaged in simple rent-seeking activity via corruption as now developing the investment interests of entrepreneurs.[34]

For present purposes the key question centres around the nature of links between this capitalist class and the state. Is it able to influence policy outcomes significantly, and if so, how? In this regard Robison's account of the nature of interest intermediation and the linkages between state and society in Indonesia shares important elements with that of Dwight King. Specifically, he sees the New Order's strategy of developing corporatist structures as being designed to contain and control the political energies of such key sectors in society as capital and labour.[35] The exclusionary nature of this corporatist network has served, Robison argues, to largely shut even the monied classes out of the processes of government.

Although the new regime of General Suharto had the political support of the land-owning and capital owning classes and the middle classes these were quickly disabused of any expectations that they would participate in government. Control of the state apparatus was rapidly assumed by the military and selected civilian bureaucrats. Authoritarian rule was reinforced by the consolidation of corporatist institutions and ideologies.[36]

Robison thus makes it clear that he does not regard major societal interests, including business, as having any direct influence over, or participation in, policy formation. But in this, as he himself is aware, he confronts a theoretical dilemma. If the bourgeoisie does not yet exert instrumental influence over policy (in part because the great majority are Chinese, and thus politically vulnerable), what then is its political significance? In seeking to explain this seemingly paradoxical situation in which 'the ruling class does not rule', he adopts what is essentially a structuralist framework in which the principal constraint upon policy-makers is not the direct or instrumental pressuring of capitalist groups, but rather the underlying dynamics of the local and international economies which cannot be ignored by state leaders if long term economic growth and development are to be achieved. While clearly very conscious[37] of the growth of business organisations such as the Chamber of Commerce and Industry (KADIN) and the possibility of increased business links with the state political party GOLKAR, Robison sees the Indonesian state as relatively autonomous and largely immune to direct political action by capitalist groups seeking to shape government policy. This is not to suggest that Robison regards class and other societal forces as unimportant; clearly he does not as his detailed study of the rise of business groups in Indonesia testifies. Rather, it is to make the point that for Robison, the principal external constraints on policy-makers arise from the tensions and problems embedded in the structure of the local and wider global economy rather than the direct political action of societal groups.[38]

Robison offers a distinctive theoretical approach to the study of Indonesian politics. While his work has quite different philosophical foundations to that of other writers discussed here, Robison does concur with others on a number of important issues. Along with most other observers, Robison's interpretation of Indonesian politics is very much state-centred. He sees influence over public policy to be concentrated in the hands of state leaders. Though on the one hand he has argued the importance of an emerging bourgeoisie as the most significant domestic extra-state interest, on the other he has said that it is not yet able to influence policy itself in a direct or systematic way. Importantly, in so far as he addresses the question of the actual political linkages between state and society in Indonesia, he sees

patrimonial connections and corporatist associations as the principal
means by which societal interests might be transmitted into the policy
process.[39]

Restricted Pluralism

Finally, an important contribution to the debate, representing a
position towards the pluralist-end of the spectrum is that advanced by
William Liddle which we might term 'restricted pluralism'.[40] Liddle is
the only major foreign observer of Indonesia to examine policy
formation processes in terms which allow for some significant inter-
play of both state and extra-state interests.

Like a number of the other scholars discussed here, Liddle seeks to
differentiate his interpretation from the various other approaches
already outlined. The gist of Liddle's contribution is a claim that
politics generally, and influence over policy in particular, is considerably more pluralistic in Indonesia than is normally acknowledged. He
certainly agrees with Emmerson that there can be a range of different
actors within the state structure involved in policy formation and
that, with the exception of sensitive 'high politics' matters, substantive policy debate does indeed take place. Where he differs markedly
from Emmerson (and virtually everyone else) is in his argument that
there is a wide variety of *extra*-state actors which may at times
influence policy outcomes.[41]

He identifies, for example, the press, intellectuals, individual
Members of Parliament, producer and consumer interests, as well as
local level officials as often having significant, albeit varying, degrees
of influence. (Note however, that some of these—Parliamentarians
and local officials—though typically overlooked by other analysts,
should still be considered as members of the state apparatus, even
though their interests may in some respects vary substantially from
those of the government.) Liddle's arguments are based on a series of
case-studies of agricultural policy formation which highlight competing actors and demands. Many of the arguments Liddle makes about
the potential significance of extra-state groups in the policy process
are supported by valuable case-study material provided Makarim
Wibisono.[42]

Beyond claiming that influence over policy is not narrowly monopolised by the upper echelons of the state structure, Liddle seeks to
identify some of the mechanisms by which these 'outside' actors are
able to achieve a measure of influence.[43] While he finds some signs of
extra-state groups being able to achieve *direct* influence on particular
policy issues, he concludes that *indirect* influence is more character-

istic. To illustrate this notion of indirect influence, he points in his case-studies to instances where decision-makers anticipate societal demands and adjust policy sufficiently to pre-empt representational activity by the groups concerned.[44] Thus, for instance, the government tries to satisfy at least the minimum interests of farmers in advance of their grievances resulting in rural unrest. Liddle also sees ideology, or more broadly, the climate of ideas, as playing an important part in the policy process by influencing political discourse and constraining policy-makers, sometimes to the advantage of weak groups in society.

Liddle offers a distinctive picture of the nature of interest intermediation, and by extension, the political system. He sees a restricted pluralism—certainly not a uniform or egalitarian distribution of opportunity for influencing policy outcomes—but a political system in which some measure of extra-state pluralism can be found. He is the only major analyst of Indonesian politics who explicitly points to non-state actors as having a capacity to influence policy formation in other than a clientelistic fashion. Although still maintaining a state-centred approach, Liddle is the writer who seems most concerned to delineate the possible significance of at least some societal actors in the shaping of policy.

Conclusion

The problem of interpreting New Order politics has given rise to a range of different approaches to the subject. And yet, overall, the striking feature about the academic debates on the nature of contemporary Indonesian politics is not the divergence, but rather the *convergence* of opinion. Certainly a number of the people discussed here are working from fundamentally different philosophical premises and have varying purposes in mind, and certainly there is ongoing disagreement among academics about how best to explain the system of governance in Indonesia. Yet, in spite of this, it remains inescapable that there is an underlying consensus centring around the idea that the state is largely unfettered by societal interests in the determination of policy. With the partial exception of Liddle, all the approaches are very heavily state-centred in their focus: very little scope is allowed for the possibility that extra-state actors have a major role in policy formation. This is not surprising given that scant attention is given in the literature to the structure and processes of political representation: it is difficult to talk of societal inputs into policy if one has little knowledge of the means by which this might be taking place. Such differences as there are among the various approaches in this regard are differences of degree; the earlier they appear in the theoretical spectrum outlined above the less scope they allow for societal input into policy formation (and correspondingly, the less attention they give to the subject).

Picking over the academic literature on the linkages between state and society in Indonesia, three basic types of linkage by which societal interests might be transmitted upwards to policy-makers can be identified: patron-client relationships, corporatist channels and what we might term political input by 'osmosis' or absorption. As should be evident, the prevailing view is that these linkages do not amount to a major constraint on the state's policy-makers. Patron-client connections, by definition, are restricted to personalised and particularist concessions from a patron within the state to an individual or individuals on the outside. They do not, therefore, pertain to broad-based political issues. In the case of the second possibility, there is some uncertainty as to how the corporatist structures in fact function, although the general presumption is that typically they restrict and suppress the flow of demands. Finally, in terms of 'osmosis' (Emmerson's 'vicarious representation' and Liddle's 'anticipation') it is obvious that this is heavily dependent upon the behaviour of state officials rather than societal actors themselves and that the political initiative thus lies within the state rather than society.

With this consensus as its point of departure, the argument of this study is that important change is underway in Indonesian politics, and that there is in fact considerably more political input by societal groups outside the state structure than is generally recognised. Politics and policy-making in Indonesia is not simply a matter of internal manouevering among state actors. As will be seen later, the transition underway means that near exclusive focus on the state which has prevailed is being rendered increasingly untenable.

1. Anderson (1983).
2. Roth (1968).
3. Eisenstadt (1973).
4. See Riggs (1966) and (1964).
5. For academic exemplars see Soedjatmoko (1983); Yahya Muhaimin (1980); and Fachry Ali (1986).
6. Jackson (1978).
7. Jackson (1986) p. 4.
8. Noting the continuities with Sukarno's Guided Democracy period, Jackson declares: 'Indonesia remains a bureaucratic polity—that is a political system in which power and participation in national decisions are

limited almost entirely to the employees of the state, particularly the officer corps and the highest levels of the bureaucracy . . . Although the number of bureaucrats and army officers influencing policy implementation at the local level is much larger, national policies are established by a small ruling circle whose members primarily respond, albeit it not exclusively, to the values and interests of less than one thousand persons comprising the bureaucratic, technocratic and military elite of the country . . . In bureaucratic polities the military and the bureaucracy are not accountable to other political forces such as political parties, interest groups or organised communal interests. Actions designed to influence government decisions originate entirely from within the elite itself without any need for mass participation.' Jackson (1978) p. 4.

9. Jackson (1978) p. 5.
10. Jackson (1978) p. 14 and 18.
11. See, *inter alia*, Crouch (1979), (1980), (1984), (1986) and (1987).
12. Crouch (1979) pp. 578–79.
13. Crouch (1986) pp. 46–47. As he puts it: 'the picture of government-business relations presented in the patrimonial and bureaucratic-polity models is still to a large extent valid at present despite the rise of some big [business] conglomerates and the possible long-run implications of this in the future.' (1986) p. 52.
14. Girling (1981), McVey (1982) and Mackie (1986a) and (1986 b).
15. Mackie has put this most strongly. 'For all the talk we have heard since the early years of the New Order about the close connections between wealthy Chinese *cukong* and powerful Indonesian generals, there is little evidence that any of them have been able to carry much weight in the general decision-making processes that determine the broader outlines of national economic or social policy formulation (e.g. exchange rate policies, budgetary allocations, industrial priorities etc.): at most they can exert some influence over particularistic decisions about the allocation of contracts, licences, credits and so on.' Mackie (1986 a) p. 17–18.
16. Emmerson (1983).
17. In fairness, it should be noted here that while Anderson nowhere explicitly depicts the state as a near-monistic entity, Emmerson's juxtaposition is not unreasonable, for Anderson does indeed create this impression with his emphasis on the state as an institution that has interests of its own which it wilfully pursues. Certainly he does not attempt to disaggregate the state and to draw attention to pluralism within the state.
18. In this latter respect, it should be remembered that not all of the bureaucratic polity and patrimonial cluster went as far as Jackson in stressing clientelistic competition over the perquisites of office. Crouch, for instance, while seeing clientelism as being the prevalent mode of political behaviour, explicitly pointed to a trend towards more substantive policy debate as the economy developed and became more complex. Crouch (1979) p. 579; and Crouch (1986) p. 47. This is a view

with which Emmerson is in clear agreement. Emmerson (1983) p. 1239.
19. Emmerson (1978).
20. King (1982 a).
21. Linz (1970).
22. O'Donnell (1978) and (1977).
23. Kaisiepo (1986).
24. For general overviews of the main debates see, Malloy (1977 a) and Collier (1979).
25. See also King (1977), (1979), (1982 b).
26. Stepan (1978) p. 46.
27. Malloy (1977 b) p. 4.
28. For a general overview of the theoretical debates on corporatism in Western industrialised nations, see Roger (as distinct from Dwight) King (1986) pp. 115–40; and Schmitter and Lembruch (1979).
29. Schmitter (1979 a) pp. 20–22.
30. King's evidence of the successes of these organisations in representing the interests of their membership is unclear. In the case of business, for example, he tells us that of the business association leaders he interviewed, many claimed to have successfully 'pressed upon authority groups a specific project related to their interests'. [King (1977) p. 18; and see also, King (1982 a) p. 115 fn. 32.] As will be argued later, while many association *leaders* may have secured government contracts and the like for themselves (as distinct from their members) this is a very different matter from influencing a broader policy issue. Indeed this particularistic activity (securing individual contracts or favours, etc.) is little different from the partrimonial behaviour described by the bureaucratic polity cluster. It is not clear what King means by a 'project' here.
31. The principal pieces of interest here are: Robison (1978), (1981), (1982), (1985), (1986 a),(1986 b), (1996 c) and (1988).
32. Indeed, King classified Robison under the bureaucratic polity label. See King (1982 a) pp. 106–7 and fn. 11. See also Crouch (1986) pp. 49–50.
33. Robison (1978) p. 18.
34. Robison (1985) p. 316.
35. Robison (1985) p. 316.
36. Robison (1988) p. 61.
37. Robison (1986 a) p. 396.
38. It should noted here that Robison has been accused of (among other things) being insufficiently 'state-centred' in his analysis, and indeed of being 'society-centred' [Winters (1988)]. This is an odd proposition. Undoubtedly Robison spends a great deal of time talking about an emerging bourgeoisie, but this does not mean he therefore believes that societal forces are the principal determinants of policy [which is what 'society-centred' ultimately means: see, for instance, Nordlinger (1981) & (1987) and Skocpol (1985)]. As is argued here, a close reading of Robison [especially his most recent work (1988)] reveals that he undoubtedly believes the means for transmitting societal pre-

ferences into policy to be extremely limited. As a result, he sees the state having very great autonomy in the determination of policy, with the major constraint upon its actions being the underlying structural developments in the international and domestic economies. Robison may have sins to answer for, but 'society-centredness' is not one of them.

39. As he puts it: 'For those outside the military, access to even the outer circles of power and influence is confined to informal patron-client networks or to government-controlled and sponsored corporatist organisations . . .' Robison (1985) p. 306.

40. Liddle (1985) and (1987).

41. As he puts it: 'a political system of military and bureaucratic authoritarianism, at least in Indonesia, does not preclude a policy process in which actors outside the central state apparatus play a significant role.' Liddle (1987) pp. 142–43.

42. See his very useful study of the textile industry. Wibisono (1987) and (1989).

43. Liddle (1987) pp. 142–44.

44. This proposition while clearly more 'voluntarist', is not dissimilar to Robison's argument about structural imperatives ensuring that the fundamental interests of capital are preserved by the state.

3

The Political Setting

This chapter surveys the institutional, ideological and economic landscape in New Order Indonesia, in short, the political setting. The aim is to provide a general description of the nature of political representation, as a first step towards to exploring in greater detail some of the prevailing ideas about the nature of the Indonesian political system.

As has been seen the general view to emerge from the academic literature is that the state massively dominates Indonesian political life, with societal groups having little or no scope for influencing political outcomes. As this chapter will show, it is not hard to understand why there should be such a consensus: there has indeed been a concerted drive during the New Order years to narrow the scope for political participation and enhance the state's capacity for control and social intervention. And there can be little doubt about the overall success of this endeavour. At the beginning of the New Order period the future of the government was far from certain, there being many groups with strong and independent political capabilities which operated as countervailing forces on particular policy issues. By comparison, in recent years the government has appeared reasonably secure from any conceivable society-based challenge and has been far less constrained in the development of policy.

And yet, as will be seen, the picture is not as black-and-white as much of the academic literature suggests. For in spite of the government's best efforts, there are a few institutions which, on an intermittent basis, can be effective in projecting societal interests into the policy process. In this respect we will give attention to the Parliament, the press and community-based non-governmental organisations.

After this overview of political representation, the focus of the chapter shifts to the specific circumstances of business, and the nature of relations between the private sector and the state in Indonesia. Special attention is given here to the Chamber of Commerce and Industry (KADIN). The chapter's general exploration of the political setting is completed with a survey of the country's economic circumstances in the mid-1980s. As we will see later, the economic downturn during this period proved to be a crucial factor in altering Indonesia's political matrix, for it unleashed forces which were instrumental in stimulating political change.

Political Representation in Indonesia: an Overview

In the years since the rise of the New Order in the late 1960s Indonesia has experienced a sustained and far-reaching campaign of political restructuring. Following the widespread political mobilisation that took place in the final years of Sukarno's rule and the traumatic events surrounding his demise, security planners within the state developed a corporatist strategy to handle the demands being made upon the new government by a wide spectrum of groups within society. The core of this strategy was to channel political participation away from less controllable institutions, such as the political parties, and into various state-designated representative bodies which were differentiated on a functional basis. This resulted in a steady narrowing of the scope for participation and a heavy concentration of influence over the formation of public policy in the hands of the state.

From the outset, Suharto's new military-dominated government viewed the civilian political parties with profound scepticism and was anxious to ensure that they did not come to threaten its position. Though the Communist Party had been physically eliminated, the military remained wary of the potential for mass-based political mobilisation. In this situation the prospect of developing a tightly controlled corporatist system of interest representation held much appeal for New Order security planners.

The idea of shifting away from a competitive party system to one in which corporatist organisations would be the principal form of linkage for the channeling of societal demands to policy-makers was not new. As David Reeve[1] has shown in his excellent study of the state political party, GOLKAR, the concept of corporatist representation predates the New Order. Indeed, a number of corporatist structures had already been set up during the Guided Democracy period under Sukarno. Not surprisingly, the military has been the most active proponent of a corporatist approach to the management of interest representation in recent decades, though in so doing it has been drawing on a tradition of political thought which can be traced to some of the early influential nationalist thinkers. Though the terminology of corporatism was not employed in this tradition of thought, the concepts were much the same. A network of functionally-based representative organisations which would serve as the conduits for channeling societal aspirations upwards to state leaders and which would be imbued with a collectivist spirit, was seen as both an indigenous and, more broadly, an Asian alternative to what was regarded as the divisive Western capitalist and liberal democratic thinking associated with a pluralist and competitive party system.[2]

While this tradition of political thought proved useful to the armed forces during the Guided Democracy period, it is under the New Order that the development of corporatist representation channels has reached its zenith. Following Reeve,[3] we can see that in its early years, the New Order government introduced a wide range of measures to fuse the institutions of political representation into a corporatist form. After this groundwork had been laid, the emphasis in the latter 1970s and 1980s was on consolidating the system.

The basic aim of the military's political strategists was to unfasten the links between the political parties and societal interests. This they set about doing early. In the place of parties they developed an elaborate and far-reaching network of corporatist bodies. These organisations were in turn usually fused, or brought together, under the umbrella of GOLKAR. A first step in this direction was to address the large social sectors which had been closely linked to the political parties. All existing representative bodies covering labour, peasants, fishermen, youth and women were fused into five single and officially designated organisations. These functional categories received special attention as they had in the past been a source of radicalism, a spectre which continued to haunt the New Order government. This corporatist strategy was not, however, confined solely to these mass social categories: it was extended right across the social spectrum.[4] Numerous associations were established as the sole representative bodies for particular segments of society. Priority was given to those segments which were of 'strategic' significance. So, in addition to the five major mass organisations mentioned above, civil servants, Islamic religious leaders, teachers, students, journalists, doctors, lawyers and business people, for example, also acquired a compulsory, or semi-compulsory, officially stipulated body, nominally charged with representing their collective interests. Importantly, a major reason underlying this emphasis on functional divisions, was the desire to blur class and other established social cleavages.

These corporatist institutions were not established in a sudden or dramatic way. The new representational structures were not openly or confrontationally imposed upon the various social groups. Under the guidance of the political strategists in General Ali Moertopo's Special Operations unit, feelers were put out to key elements within each group. Via a process combining patronage and political suasion, existing organisations were turned to the government's purposes, or new ones were specially created. As Reeve[5] notes, by virtue of this low-profile method, the government was able to stand back and welcome these new single vehicles as if they were spontaneous societal initiatives.

Parallel with this strategy of establishing a network of corporatist structures to cut the links between the political parties and society was an outright push to emasculate the parties themselves.[6] The nine remaining parties other than GOLKAR (which at that stage still claimed it was not a party) were fused into two new all-embracing parties; one amalgamating the former Muslim parties, and the other former nationalist and Christian parties. The titles given to the two new parties, (respectively) the Development Unity Party (PPP) and the Indonesian Democratic Party (PDI), concealed their heritage and provided little clue as to their political orientation. More important, though, was the fact that the fusion created artificial new political organisations which were fraught with internal tensions. Beyond this, security planners ensured that party leadership positions were filled with compliant individuals and, moreover, they carefully vetted all candidates wishing to stand for election. These various measures all helped to ensure that the parties would be in no position to challenge the government's authority.

The final and perhaps most decisive stroke was the introduction of regulations preventing the establishment of party offices in villages and small towns, where most of the population was located. This came about with the development of the concepts of 'depoliticisation' of the countryside and the creation of a 'floating mass'. Put simply, this meant detaching the bulk of the population from all but state-approved political channels.[7] These changes were crucial, for they placed the majority of the population beyond the effective reach of the two non-governmental parties, the PPP and the PDI. For electoral purposes, only GOLKAR was able to organise at the village-level. As a result, the only channels linking the mass of the population into the political system were within the corporatist network comprising GOLKAR and the maze of non-party functional representative organisations. Of course, this whole network was state-controlled.

Efforts to enhance political control were also directed inwards—

within the state apparatus itself. Many internal changes were wrought within the bureaucracy in a bid to transform it into a more coordinated instrument in the hands of the government instead of being simply a political arena in which uncontrolled bureaucratic fiefdoms competed. Not only were Communist Party supporters and suspected sympathisers eliminated from various government departments, but all civil servants (as well as state enterprise employees) were required to become members of the Civil Servants Corps (KORPRI)—the functional organisation nominally responsible for the representation of their interests. This was part of the drive to establish a 'monoloyalty' among state employees which would bind them to GOLKAR, and thus the government. As Emmerson has noted, KORPRI was 'meant to be the sole organisation in their lives outside the office.'[8] However, of KORPRI's five stated objectives, only the last referred to the well-being of civil servants; the others emphasised notions such as discipline and patriotism. KORPRI, being an integral component of GOLKAR, operated more as an instrument of control than representation, with all civil servants being required to vote for and support GOLKAR at elections. Apart from guaranteeing GOLKAR a portion of the voting population, this had the important benefit of allowing it to sidestep the prohibition on political parties operating at the village level, for village officials, being civil servants, were thus also members of KORPRI and GOLKAR, and therefore well placed to do GOLKAR's political bidding.

The civil service was not the only part of the overall state apparatus to be restructured. The armed forces themselves underwent a series of extensive organisational reforms aimed at tightening the lines of command and control.[9] As a result of these reforms, the days of the central government having to bargain with regional military commanders are long over. As with the restructuring to the civilian bureaucracy, these organisational changes meant that the military has become a more reliable instrument in the hands of the central government.

The effect of New Order's massive political engineering program was to eliminate, or enfeeble, less controllable (and thus possibly threatening) channels of interest articulation from the political landscape, and to replace them with a vast and authoritarian corporatist network. The implicit compact between the state and the leaders of the countless corporatist organisations was typically the provision of access to material and social rewards in exchange for stability and compliance in the sector for which they were responsible. Thus the new corporatist architecture, which had GOLKAR as its capstone, did not really serve to aggregate social demands and channel them upwards. Instead of actively promoting the interests of those it

nominally represented, GOLKAR and the corporatist network surrounding it served to restrict and contain demand-making. With little
serious commitment to promoting their member's interests, the leaders of these organisations tended to be concerned with only their own
narrow personal interests. This meant that there was typically little
political activity within these organisations beyond prominent figures
jostling for access to the benefits frequently associated with leadership positions. Lacking any greater life, the network of corporatist
bodies for the most part lay quietly on the political sidelines. And yet
this passivity did not represent a failure by its designers: quite the
opposite.

For Ali Moertopo, the principal political architect of the New
Order, this corporatist strategy was a great success. Its whole aim was
not to promote or somehow enliven the capacity of societal groups to
influence politics, but rather the very reverse: it aimed to reduce
drastically the opportunity for demands to be made upon the state by
such groups. It arose out of a conviction that stability and security
were threatened by high levels of political mobilisation and an
environment in which power was dispersed. The logic of the New
Order's corporatist strategy for political management has been to
overcome this situation. Not surprisingly then, though in formal
terms they were important advisory and consultative bodies, in
practice the corporatist representative organs were pushed to the
periphery of power. Their *de facto* role—which they performed very
effectively—was to absorb and contain the demands of extra-state
groups. With the leadership of all strategically significant organisations overseen by state officials, the pattern for them to become
merely formalistic and idle was soon established. Rather than serving
the interests of client groups by seriously promoting their demands to
policy-makers, these organisations served the interests of the New
Order's political strategists by acting as buffers between societal
interests and the state. They were, in short, a means of social and
political control.

That providing an effective interest representation network was
not one of the priorities of this approach was reflected in the junior
position GOLKAR itself held within what became known as the
Grand GOLKAR Family (*Keluarga Besar GOLKAR*). Apart from
GOLKAR itself, the other two elements of the 'family' were the
armed forces and KORPRI. This was indicative of the overall character of the New Order state—a structure controlled by a military and
bureaucratic elite.

The development of this corporatist framework continued steadily
through the late 1970s and into the 1980s. Functionally-based representational associations continued to be established, even as some

withered through inertia. Rather than operating as an organ for interest aggregation, GOLKAR functioned primarily as an electoral vehicle for the government and has secured growing majorities at five yearly intervals. During these years control of the press was tightened, with recalcitrant papers being shut down. Journalists too were brought under a single association imposing tight discipline.

The climax of this wave of corporatist restructuring came with the enshrining in law in 1985 of the requirement that all social and political organisations have as their foundation the state ideology, *Pancasila*. At a formal level *Pancasila* enunciates five social and humanitarian principles. However, the term has come to be so loosely used that it functions primarily as a hazy ideological shroud in which the government cloaks itself to legitimise its corporatist strategies for political management. All interest associations in the community (including the various religious groups) were formally required to acknowledge *Pancasila* as their sole ideological foundation. The Muslim-based party, the PPP, in particular, had conspicuous difficulty in reconciling this with its religious affiliations. The principal connotations flowing from it are the importance of unanimity and consensus and the state's monopolisation of the right to divine this consensus. In an earlier lead-up to the 1985 law, a compulsory intensive training program had been introduced into the civil service, universities and schools in order to inculcate the civic obligations *Pancasila* entails.[10] By promoting *Pancasila* in this way, the government was, in effect, seeking to achieve widespread acceptance of its authoritarian corporatist orientation. The wider significance of the 1985 law is that it represents the highwater mark of the New Order's restrictive corporatist strategy for the management of political life in Indonesia.

With the passage in 1985 of the ideological foundations law, the New Order's enormous corporatist restructuring program was more or less complete. All the major pieces were now in place. There can be little doubt that this corporatist strategy has achieved its aim of greatly reducing the capacity for political participation by extra-state groups. Political activity has been contained and restricted to a far greater degree than it was at the beginning of the New Order period. As such, societal constraints on policy-making have been much reduced. In this more ordered and regulated environment, the focus in recent years has been on keeping political activity contained within the new parameters. Much emphasis has been given to promoting the image of a national political consensus arrived at through a consultative process between the state and the corporatist representative bodies. Political debate outside the consultative process, especially party-political debate, is branded as inappropriate and illegitimate.

The centre-piece of this corporatist consultative process is the government's State Policy Outline document (GBHN).[11] After the Constitution, the GBHN is officially the most important set of guidelines for all government policy initiatives. A new GBHN document is developed every five years, corresponding with the formulation of the REPELITA, the Five Year Development Plans. While the REPELITA is more significant in terms of actual policy implications, the GBHN is seen to be of considerable symbolic and ideological significance, supposedly representing a distillation of national aspirations. To this end the GBHN is drawn up by a special government-appointed team. The members of this team are all senior government officials—reflecting the fact that it is an executive-controlled exercise. Ultimately, a wide-ranging document is considered (sometimes heatedly) by the People's Consultative Assembly (MPR) before being ratified.

In preparation for the 1988 GBHN, in late 1986 the People's Consultative Assembly sent out a questionnaire to 229 state institutions and prominent individuals seeking their views on a broad range of national issues.[12] In a revealing acknowledgement, the Deputy Head of the Consultative Assembly said that this was to try to overcome the impression that the GBHN was merely a product of the executive. While in principle the Consultative Assembly may reject or amend the document that is ultimately submitted to it, in practice—as is openly acknowledged—this is politically inconceivable in the existing political environment.[13] The inevitability of the MPR's endorsement of the GBHN neatly captures some of the ambiguity of Indonesian political life. Straight-forward authoritarian control interweaves a political culture which, at least nominally, is uncomfortable with adversarial conflict and places great store in consensus.

The GBHN is of great symbolic importance, but its actual impact upon policy is limited. This is not to say that the GBHN is insignificant, but simply to note that it acts as a 'negative' rather than 'positive' constraint upon policy. In other words, the fact that an idea or principle is included in the GBHN does not ensure policy action to implement it, but rather serves to prevent, or make difficult, any policy initiatives in contravention of it. This is not without political significance. As will be seen later, securing recognition of a principle in the GBHN can be a valuable strategy for protecting it from political opponents. The symbolic importance of the GBHN lies in the fact that it has been endorsed by the Consultative Assembly, and thus supposedly expresses the people's will. The GBHN is a broad statement of policy directions of which the government approves, although in a less focused way than the President's annual national address, or even the REPELITA. A principle acknowledged in the

GBHN bears the state imprimatur and is thus invested with something approaching ideological sanctity.

The Cabinet is another prominent political institution in which, like the GBHN, the appearance of unanimity is all-important.[14] In keeping with the overall political style of the New Order, political debate and conflict among ministers is suppressed in the Cabinet. The full Cabinet meets only once a year in the largely formal plenary session which reports on the annual budget. Much more frequent are the three categories of restricted sessions which comprise, respectively, ministers in the areas of economic, political and social affairs. The President will always attend the economic and political gatherings, but rarely those for social affairs. Even at these limited sessions, however, serious debate is very uncommon. Instead, discussion usually takes the form of presentations 'before' the President. Priority is given to avoiding the appearance of disharmony in the presence of Suharto, for this would require acknowledgment of the existence of conflict within the government. If a particular minister has an unsatisfied concern, rather than raise it at a restricted session of Cabinet, he or she is likely to pursue this in the context of a private bilateral meeting with the President. Not only does this avoid embarrassment for the minister concerned, more importantly, it obviates the need for open presidential acknowledgment of discord. It is not that the President cannot be informed of bad news or conflict, but rather that this must not take place openly. Suharto is, apparently, quite accessible to ministers wishing to come to him. Whereas some senior figures (such as Cabinet Secretary, Moerdiono; Armed Forces Chief, Try Sutrisno; and Research and Technology, Minister Habibie) are seen to have almost unlimited access, most ministers would only go to the President directly to complain about a dispute with another minister on a very serious matter.

Substantive policy debate among ministers takes place away from the President. Special working meetings are convened on an *ad hoc* basis by individual ministers, sometimes as frequently as several times in one week. Meetings of this sort tend to be very small, involving only those few ministers immediately concerned with a particular issue (officials do not attend). In addition to these *ad hoc* gatherings, there are also more structured meetings which, while being of a more formal nature, are nevertheless still more free and frank forums than actual Cabinet meetings. For instance, prior to the monthly Cabinet meeting on economic matters (traditionally the first Wednesday of the month) there is a meeting of the Economic Coordinating Ministry (on the Monday) which is led by the Economic Coordinating Minister and attended by all the economics-related ministries and agencies. Similarly, the Economic Coordinating Minister also heads the regular meetings of the Monetary Board at which the most senior economic officials discuss the framework for macro-economic planning. These various formal and informal meetings provide opportunities for ministers to delve gently into developments taking place in each others' portfolios and are used to thrash out policy compromises which can then be taken to the President. Importantly, the conflict and bargaining over policy matters in these forums always takes place within the parameters of what is thought to be acceptable to the President.

In all formal political institutions—right up to the Cabinet—priority is given to minimising the appearance of political differences. Though the process for the limitation of pluralism is more refined at cabinet-level, the principal is the same as that which underlies the GBHN, and, ultimately, the vast network of corporatist structures; formal political participation must be via the designated channels—channels which are themselves carefully filtered.

So far, this discussion has concentrated on the decline of the political parties and the recasting of the representative framework in a restrictive corporatist form. Emphasis has been given to the government's efforts to tighten control of political life by excluding societal groups from access to the policy-making system. But having made this point, it is necessary to pause and ask whether, in fact, societal groups have been as thoroughly excluded as most of the academic literature would lead one to expect. To this end, consideration will now be given to three institutions which are often overlooked in Indonesia, and yet to varying degrees, *do* serve to feed societal demands up to policy-makers: the Parliament, the press, and community-based non-governmental organisations. Each is considered below.

The Parliament

One institution in the Indonesian political system which is conspicuously and almost universally ignored as a vehicle for interest representation is the national Parliament. The Parliament comprises two bodies, the People's Consultative Assembly (MPR) and the House of Representatives (DPR), with the latter normally being thought of as the Parliament proper.

In theory the People's Consultative Assembly is the highest authority in the land, being responsible for the election of the President and Vice President, and, as discussed earlier, the production of the GBHN. In practice, however, the Consultative Assembly is controlled by the government, with more than half of its members being government appointed.[15] New Order practice has been for the Consultative Assembly to meet only once every five years, at which time the GBHN is debated and then ratified and the reappointment of Suharto as President (along with his nominee for Vice President) is confirmed.

Despite having great potential powers under the Constitution, the People's Consultative Assembly is thus a body which receives almost no thought except for the short period when it comes together. Rather than the Consultative Assembly, it is the House of Representatives—the legislature—which attracts greater attention. (For this reason, as well as for convenience, the House of Representatives will henceforth be referred to as the Parliament.) Most foreign observers of Indonesian politics, and indeed, many Indonesians themselves are dismissive of the Parliament. There is a presumption that the Parliament is, at best, only a marginal political arena, and is generally irrelevant to the determination of policy outcomes. Many Indonesians describe it as little more than a charade. This attitude is epitomised by former Vice President Adam Malik's description of a Parliamentarian's life as consisting of the 'four D's': *daftar, duit, duduk, diam* (clock in, collect your pay, sit back and keep quiet.)[16]

Such widespread derision is not without foundation: the Parliament is indeed very largely dominated by the government. The locus of power in Indonesia centres around the President and his ministers—none of whom sits in the Parliament. Although the Parliament is constitutionally empowered to initiate and review legislation, the New Order practice has been for all legislation to originate from the executive branch, and for the legislature to play only a tame review role. Underlying the weakness of the Parliament is the emasculated nature of the Indonesian party system. The party system in Indonesia does not serve to aggregate societal interests and transform demands into policy options. The two non-government parties, and indeed, GOLKAR itself, are devoid of distinctive party platforms or policy orientations. We have already seen that the electoral process is thoroughly 'managed' by the government, and that the possibility of an unfavourable political outcome is remote. Furthermore, of the 500 members of the Parliament, 100 are from the armed forces and are appointed by the government. This, together with the general inertia of the two minor parties and the fact that GOLKAR holds the great majority of the 400 elected seats, does indeed ensure that the Parliament is not a forum in which the government's policies are subject to vigorous scrutiny.

Having said this, however, it nonetheless remains the case that the Parliament can, in a limited and sporadic fashion, exercise some influence on legislation and perform some oversight functions. The focus of attention here is not on the Parliament as a whole, but on the activities of the various committees within it. Members of the Parliament sit on one of eleven specialist committees, each of which has a designated area of responsibility such as defence and security, trade and commerce, public health, agriculture and so on. Some of these have, on occasion, delayed or indirectly forced alterations to government legislation. In such situations, the stalling of a bill typically takes place before it is even submitted to the Parliament for deliberation. Usually this would occur when senior officials from the relevant section of the bureaucracy approach the appropriate committee to discuss the issue and gauge their reaction. This is the one significant opportunity Members have to 'oppose' legislation. A bill to which the government is committed would, however, never actually be overturned. And yet, paradoxically, it is precisely because of this that the occurrence of delays is interpreted as indicating serious opposition. If reservations are voiced which cannot be resolved by negotiation with departmental officials, the matter is passed up the state hierarchy, on one side through departmental channels, and on the other through party, or Fraksi,[17] channels, to be determined at a ministerial, or, if necessary, presidential level. Expressions of concern about government legislation can range from the mild probing of an issue through to vigorous debate and opposition. Interestingly, and contrary to expectations, of the four *Fraksi* in the Parliament, it is the GOLKAR and Armed Forces representatives who are the most likely to take the initiative in expressing concern about aspects of proposed legislation. As a generalisation, when compared with the non-government *Fraksi* in the Parliament (those representing the PPP and the PDI), the GOLKAR and Armed Forces *Fraksi* seem relatively less constrained by a paucity of talent or the prospect of government oversight and intervention.

The other potential opportunity Members of Parliament have for some input to policy debates is through Committee hearings on specific issues.[18] The agenda of matters to be considered by a committee is set following discussion amongst the leadership groups of the four *Fraksi* in the Committees prior to each sitting of the Parliament. The agenda is thus usually a matter of compromise and any *Fraksi* leader can veto an issue he or she does not want aired. The public is able to request that an issue be addressed, there being around two or three such requests from the public to a committee per session (depending on the policy area). There are four two-month sittings of the Parliament per year, with about three weeks being devoted to public hearings each time. At the public hearings the Committees may invite senior government officials and even ministers, as well as members of the public to appear before it. Depending on the interests and determination of the Committee leadership, these can be valuable opportunities to question government leaders about policy issues. While the Committees have no power to force officials to cooperate or provide information, it does appear that most committees are of sufficient standing that an appearance before them is not treated lightly. The presence of journalists covering issues greatly strengthens these public meetings, as all government representatives are wary of receiving negative press coverage. In addition, these meetings can provide a forum in which societal interests can broadcast their viewpoint, again because the hearings are usually covered by the press.

A striking example of the impact a Parliamentary Committee can have in this way is the enquiry held in July 1989 by the Committee (number II) responsible for public administration and home affairs.[19] The enquiry explored the need for greater 'openness' (*keterbukaan*) in Indonesian political life—a catchcry roughly corresponding to the term *glasnost* in the Soviet Union. The enquiry was a media sensation and, even if nothing else, seems likely to have lodged the question of political reform firmly on the public agenda.

Beyond these formal channels, prominent Members can receive numerous calls for assistance from individual members of the public. According to official records, in the period between October 1987 and July 1989 members of the GOLKAR *Fraksi* received eighty four approaches by complainants, the Armed Forces *Fraksi* sixty one and the PPP *Fraksi* thirty seven. (No records are available for the PDI *Fraksi*.)[20] Typically these sporadic pleas for assistance are from people with medium size businesses with grievances about alleged mistreatment by state officials or from low income groups who are being forcibly uprooted as a result of land redevelopment. If a Member is willing to take up an issue, there is some scope for bringing about redress by using his or her status to induce a government official to review the matter. In this respect, it seems that Members of the Parliament are more approachable for aggrieved people with limited political resources than are the government departments responsible for the matter.

For most of the New Order period the Indonesian Parliament has been thoroughly overshadowed by the government. Indeed, if nothing else, its lack of widespread public prestige is testimony to this. The point to be made, though, is that the Parliament is not as irrelevant to the policy-making process as is usually supposed. It is an institution to which groups and individuals in society can and sometimes do look in seeking to have a grievance redressed.

There are very clear constraints on the Parliament's capacity to influence government. The first problem is the question of the quality, convictions and determination of individual Members. Many are seen to be compliant and docile. Some are willing to take up issues or causes that are brought to them, but few are prepared to push a matter in the face of governmental opposition. Those that do attempt to do so, and thereby embarrass the government, run the risk of being declared ineligible for the next election. More generally it can be said that the Parliament largely remains a forum of the weak; groups or individuals that have substantial political resources, and more importantly, the option of dealing directly with senior government officials, will not need to use it. For those without this luxury, it can sometimes be of value.

Despite all the limitations of the Parliament, activist members—especially those with the GOLKAR and Armed Forces *Fraksi*—have managed gradually to boost the institution's profile. As the respected Secretary-General of GOLKAR, Rachmat Witoelar, put it: 'We [the Parliamentarians] have gained a lot of ground. Ten years ago it was very different. We have managed to impose our presence on the political scene without antagonising those who hold power.'[21] The Parliament has become more active in recent years, even if its ability to act as a direct check to the government remains very limited. Mention has already been made of the dramatic enquiry into political 'openness' held by a Parliamentary Committee in July 1989. Other noteworthy instances of high-profile parliamentary activity include the 1988 campaign against government-backed public lotteries and the 1989 criticism of increases in electricity prices.[22] The heightened activism of the House of Representatives in the last few years even spilled over into the People's Consultative Assembly when it convened for its five-yearly meeting in 1988 to ratify the GBHN and confirm the reappointment of President Suharto. Significantly, aspects of the government's draft of the GBHN had to be put to a vote as consensus proved elusive in negotiations. Recourse to voting in this highly symbolic forum was conspicuously at odds with the New Order style of suppressing partisan conflict to achieve ostensible consensus.

Though none of these initiatives by Parliamentarians resulted in actual changes to government policy, they were widely seen as indicative of growing activism within the Parliament and a commitment to reclaiming some of political autonomy as well as rudimentary powers of oversight.

The Press

A second institution given insufficient attention in terms of political representation in Indonesia, is the press.[23] Of the three institutions discussed here—the Parliament, the press and community-based non-governmental organisations—the press is undoubtedly the most potent. Most of what has been written about the press in Indonesia concerns the constraints under which it operates.[24] We thus know a good deal about formal and informal censorship as well as the self-censorship patterns among magazine and newspaper editors. Certain sensitive issues are simply not reported in the press. The government continually stresses that journalism must be 'responsible' and supportive of its development plans.

Most newspaper editors have few qualms about delaying and down-playing coverage of communally divisive issues such as race tensions. More problematic are the unwritten rules that no criticism should be voiced about matters such as the President and his family or security policy. The usual procedure is for the Armed Forces Information Office or the Department of Information to contact editors if there is an issue which key figures in the government do not want reported. Interestingly though, it is often not the major political controversies which attract censorial intervention (these may usually be reported after a short time lag), but rather matters which though nationally insignificant are personally embarrassing for senior military figures.

Many publications have fallen foul of the censorship ground rules. While there has not in recent years been the large scale banning of papers that took place in connection with the Malari riots of 1974 and the general election of 1978, newspapers are periodically forced to close down if they are seen to be too provocative or questioning of government rule. The closure of the very influential *Sinar Harapan* in late 1986 and the more sensational *Prioritas* in mid-1987 are recent examples. A more systematic restriction on the press is the limitation on newspaper size and advertising levels. Since 1980 the maximum length of any daily paper has been twelve pages, with not more than 30 per cent of the total page space to be used for advertising. While the restriction was officially justified in terms of protecting the smaller publications, it seems clear that the real aim was to prevent the largest newspapers from expanding their circulation and influence.[25] Similarly, Jakarta national dailies may not be printed outside the capital itself, thereby restricting their regional reach.[26]

Nevertheless, as Rodgers argues[27]

> . . . newspapers have pride of place in reflecting and moulding attitudes of Indonesia's national political elite and as barometers of the political and socio-economic weather in Indonesia. And in spite of the various formal, 'informal', and financial pressures upon them, Indonesia's more independent newspapers maintain fairly high reporting standards, probably conducting the most sophisticated political debate of any domestic ASEAN press.

Providing they avoid the most sensitive 'high politics' issues, news-papers in Indonesia are able to maintain a very lively and often surprisingly critical coverage of political affairs. As the electronic media is state-controlled (apart from Citizen Band radio), the quality press is essential reading for the political elite. While the daily, *Kompas*, stands out as the premier newspaper (circulation: over 500,000) there are others that are both respected and influential. Among them are *Suara Pembaruan* (formerly *Sinar Harapan*, circu-lation 50,000); the GOLKAR-controlled, yet relatively independent *Suara Karya* (60,000); *Merdeka* and *Business News* (both of which have small circulations) and the widely read weekly magazine *Tempo*. Different publications reach different audiences. Thus some of the military-linked newspapers such as *Berita Buana*, *Berita Yudha* and *Angkatan Bersenjata*, while not major papers, do reach a specifi-cally military audience.[28]

In the absence of other sources of open political debate, press commentary assumes particular importance in influencing the politi-cal agenda.[29] Indeed, in the absence of any formal parliamentary 'Opposition', the press is often seen as assuming this role in a de facto fashion. It is generally recognised that government ministers and senior officials are quite sensitive to press coverage which points to controversy or mismanagement in their area of responsibility. Even more pointed are 'letters to the editor', which very often enable newspapers to print criticism they would not be willing to write themselves. The importance of critical press coverage to government decision-makers lies in its ability to draw areas of controversy or mismanagement in their bailiwick to the attention of their superiors and/or opponents. Most worrying of all is the possibility of such coverage prompting presidential censure, for, by all accounts, Su-harto views the appearance of controversy in political management with considerable disfavour. Another way in which press coverage may have influence over policy issues is by providing ammunition which a faction within the state elite can invoke in policy debates. Thus for example, a minister opposed to the policy initiatives of another, might bring in copies of newspaper headlines criticising the policy in question and use them to embarrass his opponent, or at least stimulate debate.

Perhaps the clearest testimony to the influence of the press in reaching up to the most senior echelons of the government is the comment made to the author by the editor of one of the leading national newspapers, that he is approached a number of times each year by ministers asking him to give prominent coverage to an issue so as to strengthen one side of a policy debate.

The significance of the press in Indonesian political life is thus that it provides a potentially effective channel for groups or individuals wanting to influence the shaping of public policy. In this, it is of value not just to competing groups within the state elite, but also to those outside the state structure seeking to influence some facet of politics. In much the same way as a minister might approach a newspaper editor, groups and individuals in the community approach journalists and editors to promote a cause. If a story seems of sufficient interest, it stands a good chance of being published. Sometimes the individual or group concerned will pay a journalist to write a favourable story—the so-called 'envelope syndrome' (from envelopes full of banknotes). At other times a story will get coverage because a journalist, or editor, is sympathetic. At still other times, it is simple 'newsworthiness' which determines whether a story is taken up. The more sophisticated the newspaper or magazine, the greater the likelihood that the matter will be researched and checked prior to publication.

The press is, within certain limitations, a potentially effective conduit for the channeling of ideas and arguments from motivated societal groups to senior political circles. The press seeks issues and stories itself, but is also sought out by interests in society wishing to use it. The press is a more wide-ranging, more accessible and more influential channel than the Parliament which itself, it should be remembered, is largely dependent on the press for much of its limited ability to influence matters.

Non-Governmental Organisations

The Parliament and the press are two institutional means standing somewhat independently of the atrophied corporatist network by which the interests of groups or individuals outside the state can be prejected into the policy-making process. A third such avenue are community-based non-governmental organisations (NGOs).[30] Surprisingly, perhaps, NGOs have generally managed to preserve considerable independence from the state. NGOs sprang up in Indonesia during the early 1970s, with new trends in development theory at that time being an important stimulus. Often, they were established by intellectuals or student activists. Since then, the number of NGOs in Indonesia has grown markedly, though they have faced a continual balancing-act in seeking to pursue their ideals while avoiding the censure of the security organisations.

The delicate status of the NGOs is reflected in their Indonesian title, *Lembaga Swadaya Masyarakat*: Communal Self-Help Organisations. This was deliberately chosen to avoid political, or opposi-tional connotations. Among the most prominent NGOs are the Legal Aid Institute, the Institute for Economic and Social Research, Education and Information (LP3ES, which publishes the respected journal, *Prisma*), the Consumers' Association, the Environmental As-sociation and the Development Studies Institute. Beyond the fifteen-odd large NGOs which operate at the national level, there are also several hundred small grass-roots organisations at the local level.[31] The most active and controversial of the NGOs is the Legal Aid Institute which has clashed openly with the government—especially on human rights issues—by providing legal representation for de-fendants in politically sensitive trials.[32]

Generally, NGOs have two main sorts of potential influence on policy outcomes. The first is through acting directly as professional consultants to various government departments on technical policy questions. This is a role which has increased in recent years. Second, they can have indirect influence via the press attention which their activities readily attract.

The issue of political control, or state guidance, has come to assume increasing prominence for NGOs in Indonesia since the 1985 Mass Organisations (ORMAS) Legislation was introduced.[33] The purpose of the controversial ORMAS legislation was to limit the scope for independent political action outside state-sanctioned guidelines. It is now, for instance, less easy for some NGOs to receive foreign assistance. In addition, anyone wishing to establish a new NGO will be required to obtain a special government permit (in the past this could be done simply by lodging a declaration with a notary). To date, however, the government has not moved to imple-ment the provisions of the ORMAS law in relation to the NGOs in any systematic fashion. This appears to reflect ambivalence within the government towards the NGOs. While the security organisations are less well-disposed to them, in some quarters (such as the Depart-ment of the Environment, the Department of Public Works, and also, apparently, the Cabinet Secretariat and the Department of Internal Affairs) the NGOs are viewed with favour. This depends, however, on the individual organisation and the particular issue. For present purposes, the significance of the NGOs is that they represent another potential channel for the articulation of extra-state interests. While some, such as the Legal Aid Institute and the Consumers Association, do take up the grievances of individuals, NGOs tend to represent collective societal interests. Broadly speaking, they also tend to promote ideas supportive of weaker groups in society. Their influence is limited and sporadic but, nevertheless, most of the large

NGOs have managed to achieve some notable victories. This, of course, is dependent on their operating within limits acceptable to the government.

Business Representation

Up to this point consideration of political representation has been at a very broad level. Attention will now be shifted to links between the state and one particular segment of society: business. In this way it is possible to examine in greater detail some of the dynamics of political life in Indonesia.

A general argument·has been made here that the three political parties in Indonesia are of little significance in terms of aggregating societal interests and channeling them into the policy-making system. This is no less true for business than for other sectors of society. Business groups neither pay much attention to the parties nor, more tellingly, seek to make financial donations to them on any widespread basis. This is not simply a product of the fact that GOLKAR and the two minor parties are all subsidised by the government. Though key individual parliamentarians might be approached occasionally for assistance on specific matters, in general, business well recognises that the parties themselves are not significant institutions in the Indonesian political system, and as such are unlikely to waste resources on them. This differs from the situation in other countries in the region such as Thailand, South Korea or Japan, where in differing ways business makes extensive contributions to political parties.[34]

In so far as political representation and the shaping of public policy outcomes are concerned, then, the parties are of little interest to business in Indonesia. The same can be said for the NGOs since their orientation towards less privileged groups in the community makes them unlikely vehicles for business interests. Mention has already been made of individual Parliamentarians and, particularly, the press as being of potential assistance to business. But what of those bodies formally responsible for the representation of business interests? It is to the business associations that attention will now be turned.

Making up part of the vast state-sponsored corporatist representational network are several hundred business associations operating at the national level of politics in Indonesia. For virtually every sector, and then sub-sector of business, there is a separate association. A small, random selection might include—the Architects' Association, the Shipowners' Association, the Coffee Exporters' Association, the Real Estate Association, the Car Tyre Manufacturers' Association, the Pesticide Producers' Association, the Tooth Paste Manufacturers' Association and (intriguingly) a separate Association for Tooth *Brush* Manufacturers.[35] Standing at the centre of the field is KADIN (the Indonesian Chamber of Commerce and Industry)—the peak organisation for the articulation of business interests.

Historical Background

KADIN is a creation of the New Order period, having been established in 1968. A variety of business associations had preceded it. During the period of Parliamentary Democracy in the 1950s the Central Economic Council of Indonesia (DEIP) operated as the peak business organisation, with numerous sectoral associations affiliated to it. By 1956 this was in decline and was subsumed within the Council of Business and Trade (DPP) at the national level and the Assembly of Business and Trade (MPP) at the regional level. These two bodies were created by government decree and were aimed at introducing greater regulation of business representation. This, however, did not prevent the proliferation of other independent business associations. The intense and fragmented political party competition of the period encouraged the multiplication of such organisations. Among others to spring up around this time were the All Indonesia National Economic Congress (KENSI); the Indonesian Union of Middle Traders (SPMI); and the All Indonesia National Importers' Congress (KINSI). A central aim of many of these was to oppose Chinese domination of the economy.[36]

In the Guided Democracy years Sukarno attempted to reform the business representation structures with a view to increasing the state's capacity to control the business sector. Presidential Decree no. 2 of 1964 established the National Business Council (BAMUNAS) as the peak association through which business could communicate with the state. This was clearly a forerunner to the corporatist organisations of later years. In practice, however, as Robison reports, BAMUNAS tended to function primarily as a fund-raising organisation for the government. In addition to BAMUNAS, two further types of state-sponsored bodies were set up to oversee industry: the Federation of Homogenous Enterprises (GPS) which operated at a sectoral level, and the Organisation of Homogenous Enterprises (OPS) which operated at a sub-sectoral level. These took over roles that had been performed earlier by the Council of Business and Trade (DPP) and the Assembly of Business and Trade (MPP).[37]

Following the fall of Sukarno and the emergence of the New Order, business representation structures changed yet again. In the wake of the 1965 coup, a new business grouping known as the National Business Action Front (KAPNI) was formed. It was, however, more concerned with supporting the new regime than promoting business demands, and lasted only a short time before its momentum dissipated.[38]

As the New Order government became more established, it set about remodeling the channels for business representation along the lines of the military's favoured corporatist strategies. In June 1967 Presidential Decision no. 84 abolished the Sukarno-created BAMU-NAS. A number of associations attempted to fill this void. The most significant of these was *Forum Swasta* (the Private Entrepreneurs Forum), set up under the leadership of the prominent textile industrialist, Hussein Aminuddin, in February 1968.[39] *Forum Swasta* was, however, unable to establish itself as the pre-eminent business representative organisation because it met with heavy opposition from Soedjono Hoemardhani, a retired military officer who was a close adviser of Suharto. The government's choice for the task of peak business organisation emerged in September 1968, with the formation of KADIN Indonesia as a national business association. The basis for this was laid with the creation in November the year before of KADIN Jakarta, a purely Jakarta-based business organisation sponsored by the city's Governor, Ali Sadikin. Within a few months of the founding of KADIN Jakarta (or KADIN Jaya, as it became known) the government sponsored the formation of regional equivalents in the provinces. At a congress convened among the various regional KADINs in September 1968 the creation of KADIN Indonesia as the peak national body was formalised, thus marking the birth of the organisation which henceforth became the officially designated conduit for intermediation between the state and the business community.[40] The business community was not subjected to the same degree of corporatist restructuring as, for example, the labour movement (where the Communist Party had been strong). While KADIN and many other sectoral business associations were deliberately created, or induced, some associations which had been in existence for many years were permitted to continue.[41] On the whole, however, such bodies gradually acquired corporatist characteristics during the 1970s.

Leadership of KADIN was initially in the hands of senior military figures involved in business. The first three chairmen, from 1968 until 1979, were military figures.[42] Since then two prominent civilian *pribumi* businessmen, Hasjim Ning and Sukamdani Gitosardjono, and a civil servant, Sotion Ardjanggi, have occupied the top position.

While there may have been symbolic significance in the government allowing private business figures rather than state officials to fill the position, there has, in practice, been no effective distancing of the KADIN leadership from the state, as both Hasjim Ning and, especially, Sukamdani were very closely interlocked with the state's political leadership. During this period the position of KADIN as the peak association for business representation was given statutory recognition with Presidential Decision no. 49 in December 1973. This official recognition, or affirmation, of KADIN's position as the pre-eminent business association was (at KADIN's urging) enhanced further in 1983 with specific mention in the State Policy Outline document (the GBHN) and then in 1984 in the fourth Five Year Development Plan (REPELITA IV). Specific reference was made in these two important policy outlines to the role to be played by KADIN in participating actively in national economic development.[43] More importantly still (as will be discussed below) in 1987 KADIN finally secured the ultimate formal endorsement when a special act of Parliament was passed which gave official recognition to its role as the sole peak business organisation.

KADIN: Dynamics and Structure

Despite moves such as these to enhance the standing of KADIN, it has never commanded a good reputation in the eyes of either the business community or the state. Put bluntly, the business community has tended to see KADIN, or more specifically its leadership, as self-serving and virtually a tool of the government rather than as a representative of industry interests. Evidence of the currency of such attitudes is not hard to find. Almost all business figures interviewed by the author, including those who were themselves in senior positions within KADIN, were openly dismissive of it.[44]

Public criticism of KADIN is common as well. Prominent Jakarta businessman Abdul Latief has frequently lambasted the KADIN leadership for its failure to represent business interests. In a speech in August 1987 he called for a more professional KADIN and argued that: 'The business community clearly wants a [KADIN] leadership which genuinely understands their interests, and does not simply promote its own private interests while proclaiming that it represents those of its membership.'[45]

A perusal of the press often reveals statements of dissatisfaction from both business figures and editorial writers. Indicative was a report which, having opened with an account of a bitterly disappointed businessman's experience with KADIN, went on to argue:[46]

Complaints such as this are becoming increasingly common, not just in business circles in Jakarta, but also in the provinces. They believe that all of KADIN's activities are just for show, and aimed only at promoting the KADIN leadership. Meanwhile KADIN's true role, to serve the interest of the business world, has been forgotten.

Membership of KADIN and of many of the sectoral industry associations gathered beneath its umbrella, appears to be generally seen by business as an unavoidable burden. Membership involves the payment of fees and investment of time for very little return. Meetings held by KADIN and the industry associations were often dismissed as being little more than talk-fests.[47]

Perhaps the most telling indication of the low esteem in which KADIN is held by the business community, is the fact that very few of the major Chinese business people bother to join it. This is particularly true of the giant Chinese corporate groups, which have their own individual patron-client links to decision-makers within the state. While there are a small number of the largest Chinese businessmen in KADIN, their involvement is via the Advisory Council and largely formalistic. Liem Soe Liong, the head of Indonesia's largest business conglomerate, is of special importance of KADIN as he, in effect, subsidises its running costs—apparently at the behest of the President. Observers say that Liem derives little direct benefit from these outlays, other than the expectation that the *pribumi* dominated KADIN will not interfere with, or, criticise his business activities.

Apart from irritation with its ineffectiveness, the other widely found concern about KADIN among the business community is that it is too close to the government. Despite occasional public calls for macroeconomic reforms by the KADIN leadership, it is generally regarded as merely reflecting government wishes. The appointment of former bureaucrat, Sotion Ardjanggi, to the chairmanship in 1988 did nothing to ease this concern. Many of KADIN's public pronouncements about the need to help small (and by implication, struggling *pribumi*) business people are often pointed to as evidence of empty rhetoric designed to harmonise KADIN with state ideology. Efforts to conform with government interests are often seen to be at the expense of those of business.

It is not only its client group, the business community, which holds KADIN in low esteem; it also appears to be held in low regard by many sections of the government. Despite statutory recognition and public statements[48] by the President that if KADIN was not satisfied with cooperation and consultation by senior officials or ministers, it could report directly to him, the KADIN leadership is effectively marginalised by policy-makers. Indeed the most commonly heard refrain from the KADIN executive is that the government does not take it seriously or pay attention to its viewpoint.[49] Under Sukamdani's leadership, the KADIN executive did not have close relations with the key economic ministers, the policy-makers in the area most relevant to the interests of business. While Sukamdani and the Deputy Chairman, Probobsutedjo, enjoyed direct personal links to President Suharto, this did not equate to significant influence over economic policy. (No doubt, however, these clientelistic connections were of considerable personal benefit in terms of patronage and the securing of government contracts.)

KADIN has had an institutionalised 'dialogue' with the economic ministers, but this has only been taking place once a year. Moreover, as Sukamdani explained in a press interview, these meetings amounted to little more than a statement by economic ministers on the broad directions of government fiscal planning.[50] They provided virtually no scope for policy input by KADIN on behalf of business. Symbolic of KADIN's impotence was a remark to the international press by Sukamdani saying that KADIN was rarely consulted before or even after the government introduced new economic policies.[51]

There are at least five broad reasons for this reluctance on the part of ministers and senior officials to treat KADIN as a serious contributor to policy formation. The first relates to elements of the world-view of the traditional *priyayi* aristocracy in Java, which endure among senior officials, and mark out the modern bureaucracy as a direct descendant of the feudal court, or *kraton*. Central to this world-view is a paternalistic attitude towards those outside official-dom. Members of the business class, in particular, are viewed as occupying an inferior social position. This traditional disdain towards business is, of course, sharpened greatly by the fact that the business community is dominated by Chinese Indonesians. Nevertheless, it is a problem for both Chinese and *pribumi* business people. Sukamdani (a *pribumi*) openly complained of state officials regarding themselves as being above business people.[52] Certainly this is a complaint commonly heard in Jakarta's business community.

A second barrier to greater influence by KADIN (and business generally), which is also of an intangible nature, concerns the anti-pathy of post-independence Indonesian state ideology towards profit-making and the private sector.[53] Drawing directly on Section 33 of the Constitution and the GBHN, the Indonesian economic system is always described glowingly in official rhetoric as a 'democratic' or *Pancasila* economic system, as opposed to a 'free fight liberal' or market-based system. Section 33 of the Constitution, which carries great ideological weight, emphasises the centrality of the *sistim kekeluargan*, literally, the family system. This invokes

notions of economic collectivism and cooperation. Terminology such
as *kebersamaan* (equality), *kerjasama* (cooperation), *kekeluargaan*
(family spirit), *kerukunan* (harmony) and *persaingan tidak sehat*
(unhealthy competition) is ubiquitous in official rhetoric.[54] These
social justice ideals underlie the government's ideological justification of cooperatives and state enterprises as forms of economic
organisation. While much of this rhetoric is obviously a poor guide to
the reality of the Indonesian economy, since private enterprise and
private capital formation play a large and growing part in the country's economic development, it nevertheless has considerable political force, especially as the President appears to be its most committed
advocate. Though intangible, these cultural and ideological factors
are nonetheless widely seen as having real significance. Jamie Mackie
has argued that this ideological distaste for profit seeking is an
essential reason for what he sees as the weakness of economic
interests in Indonesia.[55]

   A third reason concerns questions about KADIN's credibility as
the peak business association. This problem is of a double edged
nature. On one hand KADIN is seen as lacking in substance because
some of the largest Chinese business conglomerates either bypass it
altogether or else have only token involvement in it. On the other
hand, however, a number of the prominent *pribumi* business figures
within the KADIN leadership group are generally seen to have
dubious commercial credentials as their prosperity has been heavily
dependent on special government patronage. Combined, these two
elements have rendered KADIN's claim to be the spokesman of the
business world rather suspect.

   A fourth factor underlying the disdainful attitude of important
sections of the bureaucracy towards KADIN centres around the
perceived lack of professionalism and seriousness on the part of
KADIN's leaders. It has only been through the establishment of the
Institute for Economic Research and Development (LP3E) within
KADIN as an economic 'think tank' under the leadership of the
respected former minister, Mohammad Sadli, that KADIN's executive has accrued any credibility on macroeconomic matters. LP3E
was formed at Sukamdani's initiative to equip the KADIN leadership
to address broad problems confronting business. While the LP3E has
reportedly generated useful papers on economic issues under the
guidance of people like Sadli and Suryo Sediono, this resource has
not always been exploited by the KADIN leadership. The LP3E, for
example, conducts monthly meetings to address major issues which
have been attended only on an irregular basis by KADIN leaders.
Economic policy-makers are unlikely to be willing to listen to

KADIN leaders if they are ill-informed or appear to be dilettantes on matters of national economic development and planning.

A final and more general reason for the unwillingness of policy-makers to heed KADIN, is that it would run completely against the grain of the New Order's corporatist approach to political management were they to do so. The political architects of the New Order did not intend that state-designated interest organisations, such as KADIN, should be active participants in the shaping of public policy. Put bluntly, they were to be seen, but not heard; for if institutions such as KADIN were to become seriously involved in the policy process, it would inevitably mean a diminution of the government's control over policy directions. As Sukamdani himself declared, the relationship between KADIN and the government was unlike that between industry peak associations in either the Anglo-Saxon or continental countries of the West. Instead, he said, it was based upon the Indonesian principles of *Pancasila*.[56] This was little more than a coded acknowledgment that KADIN does not serve as an effective channel for business interests. Instead, in keeping with the government's corporatist design, it serves to regulate and restrict business demands upon the state.

There is, then, a number of reasons for the unwillingness of state officials to treat KADIN representations with great seriousness. If KADIN has any influence at all upon government policy it is only as one of many actors shaping the climate of ideas in which politics takes place. For example, public statements by the KADIN executive supporting deregulation of certain facets of the economy presumably do help to sustain the momentum of that particular policy reform movement. Certainly under Sukamdani's leadership KADIN developed a higher profile than previously. And this, presumably, has boosted the organisation's ability to contribute to the *public* discourse on economic issues and the climate of ideas. But even here KADIN's influence is very limited: it does not set or even shape the agenda for policy debate. In terms of influencing the climate of ideas, KADIN's voice is still weak compared with those of the key economic policy segments of the state elite, the press and foreign institutions such as the World Bank and the International Monetary Fund.

Emphasis has been given to establishing the claim that while KADIN may considerably benefit the fortunes of its individual leaders, it is not important as a vehicle for the advancement of broad business interests. This proposition requires qualification though, for when people speak of KADIN they usually have in mind the national executive. There is, however, much more to the organisation than this. Aside from the executive, KADIN is made up of three strands:

the regional KADIN branches (the KADINDA), the 'aspiration groups', and the sectoral and sub-sectoral industry associations. A little should be said about each as there are quite separate sets of interests involved.

The dominant strand is that of the KADINDA. While KADIN is the national organisation, it has regional and district branches below, scattered throughout the country. Many of the regional and district KADINDA exist almost in name only, having little membership or organisational depth. Lacking any dynamism of their own, in most cases, the KADINDA tend to be steered by the regional GOLKAR officials, who are themselves usually the regional political administrators. Thus, at the regional level the KADIN network is primarily an instrument of control for the political authorities, herding business people into a single corporatist pen. With some exceptions,[57] the KADINDA are generally seen as passive and pliant organisations, whose membership tends to be dominated by building contractors. (The dominance of building contractors is due to the fact that public sector work, which represents a huge slice of the industry, is unobtainable unless they are member of KADIN.)

A second strand of the KADIN structure is made up of the so-called 'aspiration groups'. There are only a few organisations in this category, most of which emerged during the 1970s. Basically, they are very loose bodies representing different 'classes' of business people. The term 'aspiration group' is an ideological nicety, referring to the fact that these nominally represent weak economic interests. Thus, for example, there is the Veterans' Business Organisation (DEVI), the All Indonesia Small Business Organisation (HIKSI), the Indonesian Small and Medium Business Organisation (KUKMI), the Indonesian Weak Business Organisation (HIPLI), the Indonesian Indigenous Entrepreneurs Organisation (HIPPI) and the Indonesian Young Entrepreneurs Organisation (HIPMI). Except for the last two organisations, these aspiration groups are insignificant, merely standing as testimony to the government's corporatist strategy of providing an official body with the nominal responsibility of acting as a conduit to interests in society.

HIPPI (indigenous entrepreneurs) and HIPMI (young entrepreneurs) are of some importance; the former due to the fact that it is sponsored by Probosutedjo, Suharto's half-brother and the Deputy Chairman of KADIN. A political maverick, Probosutedjo has used this as a forum from which to criticise the dominant position of Chinese capital in Indonesia, a perennial and sensitive subject. Only his unassailable position as a member of the President's family has allowed him to do this, even though it is a theme which enjoys much support among non-Chinese business people.

More noteworthy in terms of business representation is the Young Entrepreneurs Association, HIPMI. This was formed in the early 1970s by Abdul Latief and other prominent young business figures such as Aburizal Bakrie, Tanri Abeng and Ponco Sutowo (most of whom were associated with the Muslim Students' Association, HMI). In its early days, HIPMI developed an image as a group of outspoken 'young turks'. They were seen as more willing to confront the government and speak out on behalf of business, so much so that they antagonised General Ali Moertopo and other senior security managers.[58] In the absence of KADIN acting as an effective petitioner for business, HIPMI has sometimes been seen as an emerging forum for business activists.[59] This, however, appears very unlikely to be the case. Despite the fact that HIPMI has established a 'think tank' of its own (following KADIN's LP3E), it remains little more than a small and occasionally brash version of KADIN. It is widely seen (like KADIN) to be primarily generating business opportunities for its leadership, rather than promoting the broad interests of its constituency.[60] Furthermore, it is today less outspoken than in the past, having been coopted by the government within the KADIN and GOLKAR network.[61]

Apart from HIPPI and HIPMI which are only significant at the level of rhetoric, the aspiration-group strand of KADIN is of no major importance. The third strand, the industry associations, however, demand serious attention.

It is widely recognised in Jakarta that the only real representation of business interests lies with the individual sector-specific industry associations.[62] It is at this association level, for example, that foreign firms in joint ventures are most likely to have membership. As mentioned earlier, there are some 350 industry associations registered in Indonesia, although only about two thirds are actually members of KADIN. The associations which are members, are grouped into various sections. There is, for instance, a financial services section, a basic chemicals section, a metal and motor industries section, a mining and energy section and so on. Each section has its own administration and leadership and subsumes numerous sector-related industry associations.

While many of the associations are as docile as the rest of the business representational structures, there are some which do actively promote the interests of their sectoral constituency. KADIN leaders, together with the government's political strategists, have wanted individual business people to become KADIN members via the KADINDA rather than via sectoral industry associations. This is because the associations are often less amenable to control by either the government or the KADIN executive than the KADINDA.

While many associations are passive and unthreatening, those which are active are seen as unwilling to accept quietly an unfavourable policy environment.

So stark is this contrast that it represents a fundamental cleavage within KADIN. On one side there are the activist industry associations, while on the other, lined up against them, are the KADINDA, the mainstay of support for the executive. The two sides are representative of the forces of assertive business as opposed to those of state corporatist political engineering. Since the early 1970s there has been continued tension between the two. The activist associations have pushed against what they have seen as the weak and ineffective leadership of successive KADIN leaderships by seeking greater influence within the KADIN structure. Consistently, however, they have been thwarted by an internal power distribution which sees the first strand of KADIN, the KADINDA, controlling the election of the KADIN executive. Until recently it has been only the KADINDA which have been entitled to participate in the ballot to elect the executive board every five years. The associations were permitted to nominate some candidates for the ballot, but not to vote. Thus, in view of the fact that strong links existed between GOLKAR and the KADINDA, the scope for the election of a candidate unpalatable to the government was much reduced. Unlike the associations, the KADINDA could be orchestrated without great difficulty. Nevertheless, the government has always carefully monitored the election of the KADIN executive, with all candidates being first interviewed individually by the State Secretary.[63] Moreover, when there has been controversy over the chairmanship of the organisation, Presidential 'guidance' has resolved the matter.[64]

The persistent pressuring by the activist associations to have KADIN's constitution amended to allow them voting rights is symbolic of attempts by some industry activists to shake off the corporatist shackles encumbering KADIN and turn the organisation to their own purposes, as an effective vehicle for the articulation and promotion of business interests.[65] This struggle was captured nicely in one newspaper editorial:

> . . . they (the genuine entrepreneurs) should determine KADIN policy, not the pseudo-entrepreneurs. The voice of the genuine entrepreneurs must be heard, and the sectoral business associations, which represent the crest of the wave, must be given a real role and decisive say.[66]

KADIN's Search for Legitimacy: The Law of 1987

Recognising its limitations, as well as public consciousness of them, the KADIN leadership has consistently sought a stronger legal basis for the organisation. The earlier mentioned attainment of recognition in the State Policy Outline document (the GBHN) and the fourth Five Year Plan (REPELITA IV), represented partial fulfilment of this aim. The ultimate target, however, was the enactment by the Parliament of a law which would specify KADIN as the sole peak business organisation and hopefully enhance its authority and influence. An act of Parliament would be a stronger statutory basis than an executive decree, being less readily amenable to reversal by the government. Great expectations were held for such a legislative basis. First, it was hoped that it would eliminate the possibility of any threat to KADIN's position as the pre-eminent business association; secondly, that it would resolve KADIN's most serious weakness—an inability to raise sufficient funding to operate effectively and autonomously; and thirdly, that it would improve the organisation's standing—and thus its capacity to deal on a more equal basis with state officials and government leaders.

The first of these motivations, KADIN's interest in self-preservation, reflected a concern about the typically short life-span of business associations in Indonesia. As already seen, there have been numerous business peak associations in Indonesia. The KADIN executive was anxious to reduce the risk of another state-approved association emerging to challenge or supplant it. KADIN had long sought to increase its authority through the introduction of compulsory membership for all firms and sectoral business associations.[67] If all firms and business associations were roped in under KADIN's umbrella, the scope for challenges to the organisation's position as the pre-eminent body would be reduced. Many sub-sections within the business community were conspicuously unhappy with KADIN's performance and leadership, and thus either withheld their support or were, in some cases, openly critical. In 1982, for example, there was great controversy over reforms to KADIN's constitution. Some factions were very hostile to proposals by the KADIN leadership and openly signalled a split with the organisation. This resulted in the formation in early 1983 of the Federation of Industry Associations (BMAI) by a range of business groups, especially those in the metal and chemical industries. This took place with the support of then Industry Minister, Suhud.[68] While this schism ultimately came to nothing (the BMAI later faded away, in large part because of a change in Industry Minister), it was a clear indication of the serious discontent with existing industry representation arrangements.

KADIN's interest in compulsory, or at least greatly expanded, membership was twofold. On one hand it wanted to secure its position against possible rival institutions, while on the other, if its membership was near-to-universal rather than fragmentary, its bargaining position with the government would be enhanced.

Interestingly, the government appears to have been wary of this prospect. Trade Minister Rachmat Saleh was reported as telling the Parliament during a hearing on the KADIN law that the government did not view universal compulsory membership as desirable.[69] KADIN was already the only official peak organisation for the entire business community, even though its actual membership fell far short of this. One might have expected the government to be very keen about the idea of enforcing compulsory universal membership of KADIN upon the business community. Herding *all* of the private sector business people into one pen would certainly be consistent with the expectations of corporatist theory. However the reality of the situation is rather more messy, and not entirely clear. It appears that there was some concern within the government that a larger KADIN might become a stronger KADIN, and thus more able to project its demands into the policy process. While committed to the idea of KADIN as a compliant corporatist body, the government seems to have been unwilling to allow it to expand to the point of commanding membership of *all* business people. From this viewpoint a simple majority of the business community was sufficient, and some 'leakage' of members was desirable, otherwise KADIN might possibly become stronger than its political masters intended.

The second of KADIN's ambitions in pursuing a legislative basis for itself—financial independence—was, if anything, more pressing than the first. As LP3E chairman, Mohammed Sadli, emphasised, KADIN's biggest weakness has always been its inability to finance itself from membership dues.[70] Of those individual companies and business associations which were actually members of KADIN, many did not pay their dues. While figures for individual companies are not available, it is known that approximately 350 business associations existed in 1985, with 210 of these being KADIN members. Of this total only 75 per cent paid their dues.[71] As KADIN was unable to compel fee payment, it was faced with an acute dilemma: revoke membership for non-payment of dues (and thus risk large scale disaffection) or lamely tolerate the situation. The latter option has prevailed. In consequence KADIN has been unable to fund itself adequately. In this situation it has fallen to a small number of very large Chinese business people (principally Liem Soe Liong) to subsidise the organisation's activities—apparently at the behest of the President. (Liem's son, Liem Foeng Seng, heads the KADIN treasury section.) Public statements by Sukamdani and other KADIN leaders indicated their discomfort with this arrangement. Speaking before the State Budget Committee of the Parliament, Sukamdani asked why the Government did not allocate funds to assist with the running of KADIN. He said that this would be preferable to the organisation being dependent on handouts from a few large business-men and thereby risking an impression of bias.[72] Above all, the KADIN leadership was uncomfortable with the appearance that it was beholden to a few very large *Chinese* benefactors. The general resentment felt towards the dominant commercial position of the Chinese placed the KADIN leadership in a delicate situation. The question of funding was, therefore, linked with the issue of compul-sory membership. If KADIN could obtain a larger membership, its coffers would also swell (presuming that members could be con-strained to pay their dues) and it would thereby get around the problem of relying on politically controversial benefactors.

Apart from an increased membership base, another financial plum keenly sought by the KADIN leadership was the right to administer the national company register, a function performed by the Depart-ment of Trade. KADIN hoped that this lucrative role might be ceded to it as part of the projected KADIN law.[73] Collection of a universal registration charge would provide an immediate and continuous supply of supplementary revenue. However, it was also for precisely this reason that the Trade Department was unwilling to surrender its control of the company register: it also valued the fund-raising tool highly. As a compromise, KADIN proposed that the Trade Depart-ment retain the initial registration function, but that KADIN be granted the follow-up role of re-registering firms. The Department, however, was not willing to bargain on this lucrative exercise. Trade Minister Rachmat Saleh, publicly signalled the government's unwill-ingness to compromise when he told the Parliament that the govern-ment regarded fund-raising as an internal problem for KADIN to resolve itself.[74]

As with the issue of universal membership, the government was aware of the possible implications of allowing KADIN to obtain financial independence. If it remained financially hamstrung (and dependent on the patronage of a few key Chinese businessmen, who were themselves beholden to the government) it was unlikely to be able to challenge the government's control over policy.

The third of KADIN's expected gains from a formal legislative basis was the achievement of a better footing from which to negotiate with the government on matters of concern to business. An unequi-vocal statement in law stipulating a role for KADIN as 'adviser' or 'consultative partner' to the government in the development of policy would enable it to achieve greater political influence and override the traditional disdain of state officials. This broader concern was also bound up with the two previous aspects, strength of membership and finance. If these were secured, there would be still greater pressure for change in the behaviour of state officials towards business. A law would not, of course, immediately constrain officials to treat KADIN seriously: but it could be expected that important recognition of this sort would go some distance towards slowly breaking down the status distinction between business and officialdom.

Finally, after lobbying for many years, the KADIN law was ratified by the President in January 1987.[75] KADIN had agitated for the introduction of such a law since at least the time of Hasjim Ning's leadership in the late 1970s. Under Sukamdani two major drives were mounted—the first following his attainment of the chairmanship, and the second in 1986. These involved making approaches and submissions to various government departments and the Parliamentary Committees, as well as extensive use of the press.[76]

An important factor which had delayed the law for so many years was the question of restructuring KADIN. If the government was to agree to the introduction of a specific law enshrining KADIN's position, it first wanted assurances that KADIN was the sort of organisation with which it would remain comfortable. It was for this reason that the internal struggle between the KADIN executive and the KADINDA, on one hand, and the industry activists from some of the sectoral associations, on the other, was of such importance. Upon it hung the control of KADIN, and thus the whole orientation of the organisation.

When ultimately promulgated, the KADIN law was in many respects an anti-climax. It confirmed that the government was not about to abandon its corporatist strategy for the management of interest representation. No provisions were included for compulsory membership of KADIN, and there was no provision for new funding sources. In a compromise gesture, however, the government included in the Act clauses which left open the possibility of further changes being introduced by subsequent implementing regulations both on the issue of membership and, by implication, funding.[77] The KADIN leadership, assuming that it would soon be granted such privileges, began, almost immediately after the ratification of the law, to call for the introduction of the implementing regulations which had been implied.[78] There was, however, no response from the government. Indeed, two members of the Parliament openly refuted the suggestion by KADIN leaders that membership would become compulsory as a result of the new law.[79] In reality, there seems very little likelihood that the government will meet KADIN's wishes on either front.

The aspect of the new law which attracted greatest attention was the stipulation that henceforth KADIN members would be drawn not just from the ranks of private enterprise, but also from the state enterprises and cooperatives. This was a striking change, and led to concern among business activists that it was intended to increase the government's capacity to influence KADIN activities by diluting the strength of the private sector's voice through the inclusion of public sector business. As indicated earlier, business activists in the associations wing of KADIN were already in a weak position as the organisation was effectively penetrated and managed by the state through its control of the selection of KADIN leaders. The activists feared that this situation would only be worsened once the state enterprises and the cooperatives joined the organisation.

Presented with a *fait accompli*, KADIN leaders sought to downplay the significance of the inclusion of public sector enterprises, and spoke instead of a bright new future opened up for the organisation by the new law. Notwithstanding the rhetoric of KADIN leaders, it was widely believed in business circles in Jakarta that not only would the new law do relatively little to promote the representation of business interests, but that the provision for the inclusion of public sector enterprises was an actual setback. This concern about state control of the organisation nominally responsible for the representation of their collective interests was further sharpened with the selection of Sotion Ardjanggi, a senior bureaucrat, to replace Sukamdani as KADIN chairman in 1988. Though business activists had long been critical of Sukamdani for his failure to push business interests more vigorously, in hindsight he came to appear considerably more attractive, for he was at least of the private sector rather than the state.

Ironically, the one aspect of the new law which did hold out the prospect of a brighter future for KADIN in terms of interest representation and dealings with the state, received very little attention. This concerned the explicit recognition of the profit motive as the defining characteristic of economic enterprise for the first time anywhere in an official Indonesian legal statute.[80] While the existence of private enterprise has long been acknowledged, it has always lacked ideological legitimacy in Indonesia. In the Constitution and the GBHN, the key repositories of New Order ideology, profit and competition are nowhere acknowledged. Instead the language used is that of collectivism. Even more telling is the fact that prior to the 1987 law KADIN's own constitution did not attempt to legitimise these concepts.

It is possible that this recognition and legitimation of the market could come to represent an ideological turning point in the political economy of Indonesia. More than any other aspect of the KADIN law this holds the greatest potential for boosting the capacity of business to achieve greater influence on policy. Change of this nature, however, is almost certainly of a long term nature and unlikely to have an immediate impact.

The Economic Environment of the Mid-1980s

Thus far, this chapter has examined the political context in which business-government relations are located in contemporary Indonesia. However, before we proceed to the case-studies for a detailed examination of interest representation by particular sections of the business community, it is important to provide a brief overview of the economic context of the mid-1980s, for this was fundamental to much of the politics of the period.

Much has been written elsewhere on the nature of Indonesia's economic crisis of the mid-1980s, and the main elements are by now familiar.[81] Following the buoyant years of oil-led growth in the 1970s, the Indonesian economy between 1982 and 1987 has been subject to extreme buffeting from developments in the international economy. The most serious of these was the two-stage collapse in oil prices. The country's gross earnings from oil and gas exports, having reached a high-point of almost $19 billion in 1981–82, plummeted to $14.7 billion in 1982–83, slid further to $12.4 billion in 1985–86 and then dropped all the way to $6.9 billion in 1986–87. In a situation where oil receipts constituted as much as three-quarters of the country's total export earnings and two-thirds of government revenue, this was indeed an enormous blow. Figure 3.1 shows changes in the value of oil and gas both in terms of export earnings and also government revenues. (The data has been converted to US dollars to remove the disguising influence of several devaluations and to highlight international purchasing power.) In addition to a collapse in oil and gas earnings, the value of Indonesia's non-oil primary commodity exports (which represent approximately 20 per cent of export earnings in the mid 1980s) also suffered from a general tumbling in commodity prices. While not all non-oil commodity prices were affected equally, by 1985 the World Bank's international index of primary commodity prices was at a level 20 per cent below that of 1979–81.

Coinciding with this collapse in export earning potential were the flow-on effects of the international economic downturn, particularly in the United States. These factors came together to induce a recession in the Indonesian economy so that, in 1985, growth in the GDP totalled only 1.9 per cent compared with 6 per cent the year

FIGURE 3.1
Export Earnings and Government Receipts From Oil & Gas
(Constant Prices)

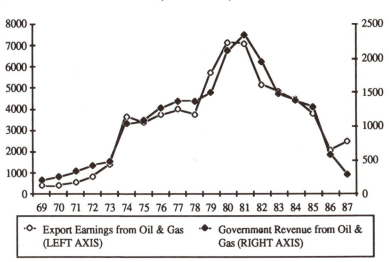

Source: Department of Finance (1988).

before. (A more telling figure, Gross Domestic Income, which makes adjustments for declining terms of trade, would reveal an even bleaker picture.) Thus at a time when economic planners were searching for alternative sources of investment to generate growth, local business activity was contracting.

In responding to this situation, the government was severely constrained by a rapidly deteriorating balance of payments and a greatly reduced revenue base. In the longer term there was the broader problem of the need to restore sustainable levels of growth in income, investment and employment. One of the first measures adopted was an austere fiscal policy, with development expenditure being cut back sharply. At the same time, to prevent the economy from stalling, greater use was made of foreign borrowings for investment in development projects. Aid came to constitute a much larger proportion of developmental expenditure. This had implications for the debt-service-ratio, however, which had been seriously affected by unfavourable international currency realignments. (The bulk of Indonesia's export earnings were denominated in the declining US dollar while, conversely, much of its imports and debt were denominated in the rapidly strengthening Japanese yen and European currencies.) In an inevitably unpopular bid to prevent the balance of payments deficit from getting out of control, the rupiah was devalued sharply by a nominal 45 per cent in September 1986.

In addition to these macroeconomic adjustments, important structural change was also undertaken to boost desperately needed foreign exchange earnings. A range of measures was introduced to reform the country's restrictive trade regime (*tata niaga*) especially in the area of government-created import monopolies. The import monopolies had become very controversial both because they undermined the international competitiveness of downstream exporters, and because of their links in many cases to senior political figures and exorbitant rent-taking practices. Movement in the direction of tariff rather than non-tariff barriers, as well as the overall reduction of dispersal in trade protection levels was therefore introduced only slowly.[82] In addition to measures seeking to facilitate non-oil exports through the lowering of cost inputs, deregulatory reforms were also undertaken to encourage increased foreign investment to assist in economic regeneration.

Many of these reform measures were politically very contentious, as they represented virtually a 'U-turn' on various key elements of economic policy during the booming years of the 1970s and early 1980s. During the oil-rich years an over-valued exchange rate had obstructed non-oil exports while encouraging imports. In this period of prosperity, lax financial discipline and the establishment of import monopolies attracted less controversy. The onset of hard times provided the stimulus for serious consideration of how to address the problem of an over-regulated, 'high-cost' economy. The balance-of-payments crisis of the mid-1980s brought the arguments for the promotion of non-oil exports into sharp focus.

The pressing economic problems of this period provided much needed support for the so-called 'technocrats' (the liberal economists in the government who favoured deregulation) in their perennial policy struggles with opposing officials committed to a more nationalistic and interventionist economic outlook. The technocrats were able to capitalise on the country's economic difficulties and make considerable progress in bringing about a shift from reliance upon import-substitution measures towards a more export-oriented trade and industry policy.

As Robison has argued, many of the deregulatory measures so introduced directly threatened the interests of major corporate groups engaged in upstream production and the importation of similar industrial inputs, together with those of some powerful elements within the state structure who were financially linked to these ventures through their involvement in the initial granting of monopolies and other concessions.[83] Inevitably, this imbued almost all discussion of the restrictive trade regime (*tata niaga*) with considerable political sensitivity.

Many of these issues will be illustrated in the course of the case-studies. The point of this overview has been to emphasise the acuteness of the economic crisis that confronted the government, especially between 1985 and 1987. Much political debate emerged during this period over the impact of economic conditions and of some of the bold policy reforms aimed at tackling the situation. Policy-makers were caught between the macroeconomic imperatives, which manifested themselves in ways ranging from catastrophic reports of a balance of payments deficit to the increasingly conspicuous need for employment creation, and the less obvious, but no less real, political resistance from a variety of sources opposed to the reforms. In short, the politico-economic setting for the three case-studies which now follow, was, to say the least, turbulent.

1. Reeve (1985). It must be stressed that Reeve, an historian, does not himself talk in terms of corporatism. He analyses the emergence of GOLKAR in terms of traditional Javanese ideas about political representation. That the picture he puts forward matches corporatist models is, however, quite clear.
2. Reeve (1985) especially pages xiii–47.
3. Reeve (1985) pp. 322–65.
4. In addition to Reeve, see also Mohtar Mas'oed (1989) and Dwight King (1977).
5. Reeve (1985) p. 131.
6. For a thorough study of the position of parties in Indonesian politics during these years see, among others, Liddle (1978), Crouch (1978), and Ward (1974).
7. See Ward (1974).
8. Emmerson (1978) p. 107. See Emmerson for a more detailed account of the development of KORPRI, especially pp. 101–9.
9. Haseman (1986).
10. For further details on this enormous social and political education program see, Morfit (1981), Weatherbee (1985) and Watson (1987).
11. For some insight into the background of the GBHN see Rufinus Lahur (1973).
12. 'MPR Sebarkan Kuesioner Untuk Himpun Bahan GBHN 1988–1993', *Kompas*, 26 November 1986.
13. See 'Siapapun Boleh Sumbang Pemikiran Untuk GBHN', *Kompas*, 5 June 1987.
14. This discussion of the Cabinet draws on interviews with three former

New Order ministers, Mohammad Sadli (22 April & 24 August 1987); Daoud Joesoef (20 August 1987), and Frans Seda (4 May 1987) and the attachments accompanying Pangestu (1989).

15. Following a constitutional amendment in 1985, the People's Consultative Assembly is made up of 1,000 members. 500 of these are especially appointed by the government, while the remaining 500 comprise the full membership of the House of Representatives. However 100 of the 500 members of the House of Representatives are also appointed by the government, being drawn from the ranks of the armed forces.

16. 'View from the Pinnacle', *Indonesian Observer*, 22 July 1987.

17. *Fraksi*, the term officially used, refers to the four divisions into which members of the House of Representatives are divided. The four *Fraksi* are formal institutional divisions corresponding to the three parties (GOLKAR, the PPP and the PDI) and the armed forces appointees. In the parliamentary context the term 'party' is eschewed, because the 100 armed forces representatives are neither elected nor members of any party, and also because GOLKAR itself resisted the label of 'party' for many years. In theory this semantic distinction also helps to blur the appearance of partisan conflict.

18. For much of the information here, I am grateful to Djoko Sudjatmiko (Committee VI, Deputy Leader GOLKAR *Fraksi*—interview 6 June 1987); Hamzah Haz (Committee XI, Leader PPP *Fraksi*—interview 9 June 1987); and Beren Ginting (Committee VII, Deputy Leader GOLKAR *Fraksi*—interviews 13 June & 19 August 1987).

19. See 'Keterbukaan: Mari Bicarakan Bersama', *Tempo*, 8 July 1989, pp. 22–31; and 'Maka, Sebuah Harapan Baru pun Lahir', *Tempo*, 15 July 1989, pp. 22–34.

20. 'Pagar-Pagar di Dalam DPR', *Tempo*, 15 July 1989, p. 27.

21. Quoted in Vatikiotis M., 'Caution is the Catchword for Political Rejuvenation', *Far Eastern Economic Review*, 20 April 1988, pp. 20–21.

22. On the lottery controversy, see 'Desa Matikan Karena Angan-Angan', *Tempo*, 9 July 1988, pp. 22–30 and 'Soal Kupon, Sampai di Sini', *Tempo*, 23 July 1988, pp. 23–25; while for the question of electricity prices, see Vatikitotis M., 'Galvanising Politics: GOLKAR Uses Electricity to Redefine Role', *Far Eastern Economic Review*, 20 April 1989, p. 27.

23. Much of the material in this section draws on interviews with Yakob Oetama (Chief Editor of *Kompas*) 24 April 1987; August Parengkuan (a *Kompas* editor) 8 September 1987; Sanyoto (Chief Editor of *Business New*) 2 February & 2 September 1987: Mohammad Chudori (General Manager of the *Jakarta Post* and Chairman of the Indonesian Journalists' Association) 10 March 1987; Endang Ahmadi (Deputy Chief Editor *Berita Yudha*) 8 April 1987; and Suwachman (Managing Editor of *Prioritas*) 8 April 1987; as well as numerous other journalists.

24. In this regard see Peter Rodgers' (1980) very useful monograph; Nono Anwar Makarim (1985); and Tjipta Lesmana (1985). For a recent overview of the newspaper industry see 'The Killing Business' and

Christianto Wibisono's 'Siapa Raja Pers Indonesia', *Swasembada*, vol. 12, no. III, April 1988.
25. Rodgers (1980) p. 17.
26. Goenawan Mohamad (Chief Editor of *Tempo*), 'The Press in Indonesia', seminar in the Department of Political & Social Change, the Australian National University, 23 March 1988.
27. Rodgers (1980) p. 4.
28. This section draws on Goenawan Mohamad (1988).
29. The following draws on interviews with three former New Order ministers—Mohammad Sadli (22 April & 24 August 1987); Daoud Joesoef (20 August 1987) and Frans Seda (4 May 1987).
30. This section draws on interviews with Aswab Mahasin (Director of the LP3ES—the Institute for Social & Economic Research, Education & Information) 14 February 1988; Erna Witoelar (former head of the Environmental Association & current head of the Consumers' Association) 15 August 1987; Tini Hadad (Secretary of the Consumers' Association) 18 August 1987; and Permadi (former head of the Consumers' Association) 24 May 1987. For a general overview of the position of NGOs in Indonesian political life, see Eldridge (1984–85).
31. Technically the largest NGOs are known as *Lembaga Swadaya Pembangunan Masyarakat* (Communal Development Self-Help Organisations) with the term *Lembaga Swadaya Masyarakat* being reserved for the numerous small local-level organisations. In practice, the latter term is often used as a generic label for them all.
32. For a useful study of the Legal Aid Institute, see Lev (1987).
33. For a critical review of the implications of the ORMAS law for NGOs see, Rickard (1987).
34. Compare, for example, Johnson (1987) pp. 156–57 with Ramsay (1987) pp. 256–57; Jones & Sakong (1980) pp. 67–69; Curtis (1975); Allinson (1987) and MacIntyre (1990), forthcoming.
35. For a much more extensive list see, KADIN (1987 a) pp. 111–21.
36. For further details see Robison (1986 a) pp. 60–61; and the useful three part article by Amaludin Ganie (the first Secretary General of KADIN): 'KADIN dan Sejarahnya', *Merdeka*, 20–22 September 1982.
37. See KADIN (1987) pp. 2–3; and Robison (1986 a) p. 81.
38. Amaludin Ganie (1982) and KADIN (1987 a) pp. 3–4.
39. For some reference to *Forum Swasta* see, 'Meningaktkan Kedudukan dan Peranan KADIN Sebagai Organisasi Dunia Usaha Nasional Dalam Kerjasama Dengan Pemerintah', *Suara Karya*, 13 September 1984; and Robison (1986 a) p. 367 fn 3.
40. Amaludin Ganie 1982, *op.cit.*
41. See King (1977) pp. 14–16.
42. These were, Brigadier General Usman Ismail, Brigadier General Sofyar and Air Marshall Suwoto Sukendar.
43. For further details see, KADIN (1987 b) p. 18.
44. Robison encountered a similar reaction, and noted that: 'KADIN is widely regarded as a collection of business failures scrabbling for the

crumbs of patronage who hypocritically set themselves up as leaders of business in Indonesia . . . [and] as a club dominated by self-seeking and well-connected businessmen . . .' Robison (1986 b) p. 45.

45. Abdul Latief 'KADIN Untuk Mempersatukan Dunia Usaha, Sentuhan Profesionalisme dan Transparansi Bisnis di Indonesia,' presented to a forum on Professionalism and the Business Environment, Jakarta, 4 August 1987.

46. 'KADIN Harus Membenahi Diri', *Kompas*, 15 September 1984. Among many others, see also, for example, 'Musyawarah Pengusaha Indonesia' (editorial), *Berita Yudha*, 23 September 1987; 'Pergulatan KADIN Indonesia Dengan Asosiasi Berlangsung Hangat', *Prioritas*, 16 June 1987; 'Bolstering the Chamber' (editorial), *Jakarta Post*, 25 September 1985; and 'KADIN's Leadership Role' (editorial), *Jakarta Post*, 23 April 1984.

47. As one newspaper put it: 'The majority of business people are fed-up with [business] organisations, with their levies and dues for which there is little clear benefit.' 'Banyak Pungutan Dari Asosiasi Termasuk Dari KADIN Sendiri', *Pelita*, 15 July 1985.

48. See 'KADIN Indonesia Dapat Beri Laporan Langsung Kepada Presiden', *Kompas*, 18 May 1983.

49. See, for example, 'Keluh Kesah KADIN Yang Cukup Panjang' (editorial), *Kompas*, 21 June 1986; 'Pemerintah dan Swasta' (editorial), *Kompas*, 10 September 1983; and, 'Pemerintah Belum Sepenuh Hati Mau Bekerjasama Dengan KADIN Indonesia: Sukamdani—Banyak Pejabat Masih Bersikap 'Atasan' Dengan 'Bawahan' Terhadap Swasta', *Kompas*, 9 September 1983.

50. See 'Kerjasama Pemerintah dan KADIN Belum Seperti yang Diharapkan', *Kompas*, 16 March 1985.

51. 'Suharto's Policies Lashed by Businessmen', *Sydney Morning Herald*, 20 June 1986.

52. See for example, 'Pemerintah Belum Sepenuh Hati Mau Bekerjasama Dengan KADIN Indonesia: Sukamdani—Banyak Pejabat Masih Bersikap 'Atasan' Dengan 'Bawahan' Terhadap Swasta', *Kompas*, 9 September 1983.

53. For a broad discussion of ideas about economic organisation in Indonesia, see Rice (1983).

54. For an overview of this see the KADIN commissioned report by the University of Indonesia's LPEM (1987) pp. x–xvii.

55. 'The reasons for this curious flaccidity of interest groups in Indonesia must again be sought in the political and ideological-cultural domain, I believe, far more than on the economic or structural side. . . . many of the principal tenets of capitalist ideology are still not widely accepted as legitimate or appropriate for Indonesian society; both acquisitiveness and self-interest are widely regarded as reprehensible qualities in traditional Indonesian value-systems and they have not yet been incorporated into the national ideology as desiderata for the sake of achieving development.' Mackie (1986 a) pp. 22–23.

56. See 'Struktur Organisasi KADIN Indonesia, Akan Tetap Sama', *Suara Karya*, 5 March 1987.

57. For a fascinating analysis of politics at the regional level, see Jim Schiller's study of Jepara: *State Formation in New Order Indonesia: The Powerhouse State in Jepara*, Ph.D. dissertation, Monash University Press, Melbourne 1986. Schiller's study is particularly interesting for in Jepara there appears to be an unusually coherent and active business community which has meant that considerable life is breathed into the local KADIN branch.
58. Interview with Abdul Latief, 1 September 1987.
59. see, for instance, Robison (1986 b) pp. 46–47.
60. For public reference to this attitude see, for example, 'Wapres Kepada HIPMI: Jangan Menjadi Pengusaha Fasilitas', *Suara Karya*, 30 June 1983; and 'Fasilitas Pemerintah Membuat Orang Berebut Kursi Kepimpinan HIPMI', *Sinar Harapan*, 18 April 1986.
61. Interview with Abdul Latief, 1 September 1987.
62. Interviews with, among many others, Mohammed Sadli (Chairman of KADIN's LP3E) 22 April & 24 August 1987; Sjahfiri Alim (President Director of Goodyear Pty Ltd & Head of KADIN's Chemical Industries Section) 25 August 1987; Sjahrir (Chief Economist for Centre for Policy Studies) 4 September 1987; Sanyoto (Chief Editor of *Business News*) 4 September 1987; Dr Dorodjatun Kuntjoro-Jakti (Director of the LPEM, University of Indonesia) 28 August 1987; and Abdul Latief (President Director of Sarinah Jaya Pty Ltd) 1 September 1987.
63. Interviews with Sjahfiri Alim (President Director of Goodyear Pty Ltd & Head of KADIN's Chemical Industries Section) 25 August & 10 September 1987.
64. The conflict over the leadership positions is usually simply a case of different individuals scrambling for positions offering great patronage potential. In 1985 Sukamdani was locked in a close and bitter battle with Probosutedjo for the leadership, and it was only the intervention of State Secretary Sudharmono, indicating that the President wished to see Sukamdani re-elected, which sealed the contest. In the two previous elections at which civilians were chosen (Sukamdani 1982, and Hasjim Ning 1979) indications of Presidential preference had also been crucial to the resolution of the battles among the contestants, all of which had powerful backers within the state elite. [See for example, Handley P., 'A Matter of Influence', *Far Eastern Economic Review*, 17 October 1985, p. 64; and 'KADIN re-elects Sukamdani Chairman for Next 4 Years', *Jakarta Post*, 30 September 1985.] Interestingly, this is true of the HIPMI leadership elections as well. The HIPMI election of April 1986 reduced to a contest between Gunariyah Mochdie and Sharif (Cicip) Sutardjo. The former was the younger sister of the Minister for the Promotion of Local Products, Ginandjar Kartasasmita, and was strongly backed by Sudharmono, whereas the latter was backed by Co-operatives Minister, Bustanil Arifin. Reportedly, the contest was decided at the eleventh hour when President Suharto's second son, Bambang Trihatmodjo, arrived at the convention in Bali and conspicuously joined Sharif Sutardjo for lunch. This act, according to an eyewitness, was sufficient to influence the contest decisively, as electors rapidly recalculated their prospects for business patronage.

65. For an overview of this conflict see, 'Perang Saudara Perlu Diakhiri', *Sinar Harapan*, 20 September 1982; and 'Kepentingan Perjuangan Barisan KADIN dan KADIN Indonesia', *Business News*, 27 April 1984.
66. 'Musyawarah Pengusaha Indonesia' (editorial), *Berita Yudha*, 23 September 1987.
67. For reference to public calls by Sukamdani for compulsory membership, see 'Diharapkan Semua Pengusaha Jadi Anggota KADIN', *Suara Karya*, 17 March 1987. In 1984, he urged that companies not members of KADIN be removed from the state register of firms eligible to tender for government contracts. See 'Harapan KADIN: Pengusaha Bukan Angotta KADIN Tidak Diikutkan Dalam DRM [Daftar Rekanan Mampu]', *Suara Karya*, 25 September 1984.
68. For an insight into this episode see, for instance, 'Grup Musa Ikut Beraksi: Menolak Rancangan AD/ART KADIN', *Jurnal Ekuin*, 6 July 1982; 'Musa Grup: Frans Seda & Probosutedjo Cocok Untuk Ketua Umum KADIN', *Jurnal Ekuin*, 6 September 1982; 'Menteri Suhud Anjurkan BMAI Himpun Dana Untuk Biaya Kegiatan-Kegiatan', *Sinar Harapan*, 3 January 1983; and 'BMAI Ganti Nama', *Kompas*, 27 January 1983.
69. 'KADIN Terbuka Bagi Pengusaha Anggota GOLKAR, PPP dan PDI', *Suara Karya*, 6 October 1986.
70. Interviews with Mohammed Sadli, 22 April 1987 & 24 August 1987.
71. '25 Persen Anggota KADIN Menungguk Bayar Iuran', *Merdeka*, 19 September 1985.
72. 'Kerjasama Pemerintah dan KADIN Belum Seperti Diharapkan', *Kompas*, 16 March 1985. See also similar statements by KADIN Deputy Chairman, Arnold Baramuli, in 'Kerjasama Pemerintah dan KADIN Belum Seperti yang Diharapkan', *Kompas*, 16 March 1985.
73. 'KADIN Minta Wewenang Atur Dunia Usaha', *Kompas*, 13 April 1984.
74. 'KADIN Terbuka Bagi Pengusaha Anggota GOLKAR, PPP and PDI', *Suara Karya*, 6 October 1986.
75. Undang-Undang no. 1 1987 Tentang Kamar Dagang dan Industri, 28 January 1987.
76. Interviews with Probosutedjo (Deputy Chairman of KADIN) 8 September 1987; and Beren Ginting (Deputy Head of Parliamentary Committee VII, GOLKAR *Fraksi*) 19 August 1987. For some insight into KADIN's long-running campaign for a legislative basis, see for instance, 'RUU KADIN Merupakan Impian Yang Sudah Lama Ditunggu', *Sinar Harapan*, 6 August 1986; 'Sukamdani: Ada Petugas Yang Suka Mengutit Barang', *Kompas*, 28 July 1986; 'Menteri Radius Prawiro Sambut Baik Rancangan AD/ART KADIN', *Antara*, 28 May 1983; and 'Mengisi Epilog Munas Khusus KADIN 1981', *Kompas*, 14 May 1981.
77. See Articles 8 and 10, Undang-Undang Tentang Kamar Dagang dan Industri, no. 1 1987. With regard to funding, the relevant clause explicitly left open the possibility of KADIN being granted special duties by the government in the future. 'Special duties' was interpreted

as possibly meaning administering the lucrative company registration process.

78. See, for example, 'KADIN Segera Siap Sesuaikan Organisasi Dengan UU no. 1 Tahun 1987', *Business News*, 2 February 1987; and 'UU KADIN Diharapkan Mampu Meningkatkan Peran Koperasi', *Priori-tas*, 23 February 1987.

79. 'Tak Ada Kewajiban Untuk Menjadi Anggota KADIN', *Suara Karya*, 17 June 1987.

80. Article 1, Paragraphs b and d, *Undang Undang Tentang Kamar Dagang dan Industri*, no. 1, 1987. See also, LPEM (1987) pp. xv–xvi.

81. Among the many useful sources on the subject, those drawn-on here include the World Bank (1987), and (1986), Robison (1987) as well as the regular surveys of economic developments in the *Bulletin of Indonesian Economic Studies*, Australian National University, Canberra; and *Ekonomi dan Keuangan Indonesia*, LPEM, University of Indonesia.

82. For valuable discussion of the problems of economic deregulation and reform efforts surrounding the *tata niaga* trade regime, see Soesastro (1989) and Pangestu (1987) pp. 27–35.

83. See Soesastro (1989) and Robison (1988) for more detailed discussions of this issue.

4

The Textile Industry and the Conflict over Import Monopolies

This chapter focuses on a policy conflict relating to the textile industry or, more particularly, the spinning industry. It is an intriguing, if at times complex case-study, which has at its crux a conflict concerning the Department of Trade's decision to grant a particular company a monopoly over the procurement of raw materials for the spinning industry. The company, CBTI (Indonesian Textile Fibre Development Ltd.), was controlled by the leadership of the Indonesian Textile Association (API), the peak representative organisation for the entire textile industry. Many within the spinning industry regarded CBTI's operations, and its links to API, as highly threatening. This led to the formation of a new representative association, the Spinning Industry Joint Secretariat, or SEKBERTAL, which mounted a long and hard-fought campaign during 1986–88 to have the bundle of policies empowering CBTI reversed.

The significance of this case-study for our theoretical concerns is that it offers much illuminating material on some of the processes of interest intermediation between business and the state. In particular, aspects of this case challenge the idea that extra-state actors are of little significance in the determination of policy.

The chapter begins with a profile of the textile industry, especially the spinning sub-sector, and then proceeds to an overview of the interest representation structures within the textile industry. This is followed by a short outline of the background to the conflict that erupted over CBTI, after which the details of the story itself are unfolded. The chapter concludes by relating the material from this case-study back to the underlying theme of the book, namely the question of political representation by business and, more generally, relations between state and society.

FIGURE 4.1

Structural Overview of the Textile Industry

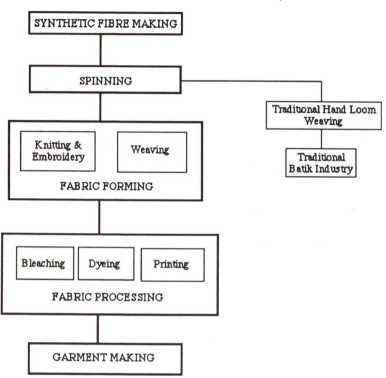

A Profile of the Textile Industry

The textile industry is often one of the first parts of the manufacturing sector to experience rapid growth in newly industrialising countries. It is made up of a number of distinct sub-sectors. A simple functional diagram of the entire textile industry from the upstream synthetic fibre makers through to the garment makers, at the downstream end of the production line, is set out in Figure 4.1. Note that the diagram also includes the traditional weaving and batik cloth-making industries. In the past these traditional manufactures have tended to be small scale and scattered throughout rural areas, but this is changing. However, at each level they are still quite separate from the mainstream modern textile industry, which is, of course, technologically more advanced and has a vastly greater production capacity.

Our concern in this chapter is with the modern textile sector and, in particular, the spinning industry.

Prior to the more liberal economic policies introduced in the early years of the New Order government, the bulk of productive activity in the textile industry (apart from the traditional cottage-based sector) was confined to weaving and, to a lesser extent, spinning. During the 1950s and early 1960s, state enterprises came to assume a dominant role within the textile industry. The commitment to economic interventionism under Sukarno saw the state become heavily involved in the production of yarn and fabric as well as controlling the importation of cotton. A number of state-owned spinning mills and weaving factories were established during this period and scattered around the country.[1] The modern-sector textile industry in Indonesia only really began to flourish from the early 1970s onwards. In the spinning industry, for example, the total number of spindles did not much exceed 500,000 until 1970. By 1979, this figure had risen to about 1.7 million spindles, and by 1985 to 2.5 million. Similarly in the weaving industry, the total number of mechanical looms in 1970 was approximately 35,000, whereas by 1984 there were around 82,000. Following this rapid growth in the productive capacity of the yarn and fabric forming industries, there was a resultant expansion and development of fabric processing industries such as bleaching, dyeing and printing. Synthetic fibre manufacturing varied somewhat, in that production only began in 1973, and then at the modest level of 4,000 tons per year. However, by 1985 this had already grown to over 200,000 tons.[2]

The rapid growth of the textile industry during the 1970s was largely a product of the government's various forms of protection for local producers. As a result of these measures, traders and wholesalers who had hitherto concentrated on importing, switched to local manufacture. Large scale foreign investment, particularly by Japanese firms, also played a key role in the expansion of the industry, especially during the first half of the 1970s. Indeed, foreign investment in the textile industry accounted for more than one third of total foreign investment in manufacturing in Indonesia up until 1977. As Hal Hill has explained, this level declined somewhat once the early 'easy phase' of import substitution passed.[3]

Table 4.1 compares the three major sub-sectors within the textile industry, and contrasts them with the total figures for all manufacturing in Indonesia.

This case-study is principally concerned with the spinning industry. The spinning industry occupies a strategic position in the overall scheme as nearly 80 per cent of all the fibre used in Indonesia is in staple form (whether cotton or synthetic) and thus must be converted

TABLE 4.1

Profile of Selected Sub-Sectors of the Textile Industry, 1985

(Prices in millions of Rupiah)

	NUMBER OF FIRMS	EMPLOYMENT	VALUE OF GROSS OUTPUT	VALUE ADDED (AT FACTOR COST)
SPINNING	94	66,586	889,840	285,170
WEAVING	1030	155,025	1,063,299	336,664
TEXTILES & GARMENTS	775	80,800	373,503	131,632
ALL MANUFACTURING	12,909	1,672,162	23,027,322	7,203,692

Source: Bureau of Statistics (1987).

into spun yarn.[4] In other words, the downstream manufacturing sectors rely to a large extent on local yarn production. In 1987 there were eighty-eight spinning mills, of which eighty-two were operational. The spinning industry is very heavily concentrated in Java (97 per cent of all spindles), particularly around Bandung and Jakarta. Table 4.2 details size and ownership of firms in the spinning industry in 1987. From this it can be seen that local private firms dominate the market with approximately 47 per cent of spindle capacity, followed by a combined total of 27 per cent among the joint ventures, with the state firms holding 26 per cent of spindles. It should be noted, however, that the state-owned spinning mills operate for a substantially shorter number of average hours per year (4,000–5,000) than the privately-owned mills (8,000–8,400).[5] This means that their share of total yarn actually produced is likely to be somewhat smaller. Table 4.2 also makes clear that the local private spinning industry is heavily dominated by Chinese Indonesian firms. In addition, the table also distinguishes those firms (a total of thirty-five) which have integrated production facilities. Rather than just specialising in yarn production, integrated factories engage in fabric forming and, in some cases, fabric processing as well.

Within the textile industry, spinning is one of the most technologically sophisticated sub-sectors. The available data suggests that the technological base for the Indonesian spinning industry is very modern, rating only behind South Korea in terms of the age of the machinery installed.[6] While clear statistics are unavailable, it seems that roughly half of the total yarn produced is derived from cotton, and half from synthetic fibres. About 80 per cent of the spinning industry's synthetic fibre needs are satisfied by the eleven local producers. In the case of cotton, however, the local supply is extremely limited, and as a result, around 95 per cent of total cotton requirements are imported.[7] The Indonesian government has been very keen to develop a local cotton industry, both for reasons of

TABLE 4.2

The Spinning Industry by Size and Ownership, 1987
(Size measured by total number of spindles)

	LOCAL COMPANIES			JOINT VENTURES		
	STATE *	PRIVATE	(ETHNICITY)	JAPAN	HONG KONG	INDIA
A.C.T.E.M.	-	-	-	3,600	-	-
Adetex	-	48,864	(Chinese)	-	-	-
Argopantes***	-	89,856	(Chinese)	-	-	-
Banjaran	64,480	-	-	-	-	-
Bapintri	-	47,008	(Chinese)	-	-	-
Batamtex**	-	43,216	(Chinese)	-	-	-
Bekasi	39,806	-	-	-	-	-
Bitratex	-	-	-	-	-	24,000
Centex***	-	-	-	31,536	-	-
Cilacap	60,000	-	-	-	-	-
Cimanggis	-	19,968	(Chinese)	-	-	-
Cipadung	34,188	-	-	-	-	-
Dan Liris***	-	81,168	(Chinese)	-	-	-
Dasatex	-	24,468	(Chinese)	-	-	-
Dayasamatex	-	28,520	(Chinese)	-	-	-
Dharma Kalimas	-	11,520	(Chinese)	-	-	-
Dharma Manunggal	-	34,992	(Chinese)	-	-	-
Djantra	33,184	-	-	-	-	-
Easterntex***	-	-	-	31,344	-	-
Edi Sandang	-	2,660	(Chinese)	-	-	-
Elegant	-	-	-	-	-	26,760
Eratex Jaya**	-	-	-	-	30,352	-
Famatex***	-	30,720	(Chinese)	-	-	-
Five Star***	-	-	-	-	-	15,360
G.K.B.I. Cirebon	38,016	-	-	-	-	-
G.K.B.I. Medari***	47,808	-	-	-	-	-
Gokak Indonesia	-	-	-	-	-	31,520
Grati	41,172	-	-	-	-	-
Horizon Syntex**	-	-	-	-	-	21,008
Imogari***	-	832	(pribumi)	-	-	-
Inbritex***	29,032	-	-	-	-	-
Indaci	-	-	-	5,888	-	-
Indonesia Baru	-	23,296	(Chinese)	-	-	-
Indorama	-	-	-	-	-	44,064
Intra Troika	-	8,000	(Chinese)	-	-	-
Isada	-	1,952	(Chinese)	-	-	-
Istem***	-	-	-	20,400	-	-
I.T.T. Bandung	8,400	-	-	-	-	-
Kahatex***	-	6,652	(Chinese)	-	-	-
Kamaltex	-	28,800	(Chinese)	-	-	-
Kasta Timbul	-	45,144	(Chinese)	-	-	-
Kewalram	-	-	-	-	-	22,000
K.T.S.M.***	29,376	-	-	-	—	-
Kumatex	-	-	-	29,536	-	-
Lawang	34,784	-	-	-	-	-
Lucky Abadi***	-	19,392	(Chinese)	-	-	-
Malaktex	-	-	-	5,200	-	-
Maligi	-	60,960	(Chinese)	-	-	-
Mertex***	-	-	-	20,000	-	-
Misutex	-	18,304	(Chinese)	-	-	-
Naintex Dua	-	25,000	(Chinese)	-	-	-
Oceanic	-	-	-	-	17,676	-

TABLE 4.2

	LOCAL COMPANIES			JOINT VENTURES		
	STATE *	PRIVATE	(ETHNICITY)	JAPAN	HONG KONG	INDIA
Palembang	30,000	-		-	-	-
Pancatex	-	44,560	(Chinese)	-	-	-
Pardedetex***	-	10,000	(pribumi)	-	-	-
Peony Blanket**	-	2,180	(Chinese)	-	-	-
Primatexco**	-	-		49,872	-	-
Primissima**	36,288	-		-	-	-
Putra Sejati	-	37,552	(Chinese)	-	-	-
Sandratex***	-	65,760	(Chinese)	-	-	-
Sari Warna**	-	30,240	(Chinese)	-	-	-
Secang	36,372	-		-	-	-
S.C.T.I.***	-	-		22,080	-	-
Senayan***	60,000	-		-	-	-
South Grandtex***	-	53,312	(Chinese)	-	-	-
Sukuntex	-	15,000	(pribumi)	-	-	-
Sunrise	-	-		-	-	25,920
Superbtex	-	-		-	20,280	-
Tarumatex	-	40,000	(Chinese)	-	-	-
Texin***	11,560	-		-	-	-
Textra Amspin**	-	55,296	(pribumi)	-	-	-
Tohpati	20,400	-		-	-	-
Tristate**	-	23,200	(Chinese)	-	-	-
Tubantia	-	36,480	(Chinese)	-	-	-
Tyfountex***	-	-		-	64,176	-
Unilon***	-	-		23,328	-	-
Unitex***	-	-		22,000	-	-
Vonex	-	-		8,000	-	-
Wastra Indah**	-	37,560	(Chinese)	-	-	-
Wing Indotex**	-	-		-	12,800	-
World Yamatex	-	20,160	(Chinese)	-	-	-
Young Indonesia**	-	-		-	31,9788	-
TOTAL	654,866	1,172,592		272,784	177,262	210,632
(100 per cent)	(26 per cent)	(47 per cent)		(11 per cent)	(7 per cent)	(9 per cent)

*   A small number of the mills listed under the state category are in fact either cooperatives or semi-state
     enterprises. For present purposes these sub-categories are not significant.
**   Denotes integrated mills conducting both spinning and weaving activities
*** Denotes integrated mills conducting both spinning, weaving and finishing activities.

Source: API, SEKBERTAL and the Department of Industry.

economic self-sufficiency, and because of an official commitment to assisting small scale farmers. In 1978–79 there were some 1,500 hectares under cultivation, and by 1984–85 this had grown to over 30,000 hectares. Nevertheless, cotton's record in Indonesia is not encouraging as yields-per-hectare have been declining rather than improving.[8] In late 1987, for example, there was open discussion of the failure of the government's smallholder cotton intensification program to achieve its targets. The average yield in 1986–87 was only 359 kilograms per hectare (the lowest in the nine years of the program) and far short of the projected levels of 2,000–3,000 kilograms per hectare.[9] Aside from the economic difficulties confronting cotton growing in Indonesia, the climatic conditions are not especially suited to the crop.

Interest Representation in the Textile Industry

Like most other sectors of business in Indonesia, the textile industry has a government-designated representative body, nominally charged with promoting industry interests. One of the difficulties in attempting to organise all business people in the textile industry into a single association is that because the industry embraces such a range of manufacturing stages, the interests of the various sub-sectors frequently diverge. At the most simple level, upstream producers naturally want a guaranteed market downstream. On the other hand, downstream producers usually prefer to import their raw materials rather than use local products if the latter are more expensive. The diversity of interests between the different sub-sectors of the textile industry is reflected in its representational structures. The tangled web of representational arrangements in the textile industry was one of the contributing factors to the conflicts with which we are concerned in this chapter. As such, it will be helpful to review briefly the way in which they developed.

Following the rapid growth in the textile industry during the 1970s, a number of representative associations were established—the Indonesian Garment Makers' Association (PIBTI), the Indonesian Synthetic Fibre Makers' Association (APSYFI), the Indonesian Spinners' Association (ASPI), and the Textile Club (an informal group of a few large spinning and weaving companies, most of which were joint-ventures with Japanese firms). As PIBTI, APSYFI, ASPI were all sector-based, they had little concern with developments in other areas of the textile industry. An organisation which was a partial exception to this pattern was the All-Indonesia Union of Textile Companies (PERTEKSI). In theory, PERTEKSI was representative of the entire Indonesian textile industry. In practice, however, PERTEKSI tended to represent only a selection of spinning and weaving companies, mostly in West Java. Its only significant representational function was (and is) to present the employers' case at annual wage negotiations with the textile worker's union.

A catalyst which brought change to these representational arrangements was introduced in 1978 when the various ASEAN governments decided to form an ASEAN-wide textile organisation as a step towards greater regional cooperation. Suddenly, there was a need for a national textile organisation to represent Indonesia within the region. To this end, the Federation of Indonesian Textile Associations (F-API) was formed in October 1978 as an umbrella organisation to represent the entire textile industry.

Apart from the actual creation of F-API, another important development at this stage was the involvement of Frans Seda in the representational processes of the textile industry. Seda was to play an important part in subsequent events. A former cabinet minister in both the Old Order and early New Order governments[10] and an outspoken *pribumi* figure, he was judged to be a potential asset as an articulate and well-connected industry spokesman. Seda, however, was a relative newcomer to the industry and some difficulties had to be overcome to find him a position of appropriate standing within its forums. His own company was in the garment-making sector; but as the garment-makers' association, PIBTI, was headed by Arnold Baramuli, another well-established and influential *pribumi* figure within KADIN, it was nòt possible to give Seda the leadership of that body. A solution was found in the creation of a new and otherwise unimportant body—the Indonesian Textile Products Trade Association.[11]

As the new peak organisation for the textile industry, F-API embraced all sectoral textile associations. Apart from those pre-existing associations which chose to join the new federation (the already mentioned PIBTI, APSYFI, ASPI and PERTEKSI) a number of other associations were also created and brought into the F-API fold.[12] Partly as a result of its multiple constituent parts, F-API was riven with factional differences and conflicting sets of interests. Within a year of being established it was in turmoil because of the various divisions among the sub-groupings of the organisation. The inability of the F-API leadership's to stabilise the situation, led to Frans Seda being invited to lead the organisation. It was hoped that he could overcome the problems bedevilling F-API and also help to promote textile industry interests through his wider political connections.

Apart from Frans Seda, two other prominent *pribumi* figures in the new leadership group were Fahmy Chatib and Musa. All three were widely regarded as 'political' figures rather than entrepreneurs. None was actively involved in company management. Musa, for example, had an enduring association with the Chinese textile magnate, Thee Nian King, who controlled the largest and most widespread corporate network in the Indonesian textile industry.[13] Thee Nian King, himself, maintained a very low profile, relying on Musa as his *pribumi* spokesman. Despite this, Thee was nevertheless very closely associated with the F-API leadership. Fahmy Chatib played a similar role to Musa and was retained by another Chinese textile entrepreneur,

Max Mulyadi Supangkat, owner of a large knitting firm. Another key figure in this leadership group was Handoko Tjokrosaputro. Handoko was another very large Chinese producer, having interests (like Thee Nian King) which were spread from synthetic fibre-making, through integrated spinning and weaving, to batik and garment manufacturing.[14]

These men were the principal figures in F-API's new leadership clique. Apart from their standing as leading identities within the textile industry, a vital aspect of their power-base was their close ties with the Department of Trade.[15] All of these members of the F-API leadership were to play an important role in the conflicts that emerged within the industry during 1986–88.

As head of F-API, one of Frans Seda's first priorities in seeking to strengthen both his own leadership and the organisation's representational capabilities was to locate a source of revenue. Ordinary membership fees apparently did not generate sufficient funds. The difficulty he faced was that many textile producers were sceptical about the purposes to which any such revenue would be put, and so the issue dragged on for some time. In order to overcome resistance within the textile industry, the F-API leadership, in conjunction with the Trade Department, determined a policy whereby a compulsory levy would be applied on all textile and garment exports to Western countries for which quota restrictions applied. Under this arrangement, exporters could only obtain the necessary clearance permits from the Department of Trade after providing proof that they had deposited the required levy in F-API's bank account.[16]

This was a very odd policy to introduce at a time when the government was increasingly looking to promote non-oil exports. The rationale provided for it was that the money raised (a sizeable sum) would be used by F-API to assist in the further development of the textile industry. Garment exporters within PIBTI (the garment makers' association) were very strongly opposed to the policy. In spite of this, the combined will of the F-API leadership group and the Department of Trade prevailed. This episode marked an important point in the growth of disaffection among sections of the textile industry towards the F-API leaders.[17]

The episode is also important because it marks the beginning of the F-API executive's ability to raise funds on a very substantial scale. This, in turn, gave it increased organisational flexibility and enhanced its capacity for action. The achievement of this capability, however, was not without problems. While the levying of export charges, which F-API called dues (*iuran*), had been sanctioned by the Department of Trade, there remained some technical debate over the legality of the procedure. This stemmed from the fact that F-API was only legally entitled to levy dues from its own members. As a federation of associations, rather than an association itself, F-API was, therefore, technically entitled to collect dues only from its constituent associations, and not from individual companies. (The individual companies were members of the various specific sectoral associations rather than of F-API, and hence if individual companies were to be levied it could only be via their specific associations.)

In a bid to overcome this legal difficulty, the F-API executive convened a special national congress of the organisation in March 1985 and effected changes to its constitution so that the Federation of Indonesian Textile Associations became *the* Indonesian Textile Association. In short, F-API became API. Instead of being a federation of individual associations, it became one giant association itself. This was achieved by fusing the various sectoral associations together to create a new transformed unity—API. The various individual sectoral associations within the old F-API ceased to exist, their functions being performed instead by a number of sector-oriented compartments within the new organisation.

The significance of this move was that API members now became individual companies rather than sectoral associations and, as such, the executive was legally entitled to collect dues from them. The controlling group in the leadership of F-API, centring around Frans Seda and Musa, naturally ensured that they remained at the helm of the new API.

This transformation, or 'fusion' of F-API into API was very controversial. Not surprisingly, those groups opposed to the export levy, or dues, were also strongly opposed to this move, as it would strengthen that policy and entrench Frans Seda's group in leadership positions. PIBTI, PERTEKSI and APSYFI refused to join the new API, and so remained as autonomous bodies outside its jurisdiction. The refusal of APSYFI (the synthetic fibre makers' association) to participate in the new API had less to do with the issue of levies (synthetic fibre-makers were selling to the local market and thus were not greatly affected) than with the fact that the head of PIBTI, Arnold Baramuli, also happened to be the head of APSYFI. Baramuli was therefore in a position to bring APSYFI in behind PIBTI and PERTEKSI in opposing the new API. More generally, the leadership of all three of these associations were concerned to preserve their own institutional autonomy, as they were not part of the leadership group in API and were generally unhappy with its *modus operandi*.

Further controversy resulted from the manner in which the fusion and the special national congress had been conducted. Many people emphasised that the whole procedure was very carefully stage-managed by the API executive to eliminate dissent, and certain questions were raised about the legality of the exercise. The weaving association, ASPINDO, had not formally opposed the change, but neither had it dissolved itself following the fusion, and thus remained in limbo. The spinning association (ASPI), on the other hand, did formally fuse into API and dissolve itself, but did so with little membership support. Moreover, as already seen, three major groups had boycotted the whole exercise.

The controversy over the legitimacy of the new API received considerable press coverage, following a vigorous attack on the proceedings of the congress by Baramuli in another of his capacities as Deputy Head of KADIN. Speaking at a KADIN press conference, Baramuli lashed out at the API leaders, alleging they had employed illegitimate and unconstitutional practices to bring about the fusion. The API executive, assured of Trade Department support, denied all these allegations.[18]

The protests of people such as Baramuli were insufficient to impede the transformation of API or the progress of the leadership group. This was in part because he received little public support. As in many areas of business representation in Indonesia, most producers were not alarmed by the whole exercise, regarding it as competition for the spoils of office: effective representation of industry interests was not a question. While some sections of the textile industry were already dominated by the API leadership clique (principally the large scale integrated spinning and weaving operations), others were co-opted, and still others were simply apathetic. Of those which strongly opposed, only Baramuli spoke out; PERTEKSI, as usual, remained fairly quiet. Underlying all of this was the realisation that the API transformation was backed by the Trade Department. Furthermore, the fusion enjoyed a certain superficial legitimacy in so far as it brought a multiplicity of business associations together under one tight lid, something very much in line with the government's broad corporatist approach to the management of interest intermediation.

Within the textile industry, this episode marked another important stage in the alienation of rank-and-file manufacturers from the API leaders. There was concern among some people that the transformation of F-API into API had been carried out purely to strengthen the political and financial position of the organisation's leaders, and that by questionable means.

The purpose of this discussion has been to provide an overview of the representational structure in the textile industry. As has been seen, a striking feature of the textile sector is the significance of sub-sectoral divisions. Inspired by the needs of an ASEAN cooperation exercise, F-API was formed as a national umbrella organisation, bringing the various sectoral associations together. But beyond being desirable for reasons of regional cooperation, the establishment of a single corporatist body as the sole designated representative association was entirely consistent with the pattern elsewhere in the Indonesian business world. What set the textile industry somewhat apart was the fact that the constituent sectoral associations within F-API had a life of their own, and were, in some cases, reluctant to sacrifice authority to the peak body.

This became of special significance following the rise of the group within F-API centring around Frans Seda, Musa, Handoko Tjokrosaputro and Thee Nian King, all of them well-connected and prominent figures in the business community. Following this group's success in securing the leadership of F-API, they introduced—in cooperation with the Department of Trade—a levy on exporters, ostensibly designed to generate operational funds for the organisation. This policy, together with the transformation of F-API into the consolidated API, resulted in the alienation of many of those producers not associated with the leadership group. Those who did not enjoy the benefits of these changes began to drift away from API, usually through non-payment of membership fees[19] and decreased participation in its activities. This alienation process was gradual and sporadic. Three sectoral associations, PIBTI, APSYFI and PERTEKSI, stood defiantly apart from the peak body.[20] However, of these, only PIBTI was a serious critic of API.

Apart from illustrating the corporatist characteristics of API, this picture is important as many of the tensions within the textile industry's representative structure were integral to the bitter dispute over the monopoly powers of CBTI which arose in early 1986 (less than a year after the formation of API). As will become clear, CBTI, an import company, was the agent of API leaders. For the present, all that needs to be remembered is that even before the eruption of the conflict over CBTI, there was already a good deal of scepticism and discontent with API and the representational services it was supposed to offer the industry. It is to the background of the specific conflict over CBTI that we now turn.

The Background to the Conflict Over CBTI

In one sense the CBTI affair began with a series of Ministerial decrees by the Trade Minister, Rachmat Saleh, in late 1985 and early 1986. However, the real genesis lies a little further back, and centres around two main factors—fluctuations in the international price of cotton, and the domestic ramifications of the negotiations over the General Agreement On Tariffs and Trade (GATT) on reducing trade protection. This backdrop merits brief consideration.

The raw materials of the spinning industry in Indonesia are cotton fibre, polyester staple fibre and rayon staple fibre, and individual firms may produce pure cotton, synthetic, or a blended yarn. While about 85 per cent of the spinning industry's synthetic raw materials are supplied locally, in the case of cotton, 95 per cent is imported. Local cotton had been cheaper than imported cotton prior to late 1984, but its quality was generally regarded as being inferior to that obtained overseas. As a result, local cotton was mostly consumed by the state-owned spinning mills, with private spinners preferring to buy their cotton internationally. The purchase of cotton, whether local or imported, was conducted on an unrestricted and autonomous basis by individual companies.

This system worked relatively well in so far as all spinners were able to purchase the type and quality of cotton they wanted at the market price. At the same time Indonesia's fledgling cotton growing industry could be confident that all its produce would be absorbed, largely because of the price advantage it enjoyed over the better quality cotton on the world market. However, disruption came suddenly in 1985 when the international price of cotton fell sharply. The local cotton growing industry, beset with many inefficiencies, was unable to reduce its costs sufficiently to remain competitive. As a result, consumers of local cotton suddenly found the more desirable imported cotton to be cheaper than the local product. Predictably, falling demand for local cotton soon led to the rapid build-up of unsold stockpiles.

These developments in turn had political repercussions. The Directorate General for Plantations (within the Agriculture Department) became alarmed about the future of the cotton growing estates. Falling demand for cotton was endangering the small scale cotton growers—to which the government, and the President in particular, had a strong commitment. At this stage, seeing an opportunity for itself, API became involved. Following discussions among API, the Directorate General for Plantations and the Department of Trade, it was agreed that API would undertake to guarantee the absorption of all local cotton by the spinning industry.[21]

Following on from this, the Trade Minister, Rachmat Saleh, issued two decrees on 5 December 1985 requiring all spinning companies to use local cotton in a ratio of 1:10 with imported cotton. Spinners were henceforth only permitted to import cotton after demonstrating that they had purchased a volume of local cotton equal to one tenth of the amount they wished to import.[22] By this means it was expected that the absorption of all local cotton would be assured, since it amounted to only 5 per cent of total cotton consumption.

In the wake of these momentous decrees, API moved to cement its position as the implementing agent for the new regulations. In a forcefully worded letter to all spinners, it argued that the new regulations necessitated collective action by the spinning industry, and hence, all spinners would have to sign what was in effect a formalised *carte blanche*. In short, they were required to agree, in advance, to any measures taken by API, or an organ appointed by the API executive. Failure to comply, the letter emphasised, would result in sanctions being applied against offending companies.[23]

This chain of events was one of the catalysts for the conflict which gripped the spinning industry in 1986. The second catalyst, though concurrent, was quite separate. It concerned the subsidies on fabric and garment exports paid by the Indonesian government.

Indonesia produces around 2.5 billion metres of cloth per year, of which 75 per cent is sold on the domestic market and the remainder exported. These exports (until mid-1986) were supported by government subsidies to the textile industry totalling US$120 million.[24] However, as an immediate consequence of becoming a signatory to the GATT code on Subsidies and Countervailing Duties, Indonesia was obliged to terminate its direct state subsidisation of garment and fabric exports. As 1985 progressed, the government thus emphasised to the textile industry that the existing SE (Sertifikat Eksport) system of export subsidies would stop on 30 March 1986 in order to bring Indonesia into line with the GATT.

The Minister for Industry, Hartarto, called in both API and the Garment Manufacturers' Association (PIBTI) for consultations in late 1985 so as to gauge industry attitudes towards the prospect of the withdrawal of the SE subsidy. (PIBTI, it will be recalled, was one of the associations which refused to join the new API following the March 1985 fusion.) In the course of these discussions, Hartarto is said to have mentioned in passing the idea of a 'cross-subsidy', referring to the arrangement in the glass industry where a large Japanese company, Asahimas Pty Ltd, subsidised the operations of its export-oriented downstream divisions with some of the profits of its successful upstream, locally-oriented division.[25]

In the weeks that followed, API went on to develop an idea for a scheme under which export-oriented garment manufacturers would, ostensibly, be subsidised by the upstream spinning industry. While API adopted the term 'cross-subsidy', mentioned by Hartarto, their proposal was fundamentally different, as the cross subsidy would not be 'intra-firm', but 'inter-firm': the subsidy would not come from one branch of a firm's activities and go to another, but instead would go from one firm to another quite separate firm. In other words, under an API-controlled scheme, firms in the spinning industry would be required to subsidise unrelated firms in the garment manufacturing industry through a levy on all the raw materials they purchased, especially cotton.[26] The actual details about how the revenue raised by this levy would be transferred to the garment manufacturers were, however, never made clear. The only implication to be drawn was that API, or an agent of it (CBTI), would somehow distribute the money among garment exporters.

On the surface, at least, the idea of some form of indirect subsidy seemed attractive to the garment manufacturers in PIBTI. After all, it was the spinners, and not them, who would bear the cost of the scheme. There was little scope for protest by the spinners as the former spinning association, ASPI (which had been headed by Musa), had officially fused itself into the new API structure in 1985. The API executive seems to have calculated that Musa, now the head of the spinning section in API, could be relied upon to control any debate and unrest among spinners and contain it within API's walls. One of the aspects of this plan, then, was to placate the hostility of PIBTI (hitherto the principal opponent of the API executive), but at the expense of the spinners.

API then approached Trade Minister Rachmat Saleh with the idea in December 1985, offering it as an attractive solution to the govern-ment's GATT headaches. The scheme had appeal to the Trade Department, for not only did it apparently provide a way out of the GATT problem[27] while helping to underwrite a very valuable export industry, but also it did not require any outlay of government rev-enue. (This was of added significance in view of the general climate of fiscal austerity enforced by the country's deteriorating terms of trade.) In short, API was apparently offering to take the problem off the government's hands. To put a further shine on the plan, API was able to imply that the idea had been endorsed by Industry Minister Hartarto, and to claim that, as the national textile organisation, it (API) represented the overall will and interests of the indusry. As we shall see, however, not only was Hartarto unenthusiastic about API's particular notion of cross-subsidy, but much of the spinning industry was vehemently opposed to it.

Rachmat Saleh and the Department of Trade evidently supported the plan.[28] Following the formation of the API-controlled company, CBTI, in January 1986, Rachmat Saleh issued a decree in February granting CBTI the sole rights and responsibilities for the procure-ment of all local and imported cotton. A few weeks later this was followed by two corresponding decrees giving CBTI sole authority over the procurement of the main synthetic fibres used by the spinning industry—polyester staple fibre and rayon staple fibre.[29] The granting of such import monopolies was quite consistent with the Department of Trade's restrictive trade regime or *tata niaga* (referred to at the end of Chapter 3): many other similar monopolies had already been created in different parts of the manufacturing sector. That it was consistent with other similar decisions did not, however, make it uncontroversial. Plainly, all such restrictive measures ran counter to the deregulatory spirit of the reform drive being mounted by other economic ministers in the government. The justification offered in this instance was that CBTI's monopolies were intended to help to promote garment and fabric exports.

CBTI was the product of API's involvement in two separate policy problems: the surplus of locally-grown cotton and the question about export subsidies for textile products. It was presented as the vehicle with which API would resolve both these issues. On the one hand CBTI would directly oversee the utilisation of all local cotton as well as acting as a national trading company, buying cotton in bulk on the world market. In this respect it would, ostensibly, help both local cotton growers (by guaranteeing the absorption of their entire crop) and also the spinning industry (by obtaining cheaper cotton prices through international bulk-buying). In addition to all of this, CBTI would also assist fabric and garment exporters through the provision of a cross-subsidy to be based on a levy applied to all fibre purchases by spinning mills. At first glance, then, API's various plans seemed quite respectable: here was a case of a business association, in conjunction with the Department of Trade, working to serve the national interest by promoting cooperation among its members. However, as 1986 progressed it became clear that the spinning industry, in particular, took a somewhat less benign view of the situation.

The three ministerial decrees in January and February 1986 (granting the monopoly rights) along with the two issued in December 1985 (requiring consumption of local cotton) gave API and CBTI great power over the spinning industry. Spinners had to make all purchases of cotton and synthetic fibre via CBTI and, moreover, were required to purchase 10 per cent of their cotton needs from local stock before they were able to import cotton—both at prices determined by CBTI. These were the core issues in the dispute that subsequently unfolded.

The Conflict Over CBTI

The formation of CBTI on 1 January 1986 was a low-profile event and attracted little attention. Of greater significance, however, was the equity structure of the new company. The initial equity capital of the company was Rp. 10 billion, spread among 100 priority shares and 900 ordinary shares. The company was founded by ten prominent individuals in the textile industry, each of whom purchased ten priority shares (thus together consuming all 100 of them) and ten ordinary (or lesser) shares. The ten founders of the company also made up its board of directors. This was crucial as all ten of these individuals either belonged to the API leadership group themselves, or else were very closely linked with it. Prominent among them were Handoko Tjokrosaputro (the president director), Musa (the *pribumi* representative of Thee Nian King[30]) and Fahmy Chatib (the *pribumi* Secretary General of API).

In short, the equity in CBTI was very largely held by the API leadership. This crucial fact suddenly came to light several weeks later when Trade Minister Rachmat Saleh awarded CBTI sole control over cotton procurement.

The immediate reaction of anonymous textile industry sources quoted in the Jakarta press was one of incredulity that the government had bestowed this authority on a company which was barely a month old.[31] This was immediately followed by questions about the appropriateness of a small group of senior API people having such a tight control over this new company which had been given far-reaching powers. These concerns were voiced by individual spinners as well as PIBTI, which, at this stage, was still the main institutional opponent to API. However, this expression of concern took place in a very *ad hoc* and uncoordinated way, reflecting in part the fact that little was yet known about CBTI or its plans.

In response to criticism that CBTI existed only for the benefit of its leadership, in a late February press interview, Fahmy Chatib said that all business people in the textile industry were welcome to buy (ordinary, as opposed to priority) shares in CBTI. He went on to emphasise that there were no provisions restricting shareholding in CBTI to API members.[32]

Evidence of the disquiet on the matter can be gleaned from the fact that Trade Minister Rachmat Saleh apparently felt the need to comment on the subject of perceived inequity. He was quoted in the press as saying that CBTI should review its articles of association and remove the distinction between priority and ordinary share holdings.[33] If in fact carried out, this would place the company's leadership (who held all 100 of the priority shares) on a more equal footing with regular shareholders and broaden the equity base.

The first open and public attack on CBTI came several days later when, on 4 March, the head of the Indonesian Importers' Association (GINSI) told a press conference that the appointment of CBTI as the sole importer of cotton was a regrettable decision. He argued that such decisions inevitably resulted in higher prices and a concentration of economic power to the detriment of the rest of the industry, and was, moreover, in contravention of the GBHN.[34]

GINSI's role here is interesting since its direct involvement in the matter was limited. GINSI is an organisation representing the interests of importers in general, and as such, the affairs of the spinning industry concerned only a small percentage of its total membership.[35] Rather than being motivated by the particular interests of spinners, GINSI was concerned by the broader problem of the growing network of restrictive import and export regulations, loosely referred to as the *tata niaga*. Though actually covering a large body of restrictive trade regulations, the term *tata niaga* was frequently used in public discourse as a sort of code word for unpopular import monopolies. This was because the whole question of import monopolies was infused with considerable political sensitivity arising from the fact that the principal beneficiaries of the import monopolies were frequently connected to senior government figures, including the President. As emphasised at the close of Chapter 3, the *tata niaga* issue was probably the single most controversial aspect of government policy vis-a-vis the business world. The reform-minded technocrats in the government who were anxious to restructure the Indonesian economy, were keen to remove the upstream impediments that the *tata niaga* system imposed on a wide range of industries, especially those which had implications for exports. In this policy environment CBTI's monopolies were bound to attract great attention.

An illustration of this came the day after the GINSI comments, on 5 March, when Rachmat Saleh's decree granting CBTI the cotton procurement monopoly was reported to an economic and finance session of the Cabinet attended by the President. At a press conference afterwards Information Minister, Harmoko, apparently saw a need to defend the government's decision on CBTI.[36]

That the issue reached cabinet level was itself telling. Only a very small percentage of Ministerial decrees are reported to the Cabinet, as ministers are empowered to issue these independently. Normally, only decrees of great weight or wide implication are taken to the Cabinet. Interestingly, however, in this case the matter was endorsed by the Cabinet several weeks after the decree had been issued. GINSI officials later speculated that this was because the matter was proving more controversial than expected and Rachmat Saleh felt the need to have the policy endorsed by the Cabinet, thereby strengthening its authority. Rather than being merely the decision of a single minister, responsibility for it was broadened to include the whole government.[37] Another factor involved in the decision by Rachmat

Saleh to seek Cabinet endorsement probably lay in his desire for political backing, as the following day he was to issue the two further decrees (mentioned earlier) extending CBTI's monopoly rights over the procurement of cotton to include rayon and polyester staple fibre as well.

One of the factors about this case which perplexed many observers was that Rachmat Saleh, as minister in charge of an economic portfolio, was widely held to be one of the liberal technocrats. It thus seemed strange that he should be promoting a policy which was so plainly at odds with the whole deregulatory drive of his colleagues. Furthermore, he had himself been active in the mid-1970s in challenging the massive misuse of funds in the state oil company, Pertamina. No entirely persuasive explanation of his behaviour in regard to CBTI has been put forward.[38]

In addition to the Information Minister defending CBTI, API itself was also actively involved. In a press conference, Frans Seda rejected GINSI's criticism of CBTI, claiming instead that it was set up collectively by people in the industry and would only serve to promote efficiency and lower costs.[39]

In mid-March an important development in the story took place when Husein Aminuddin became involved. Aminuddin, the head of one of the large spinning mills (Textra Amspin Pty Ltd), had been active in textile industry affairs in the 1960s.[40] The immediate significance of Aminuddin's involvement in the imbroglio was that he was a *pribumi* producer of sufficient standing to command some attention. His first step was to send a letter to Industry Minister Hartarto on 15 March. Officially registered copies were also sent to the Coordinating Minister for Economics, Finance and Industry, the Finance Minister, the Trade Minister, the Cooperatives Minister, the Research and Technology Minister, the Governor of Bank Indonesia and the Minister for State Apparatus. This was a procedure he was to use to great effect throughout the months that followed.

This was, to say the least, an extremely bold move by an individual business person who did not hold any formal office. The letter was a lengthy and detailed argument questioning the awarding of sole procurement rights to CBTI and the procedure for the absorption of local cotton. It claimed that CBTI's status as sole importer of cotton would only harm Indonesia's trading position by further contributing to the 'high-cost-economy' problem, and at the same time it would force up the price of textile products locally. The letter also drew attention to the fact that CBTI's legal foundations were invalid because the company had not been registered with the Justice Department prior to the sale of its shares. Finally, the letter called for the replacement of the new 1:10 requirement for local cotton consumption with a 'proportional' system allocating local cotton to all spinners on the basis of their production capacity. This was of special importance. Since only 5 per cent of industry cotton needs could be satisfied by local growers, there were obvious contradictions in permitting spinners to import only on a 1:10 basis (instead of, say, 1:20). It meant either that the level of spinning output must inevitably fall, or, more likely, that the regulation would not be applied uniformly. In other words, CBTI would force some mills to buy on a 1:10 basis, while exempting certain others. If the obligation to consume local cotton was dispersed proportionately (using the more objective measure of the number of spindles per mill) the scope for manipulation by CBTI would be reduced.

These arguments came to form the basis of Aminuddin's campaign to persuade the government to reconsider its policy on CBTI. This letter, like subsequent ones, was buttressed with an array of appendices including supporting press articles, copies of relevant government decrees, copies of letters from API or CBTI to spinners, copies of the legal acts for CBTI's formation as a company, as well as detailed outlines of how a proportional scheme for the absorption of cotton might work.

Four days after this first letter to Hartarto, Aminuddin sent a second, with registered copies again going to a range of other senior economic ministers. After emphasising the issues raised in the previous letter, he went on the decry CBTI's introduction of a levy of .125 per cent of the value of cotton to be imported by spinners. Imports could not proceed without endorsement by API of the importer's Letter of Credit, and this could not be obtained without payment of the CBTI levy. The letter also argued that a conflict of interest existed for the leadership of API as it also, in effect, constituted the executive of CBTI.

These letters were studded with statements seeking to cloak Aminuddin's position with the legitimacy of official government rhetoric. He emphasised, for instance, his commitment to the success of the local small scale cotton growing industry and constantly invoked the government's own rhetoric on the need to promote export industries and tackle the problems of a high cost economy. In short, he presented his case in a fashion eminently acceptable to government leaders.

In response to the various forms of criticism that had been levelled against it in the preceding weeks, CBTI reformed its articles of association on 22 March, in a bid to stop the allegations about the differences between priority and ordinary shares. Announcing this change, CBTI president, Handoko, told the press that this move would allow wider ownership of the company, and that regardless of who actually held shares, it would strive to serve the entire textile industry equally.[41] He went on to reject the use of the word 'monopoly' to describe CBTI's operations, arguing that everyone would benefit from the cost savings that could be achieved by CBTI's bulk-buying of cotton on behalf of the spinning industry. Plainly, the use of the term 'monopoly', alluding as it did to the broader *tata niaga* debate, had more to do with corruption than concentration of ownership.

Throughout April and into early May, CBTI leaders met with the spinners on various occasions and outlined their plans for the introduction of the cross-subsidy to replace the SE system of subsidies to the fabric and garment industries. Again, however, all the emphasis was on how the funds would be collected, rather than distributed. The CBTI executive had originally planned to impose a Rp. 900 per kilogram levy on cotton fibre and only Rp. 100 per kilogram levy on synthetic fibres. This was plainly an attempt to control the spinning industry by divide-and-rule tactics.[42] After further negotiations, however, the CBTI executive appears to have concluded that the Rp. 900 figure was untenable, and instead decided on a figure of Rp. 450 for all raw materials, whether cotton or polyester. A decision was taken on 28 April to impose a flat fee of Rp. 450 per kilogram on both cotton and synthetic fibre purchases.[43] This would have represented a huge financial drain for spinners. For instance, a company using 600,000 kilograms of cotton per month, would be liable to pay Rp. 270 million (US$ 238,000) per month in levies. The decision was followed the next day with a telex to all spinners explaining that CBTI would not process the Letters of Credit for imports of any company that did not forward a signed statement acceding to all decisions taken by CBTI in connection with the promotion of fabric and garment exports.[44] In other words, should any mill owner resist, CBTI was threatening to withhold the all-important authority to import raw materials.

In doing this the CBTI leadership was taking a risk. It was still seeking to impose a very heavy levy, but instead of isolating cotton-using spinners from polyester-using spinners by a price differential and placing a very much greater burden on the former, it bound them all together by imposing a standard fee on all raw material purchases. This, as we have seen, was buttressed by the threat of withholding the authority to import should any spinning company seek to resist.

The spinners now found themselves in an extremely difficult situation. CBTI, a company owned by their business rivals, was seeking to impose a levy which would cut severely into their profitability (and in some cases, allegedly, jeopardise actual business viability); yet the prospect of opposing CBTI, and thus API, seemed unthinkable.

Many spinners emphasised that CBTI's position at this stage seemed, quite simply, unassailable. There were a number of facets to this.

- CBTI was able to point to the various ministerial and Cabinet decisions which explicitly provided them with wide-ranging powers. Equally CBTI could insist that it was government policy both to guarantee the absorption of local cotton, and to replace the SE subsidy system, with an industry-run cross-subsidy.
- There was the knowledge that CBTI and API enjoyed very close links with key officials in the Department of Trade.
- The President of CBTI, Handoko, was widely perceived to have (and frequently boasted of) close business connections with President Suharto's family.[45]
- Private spinning mills that were not a part of the CBTI group were almost exclusively owned by local Chinese, or were joint ventures involving Indian or Hong Kong companies, none of which were in a politically strong position. This was especially so in comparison with the high profile *pribumi* figures in the API/CBTI leadership. Local Chinese spinners, in particular, emphasised that it would be unthinkable for them to stand up against Frans Seda or Musa.
- The CBTI leaders frequently made it plain that the spinners should be *grateful* that it was CBTI which had been granted the monopoly control of raw materials, suggesting strongly that business interests associated with the President's family (who have had reputations for being extraordinarily rapacious)[46] had also been keen to obtain the monopoly. In short, the spinners would be well-advised to remain silent and accept the situation as it could be much worse.[47]

Almost any one of these factors on its own would have been sufficient to intimidate the majority of spinners. Faced with all of them at once, the spinners simply could not conceive of opposing CBTI.[48] Conversely, it was also manifested in the very confident and high-handed manner in which the CBTI leadership dealt with them. A number of them recounted situations in which Handoko would disdainfully tell meetings with the spinners that if they did not like what CBTI was doing, then it was their bad luck, as they would have to go against Cabinet policy if they wished to do anything about it.

A clear illustration of the confidence with which CBTI viewed its position was its persistence with the plan to introduce a Rp. 450 cross-subsidy levy. The CBTI executive persevered with this, despite direct opposition from the Minister and Department of Industry. In a meeting with CBTI leaders on 28 April, Industry Minister Hartarto had explained that the government would shortly unveil a new policy initiative (the so-called 'May 6 Package' of reforms) aimed at tackling the country's trade problems and that CBTI should avoid taking any steps which would be in conflict with the spirit of these policy reforms. This was followed up on 6 May by a telex from the Director General for Multifarious Industries (the most senior official in the Department of Industry responsible for the textile industry) to CBTI reminding it of the meeting with Hartarto and warning against the introduction of measures conflicting with the government's new trade reform package.[49] In spite of this, CBTI not only took the decision to introduce the Rp. 450 levy, but on the very same day as it received the telex from the Director General it convened a meeting with the spinners to ratify the decision. This extraordinary show of confidence—blatantly disregarding directives from Hartarto and his department—simply reflected API/CBTI's confidence that it enjoyed the full backing of the Minister and Department of Trade and, by implication, the endorsement of President Suharto.

The Rise of SEKBERTAL

The first signs of possible CBTI miscalculation emerged at the CBTI meeting called on 6 May to ratify the new Rp. 450 levy. Part way through the meeting Aminuddin, who surprised many people by attending, openly challenged the CBTI leadership, and called on all other spinners in attendance who were opposed to the levy to join him in signing a petition declaring their refusal to pay it. Of the approximately fifty spinners present, only six were prepared to commit themselves openly by joining Aminuddin. The rest remained silent.[50]

While Aminuddin failed in this gambit, a new element had clearly been introduced into the equation: for the first time CBTI had been openly challenged by someone in the spinning industry. That same evening, immediately following the CBTI meeting, Aminuddin and the six spinners who supported his move, met again and decided to set up a formal group to lobby the government in a campaign against CBTI.[51] The new organisation was to be known as SEKBERTAL, or the Spinning Industry Joint Secretariat, with Aminuddin its head.

As a first step, SEKBERTAL wrote on 16 May to the four leading economic ministers Ali Wardhana, Radius Prawiro, Rachmat Saleh and Hartarto, reiterating the concerns raised by Aminuddin in his earlier letters, and informing them of the establishment of SEKBERTAL. The letter argued that SEKBERTAL was not a narrowly based set of interests, but represented a majority of large scale spinners, both local and foreign. It set out detailed calculations of the projected costs to the spinning industry of CBTI's Rp. 450

levy. (A reasonably-sized firm would have to pay around US$238,000 per month, or US$2.9 million per year.)[52]

It is important to remember that open and formally organised lobbying does not fit well with the Suharto government's preferred mode of interest representation, namely via the corporatist network of organisations described in Chapter 3. Aminuddin's open challenge to CBTI—and by extension the government—was certainly not without political risk, as indicated by the unwillingness of other spinners to support him at the outset. This was even more the case, as SEKBERTAL, unlike API, was not an officially recognised or sanctioned business organisation. Indeed, in many respects SEKBERTAL had all the hallmarks of a renegade group that would not only be unsuccessful, but might well find itself abruptly closed down following intercession by security officials. It is in this context that the tactics and style adopted by SEKBERTAL became important.

One of the very first steps taken by Aminuddin after SEKBERTAL was formed was to report the fact to the Jakarta office of the national security agency, KOPKAMTIB. This was a technically necessary (though frequently overlooked) requirement for any newly-formed organisation. SEKBERTAL's aim in registering itself with the security forces was to reduce its vulnerability to accusations by its opponents that it was a politically destabilising or subversive group. This step was taken very consciously in light of the fact that SEKBERTAL was seeking to overturn government policy. Similarly, the name SEKBERTAL itself was carefully chosen to evoke association with the state political party GOLKAR, which had earlier been known as SEKBER-GOLKAR.[53]

Equally, the presentation of SEKBERTAL's case in the numerous letters sent to the government was always very respectful, with caution being taken to allege that it was CBTI, rather than the policies of Trade Minister Rachmat Saleh or his department, which was at fault. For instance, the SEKBERTAL letter of 16 May sent to the four economic ministers argued that CBTI was in contravention of Rachmat Saleh's Ministerial Decision no. 70 (which established the cotton monopoly), creating the impression that their grievance was not with the actual policy but the way in which it was being improperly implemented by CBTI. In fact, of course, they sought the elimination of both CBTI and the policy.[54] Further, as mentioned earlier, the letters were studded with phrases invoking the government's own rhetoric, promoting the image that their views were in concert with government policies, rather than challenging the government and important elements of what it stood for. Registered copies were also sent to a wide range of senior government ministers. A list of those officially receiving the letter was always included at the end of the letter. This served to emphasise the fact that SEKBER-TAL was seeking to deal with as many senior people in government as possible, and was also suggestive of wide-ranging access to people at top political levels. Equally, this put some pressure on the person or persons to whom the letter was addressed to take the matter seriously, as many of their colleagues would be in receipt of copies.[55]

In the light of SEKBERTAL's demonstrated willingness to oppose CBTI's cross-subsidy measures, the Director General for Multi-farious Industries convened a meeting between the two sides on 20 May. The following day, the Director General sent a telex to CBTI, stressing that CBTI should take immediate steps to revoke its decision of 28 April regarding the Rp. 450 levy on raw material purchases and avoid introducing measures with destabilising consequences for the industry.[56]

The remarkable feature about the Director General's action is that it illustrates the extent to which the Department of Industry was willing to go in support of the interests of the spinners gathered in SEKBERTAL in opposition to CBTI and API. Several factors help to explain this. First, there was a good deal of rivalry between the Industry Department and the more senior Trade Department. The former was thus predisposed towards any group which was in conflict with the Trade Department or one of its client groups (in this case API and CBTI). Second, Aminuddin enjoyed a good personal relationship with both the Director General for Multifarious Industries and his assistant, the Director for the Textile Industry, and this naturally facilitated his lines of communication. Third, both the Director General and the Director appear to have been objectively opposed to CBTI's operations because it ran counter to efforts to rationalise the economy and eliminate rent-taking practices.[57]

Yet if the Director General's intervention illustrated his support for the SEKBERTAL position, it also illustrated the strength of CBTI; for CBTI merely ignored the directives contained in the telex. In short, the CBTI leadership apparently thought their backing from the Trade Department (and by implication, the President) to be so secure that they could simply disregard instructions from the Industry Department.

Several days after this telex, SEKBERTAL sent a second letter to the economic ministers. It followed the same format as the first, though going into greater detail about complaints against CBTI and the two types of levy it was now seeking to impose on the spinning industry (the .125 per cent levy on the value of imports, and the flat Rp. 450 per kilogram levy on cotton, polyester and rayon purchases). The letter also contained a copy of the Director General's telex, inviting the interpretation that CBTI was ignoring government instructions. It specifically noted that CBTI claimed that all its actions were taken with the knowledge and blessing of the Trade Minister and that as such they (the spinners of SEKBERTAL) had no option but to form themselves into a 'forum lobby'. This terminology left no doubt as to how they saw themselves and what they intended to do. The reference to the Trade Minister was deft in the ambiguity of its implications—either Rachmat Saleh was inappropriately linked to a dubious business venture, or a dubious business venture was unrightfully invoking his name to legitimise its actions. A final noteworthy feature of the letter, was the short but politically-charged reference to the likelihood of CBTI's policies resulting in higher clothing prices for the Indonesian people in the lead-up period to the 1987 general election.[58]

In response to this wholly unexpected frontal challenge, CBTI began to pressure the still small group of spinners associated with Aminuddin in SEKBERTAL, while also seeking to limit any criticism of CBTI and API. This was attempted by, for example, holding up the applications for the opening of Letters of Credit for imports of Dasatex Pty Ltd, one of the local companies involved in the foundation of SEKBERTAL. Measures such as this were meant to dissuade spinners from associating with SEKBERTAL.[59] SEKBERTAL responded immediately with another detailed letter to the economic ministers outlining the problems being experienced by Dasatex Pty Ltd.[60] The delays soon ceased.

In a bid to pre-empt any other possible outbreaks of dissent within the textile industry CBTI and API adopted a number of measures. Producers in the garment industry were wooed with the prospect of a subsidy for their exports from the revenue gathered by the Rp. 450 levy on spinners. The garment manufacturers were not averse to any windfall benefit such as this, even if it was at the spinners' expense. The API leadership surmised that by this means they could prevent the possibility of any cooperation between SEKBERTAL and already disenchanted producers in the garment industry under PIBTI's umbrella. This approach was coupled with a campaign to encourage those presently outside API to join that organisation.[61]

Another measure adopted by the API/CBTI leadership was to encourage others to buy shares in CBTI. This would help to bind more people to the CBTI venture at the same time as helping to raise further capital. While they would certainly not be given a controlling influence in the company, it might constrain them from opposing it. A broader equity base would also help overcome the image of CBTI as a company acting solely in the interests of a narrow group centring around the API executive. Garment and fabric makers who hoped to benefit from the cross-subsidy were encouraged to buy CBTI shares. At the same time, many spinners who were otherwise reluctant to invest in the company were strongly encouraged to purchase CBTI shares. A considerable number did so, as they apparently felt there was nothing to be gained from opposing CBTI. This was especially so in the case of the Japanese joint ventures in the spinning industry.[62]

CBTI took matters one step further on 3 June by arranging a press conference to publicise their position. Musa and Handoko were reported as arguing that the Rp. 450 surcharge on raw materials was needed to replace the SE subsidy arrangement if Indonesia's garment and fabric exporters were to compete internationally. Further, they claimed that spinning companies should not complain about this, as it was intended to help the entire textile industry, as well as farmers growing cotton.[63] That CBTI took these steps suggests that they judged their position to be appreciably less secure than they had earlier believed it to be, and they apparently felt the need to explain and justify their position.

SEKBERTAL escalated its confrontation with CBTI at a Share-holders' General Meeting of the latter on 3 June. Aminuddin, who did not himself hold shares in CBTI, attended as the proxy representative of a supporter who did. Part way through the meeting Aminuddin challenged the legality of the meeting, as CBTI had sold shares, but was not legally registered with the Justice Department. Following legal advice, an apparently embarrassed CBTI executive had to declare the meeting closed.[64]

This event was significant for a number of reasons. First, it marked a more confident and aggressive approach by SEKBERTAL. Second, it constituted a public victory for SEKBERTAL and a conspicuous humiliation of CBTI, as it had been shown to be operating in technical breach of the law. And third, this small tactical victory by SEKBERTAL served to accelerate the movement of other spinners away from a resigned acceptance of CBTI and API, and into the SEKBERTAL camp. Aminuddin capitalised on the event by using it as the pretext for another letter to the government.[65]

SEKBERTAL now became increasingly bold, taking the issue openly to the media. On 18 June it held a press conference, distributing the first of what was to become a lengthy line of press releases to journalists. The 18 June press release summarised SEKBERTAL's general position, and included the most recent developments that had been raised in its last letter (14 June) to the government. This was followed by widespread and favourable press coverage of the SEKBERTAL case.[66]

SEKBERTAL's aggressive approach, characterised by its pre-paredness to make vigorous use of the press, was not something undertaken lightly. High-profile public attacks on government policy, or in this case, attacks on a body created by an act of government, are certainly not everyday occurrences in Indonesia, especially on an issue of such political sensitivity as reform of the *tata niaga* import monopoly system. Direct use of the media constituted a new tactic for SEKBERTAL, as it had previously concentrated on more private attempts to influence the government, through its letter writing campaign. SEKBERTAL was encouraged in its decision to diversify its tactics and make systematic use of the press by confidential advice to Aminuddin from senior political figures. Apparently, Sumarlin, the influential head of the Economic Planning Board (BAPPENAS), indicated that it would be easier for those who were inside the government and sympathetic to SEKBERTAL's position (in so far as it sought economic deregulation) to lend their support if the CBTI controversy received wide publicity. In short, Sumarlin's advice was to push the issue in the media so as to place it prominently on the political agenda, thus requiring the government to take notice. If the matter came to the President's attention, there would be pressure at the ministerial level to explain the reason for the discord. At the same time, it also provided a pretext for other sympathetically disposed ministers such as Sumarlin to raise the issue at meetings of the economic ministers. If there was no critical press attention being directed to the matter, it would be more difficult for sympathetic ministers to attempt to intervene in Trade Minister Rachmat Saleh's area of responsibility. The press thus assumed great importance as a means by which SEKBERTAL could hope to publicise its grievances and lodge them on the political agenda.

SEKBERTAL's press releases themselves deserve mention, if only because of their very professional nature. All releases were carefully set out to be immediately usable by journalists. This was reflected in the fact that newspaper articles, dealing with the spinning industry conflict, frequently just reproduced large slabs of the material in the SEKBERTAL press releases. Similarly, evocative and sensational labels were concocted by the SEKBERTAL leadership to attract the attention of journalists and editors.[67] By treating journalists well, SEKBERTAL encouraged favourable press treatment of its cause.[68] This was a very deliberate tactic designed to help overcome the steep political odds faced.[69]

The battle lines in the conflict between SEKBERTAL and CBTI had become clearer by mid-1986. Press reports at this stage suggested that 60 per cent of spinning companies supported SEKBERTAL against CBTI.[70] A confidential memo prepared by the Department of Industry estimated the division of support within the industry to be as follows.[71]

Pro CBTI	± 650,000 spindles	(26 per cent)
Contra CBTI	± 1,240,000 spindles	(50 per cent)
Neutral	± 610,000 spindles	(24 per cent)

Estimation of actual loyalty was quite difficult as some companies retained their shares in CBTI or else continued to be members of API even though they were politically active in supporting SEKBERTAL.[72] Ambiguity of this sort was quite common during these early stages of the conflict when many of the smaller companies, while supporting SEKBERTAL, were still afraid to formally sever links with API and CBTI in case SEKBERTAL was unsuccessful, or worse, crushed.

The position of those companies considered neutral in the dispute was a little more complex in that they fell into two groups. The first included those mills which were state-owned, or semi-state-owned. As public enterprises they could not formally comment on the conflict between the two industry groups because of the wider political implications of being seen to be opposed to official government policy. Nevertheless it seems clear that their actual sympathies were with those opposed to CBTI, if only because they were controlled by the Department of Industry, which was itself sympathetic to SEKBERTAL.

The second group of nominally neutral companies was made up of the Japanese spinning mills.[73] This group was less homogeneous in its attitudes towards the conflict. A number of the big Japanese mills were actually in joint venture with Indonesian companies directly linked to API and CBTI (primarily via Thee Nian King's extensive group of companies) and were very unlikely to oppose CBTI policy openly. More generally, Japanese firms were reluctant to engage in open and direct politicking, regarding it as politically dangerous and possibly injurious to company prosperity.[74] Typically, Japanese spinning companies, when confronted with a political problem, would consider the matter privately among themselves (in an organisation known as *Akhir Kai*) and then approach either the Embassy or the Japan External Trade Organisation (JETRO) to convey their grievances to the government. On the CBTI issue, however, they were internally divided. Some firms, especially those that were linked financially to Thee Nian King supported CBTI. Others that were either seriously hurt by CBTI policies or that did not stand to derive any of the CBTI spoils, remained quite opposed to its existence and operations.

TABLE 4.3

Company Allegiance in the CBTI Dispute
(numbers of individual firms)

OWNERSHIP	CBTI		SEKBERTAL		NEUTRAL	
STATE	-		-		18	
PRIVATE	14		23		-	
JAPANESE	-		-		13	
HONG KONG	-		6		-	
INDIAN	-		8		-	
TOTAL	14	(17 PER CENT)	37	(45 PER CENT)	31	(38 PER CENT)

Source: API, SEKBERTAL and the Department of Industry.

As a result of this internal division within the *Akhir Kai* ranks, the Japanese Embassy declined to take up the matter with the Indonesian government.[75] In consequence, those Japanese companies opposed to CBTI did not participate in the political conflict in any systematic or very effective way. This is not to say that the Japanese remained completely on the sidelines. Some of those companies most concerned about CBTI had approached the Director General for Multifarious Industries early in the conflict to seek his assistance. At that stage (prior to the formation of SEKBERTAL), the Department of Industry was apparently quite hesitant about lending its support to any moves to oppose CBTI, API and the Department of Trade, believing them to be too powerful.[76] The Japanese did later express some concern about the situation during meetings arranged with the head of the Foreign Investment Board Ginandjar Kartasasmita (29 July 1986) and Industry Minister Hartarto (29 August 1986). However, these meetings were designed to cover the whole range of Japanese investments in Indonesia, of which the spinning industry was just one small part.[77]

Overall, the Japanese companies opposed to CBTI did not participate very effectively in the political conflict over this issue. Indeed, even those companies that were very strongly opposed to CBTI were unwilling to openly link themselves with SEKBERTAL, being wary of Aminuddin's confrontational style or of being seen to be engaging in local politics. Usually the most that was done was to communicate privately with the SEKBERTAL leadership and convey sentiments of support. With these various considerations in mind, a more precise picture of the division of political loyalties within the spinning industry is presented in Table 4.3.[78]

The Tide Begins to Turn

The first sign that SEKBERTAL's campaign was having an effect came with the convening of a two day meeting between the two sides on 23–24 June. The meeting was called by Bustanil Arifin, an influential minister close to the President, who was acting as Trade Minister while Rachmat Saleh was overseas. The negotiations were intended to reach a settlement of the conflict, which had by now received considerable media coverage.

Immediately before the meeting, SEKBERTAL had sent Bustanil Arifin a lengthy and detailed letter setting out their grievances. It emphasised the economic costs CBTI policies were imposing on the industry, and suggested that the cross-subsidy proposal might still leave Indonesia in breach of the GATT Code of Subsidies and Countervailing Duties (assuming any revenues collected were actually distributed).[79]

The negotiations were apparently conducted in a very vigorous fashion. Bustanil Arifin's main concern seems to have been to settle the matter one way or another and ensure that it ceased to be a source of controversy. Indeed, he reportedly suggested to Aminuddin that instead of continually attacking CBTI, a compromise be found whereby he join, or even lead CBTI, thereby himself deriving the material benefits to be had from its revenue-raising activities.

The agreement ultimately hammered-out represented an important victory for SEKBERTAL, due partly to the chance occurrence that Bustanil Arifin chaired the proceedings rather Rachmat Saleh (who was absent on the pilgrimage to Mecca). As Minister for Cooperatives and Head of the Logistics Board, he had had little association with the industry or API, and had no particular predisposition to support them.

The following day SEKBERTAL sent a further letter to Bustanil Arifin outlining what it understood to be the terms of the agreement that had been reached.[80] Significantly, registered copies of the letter were also sent to General Benny Murdani, head of the Armed Forces and the security organisation KOPKAMTIB, the Coordinating Minister for Defence and Security General Surono, Manpower Minister Sudomo, Research and Technology Minister Habibie, Cabinet Secretary Murdiono and various others, as well as the (by now) customary list of economic ministers. The preamble to the letter stated that the spinners gathered in SEKBERTAL trusted that this agreement would overcome the chaos that had prevailed in the industry as a result of CBTI's activities and which had led to an inflation of textile and clothing prices during the *Lebaran* festive period and in the lead up to the 1987 general election. This apparently had some effect, as

General Murdani is said to have sent a personal aide to meet SEKBERTAL leaders and discuss their grievances.[81]

Of the various terms listed in the letter, the most salient were as follows:

- CBTI could only levy surcharges on the industry with the *express* approval of the government.
- the Rp. 450 levy on all raw material purchases (reputedly to fund the cross-subsidy) was not to go ahead.
- the .125 per cent fee charged by CBTI on all cotton imports was to be halved to .0625 per cent.
- the structure of CBTI was to be reformed so that it more accurately reflected the interests of the spinning industry.
- the spinning industry accepted the need to consume all locally grown cotton, but welcomed the decision that henceforth individual spinning mills were to be able to purchase this cotton independently. In other words, contracts would be negotiated between the banks representing individual spinning mills and the state-controlled cotton growing plantations. Most importantly, there was no longer any need for the spinners to deal via CBTI.
- each mill would be allocated an amount of local cotton to be purchased on a proportional basis (i.e. in proportion to its number of spindles). To this end SEKBERTAL was to check the validity of an allocation list drawn up by Fahmy Chatib, the Vice-President of CBTI, during the meeting.
- SEKBERTAL, at the direct request of Bustanil Arifin, was to refrain for the time being from issuing press releases concerning the meeting and its proceedings. This was the only condition constraining SEKBERTAL rather than CBTI.

The Director General for Domestic Trade (who was closely associated with the API leadership) announced some (but not all) of the terms of this agreement to the press after the conclusion of the meeting.[82]

In principle, SEKBERTAL had achieved a major triumph. Not only had a meeting chaired by the influential Bustanil Arifin acknowledged and apparently largely accepted SEKBERTAL's diagnosis of the situation, but an agreement had been reached requiring a range of specific remedial measures. SEKBERTAL had succeeded in having the idea of a cross-subsidy via a Rp. 450 levy on all raw material purchases defeated and formally revoked. This represented the elimination of a very large financial threat to most spinning mills. In addition, other very welcome developments were the reduction of the .125 per cent levy and the call for a reform of CBTI to overcome claims that it operated as a self-serving organisation controlled by a small number of people. Beyond this, the proposal for a return to a system of direct transactions between local cotton growers and spinning mills, without CBTI operating as a 'middleman', had been keenly sought. As explained earlier, if spinners were going to be required to consume local cotton, SEKBERTAL wanted it to be spread fairly and uniformly throughout the industry. Under the CBTI 1:10 formula, the allocation was much more arbitrary. Even more important than the equity issue, however, was the fact if all local cotton transactions had to take place via a middleman (CBTI) there was a great likelihood that the price paid by the spinning mills would be significantly higher than if they had bought the cotton directly from the growers themselves. The prospect of independent and direct purchasing was thus extremely welcome.

SEKBERTAL drew some pride from the fact that one of the conditions of the agreement was that it refrain from going to the press in connection with the negotiations. It suggested that their lobbying strategies were finding their mark. In short, sections of the government were becoming uncomfortable, and concerned about possible Presidential reaction to the controversy.

While SEKBERTAL was initially pleased with the outcome, it soon became apparent that not all the terms of the agreement would be respected. Certainly the cross-subsidy idea had gone, but beyond this CBTI seemed not to feel compelled to implement the agreement fully. This appeared to stem from the fact that the agreement was, after all, an intra-industry agreement, not a government decision. Bustanil Arifin had made no decree; he had merely officiated at negotiations. Furthermore, with Rachmat Saleh's return from abroad, Bustanil would no longer be supervising the matter. All of this, however, took some time to emerge.

After a lull of several weeks as both sides waited to see what would follow from the Bustanil Arifin meeting, SEKBERTAL wrote to all spinners informing them that the Director General for Multifarious Industries had drawn up an official list for the proportional allocation of cotton to all mills.[83] SEKBERTAL then tried to arrange a meeting with CBTI to follow up on the decisions that had been reached at the Bustanil Arifin meeting. When CBTI did not respond, SEKBERTAL sent another letter to its growing list of senior ministers, enclosing copies of its telex invitations to CBTI and noting the latter's lack of cooperation.[84]

Relations between CBTI and SEKBERTAL continued in a highly acrimonious vein with CBTI holding up the processing of Letters of Credit for cotton imports by several SEKBERTAL supporters. This led, in early August, to the Director General for Multifarious Industries sending a telex to the CBTI executive calling on them not to obstruct import procedures. Official copies of the telex were also sent to several senior economic ministers.[85]

The Conflict Intensifies

CBTI was by now well aware that it was facing a major challenge to its authority from SEKBERTAL and began to take the need to respond very seriously. In a revealing development, this led to CBTI Secretary-General, Fahmy Chatib, branding SEKBERTAL in the press as a *kelompok petisi* ('group of petitioners', or protesters).[86] The term was carefully chosen with the aim of portraying SEKBERTAL as political subversives challenging the government's authority and threatening the stability and proper functioning of the textile industry. The basis for this was the implicit reference in the term *kelompok petisi* to the informal political grouping known as the *Petisi Lima Puluh* (or Petition of Fifty) which had constituted an unofficial challenge to the government prior to the previous general election. In other words, CBTI was likening SEKBERTAL's letter writing campaign seeking changes in the status quo of the textile industry to the open letter the *Petisi Lima Puluh* had sent to the government in 1980 calling for change to the overall status quo in the political system. This was potentially a very damaging attack on SEKBERTAL, for if the label had 'stuck', SEKBERTAL's chances of persuading the government to alter its policies would be reduced. SEKBERTAL might thus be seen in a similar light to other supposed challenges to the prevailing political order.

From the outset, the leaders of SEKBERTAL had been anxious to guard against contingencies of just this sort, and had deliberately sought to avoid creating the impression that they were 'engaging in politics'. It was for this reason they had hitherto carefully focused their attack on CBTI and its 'improper' implementation of Rachmat Saleh's Ministerial Decrees, rather than the Decrees themselves, the Directors General for Domestic and Foreign Trade in the Department of Trade or for that matter the Minister of Trade himself—all of whom were actually regarded by SEKBERTAL as being as culpable as CBTI and API. Similarly, it was for this reason that they couched their campaign within the government's own rhetoric, explicitly linking their claims with the stated aims of current government policy. Equally, this was why they sent officially registered copies of their letters to so many senior political figures. This was also the reason that they took the meticulously correct course of reporting the formation of SEKBERTAL to the security agency, KOPKAMTIB.

Similarly, this concern lay behind SEKBERTAL's deliberate use of a number of newspapers that were closely associated with the military or the government in their ownership and readership. These included *Berita Yudha*, *Berita Buana*, *Suara Karya*, *Pelita* and *Harian Umum AB* (or *Angkatan Bersenjata* as it became known when it reverted to its old name during 1987).

SEKBERTAL's caution was due to the unstated, but widely recognised, links between their cause and the broader issue of import monopolies in Indonesia which ran right to the heart of the country's political leadership. Thus, for instance, Aminuddin was at pains to persuade journalists not to link the problems in the textile industry with those in others such as the politically sensitive plywood or plastics industries.[87] Not only would this guarantee the failure of SEKBERTAL's campaign, but it would possibly earn them the wrath of the country's security managers.

Furthermore, Aminuddin had a personal interest in this. He did not welcome attempts to portray him as an anti-government agitator. This was because he had been arrested in 1957 following charges of involvement with an assassination attempt on a senior Communist Party official and again in 1958 in connection with the secessionist movement, the Revolutionary Republican Government of Indonesia (PRRI). While he had subsequently been completely exonerated of these charges, there was still a risk that his opponents might seek to revive these past allegations.[88]

In view of all of this it was scarcely surprising that SEKBERTAL decided to strike back vigorously. Accordingly, on 9 August (the same day as the *Tempo* article containing the *kelompok petisi* reference), SEKBERTAL held a press conference and issued a lengthy press release.[89] The press release went to great lengths to dispel the *kelompok petisi* allegation, accusing CBTI instead of being the ones who wished to politicise the whole affair and claiming that SEKBERTAL sought to handle it in an 'objective' and 'technical' manner. SEKBERTAL, the press release stated, was only concerned about 'economics', not 'politics'. It called for a return to the system prior to CBTI's existence whereby spinning mills could import raw materials autonomously, saying that CBTI's activities had led to widespread increases in production costs. For added effect, several of the foreign companies which were active within SEKBERTAL attended the press conference and informed journalists that they were having to review their plans for further foreign investment in Indonesia because of the uncertainties CBTI was bringing to the textile industry.

The press release went on to attack CBTI for not abiding by the terms of the agreement reached under Bustanil Arifin, adding that until now SEKBERTAL had respected the Minister's request not to inflame the issue in the press, but that since CBTI had publicly branded them a *kelompok petisi*, they had no alternative but to respond. It decried the fact that CBTI, which was itself a private company, was seeking to regulate the rest of the spinning industry, and was invoking the name of the Department of Trade to legitimise its activities. CBTI and API were described as mere parasites which were not even members of KADIN (something expected of most business groups). Interestingly, in response to the rumours about his political past allegedly circulated by CBTI, the press release had a lengthy and laudatory description of Aminuddin's character and personal history. SEKBERTAL's press conference had great effect, for it quickly received very widespread and favourable coverage.[90] Virtually all of the aspects that had been raised at the press conference were reported. There were even glowing accounts of Aminuddin as a former guerilla fighter during the Revolution and the fact that he had been sent overseas by the government for training and had graduated from Cornell University.

Not content with its dramatic media counter-attack, SEKBERTAL then took a bolder and far more decisive step on the same day as the press conference, when it delivered to President Suharto's private residence a formal report on the situation in the spinning industry and the problems it was having with CBTI.[91] This was the first time SEKBERTAL had dared to communicate directly with the President, though he was certainly part of the audience it had been trying to reach via the media campaign.

The ramifications of SEKBERTAL's lobbying of the President were almost immediately evident. On 11 August Suharto summoned State Secretary Sudharmono, Acting Trade Minister Bustanil Arifin (Rachmat Saleh was away), Industry Minister Hartarto and the Minister for the Promotion of the Use of Domestic Products Ginandjar Kartasasmita, for a special meeting to consider the problems besetting the spinning industry.

Immediately after the meeting at the Palace, Hartarto and Ginandjar jointly addressed the press. Hartarto announced that the President had called for the reform of CBTI's structure and composition. At the same time, Hartarto said, he wanted to ensure that all domestically grown cotton was absorbed by the spinning industry so as to assist the development of the cotton growing industry. There was also a suggestion in the media reports of the press conference that the system for the absorption of local cotton required review, although it was unclear whether this represented the view of Suharto himself. The press drew attention to the fact that the 1:10 relationship was impractical when local cotton supplies amounted to only five per cent of industry needs.[92]

It is not entirely clear what instructions the President actually gave his ministers. That this should be the case is not unusual, for it is widely recognised in Jakarta that the President rarely gives direct or explicit rulings, especially when there is a conflict between two of his ministers which involves loss of face for one of them. More often, apparently, he merely indicates that he wishes the matter to be tidied up and controversy overcome. In this case, while it does appear that Suharto recommended CBTI be reformed and all local cotton be absorbed, newspaper reports seem to suggest that it was Hartarto, rather than the President, who advocated the use of a proportional system for the allocation of local cotton. (This would fit more closely with the actual course of events as they unfolded, as it was some time before the proportional system was universally recognised as the official allocation system.)

Nevertheless, what is clear is that this was an extraordinary break-through for SEKBERTAL. That the President himself should call for an overhaul of CBTI would have seemed inconceivable just a few months earlier. CBTI was a body that had been legitimised by Cabinet decision, and moreover was widely perceived to enjoy personal links to the President's own family. This was a telling indication that SEKBERTAL had come a long way.[93]

As a result of the late June meeting under Bustanil Arifin, SEKBERTAL had achieved one of its main objectives, namely the defeat of the CBTI proposal to levy the spinning industry with a Rp. 450 charge on all raw material purchases, allegedly for the purpose of a cross-subsidy. The threat of this levy had precipitated the formation of SEKBERTAL. Having achieved this aim, SEKBERTAL's next priority targets were:

• CBTI's continuing import monopoly;
• CBTI's non-compliance with the agreement for the use of a proportional scheme for the allocation of domestic cotton;
• the exclusive control by the small API clique which headed CBTI over the funds collected by compulsion from the other spinning companies.

With regard to the first of these items, CBTI had so far never actually implemented its proposal to act as a national 'trading house' and buy cotton internationally for the whole of the spinning industry. Under this scheme it was intended that spinners would buy the imported cotton directly from CBTI. It was claimed that this system would lead to great savings through CBTI's ability to make bulk purchases internationally. Instead, under the system that actually operated, spinning mills imported individually, but could only proceed to open Letters of Credit for importation with their banks *after* they had obtained an authorising stamp from CBTI. This, however, was available only to those companies which satisfied CBTI's criteria. This meant that in return for the authorising stamp on Letters of Credit, CBTI was able to demand that importers pay it .0625 per cent of every import contract.

The second problem of major concern to SEKBERTAL, the introduction of a standardised system for the proportional allocation of local cotton, was something CBTI had supposedly accepted at the June meeting. As already noted, if the spinners were to use local cotton (as was the clear wish of the President), they wanted to make sure that the burden was distributed fairly. This was not surprising in view of the fact that local cotton was selling for Rp. 1,700 per kilogram, while imported cotton cost Rp. 700 per kilogram.

The third and most irksome of SEKBERTAL's concern was the fact that their business rivals controlling CBTI were collecting money from them in a wholly unaccountable fashion. Had the industry benefited uniformly from the revenue raised, an unpopular system might have been slightly more palatable. As things stood, SEKBERTAL was profoundly suspicious of the ends to which any revenue collected by CBTI would be used. Indeed, Suharto's call for the reform of CBTI seems to have followed on from the failure of Bustanil Arifin's intervention to resolve the problem of its narrow equity base.

As an immediate consequence of Suharto's intervention, a two-day meeting was convened later that week (14–15 August) in the Department of Trade between CBTI and SEKBERTAL which was chaired by the Director General for Foreign Trade (from the Department of Trade) and the Director for Textiles (from the Department of Industry). The purpose of the meeting was to address the need for a reform of CBTI expressed by the President. Predictably, there was little willingness to compromise on either side. The CBTI executive wanted to retain control of the company, whereas SEKBERTAL wanted to wrest it from them, if not dispense with it altogether.

Ultimately, after marathon debate, the Director General for Foreign Trade, who was no friend of SEKBERTAL, decreed that the articles of association of CBTI were to be reformed so that its board be expanded from ten members to twenty-two. Ten would be the original CBTI members, and twelve would be from SEKBERTAL.[94] This was another major victory for SEKBERTAL, as the decision would give it control of the board of CBTI.

Presumably, this was a decision which the Director General for Foreign Trade did not reach easily. He was handing a victory to the group that had constantly attacked CBTI, and thus a policy with which he was closely associated. Clearly, however, it was not practicable for him to disregard such a clear signal from the President.

The issue, however, was still far from resolved. In order to formalise legally the changing of CBTI's articles of association and the inclusion of twelve of its representatives onto the company's board, SEKBERTAL sent a letter on 18 August containing the required statutory documents to CBTI's attorney. This proved to be in vain, as the existing CBTI board members failed to reciprocate by supplying the legal documentation required of them for the reform to go ahead. In short, CBTI simply did not act on the Director General's ruling. As a result, the changes to CBTI never came to pass and SEKBERTAL did not gain control of the company.[95]

In spite of this, CBTI's inaction only postponed change rather than preventing it from finally occurring. On 26 August, Trade Minister Rachmat Saleh quite unexpectedly invited Aminuddin to his home for private talks on the evening before he left the country again on official business. According to Aminuddin, Rachmat Saleh was very conciliatory during the meeting, asking Aminuddin for his reaction to the idea of a Department of Trade official being installed as caretaker-manager of CBTI. The official, Totong Kuswara, was in fact already associated with CBTI as a Departmental consultant. Nothing was decided, but Aminuddin concluded that Rachmat Saleh was being forced to alter his position in view of the President's intervention during his previous absence.[96]

Several days later, a telling editorial appeared in one of the leading daily newspapers, drawing attention to the fact that the tide was now running in SEKBERTAL's favour in its battle with CBTI.[97] The editorial provides an interesting synopsis of the situation.

> . . . The meeting between President Suharto and Minister for Industry Hartarto, State Secretary Sudharmono, Minister for the Promotion of the Use of Domestic Products Ginandjar Kartasasmita and Acting Trade Minister Bustanil Arifin on 11 August 1986, which specifically considered the case [of CBTI vs. SEKBERTAL] provides us with a strong hint that it will be resolved once and for all.
> The involvement of the Head of State himself indicates that the problem is not just a simple one. . . . Because if the apparatus below the President could have resolved the issue earlier, then of course the President would not have had to intervene. . . .
> If we examine carefully the directives which have been given by the Head of State regarding the resolution of the case, it would appear that they are in line with the ideas which have been frequently put forward by the spinning companies gathered in SEKBERTAL. The gist of the President's directives are that CBTI Pty Ltd must be overhauled (its articles of association

reformed and its shareholders increased), its organisation put in order and its cotton procurement procedures improved. . . . The Acting Trade Minister Bustanil Arifin in fact almost succeeded in resolving the crisis when, late in June, he organised a marathon two-day negotiation between CBTI Pty Ltd and SEKBERTAL. The agreement which was achieved at that stage—and which doesn't in fact differ much from the guidelines given by the Head of State—should have been sufficient to resolve the matter. And yet while that agreement still stands, it appears that it is not being implemented.

Two days after the editorial appeared, Rachmat Saleh returned to Indonesia and told journalists that the directorship of CBTI had been temporarily transferred to Totong Kuswara of the Trade Department. He said that this was in accordance with the President's directive that CBTI be reformed. He added that CBTI would be reformed, not abolished, observing that the current managers were too busy with their own companies to give sufficient attention to CBTI.[98] The pace at which steps were being taken against CBTI was gradual. In large part this was because of the perceived need to avoid loss of face for API, the Trade Department and, above all, Rachmat Saleh, the minister who endowed CBTI with its powers. This was recognised to be one of the major difficulties (apart from the sheer tenacity of the CBTI leaders) in persuading the government to take action. It was reflected also in the President's oblique references to the issue. SEKBERTAL itself knew that if change was to come at all, it would come in an incremental fashion. As such, the SEKBERTAL leadership could not afford to allow the pressure for action to abate.

The Conflict Enters a New Phase

Sudden and dramatic evidence that SEKBERTAL's efforts were finally bearing fruit came in early September when Sumarlin revealed at a conference that, following an instruction from the President, CBTI would be 'frozen'.[99] Anxious to see that this did in fact come to pass, SEKBERTAL continued to press its case with a strongly worded letter on 11 September to the six top economic ministers, with registered copies going to twenty-one of the most influential figures within the government—including conspicuously, the President, General Murdani and State Secretary Sudharmono.[100] The letter argued that CBTI's monopoly of cotton procurements was having a very harmful effect on the industry, was contributing to a high-cost economy and was in contravention of the policy aims outlined by the President in his 15 August speech to Parliament to mark Independence Day. The letter also reiterated the report that CBTI had been 'frozen' at the President's instruction. But, importantly, the letter went on to raise SEKBERTAL's sights from CBTI itself, and began to criticise the *very purpose* for which it had been set up. It argued that yarn production would be much more efficient if mills were allowed to obtain their raw materials directly, without having to go through CBTI, and if local cotton was allocated on the basis of the proportional list drawn up by the Director General for Multifarious Industries (rather than Rachmat Saleh's 1:10 ruling). This marked a very important shift in the emphasis of SEKBERTAL's campaign. It was no longer primarily attacking the conspicuous irregularities and improprieties in the behaviour of CBTI's management, but instead it was targeting the function CBTI was intended to perform and the principles that lay behind Rachmat Saleh's legislation empowering it.

SEKBERTAL had apparently succeeded in discrediting the performance of CBTI's leadership and perhaps wounding them mortally. What it was now seeking was the reversal of the policy providing for the import monopoly and the restrictive 1:10 requirement. The reason for this was that, while key CBTI leaders might well have been politically damaged, the government policies underlying the institution remained.

In the wake of Sumarlin's comments and its own strong 11 September letter, SEKBERTAL temporarily lessened the intensity of its campaign, as it waited to see what action resulted. Welcome support came at this stage from public statements by Sukar Samsudi, head of the normally quiet PERTEKSI, who said that his organisation was totally opposed to the activities of API and CBTI and that it applauded the efforts of Aminuddin and SEKBERTAL.[101] On the other hand, in something of a rearguard action, the CBTI management appeared before Committee VI of the Parliament on 27 September to defend its activities.[102]

In mid-October SEKBERTAL renewed its efforts to widen the focus of the attack by sending a letter which directly criticised API itself.[103] No reference was made to CBTI. The gist of the letter was that textile firms that were not members of API should not be bound by API rulings. This referred to the API ruling (mentioned earlier in this chapter) first introduced by Frans Seda in April 1984, and renewed in April 1986, requiring payment of a levy into an API bank account prior to the issue of export quotas for garments and fabrics. The letter said that SEKBERTAL would not object to payment of this levy if it were deemed necessary by the government, and provided that the money went directly into state revenue rather than API's own bank account. It argued that there were a number of important textile organisations outside API (such as PIBTI, PER-TEKSI, APSYFI and SEKBERTAL) which played a significant role within the industry in supporting government policy. And, further-more, these organisations, unlike API, had the added legitimacy of being members of KADIN (though SEKBERTAL itself, as a joint secretariat, was not a member of KADIN.) Finally, the letter called on the government to enter into consultation with these organisations and to remove API from the process of allocating export quotas so as to avoid a situation in which one private body, using the name of the government, sought to dictate to others. Three days after the letter, SEKBERTAL held a press conference and reiterated these various points for journalists.[104]

On October 18, Aminuddin took an extraordinary step in his efforts to promote SEKBERTAL. It centred around an invitation from Akbar Tanjung, Deputy Secretary General of GOLKAR and editor of the newspaper, *Pelita*, for SEKBERTAL to place an adver-tisement in his newspaper congratulating GOLKAR on its twenty-second anniversary. *Pelita*, a newspaper associated with leading government figures Sudharmono and Bustanil Arifin, had given SEKBERTAL favourable press coverage in recent months. Aminud-din agreed to purchase half a page of advertising space, provided that he was free to word the advertisement as he wished. The crux of the advertisement was a statement that SEKBERTAL joined with GOLKAR in striving to implement the injunction of the President in his national address of 15 August for a national commitment to efficiency, productivity and competitiveness.

While many companies and business groups had newspaper adver-tisements congratulating GOLKAR on its anniversary, it was highly unusual for them to be used for such overt and explicit political purposes. This rather daring public relations exercise 'enlisted' both GOLKAR and the President for SEKBERTAL's own lobbying efforts. There was a dangerous irony in this; Aminuddin's action could also have been interpreted as a statement that the govern-ment's rhetoric was, in fact, just that—rhetoric. After all, it was the same government that had, under the auspices of the restrictive *tata niaga* trade regime, created CBTI's monopoly, as well as those of other sole importers in other parts of the manufacturing sector.

Aminuddin was thus plainly engaged in a delicate political gamble by using the government's words more vigorously than it might have wished. That this was the case, and that the unusual political message was instantly recognisable and newsworthy, was reflected in the fact that several other major newspapers immediately contacted Aminuddin, expressing interest in it.[105]

The political sensitivity of the broader question of the *tata niaga* trade regime was thrown into sharp focus in early October by the forced closure of one of the country's foremost newspapers, *Sinar Harapan*. The reason for this action seems to have been governmental anger at a report in the paper leaking information about an intended deregulation of some trade restrictions. The article claimed that deregulation of a range of areas, including textiles, was imminent.[106]

Though *Sinar Harapan* paid a high price, its speculation about impending government policy reform was borne out, for on 25 October senior economic ministers jointly announced a range of policy changes designed to lower local production costs and boost the country's trade competitiveness. Among the most important elements of what became known as the '25 October package', were the removal or simplification of import restrictions and the reduction of tariffs for the importation of certain raw materials vital to local industry but not produced, or produced in insufficient quantity locally.[107]

For present purposes the key aspects relate to changes to the regulations governing the importing of textile raw materials. Essentially this hinged around whether an item could be imported freely by manufacturers, or only via a government registered importer. (In the textile industry, CBTI was of course the sole registered importer.) Under the newly announced policy, polyester staple fibre and rayon staple fibre could henceforth be imported freely, without any reference to CBTI. In the case of cotton, the situation was somewhat different. Cotton imports could still only be conducted via a Registered Importer (*Importir Terdaftar*). However, of critical importance was the fact that, in the ensuing implementing regulations, six state-owned companies were specified as the Registered Importers for cotton. Thus in respect of cotton imports there had also been vital changes. While cotton imports were still not free, there were now six registered importers, and CBTI was not listed among them.[108]

CBTI/API had thus been dealt a massive blow by the government. But important questions still remained.

- Why had the Director General for Foreign Trade's implementing regulations (for the new package) not stated explicitly that CBTI was no longer authorised as a Registered Importer?
- What was the status of Rachmat Saleh's Decree no. 70 of February that year which appointed CBTI the sole procurer of both imported and local cotton?
- Why had cotton imports not been liberalised completely like polyester and rayon?
- What was the official policy on the absorption of local cotton? Was

it to be consumed in a ratio of 1:10 with imports as Rachmat Saleh's Decrees of December 1985 stipulated, or was it to be on a proportional basis in accordance with the list drawn up by the Director General for Multifarious Industries following the meeting with Bustanil Arifin?

To pursue these matters, SEKBERTAL wrote yet again to the Ministers for Trade and Industry in early November, with registered copies going to sixteen other senior political figures.[109] The letter was a very detailed response to the 25 October package. It opened by thanking the government for the liberalisation of rayon and polyester fibre imports, but then asked that cotton imports be liberalised further, so that spinning mills might import either directly themselves, or via any of the six registered state-enterprise importers.

In support of this case, a range of technical arguments was deployed concerning the nature of the international futures market in cotton and the commercial advantage of being able to move quickly to take advantage of price fluctuations (rather than having to go via an approved trader). Excerpts from a supporting study by the United Nations Conference on Trade and Development were also enclosed.

The letter further argued that the government had no cause to worry about the local cotton crop as it would certainly be consumed by spinners, but that it was highly desirable this should take place on the basis of proportional allocation and that there should be direct transactions between the spinning mills and the cotton producers (rather than having to go via a middleman of any sort). This was a reference to the fact that spinning mills *still* had to deal with CBTI in order to obtain their local cotton, which, in turn, (because of the 1:10 requirement) they needed to be able to import. The letter concluded with another appeal for the prohibition of the levies API was applying to the export of fabrics and garments.

SEKBERTAL had a variety of reasons for attacking API over levies on fabric and garment exports.

- A number of SEKBERTAL members either had fully integrated factories that produced finished fabric for export, or else had financial involvements with other, separate, downstream factories.
- The spinning industry as a whole had an interest in the well-being of the downstream industries which consumed the yarn they produced. If the prosperity of the fabric and garment industries was threatened by API levies, this would in turn have ramifications for the spinners: a contraction in the downstream industries would result in a shrinking market for their own produce.
- The leadership of API was almost identical to that of CBTI; as

such SEKBERTAL was predisposed to confront them at every possible opportunity, if only because of the possibility of API attempting to introduce some other ploy detrimental to them.

• The SEKBERTAL leadership identified strongly with the plight of those companies further downstream who were having to grapple with API.

On 26 November, a variety of parties appeared before a session of Committee VI of the Parliament to give representations concerning the situation in the textile industry. Apart from the Director General for Multifarious Industries and the Director for Textiles, others to appear included the heads of PIBTI (the garment makers' association) and GINSI (the importers' association). The former launched a scathing attack on the API export levies, while the latter asked how much longer the government intended to allow import monopolies to operate. Members of the Committee reportedly called for API's levy practices to be reformed.[110]

SEKBERTAL did not appear before the Parliamentary Committee. There were two reasons for this. First, SEKBERTAL leaders judged the Committee to be a less rewarding avenue for lobbying efforts than those they already used; and secondly, they were anxious to keep SEKBERTAL far removed from any activity which might be construed as 'playing politics'.[111] While everything that SEKBERTAL was doing was of course 'political', they were concerned not to appear to be involved in things which were formally identified as political—such as lobbying in the Parliament for changes to key aspects of governmental policy. The underlying reason for this was that such action might be seen to imply not only a questioning of the appropriateness of a particular government policy, but more importantly also to imply a questioning of the government itself.

SEKBERTAL finally inched closer to another of its goals—the discarding of the 1:10 requirement—as a result of an action by the Director General for Multifarious Industries on 4 December, when he wrote to all spinning firms informing them of the release of a revised proportional allocation list for local cotton, covering the first half of 1987. The letter went on to say that, in accordance with the 25 October package, cotton transactions could take place directly between spinning mills and cotton producers, though proof of purchase of a mill's local cotton allocation would still be necessary.[112]

This action suggested that mills were now completely free to deal independently with local cotton producers without having to go through CBTI and also that the 1:10 requirement had now been superseded, with mills henceforth having only to consume their proportional allocation of local cotton before importing as much as they wished (though still via one of the six registered importers). The reality was less clear, however. The problem remained that Rachmat Saleh's Ministerial Decrees had not been revoked, and were thus presumably still in force. The policies of Trade and Industry were patently at odds with each other.

While the situation was still uncertain, the action of the Director General for Multifarious Industries was nevertheless a positive development from SEKBERTAL's point of view, as it served to increase the pressure for a firm resolution. Further progress was achieved on another front when the Director General for Foreign Trade sent a letter, on 10 December, to the country's customs agents (Societé Generale de Surveillance), stipulating that the only companies permitted to operate as registered importers of cotton were the six state-enterprises specified in the 25 October package, adding that CBTI would not be permitted to open any new Letters of Credit for imports, or increase the value of existing ones.[113]

Thus, CBTI's monopoly of raw material imports had finally been brought to an unequivocal end. This was very welcome news to SEKBERTAL. But CBTI was not yet finished, for it still existed as a company. And it remained unclear whether it was still legally empowered to act as a middleman and the sole procurer of local cotton.

SEKBERTAL held an end-of-year press conference where it was joined by PIBTI in yet another attack on API's export levies and its role in the allocation of garment export quotas. At the press conference they listed issues which they hoped the government would address. Several of these stood out. They sought complete liberalisation of cotton imports, to bring them into line with rayon and polyester fibre. They called for open publication of the criteria by which garment export quotas were determined. And finally, they appealed to the government to step in and create a proper national textile body genuinely representative of the interests of the whole textile industry. In this respect, they again drew attention to the existence of several textile organisations which were members of KADIN, but stood outside API.[114]

The last point had far-reaching implications. SEKBERTAL was now calling for API's replacement. This was an open admission of something SEKBERTAL had always wanted, but had never previously declared openly. API was a more established entity than CBTI. This was the reason for the invocation of KADIN's name, as an attempt to garner legitimacy around the non-API organisations.[115]

SEKBERTAL's continuing efforts were evidently not in vain, for following 'hard on the heels' of the 25 October and 10 December reforms, the *tata niaga* regime was given another dramatic reform by the government with the announcement of further major policy changes on 15 January. The essence of these new changes was a relaxation of the restrictions on imports in the textile and steel industries. Of the 300 classifications of import items contained in this package (the 25 October package had covered only 153 items) the textile industry was by far the major winner with 227. However, the single most dramatic item was the complete liberalisation of cotton imports. Spinners were now free to import directly if they did not wish to use any of the six registered importers. This brought cotton import procedures into line with rayon and polyester which had been freed up on 25 October.

This was widely seen as constituting a sweeping victory for SEK-BERTAL, with Aminuddin quoted in many places as expressing his gratitude to the President and the government.[116] In lobbying for these policy changes, SEKBERTAL had maintained continuous pressure from 25 October onwards. But since this particular lobbying effort had been directed exclusively at the government (rather than at API or CBTI), different tactics had been employed. A vociferous and provocative media-based campaign had no longer been appropriate. Instead, SEKBERTAL had adopted a low-profile approach, involving continuous lobbying by way of letters and frequent telephone calls providing large quantities of technical data and argument to key state officials. In all this, SEKBERTAL had found the Department of Industry, while sympathetic, rather slow-moving in pushing for change. As a result it had shifted the focus of its lobbying attention to more senior figures, such as BAPPENAS-head Sumarlin and the doyen of the technocrats, Widjoyo Nitisastro, a measure which had clearly proved successful.[117]

There can be no doubt that senior economic ministers such as Sumarlin were committed to promoting economic deregulation where ever possible. Their major problem was that they faced a combined opposition of other ministers and officials, and an accompanying web of business interests, all of whom sought to resist deregulation. While not especially interested in the affairs of the spinning industry, reformist ministers such as Sumarlin would have welcomed the actions of SEKBERTAL. Not only would they have seen SEKBERTAL as a 'force for good' in the spinning industry, but more generally it provided them with welcome evidence of clear industry support for their deregulatory drive. The policy process was becoming marked by competing alliances linking different state and industry factions together.

A Renewed Threat

By mid-January 1987 SEKBERTAL had achieved its fundamental aims, the abolition of the import monopoly on all raw materials, and the restoration of the freedom to import independently. No sooner had this victory been achieved, however, than a different dark cloud emerged on the regulatory horizon. Decrees issued by Rachmat Saleh and the Director General for Foreign Trade on 23 and 24 January determined that while spinning mills were indeed able to import cotton independently, they could only do so on a 1:10 basis with purchases of local cotton. This was a reaffirmation of Rachmat Saleh's original ruling in December 1985, and it thus served to strengthen the contradiction between the policies of the Department of Trade and the Department of Industry.[118]

The first person to draw critical attention to the implications of this situation was the head of GINSI (the importers' association), Zahri Ahmad. Speaking to the press, he said that the new regulations had the potential to do great damage to the textile industry by providing an opportunity for speculators to cause havoc with cotton purchases. He argued that because the price of local cotton had recently dipped below that of imported cotton,[119] there was a danger that certain 'unnamed groups' with large amounts of capital might purchase most, if not all, of the local cotton and use this as the basis for a new monopoly.[120]

Almost as if to confirm Zahri Achmad's concerns, API chairman, Frans Seda, announced before a Parliamentary committee on 9 February that API had submitted a request to the government for authority to purchase as much as 150,000 bales of local cotton, a figure equivalent to the total national production for a five year period. This, he argued, would greatly assist local cotton growers, as it would provide them with financial security in advance for up to five years of cultivation.[121]

GINSI's outburst was very close to what SEKBERTAL might have said. The two organisations were in fact in complete agreement in their views of what was desirable for the textile industry. Although they were in regular communication, they did not attempt to coordinate their actions, since GINSI had a much more diverse membership, and was primarily concerned with the broader milieu.[122]

That SEKBERTAL was refraining from public comment was indeed unusual. The SEKBERTAL leaders were certainly alarmed by the situation, viewing it as a deliberate attempt by the Department of Trade to leave open a window of opportunity for its opponents in API. Aminuddin insisted, however, that SEKBERTAL refrain from

further criticism of Trade Department policy so soon after the break-
through achieved with the 15 January package (following, as that did,
from the other beneficial reforms of 25 October and 10 December).
To do so, he believed, would risk causing the uppermost echelons of
the government to view SEKBERTAL as ungrateful, or worse,
simply committed to attacking governmental policy.[123]

SEKBERTAL therefore maintained a low media profile through
late January and the first half of February, concentrating on advising
and assisting PIBTI and the garment manufacturers in mounting
criticism of API's export levies, and the allocation of export quotas.
Aminuddin did, however, contact Trade Minister, Rachmat Saleh,
discreetly and obtained a meeting with him on 2 February. At this
private meeting he argued strongly against the illogical 1:10 policy,
emphasising that local cotton production could satisfy only five
percent, not ten percent, of spinning industry needs. The spinning
industry could only abide by the new regulation by halving production, something that was plainly undesirable.[124]

Following considerable press scepticism about API's new plan for
purchasing an enormous stockpile of local cotton, and more generally, of the merit of the 1:10 cotton procurement policy, Rachmat
Saleh came out and publicly defended the API proposal, insisting
that there were no monopoly plans lying behind it, as spinning mills
could import independently if local supplies were certified inadequate. (However, a mill which was given special authorisation to
import would still have to fulfil its outstanding obligations in the
following season, further compounding the situation.) He said that
API's proposal to buy a five year supply of cotton was not sinister,
and that no devious monopoly would result. Significantly, however,
he added that API would be permitted to proceed with its plan
provided that it did not inflate the price of cotton unreasonably to
secure a large windfall profit.[125]

By mid-February, SEKBERTAL was no longer willing to remain a
passive observer. In a press conference with widespread favourable
coverage, Aminuddin attacked the API plan and called on the
government to reject it. He advanced a number of reasons for this,
among them that it would ruin the good communications that had
developed between the cotton growers and the spinners under the
proportional system of the Department of Industry. He claimed that
this communication was beneficial to both sides, ensuring that the
correct quality and pricing information passed from one side to
another. This would be lost, he claimed, if API were allowed to step
in as a middleman, adding that API would surely introduce a surcharge for the resale of cotton to the spinning industry, thus grossly
increasing the price. He concluded by broadening the attack on API

and raising questions about API levies on garment exporters—a matter which was of rapidly mounting concern to the increasingly unhappy producers in the garment industry.[126]

A week later, Aminuddin took the opportunity to attack API again and speak out in support of the garment industry when commenting on a scandal that had erupted over the manipulation of garment export quotas to the United States, which had seen a number of garment manufacturers lose their export licences and five Trade Department officials relieved of their duties. He told journalists that the crisis could have been avoided if the quota allocation was conducted in a fair, open manner, asserting that the whole system would operate more smoothly if API was prevented from levying exports.[127]

That API was keen to reassert itself within the spinning industry and seize the opportunity opened by the new trade regulations was made clearer with a newspaper report on 11 March.[128] An article in *Bisnis Indonesia* (a paper sympathetic to API) reported that an agreement had been reached between Rachmat Saleh, the Director General for Multifarious Industries, cotton growers and the textile industry for the creation of a buffer stock of local cotton in order to guarantee price stability. The article noted that this was essential because the price of imported cotton had recently risen above that of local cotton. In March prices were Rp. 2,300 per kilogram and Rp. 1,986 per kilogram respectively. It stated that to further help the local cotton growers, the spinning industry would not object to paying a standardised price for local cotton, set at Rp. 100 below imported cotton, with the revenue generated as a result of the price differential being quite substantial. The article concluded that it would be desirable for a non-government body to manage the scheme, as Rachmat Saleh had indicated he wished to see the textile industry manage its own affairs.

The meaning of the article was quite clear to those involved in the spinning industry: API, possibly via a revived CBTI, would purchase a five year supply of local cotton and generate a large profit for itself by reselling it to spinning mills at a price set artificially at Rp. 100 below the international price, which was expected to continue to rise.

Developments on this front received a major setback, however, when the Director General for Multifarious Industries publicly denied both knowledge of, and support for, the notion of some form of large cotton stockpile.[129] SEKBERTAL's response was to continue to target the Trade Department's 1:10 policy, seeking its official replacement with the proportional system of the Industry Department, a system which left no scope for the sort of activity API was apparently considering as the individual allocation of cotton to each spinning mill would be predetermined.

In April, SEKBERTAL sent its strongest letter yet to the government. It was addressed solely to Rachmat Saleh, but at the end of the letter there was a staggering list of twenty-three key political figures, including the President, who had been sent registered copies.[130] Though politely worded, the letter was an unequivocal call for Rachmat Saleh to reconsider his Decree of 23 January (as well as the implementing Decree of the Director General for Foreign Trade of 24 January) which reaffirmed the 1:10 requirement. It stated openly that the regulation imposed great costs and administrative burdens upon the spinning industry, distorting the market and hampering their attempts to increase productivity and competitiveness as called for by the President in his budget speech earlier in the year.

The letter (a lengthy one, with many attachments) set out a range of arguments against the 1:10 system, and appealed for the spinning industry to be allowed to follow the proportional system designed by the Director General for Multifarious Industries. Prominent among the arguments used was the claim that domestic cotton production only amounted to five (as opposed to ten) percent of industry need. Hence in this situation the 1:10 regulation provided an opportunity for 'certain groups' seeking a monopoly to purchase a large share of the local cotton supply, thereby creating price havoc. It noted that it was administratively very costly for spinning mills to have to obtain letters of confirmation from the cotton growers that no local supply was available. (The cotton sales centre was in East Java, which necessitated a trip there by the spinners every time a letter was required.) This, it said, would all be necessary under the proportional system.

The letter argued that the Trade Department's regulation discouraged further investment and threatened the business climate in the industry, despite the fact that it was one in which Indonesia enjoyed a comparative advantage. The letter concluded with copies of letters and numerous telexes to SEKBERTAL from spinning mills complaining of great difficulties being experienced as a result of the 23–24 January regulations. One letter, from T.D. Pardede, was given particular prominence. Pardede, one of only three *pribumi* business people in the spinning industry, was a highly respected and well-known Sumatran business and political figure. Aminuddin sought to capitalise as much as possible on Pardede's letter, which detailed problems caused by the 1:10 regulation, and (very conveniently) urged Aminuddin to struggle for a review of the policy.

SEKBERTAL was clearly putting considerable pressure on the Trade Department, both with this letter and with its public campaign in support of fabric and garment exporters who were experiencing acute problems with the allocation of export quotas and the large export surcharges. As already mentioned, SEKBERTAL did not want to be seen as politically meddlesome and interfering in matters which did not directly concern it—such as the problems of the downstream industries in the textile sector. And yet, as against this, SEKBERTAL was very keen to launch what Aminuddin liked to describe as a 'second front' (i.e. in the garment industry) against API and the Department of Trade.

Traditionally, PIBTI had voiced garment manufacturer grievances, but while it had taken some action to criticise API and Trade, many garment manufacturers appear to have felt that the PIBTI leadership was not being sufficiently active.[131] In this situation, Aminuddin advised and assisted a number of garment manufacturers who came to see him for help in establishing an organisation equivalent to SEKBERTAL for their industry. This resulted in the formation of SEKBERPAK, the Garment Manufacturers' Joint Secretariat. SEKBERPAK was greatly influenced by SEKBERTAL, as indeed its very name suggests, with Aminuddin giving continual assistance and tactical advice to its leader Mrs Wien Dewanta.[132]

By this means SEKBERTAL could ensure that the pressure was maintained on the Department of Trade and API on issues over which they were currently vulnerable. Criticisms of the export quota allocation and the issue of the unaccounted levies on exports gained considerable supportive media attention. In this context, assistance came from the continuing scandal involving the manipulation of export quota documents by Trade officials, together with a fresh scandal that erupted concerning impropriety by Trade officials over coffee exports.[133]

These various factors closing in on the Department of Trade came to a head on 11 May with the announcement of a Presidential Decree replacing two of its most senior officials, the Director General for Domestic Trade and the Director General for Foreign Trade.[134] This was the first time that Suharto had simultaneously dispensed with two officials of such a senior rank. It was made more remarkable by the fact that the more senior of the two, the Director General for Domestic Trade, who was widely seen to be very closely associated with API, also reportedly had business links to the President's family.[135]

SEKBERTAL drew great encouragement from this development, interpreting it as an extraordinary and unequivocal indication that very senior sections of the government, and even the President, were not deaf to their complaints.[136] The removal of the two Director Generals was another major blow for API.

In the wake of all this, SEKBERTAL heightened its efforts to push for a reform of Rachmat Saleh's 1:10 ruling. Much confusion existed as to the legal situation with regard to the link between the purchase of local cotton and the importing of cotton. Rachmat Saleh's Decrees of December 1985 officially linked the two by a 1:10 ratio. However, following SEKBERTAL's campaign and the 25 October package, the Director General for Multifarious Industries had appeared to supersede the December 1985 ruling with his instruction, on 4 December 1986 to spinning mills that the importing of cotton would henceforth be governed by his system of proportional distribution of local cotton. As mentioned earlier, this had been followed up with a letter to the Director General for Foreign Trade, calling on him to instruct the foreign exchange banks as to these new arrangements. Then, to further confuse the whole situation, Rachmat Saleh and the Department of Trade had struck back on 23–4 January with Decrees reaffirming the authority of the original (December 1985) ruling requiring the 1:10 link.

This was a clear case of one arm of the government, the Department of Industry, saying one thing, while another, the Department of Trade, was saying something not only different, but quite contradictory. In this hapless situation, it fell to the banks to determine what they believed to be the official policy. This was because it was the foreign exchange banks, whether state, private or foreign-owned, which ultimately had to decide whether or not to proceed and open a Letter of Credit for a spinning company wanting to import cotton. In this respect they had to weigh a renewed Minister's Decree (from one department) against a slightly older Director General's instruction (from another department). The question confronting them became: which enjoyed greater political authority?[137] Not surprisingly, the result was great confusion in both the banking and spinning industries, with some banks apparently agreeing to process the applications of spinning mills, which adhered to the Department of Industry's proportional system, and others refusing, citing the Trade Department ruling. It seems that foreign banks generally adhered to the 1:10 ruling as it had the status of a Ministerial Decree, while a number of local banks judged the proportional system (even though not a Decree) to be in the political ascendancy.

The Department of Industry maintained its support for the SEKBERTAL campaign against the 1:10 regulation in 1987, despite Rachmat Saleh's 23 January Decree. The Director General for Multifarious Industries persisted in issuing his updated proportional allocation list, and Industry Minister Hartarto reiterated that local cotton production only amounted to five percent of spinning industry needs.[138]

Encouraged by the increasing support from the Department of Industry, SEKBERTAL sought a way by which the 1:10 regulation could be, if not revoked, at least superseded or side-stepped. The solution which emerged was a joint agreement between cotton growers and spinners providing for the institutionalisation of direct links between the two via the proportional system. The agreement included specific provisions to ensure that the new arrangements were clear in respect of the processing of applications for Letters of Credit by the banks.[139] It was reached after a series of negotiations initiated by SEKBERTAL, was signed by SEKBERTAL (representing the spinning industry) and executives from the cotton plantations' controlling and cotton marketing bodies on 13 July. Importantly, the signing took place in the Directorate General for Plantations and was witnessed by the Director General for Plantations and the Director General for Multifarious Industries.

This represented a very convenient solution to a delicate political situation. Rachmat Saleh's Decree had been quietly by-passed and a new procedure established in such a way as to minimise loss of face for him and the Trade Department. It was very significant that the new agreement had been endorsed by two departments. One of the two, the Department of Agriculture (under which the Directorate General for Plantations falls), was seen to be directly representing the interests of cotton growers—the same interests that the Department of Trade had been claiming to represent with the 1:10 regulation. This, together with the fact that the absorption of the local cotton crop was still guaranteed, meant that Trade and API could not readily claim that the new system would harm the interests of small cotton farmers. Furthermore, the fact that the new agreement enjoyed the support of two departments meant that in terms of political clout the balance had tilted away from the Department of Trade's ruling.

The 1:10 regulation had, *de facto*, been superseded, and the proportional system firmly established, ensuring direct links between cotton growers and users, at the same time precluding the possibility of any group buying up a large portion of the crop (and hence possibly manipulating prices). In short, the situation had been returned to the *status quo* as it was prior to Rachmat Saleh's first decrees back in December 1985. The only significant difference was that spinners were now required to use local cotton, something that had originally been optional. This was a relatively small burden, however, since the crop was distributed proportionately throughout the entire industry. It was a tiny price to pay for the victory that had been achieved.

The only potentially threatening cloud that remained on SEKBERTAL's horizon was API. This was because SEKBERTAL still believed that API might try to introduce some other venture detrimental to SEKBERTAL members (perhaps by reviving CBTI),[140] and because it continued to be a source of anxiety to SEKBERTAL's allies in the garment industry—SEKBERPAK and PIBTI. SEKBERTAL was therefore keen to see API's power reduced, if not eliminated altogether.

An opportunity to push in this direction had emerged shortly before the signing of the joint-agreement with the cotton growers. This centred around KADIN's need to review and reform its membership structure to bring itself into line with the new KADIN law (discussed in Chapter 3) ratified by the President in January 1987. One specific aspect of the law was that all member associations had to be sector-based. This meant that cross-sectoral organisations, or federations, could not be accepted as members of the newly constituted KADIN.[141]

Following the promulgation of the new law, KADIN chief Sukamdani Gitosardjono had instructed the heads of all different Sections within KADIN to examine the status of their member organisations. The textile industry fell under the jurisdiction of the Sections for Multifarious Industry, Small Industry and Pharmaceuticals, headed by Sunarto Prawirosujanto. When he came to consider the textile industry, he was immediately confronted with the problem that API was a cross-sectoral association. There was also the problem that some of the associations that had been 'fused' into the new API back in March 1985, remained as individual members of KADIN, as did PIBTI, APSYFI and PERTEKSI, the three textile associations that had boycotted the fusion. Sunarto therefore decided to create a new representational structure for the textile industry which would be in harmony with the new KADIN law.[142]

After consultations, Sunarto decide to unravel the maze of textile organisations and create a simpler four-fold division for KADIN's new textile representational structure which would embrace the main areas of production from upstream to downstream—synthetic fibre-making, spinning, weaving and garment-making. It was well-recognised that this change would be very unpopular with API. Both Aminuddin and Arnold Baramuli (who was, simultaneously, the head of both PIBTI and APSYFI, as well as the deputy head of KADIN) actively promoted this outcome, knowing full well that it would present an official representational alternative and thus a challenge to API's position as the supreme textile organisation.

It was envisaged that PIBTI[143] and APSYFI would fill the positions created for garment-maker and synthetic-fibre maker associations. This was natural, as they were already members of KADIN. SEKBERTAL, however, anxious as it was to fill the spinning vacancy, faced the problem that it could only become a part of

KADIN if it was formally constituted as an industry association. The decision to reconstitute SEKBERTAL was duly taken, and it was officially received as a member of KADIN on 25 July.[144] After the inauguration ceremony, Baramuli (acting in his capacity as deputy head of KADIN) addressed a press conference together with Aminuddin. Aminuddin used the occasion to attack API, as did Baramuli in announcing that even if API applied to join KADIN, its application would be rejected.[145]

A month later, on 21 August, KADIN head Sukamdani announced to the press that a new textile federation had been formed, the Indonesian Textile Industry Federation, or FITI. He said that FITI had been formed spontaneously by the four sectoral associations recognised by KADIN (the fourth, after APSYFI, SEKBERTAL and PIBTI, was ASPINDO,[146] representing the weaving industry). He added that the new federation would be headed by Kusnaeni, the widely respected leader of ASPINDO, with Aminuddin as deputy head (and de facto leader). In offering strong endorsement of FITI, Sukamdani declared that he would inform the ASEAN Chamber of Commerce and the ASEAN Textile Federation that FITI (and not API) was now Indonesia's sole representative for the textile industry.[147]

In doing this KADIN was clearly throwing its weight behind the new organisation and seeking to discredit API. FITI further strengthened its claims to legitimacy several days later when Aminuddin (acting in his capacity as a FITI representative) conducted a well-publicised courtesy call to Industry Minister Hartarto's office.[148] This served to create the distinct impression that Hartarto also endorsed FITI.

The tide was now running strongly against API/CBTI. In November the standing of their principal opponent, Aminuddin, was further enhanced when he was appointed to the Advisory Council of KADIN, and chosen as one of the private sector representatives for the special conference convened to transform KADIN in line with the new KADIN law. Aminuddin's appointment was welcomed in the press, as representing the rise of a new breed of entrepreneur championing the cause of business interests.[149] Through developments such as this, SEKBERTAL was gradually able to shed its reputation for rebelliousness and as a body that operated 'outside' officially approved patterns. Indicative of this was the fact that Aminuddin, as deputy-head of FITI, was invited to appear before a special Parliamentary Committee (VI) hearing into the textile industry. Whereas SEKBERTAL had earlier deliberately avoided contact with the Parliament, it now welcomed the opportunity, being more secure under the FITI umbrella.[150]

SEKBERTAL's complete victory was to be confirmed the following year, with the replacement of Rachmat Saleh by Arifin Siregar as Trade Minister in the new Cabinet. Siregar, shortly after a much publicised cordial meeting with the FITI leadership in May 1988,[151] issued a decree finally and formally revoking all the decrees that had been introduced by Rachmat Saleh that had provided for the existence and authority of CBTI.[152] The slate had now been wiped completely clean. Rachmat Saleh had been replaced as Trade Minister, the two Trade Director Generals most closely associated with API had been discharged, FITI had been successfully established as a rival to API and was moving to eclipse it, and all of CBTI's authority had now been categorically removed. Perhaps the most telling indication of the magnitude of SEKBERTAL's achievement was Frans Seda's decision in late June 1988 declining to continue as head of API.[153]

Conclusion

This case-study has been lengthy and rather complex. What have been the main elements? Briefly, the Department of Trade, responding to the initiative of a client group in the leadership of API, granted CBTI, an API-created and API-controlled company, a wide-ranging monopoly over the procurement of the raw materials used by the spinning industry. This was coupled with a further requirement that spinners import not more than ten times the amount of cotton that they purchased from local cotton growers. Once CBTI was established, it sought to introduce a *modus operandi* as well as a number of specific revenue-raising measures which large sections of the spinning industry saw as highly injurious.

The issue was politically sensitive in view of the widespread controversy over the government's agglomeration of restrictive trade regulations, the *tata niaga*. This made it hard for aggrieved spinners to protest against the decision. However, beyond the fact that the existing political climate discouraged action relating to the broader import monopoly issue, there was also a range of other important factors which suggested strongly that the spinners would be unlikely to contest the policy. First and foremost was the fact that the position of CBTI seemed almost unassailable to the majority of spinners. It was seen to have strong links to the Department of Trade and even to the President, while its position had also been sanctioned not just by a Ministerial decree, but by a formal Cabinet decision. In addition to this, CBTI was made up of influential members of the API leadership, some of whom were well-known and forceful *pribumi* figures.

As most of the spinners were less well-connected Chinese Indonesians or foreign investors, it was unlikely that they would be willing to stand up and oppose CBTI.

In spite of all of this, a small group of spinners, angered by CBTI proposals to introduce a heavy financial levy, and headed by one of the very few *pribumi* in the industry, formed an organisation with the explicit aim of persuading the government to reconsider its recently introduced bundle of policies governing the spinning industry and the procurement of its raw materials. SEKBERTAL soon grew in numbers as other spinners began to offer their support. Its strategy was, in essence, twofold. On one hand, it set out to mount an active media campaign highlighting the problems that it saw CBTI generating, and attempting in this way to discredit CBTI. On the other, it simultaneously maintained discreet lines of communication to various strategically placed figures in the state apparatus through numerous detailed letters and direct meetings. In this SEKBERTAL sought always to couch its arguments and claims in the government's own rhetoric of economic reform, so as to minimise the appearance of being a group that was challenging state authority.

Ultimately SEKBERTAL achieved sweeping success by not only persuading the government to withdraw CBTI's monopoly and review the 1:10 import requirement, but also by discrediting API as the peak organisation of the textile industry. At the time of writing, an alternative body, FITI, was well-established as a rival representative body for textile industry needs.

SEKBERTAL's success was clearly quite extraordinary in view of the circumstances. But what does this tell us about the nature of politics in Indonesia and the question of state-society relations? At the most basic level, the argument here is that this case pulls in a different direction to that of the existing interpretations of these matters. As seen in the discussion of the theoretical literature on Indonesian politics, the prevailing view is that participation in policy formation by societal interests is very limited. The only forms of linkage between state and society regarded as worthy of note were patron-client connections, state-dominated and exclusionary corporatist institutions, and what we have termed political osmosis—none of which was deemed to furnish societal groups with significant scope for direct input into the shaping of policy. Elements of each of these were woven through the fabric of this case. However, what makes the case particularly interesting is that it shows societal actors having a direct input into policy formation in novel and unexpected ways.

Over the course of the spinning industry conflict, the government reversed not only a Ministerial decree, but also a Cabinet decision within the space of twelve months. How did such an extraordinary policy reversal come about? Unquestionably, state actors played a central role in influencing the final outcome. The list of major participants from within the state apparatus included not only several departments and their senior officials, but also ministers, senior sections of the military and even the President himself. And yet quite clearly, were we to confine the list of key participants to those based within the state, a number of others who played a vital role in the story would be omitted. These are of course the societal actors. Most striking of all in this respect, was the role of SEKBERTAL. It is extremely difficult to imagine that Rachmat Saleh's policies would have been reversed in the manner that occurred, had SEKBERTAL (or some similar body) not been there to oppose them. The press also played a very important role. It was both a disseminator of societal groups' and individuals' demands, as well as an active participant itself, advancing certain preferred ideas of its own. To a lesser extent, KADIN also played a part, not so much as the standard bearer of industry interests, but rather as a sort of power broker, lending weight to SEKBERTAL and the other textile associations which sought to form an alternative peak organisation to replace API.

SEKBERTAL's success cannot be explained simply in terms of patron-client links. To do so, it would be necessary to argue that the crucial variable was Aminuddin's personal connections to key figures within the state, particularly Sumarlin and Wijoyo. No doubt these links were of considerable importance. But this in itself, cannot explain everything. Aminuddin did not have a *patrimonial* relationship with these men; it was not a case of them awarding concessions to a client. SEKBERTAL was a group-based struggle for collective goals which offered generalised benefits for all spinners, and not merely a select few. Aminuddin would have had little chance of success had he not been supported by the majority of the spinning industry, for it is highly unlikely that Aminuddin alone would have been able to overcome the political resources of the API camp. The whole logic of the SEKBERTAL argument was that API and CBTI were endangering an entire industry—an assertion attested to by the size of the SEKBERTAL membership. Moreover, the vigorous and very high-profile manner in which SEKBERTAL pursued its aims is utterly inconsistent with clientelistic behaviour. Its behaviour bore none of the hallmarks of a client seeking special favours from a patron. The controversy generated in the media was indicative of an effort to push the government into doing something it would not otherwise do.

Not only is it difficult to satisfactorily account for SEKBERTAL's behaviour in terms of patrimonial links, it does not sit well with the prevailing notions about a restrictive or exclusionary corporatist system either. Certainly there are some striking features in the representational arrangements within the textile industry which do accord with ideas about the exclusionary character of corporatist structure in Indonesia. API is a good example of an authoritative state-designated association, and the 'fusion' of 1985 served to enhance API's capacity to control its membership and suppress demands for policy reform. The cosy relationship between API leaders and key officials in the Department of Trade ensured that the API executive would not seek to alter the *status quo* in order to improve the industry's capacity to pursue collective political interests. With the rise of SEKBERTAL, however, the whole nature of interest representation in the textile industry changed radically. The conflict over CBTI generated a quite different mode of representational behaviour. Most noteworthy in this regard, was the way in which a major section of the spinning industry broke away from API and spontaneously formed an organisation with the express aim of lobbying the government, precisely because the designated corporatist body, API, had failed to represent their interests satisfactorily. This was carried even further with the moves to replace API altogether with FITI. In short, the restrictive corporatist structure of API was unable to contain industry demands, so a group of producers simply broke out of the official representative structure and sought to deal with the state on terms more satisfactory to themselves.

The behaviour of SEKBERTAL and FITI presents an interesting challenge to the usual interpretations of corporatist institutions in Indonesia, for while they both moved to formalise their position as state-recognised representative associations and have, in a sense, thus moved back into the official corporatist fold, their character is fundamentally different to many other organisations of this sort. Rather than serving to contain and restrict industry demands upon the government, their whole *raison d'etre* was precisely to reverse such a situation. SEKBERTAL and FITI were formed specifically to ensure a capacity to project member interests and demands in a vigorous and effective manner. Though recognisably corporatist in their form, these organisations functioned to facilitate rather obstruct policy input by the industry—something quite at odds with the prevailing style of corporatist arrangements in Indonesia. In short, SEKBERTAL and FITI seem to be of a more representative breed of corporatism.

Ultimately, the significance of this case-study lies in the challenge it poses to the existing, heavily state-centred, explanations of Indonesian politics; it is an argument that societal interests were in this case able to influence a major policy issue directly and decisively. Interestingly, in the context of a broader study of the political economy of the textile sector, another writer, Makarim Wibisono has drawn comparable conclusions about the political significance of SEKBERTAL in this policy conflict.[154] Nevertheless those sceptical of arguments about the possibility of extra-state groups playing a major role in the shaping of policy outcomes, might wish to argue that the major policy reversal in this case-study can be accounted for quite satisfactorily on the basis of political action *internal* to the state: in short, a policy shift already set in train by reformist economic ministers—the technocrats—with SEKBERTAL playing the role of a curious 'supporting actor'. Certainly there was significant momentum within key sections of the state apparatus for movement towards liberalisation of many aspects of economic policy, particularly in the area of trade policy. Major policy initiatives such as the sweeping banking reforms of 1983, the 1985 overhaul and privatisation of customs functions in the ports, and the 6 May package of 1986 liberalising some investment and export procedures, were all in place either before SEKBERTAL was established or before it had had any significant impact. Undoubtedly, the technocrats within the government and the corresponding sections of the bureaucracy wished to move much further in this direction. In addition, there was considerable pressure from the World Bank to accelerate the process of economic liberalisation. Moreover, all of this was taking place within the context of economic crisis following the dramatic deterioration of the country's trade position with the collapse in oil prices.

Clearly then, there was pressure for widespread economic reform. However, there were also very considerable countervailing pressures resisting economic liberalisation from those who were either sceptical of the economic arguments put forward, or more significantly, had a major material interest in the status quo. This was well illustrated by the piecemeal and often incremental nature of the reform initiatives. Thus reform of any policy area, particularly trade regulation, faced major obstacles.

But this is to focus too narrowly on the internal dynamics of the state. Why was it that the spinning industry was the major beneficiary of the 25 October and particularly the 15 January reform packages? Of the many different areas of industry in the Indonesian manufacturing sector, why did the *spinning* industry receive so much attention? In answering this, it is very hard to ignore the fact that the most prominent feature of the spinning industry in 1986 and 1987 was the political controversy generated by SEKBERTAL's pressure for a reversal of Rachmat Saleh's policies. It would have been quite extraordinary for other technocrat ministers to overturn those policies concerning the spinning industry that had only very recently been introduced by Rachmat Saleh and endorsed by the Cabinet, had there not been some very significant extraneous factor involved. There was no shortage of other import restrictions that might have been eased. That the government should act in the way that it did is, however, readily understandable if one considers SEKBERTAL's lobbying activities, and especially its apparent success in persuading the President to intervene. Of interest in this regard, is the view of Mohammed Sadli, a prominent member of the technocrat circle, that the spinning industry episode should be understood as a case of the government responding to external stimulus, rather than simply proceeding with a deliberate and pre-planned policy reform agenda of its own.[155] In sum, it is only when we take account of the tactical alliances forged between state *and* societal actors that we can make sense of the processes of policy formation illustrated here.

1. For background on the textile industry see, Wibisono (1987), Hill (1979), and Palmer (1972).
2. This data is drawn from the report on the Indonesian textile industry by the World Bank (1987), pp. 40–41.
3. Hill (1988) pp. 83–84.
4. World Bank Report (1987) p. 60. For a more complete overview of the textile industry see also pp. 43–7.
5. World Bank Report (1987) p. 61.
6. World Bank Report (1987) pp. 63 & 72.
7. World Bank Report (1987) pp. 44 & 47.
8. World Bank Report (1987) pp. 52 & 73; and Data Consult Inc. (1986) p. 7.
9. See 'Cotton Intensification Fails', *Jakarta Post*, 7 October 1987; and more generally, the report, 'Program Nasional Penelitian Tanaman Serat Buah 1988–1995', prepared by the Tobacco and Plant Fibre Research Institute (1988).
10. Among his various posts, Seda had been Minister of Finance in the late 1960s, as well as head of the Catholic Party.
11. Interview with Alif Martadi (Secretary General of PIBTI and former F-API official), 22 May 1987. I am indebted to Alif Martadi for much of the information on the background of the representative organisations in the textile industry.
12. These included, the Indonesian Weavers' Association (ASPINDO), The Indonesian Knitting and Embroidery Association (APBI), the Indonesian Batik Association (ABI), the Indonesian False Twisters' Association (APBTI), the Batik Cooperatives Association (GKBI), the Indonesian Union of Bonded Warehouse Industries (PIBWI), the All Indonesian Textile Consultants' Association (IKATSI) and Frans Seda's already mentioned Indonesian Textile Products Trade Association (APPPTI).

13. His flagship within the spinning industry is Argopantes Pty Ltd (the
largest single mill in Indonesia). His other mills include, Dharma
Kalimas Pty Ltd, Dharmatex Pty Ltd, South-Grandtex Pty Ltd, World
Yamatex Pty Ltd, as well as three joint ventures (with Japanese
firms),—ACTEM, ISTEM and Kumatex. In addition he has major
interests in synthetic fibre-making (Kuraray Manunggal Pty Ltd, a
Japanese joint venture) as well as the textile and garment sub-sectors
(Perintis Pty Ltd, Pola Sejati Pty Ltd and Timatex Pty Ltd, a Japanese
joint venture). He thus heads a vast empire, integrating upstream and
downstream functions. In addition to textiles, his major interests
include an integrated steel and rolling mill, chemicals and dyestuffs,
lease financing, poultry, and general trading.

14. Handoko's flagship is the giant Batik Keris Pty Ltd, a large producer of
batik and an exporter of batik garments. In addition, he owns Dan
Liris Pty Ltd (an integrated spinning mill only slightly smaller than
Thee Nian King's Argopantes Pty Ltd) and has a major share in the
synthetic fibre maker Tri Rempoa Pty Ltd.

15. It was widely believed in Jakarta business circles that this group enjoyed
a very close relationship with a number of the most senior officials in
the Department of Trade—notably the Director General for Internal
Trade, Kardjono Wirioprawiro, and the Director General for External
Trade, B.M. Kuntjoro-jakti. It was also widely assumed that as a
former Finance Minister, Frans Seda must have been well-known to
Trade Minister (and the former Governor of the Bank Indonesia)
Rachmat Saleh.

16. Many producers believed that both the F-API leadership and some
senior officials within the Trade Department had a mutual material
interest in this arrangement. The requirement to pay a compulsory
levy to F-API was contained in cable no. 236/DAGLU-21/
KWT/VIII/84, dated 10 July 1984, from the Director General of
External Trade to Regional Trade Department offices. Note however,
that the instruction from the Director General was preceded by an
F-API decree (no. 002/SK/Dp-API/84 of 10 April 1984), making the
same determination. This strongly suggests that the Director General's
instruction was intended to reinforce an unpopular F-API ruling.

17. Interview, Alif Martadi (Secretary General of PIBTI and former F-API
official), 30 April 1987.

18. See, for example, 'Kadin: Kongress Khusus F-API Tidak Sah', Kompas,
23 March 1985; and 'Tidak Relevan Mempersoalkan Sah Tidaknya
Kongress Khusus API', Kompas, 27 March 1985.

19. API membership fees were reportedly Rp 150,000 per month.

20. It should be noted that API was a very much larger organisation that any
of the other individual associations. Aside from the Chairman (Frans
Seda) and the full-time professional Secretary General (Fahmy Chatib), API had a total of fifteen sectoral and functional sections, each of
which had a chairman and leadership committee (for example, the
Spinning Section and the International Trade section). There was also
a separate Treasury Section. In nearly all cases, the leadership posi-

tions were filled by people closely associated with Frans Seda's group. Beyond its head-office, API also had a parallel regional structure scattered throughout the country. Indeed, it was such a large organisation that the KADIN executive viewed its failure to join KADIN with some suspicion.

21. Interviews with Husein Aminuddin (Textra Amspin Pty Ltd), 18 April 1987; Suwachman (an editor of Prioritas), 18 April 1987; Endang Achmadi (Deputy Chief Editor Berita Yudha), 18 April 1987; and Alif Martadi (Secretary General of PIBTI and former F-API official), 30 April 1987.
22. Rachmat Saleh's Ministerial Decrees no. 1066/KP/XII/85 and no. 1067/ KP/XII/85.
23. The official API letter was no. 171/API/XII/85, dated 30 December 1985.
24. This data was obtained from Fahmy Chatib (Secretary General of API), 2 April 1987.
25. Interview with Alif Martadi (Secretary General of PIBTI and former F-API official), 22 May 1987.
26. As we have seen, however, in some cases large spinning factories were 'integrated', meaning that not only did they spin yarn, but they also wove cloth, and in some instances also had garment manufacturing-related activities. Prominent API leaders were in this category.
27. As will be discussed later (see fn. 79 below), it is not all clear that the API scheme would have satisfied the requirements of GATT.
28. With hindsight, many spinners interviewed were of the opinion that at least some senior officials within the Trade Department had been involved in the development of this scheme from the outset, and that it was nothing more than a device to generate private revenue for these officials and the API leadership.
29. Decrees of the Minister of Trade, no. 70/KP/II/86 18 February 1986 (cotton fibre), no. 82/KP/III/86 6 March 1986 (polyester staple fibre) and no. 83/KP/III/86 6 March 1986 (rayon staple fibre). The fact that the company was suddenly formed just prior to Rachmat Saleh granting it the monopoly, indicates that CBTI's founders knew in advance that they were to receive this special status.
30. In addition, two other members of the board, Willy Brata and Chan Wing Wah, were also from Thee Nian King's Damatex group.
31. See for example 'Menperdag Tunjuk Pelaksana Tunggal Pengadaan Serat Kapas Untuk Industri', *Sinar Harapan*, 27 February 1986.
32. 'Salah Bila Menganggap CBTI Untuk Kepentingan Segelintir Pengusaha', *Suara Karya*, 3 March 1986.
33. This is reported in 'PT CBTI Mengubah Anggaran Dasar', *Kompas*, 24 March 1986.
34. See 'GINSI Menyesalkan Penunjukan Importir Tunggal Serat Kapas', *Sinar Harapan*, 5 March 1986.
35. GINSI is one business organisation that stretches back to the 1950s. (It is a descendent of KINSI.) Of the numerous business associations in contemporary Indonesia, GINSI can be considered as one of the more dynamic and effective. It has a staff of thirty (nine import company

heads, and twenty one support staff). It was very active, and ultimately successful, for example, in having a bonded warehouse created in Jakarta. It has also been a long standing proponent of reform of port procedures in Jakarta. An indication of its seriousness of purpose is to be found in the fact that its activities have not always endeared it to the government.

36. See 'Maret, Rapat Koordinasi Pengawasan Pembangunan', *Kompas*, 6 March 1986.

37. Interview with Zahri Achmad (head of GINSI), 29 April 1987.

38. The most unremitting critics of CBTI and API took the view that Rachmat Saleh himself had a material interest in the CBTI venture. Others found this implausible, and suggested instead that it was senior trade officials, and in particular, the Director General for Internal Trade, that stood behind it. As such, it was argued that Saleh simply turned a blind eye to the affair. Another account places a slightly less suspicious interpretation on his role, arguing that he was under intense pressure to award the import monopolies to interests associated with President Suharto's family, but that instead of acceding to this, he sought to ensure that at least the rents derived remained within the textile industry, that is CBTI and API. As will be noted below (see fn. 47) there is evidence to suggest that rumours of involvement by President Suharto's family were not only false, but deliberate red herrings.

39. See 'Monopoly of Cotton Imports Defended', *Jakarta Post*, 11 March 1986.

40. In 1963–64, at the request of Chairul Saleh (then Deputy Prime Minister for Economic Affairs) Aminuddin became the industry representative on the Textile Team in the Komando Tertinggi Operasi Ekonomi (KOTOE) appointed by President Sukarno. The Textile Team was responsible for the removal of market distortions via yarn allocations, and promoting the development of the textile industry. Following this experience, in 1967 he headed the National Textile Development Movement (Gerakan Pembangunan Sandang Nasional), an organisation of private mill owners aimed at reinvigorating the textile industry. Though it was not long lived, this was the first textile association of the New Order period. He also led the first Indonesian business promotion mission of the New Order to the United States in 1969 and was the head of Forum Swasta (the Private Entrepreneurs Forum). As mentioned in Chapter 3, this was the first business association of the New Order period. (Forum Swasta declined after it came into conflict with Soedjono Hoemardhani, a key military adviser to the President, and Bob Hassan, a close business associate.) Since the early 1970s he had refused to involve himself again in textile industry affairs, concentrating his attention instead on his own factory and its development. Partly as a result, he enjoyed a reputation for producing the finest quality yarn and having a technologically very advanced mill. In general, Aminuddin appears to have had a reputation as a lone operator (he did

not join any of the textile associations to be formed in the 1970s or 1980s) but as an individual to be reckoned with.

41. 'PT CBTI Mengubah Anggaran Dasar', *Kompas*, 24 March 1986, and 'Tidak Ada Saham Prioritas PT Cerat Bina Tekstil Indonesia', *Business News*, 24 March 1986. A newspaper article published later in the year suggested that in fact the reform of CBTI's articles of association and equity structure were only cosmetic, as the CBTI leadership continued to hold an equally large percentage of the share issue. See, 'CBTI, Wisma Dagang Yang Keabsahannya Diragukan', *Prioritas*, 4 November 1986.

42. Tactically this was a shrewd move by the CBTI executive. While a levy of Rp. 900 per kilogram would be a very large financial drain for most spinning companies (many of which consumed around 600,000 kilograms a month) a Rp. 100 kilogram levy would be quite manageable. This dual rate would serve to separate the interests of spinners who primarily used cotton fibre from those who primarily used synthetic fibre. Predictably, the cotton spinners were horrified by the proposal, whereas as the polyester spinners (most of whom were the Indian-based joint ventures) were quite willing to accept the proposed arrangement. [Interview with the head of an Indian joint venture spinning company who requested anonymity, 14 May 1987.]

43. Decree of the Board of CBTI no. 02/SK/CBTI/4/86, 28 April 1986.

44. Telex no. T-49/CBTI/4/86, 29 April 1986.

45. This stemmed from the apparent long-standing association of Mrs Tien Suharto with Batik Keris Pty. Ltd., a batik garment factory controlled by Handoko.

46. For a discussion of this, see Jones S. & Pura R., 'Suharto-Linked Monopolies Hobble Economy', *Asian Wall Street Journal*, 24–26 November 1986.

47. It was widely speculated that President Suharto's sons had been anxious to secure the monopoly rights gained by CBTI, and that the spinning industry was fortunate Rachmat Saleh made the decision he did. This seems to have been largely the result of a deliberate disinformation campaign by Handoko to intimidate the spinners. One interviewee informed me that he had personally spoken to Sudwikatmono, a foster-brother of President Suharto, very prominent in business circles, who had insisted that the President's family had been offered the monopoly rights, but declined as the spinning industry was perceived to be too politically sensitive. In other words, business interests associated with the President had the option of taking up the textile monopoly but decided, on tactical grounds, that to be seen to be deriving enormous economic benefits from the textile industry (as opposed to other industries) would be risky as clothing had come to be seen as a basic need.

48. This was later emphasised to me by many different spinners. Almost all of the many spinners interviewed, regardless of whether of Chinese, pribumi, Indian, Japanese or Hong Kong origin, emphasised that they

had been extremely concerned and felt quite helpless to do anything to preserve their financial position in the face of the CBTI proposals.

49. Telex no. 100/TLX/5/1986, DEPIND JKT, 6 May 1986.

50. Interviews with Hussein Aminuddin (President Director, Textra Amspin Pty Ltd) 23 April 1987 and Djon Wono (Executive Director, Dasatex Pty Ltd) 1 May 1987.

51. Interview with Djono Wono (Executive Director, Dasatex Pty Ltd) 1 May 1987.

52. SEKBERTAL letter, dated 16 May 1986. Public reference to this SEK-BERTAL letter can be found in the press. See, for example, 'CBTI Dituduh Lakukan Pungutan Paksa Atas Setiap Pembelian Bahan Baku Pemintalan', *Sinar Harapan*, 31 May 1986. This article actually cites a subsequent SEKBERTAL letter of 23 May (referred to below), though it in fact also contains much of the material from the 16 May letter.

53. Interview, Hussein Aminuddin (President Director, Textra Amspin Pty Ltd) 30 April 1987.

54. SEKBERTAL letter 16 May 1986, p. 1.

55. In addition to the actual addressees, and those who received officially registered copies, Aminuddin sent copies of SEKBERTAL letters to a large number of prominent business, political, media and academic figures in Jakarta to boost SEKBERTAL's profile and hopefully attract some support. See Appendix B, MacIntyre (1988) for a sample SEKBERTAL letter. A broad range of such people interviewed in Jakarta commented on how professional and impressive this letter campaign was. For example, Mohammed Sadli (Chairman of LP3E, KADIN) 22 April 1987; Sjahfiri Alim (President Director of Goodyear Indonesia Pty Ltd and head of KADIN's Basic Chemicals Industry Section) 25 August 1987; Yakob Oetama (Editor in Chief of *Kompas*) 24 April 1987; Indrawan (economics editor of *Kompas*) 8 May 1987; Marah Sakti (*Tempo* journalist) 29 April 1987; and prominent University of Indonesia economists Dr Doradjatun Kuntjoro-jakti (Director of the LPEM, University of Indonesia) 28 February 1987; and Dr Anwar Nasution (Faculty of Economics, University of Indonesia) 25 March 1987.

56. Telex no. 113/TLX/5/1986, DEPIND JKT, dated 21 May 1986. For public reference to this telex see, 'CBTI Dituduh Lakukan Pungutan Paksa Atas Setiap Pembelian Bahan Baku Pemintalan', *Sinar Hara-pan*, 31 May 1986; and 'Industri Pemintalan Bentuk SEKBERTAL Untuk Hadapi PT CBTI', *Suara Karya*, 19 June 1986.

57. Note, however, that Industry Minister Hartarto was not much involved at this stage. Further more (though this image is changing), Hartarto had been regarded as generally sympathetic to economic nationalist policies rather than liberalising and export-oriented approaches.

58. SEKBERTAL letter no. 003/SEKBER/5/1986, 23 May 1986, p. 3. For public reference to this see, 'CBTI Dituduh Lakukan Pungutan Paksa Atas Setiap Pembelian Bahan Baku Pemintalan', *Sinar Harapan*, 31 May 1986.

59. Another tactic employed was to try to entice some SEKBERTAL members away by playing upon the mercurial and sometimes abrasive personality of Aminuddin to divide the SEKBERTAL camp.

60. SEKBERTAL letter no. 004/SEKBER/5/1986, 27 May 1986.

61. The Bandung Garment Club, a loose and informal group of mostly garment manufacturers located in Bandung, was an early target for this strategy. (The Bandung Garment Club had no relationship whatsoever with the earlier mentioned Textile Club—Musa's old power base and a constituent part of API.) Members of the Bandung Garment Club were offered leadership positions in the regional branches of API together with various suggested financial incentives if they joined. In this case, the strategy was largely successful in absorbing a previously active organisation which was independent of API control. [Interview with Tigor Nasoetion (President Director, Imogari Pty Ltd) 18 April 1987.] Nasoetion was himself a member of the Bandung Garment Club who was initially attracted by the API overtures, but subsequently broke away and joined SEKBERTAL.

62. Interviews with executives from several Japanese spinning companies who requested anonymity.

63. See, for example, 'Pungutan PT CBTI Dimaksudkan Membantu Eksportir Tekstil', *Sinar Harapan*, 4 June 1986, and 'PT CBTI Tidak Lakukan Pungutan Paksa, Rinciannya Saja Belum Disepakati', *Business News*, 4–6 June 1986.

64. Interview with Husein Aminuddin, 5 May 1987.

65. SEKBERTAL letter no. 008/SEKBER/6/1986, 14 June 1986, pp. 4–5. While no direct public reference for this letter is available, much of it was repeated by Aminuddin at a press conference several days later. See fn. 66 immediately below for press references to this.

66. See, for example, 'Cara Kerja PT CBTI Mirip Syahbandar Zaman VOC', *Sinar Harapan*, 20 June 1986; 'Industri Pemintalan Bentuk Sekbertal Untuk Hadapi PT CBTI', *Suara Karya*, 19 June 1986; and 'Iklim Usaha Industri Tekstil', *Business News*, 23 June 1986.

67. For instance, Aminuddin at one stage likened CBTI's methods of operation to those of the Dutch East India company of colonial times, a simile which received widespread currency in the press. See 'Cara Kerja PT CBTI Mirip Syahbandar Zaman VOC', *Sinar Harapan*, 20 June 1986.

68. Many journalists and senior figures in press circles commented to me on the impressive and professional presentation of the SEKBERTAL case. Frequently commended was the way in which SEKBERTAL provided a great array of data to buttress its arguments. These ranged from costing estimates of the implications of CBTI policies, to the provision of specific dates of meetings, copies of signed memos or decisions by, for example, the CBTI executive or the Director General of Multifarious Industries. This information made it easier for the more professional journalists to check information, as well as providing them with hard data to enhance their stories. [Interviews with Endang Achmadi (Deputy Chief Editor of Berita Yudha) 8 April 1987;

134

BUSINESS AND POLITICS IN INDONESIA

Yakob Oetama (Chief Editor of *Kompas*) 24 April 1987; Sanyoto (Chief Editor of *Business News*) 2 February 1987; Suwachman (an editor of *Prioritas*) 8 April 1987; Indrawan (economics editor of *Kompas*) 8 May 1987, Marah Sakti (*Tempo* journalist) 29 April 1987, and Bluher Gultom (Sinar Pagi journalist) 14 March 1987.]
69. Interview with Husein Aminuddin, 30 April 1987.
70. For instance, 'Iklim Usaha Industri Tekstil', *Business News*, 23 June 1986.
71. Unpublished Directorate General of Multifarous Industries memo, of 30 June 1986, on the conflict within the spinning industry.
72. Interview with A.R.S. Djoemena (Director of Textiles, Department of Industry) 4 May 1987.
73. This information derives from interviews with Hiroshi Oshima (Director of the Japan External Trade Organisation—JETRO) 21 May 1987, Hirokai Okubo (President Director, Centex Pty Ltd) 22 May 1987 and Hideo Takei (President Director, Indachi Pty Ltd) 20 June 1987.
74. This point was emphasised by Hiroshi Oshima (Director of the Japan External Trade Organisation—JETRO), interview 21 May 1987.
75. Akhir Kai (which literally means 'last Thursday', derived from its members' regular golf match on the last Thursday of each month) could only approach the Japanese Embassy to lobby on their behalf if its members were all in agreement. It was understood that the Ambassador would not involve himself if they were internally divided.
76. Interviews with Japanese spinning company executives who requested anonymity.
77. These meetings were arranged by JETRO; the Japan-Indonesia Entrepreneurs Association (Himpunan Usahawan Indonesia-Jepang, an organisation for joint ventures only); and the Jakarta-Japan Club (an organisation for both joint ventures and wholly-owned Japanese companies). These forums were the primary conduits for the expression of broad Japanese business interests. The less formal Akhir Kai, by contrast, was specifically for the textile industry. Interviews with Hiroshi Oshima (Director, JETRO) 21 May 1987; and Hirokai Okubo (President Director, Centex Pty Ltd) 22 May 1987.
78. It will be noted that these figures vary somewhat from those quoted earlier from a Department of Industry memo. In those figures the gap between the spindle capacity supporting CBTI and SEKBERTAL was substantially greater. This was because the Department of Industry classified fewer companies as neutral. Because of the already mentioned problems in being certain of the allegiance of these companies, and more importantly what that might mean in terms of political action, the more conservative estimate contained in Table 4.3 is preferred. It should be borne in mind though, that this probably underestimates the strength of support for SEKBERTAL within the spinning industry.
79. SEKBERTAL letter no. 009/SEKBER/6/1986, 23 June 1986. The suggestion that the cross-subsidy proposal might still leave Indonesia in breach of GATT stemmed from the possibility that the whole arrange-

ment might be seen by other countries as a thinly veiled attempt to provide indirect subsidisation of exports with which the government was still involved. (In outlining its intention to impose a levy for cross-subsidy purposes, CBTI had emphasised that its authority to do so stemmed from Ministerial Decree no. 70 of Rachmat Saleh, which was the enabling legislation creating CBTI in the first place.)

80. SEKBERTAL letter no. 010/SEKBER/6/1986, 25 June 1986.
81. Interviews with various figures in textile industry circles who requested anonymity.
82. For a summary, see 'Setiap Pungutan Yang Dilakukan CBTI Harus Sepengetahuan Pemerintah', *Antara*, 24 June 1986.
83. SEKBERTAL letter no. 012/SEKBER/7/1986, 11 July 1986.
84. SEKBERTAL letter no. 013/SEKBER/7/1986, 15 July 1986.
85. Telex no. 189/TLX/VIII/1986, 6 August 1986. Reference to this can be found in 'PT CBTI Diminta Untuk Tidak Menahan Aplikasi L/C Kapas', *Sinar Harapan*, 9 August 1986.
86. See, for example, 'Bisnis Stempel', *Tempo*, 9 August 1986, p. 77.
87. In both these industries import monopolies were held either by members of the President's family or by business persons closely associated with the President. For a detailed discussion of the situation in these industries, see Jones S. & Pura R., 'Suharto-Linked Monopolies Hobble Economy', *Asian Wall Street Journal*, 24–26 November 1986.
88. According to Aminuddin, senior API figures, in an attempt to taint him politically, told a number of journalists that he had been found guilty of involvement in the PRRI affair. In order to convince journalists otherwise, he had showed them the letters of clearance from the military court examination of his case. Interview with Husein Aminuddin, 30 April 1987.
89. Press Release titled 'Sekbertal Disebut CBTI Sebagai "Kelompok Petisi"', 9 August 1986. Actual press references to this are cited in fn. 90, immediately below.
90. See, for example, 'Dampak Monopoli Impor Kapas Oleh PT CBTI: Banyak Investor Asing Tunda Investasi Dalam Pemintalan' *Merdeka*, 11 August 1986; 'SEKBERTAL: Bukan Petisi, Hanya Laporan Berkala', *Business News*, 11 August 1986; and 'CBTI Nekad Langgar Kesepakatan Bersama', *Pelita*, 11 August 1986.
91. Though not reported in the press, this action was corroborated by a number of separate interviews. For instance, Husein Aminuddin 5 May 1987; Indrawan (economics editor of *Kompas*) 8 May 1987; Djon Wono (Executive Director, Dasatex Pty Ltd) 1 May 1987; and Sital Roesminem (President Director, Kewalram Pty Ltd) 21 May 1987. According to Aminuddin, the report to the President was a compilation of material already used in previous letters to the Government, as well as material that was used subsequently in others. Certainly SEKBERTAL letter no. 017/SEKBER/9/1986 of 11 September 1986 listed the President as being one of its registered recipients.
92. See 'Presiden Minta PT CBTI Dibenahi', *Prioritas*, 12 August 1986; 'Presiden Minta Industri Tekstil Gunakan Kapas DN', *Suara Karya*,

12 August 1986, and 'Organisasi PT CBTI Akan Disempurnakan: Secara Bertahap Kita Mengurangi Ketergantungan Pada Kapas Impor', *Sinar Harapan*, 12 August 1986.

93. SEKBERTAL took great comfort from its own 'intelligence sources' that Suharto had been impressed by their submission, and was apparently not unsympathetic to their cause. Indeed they were told that Suharto had expressed the wish to all the Ministers at the meeting that the issue was to be 'diselesaikan secara baik-baik', which was taken by SEKBERTAL to mean that it should be resolved in a manner not prejudicial to SEKBERTAL. SEKBERTAL further believed that the President had asked General Murdani to monitor the situation. If true, this presumably related to potential political implications should the price of textiles and clothing rise inordinately in the months leading up to the coming general election, as well as any possibility of wider agitation, especially with regard to the sensitive monopoly issue. Certainly, as mentioned earlier, Murdani had sent a personal aide to meet the SEKBERTAL leadership to enquire about the controversy after his receipt of SEKBERTAL letters.

94. Public reference to this outcome can be found in 'Sekitar Adanya Kesepakatan Untuk Mengubah Anggaran Dasar PT CBTI', *Sinar Harapan*, 30 August 1986.

95. SEKBERTAL letter no. 14/SEKBER/8/1986, 18 August 1986. Some public reference to the issue is made in 'Penyempurnaan AD/ART PT CBTI Tak Peroleh Dukungan Pengurus', *Suara Karya*, 25 August 1986.

96. Interview, Husein Aminuddin, 30 April 1987.

97. 'Mempercepat Penyelesaian Kasus PT. CBTI-SEKBERTAL' (editorial), *Sinar Harapan*, 29 August 1986.

98. 'Tugas-Tugas Direksi CBTI Untuk Sementara Di Tangan Totong', *Suara Karya*, 1 September 1986.

99. For reference to this, see 'Industri Tekstil Bagai "Jatuh Terhimpit Tangga"', *Prioritas*, 24 September 1986 and 'Handoko Tjokroseputro: Paket Enam Mei Ancam Kematian 25 Persen Dari Industri Pertekstilan', *Angkatan Bersenjata*, 26 September 1986.

100. SEKBERTAL letter no. 017/SEKBER/9/1986, 11 September 1986. Public reference to several (though not all) aspects of the letter can be found in 'Sedang Dilihat, Kemungkinan Dirubah Atau Tidaknya Tata Niaga Terkendali', *Merdeka*, 24 September 1986.

101. See 'Pembinaan Industri Pertekstilan Nasional Sepenuhnya Harus Oleh Pemerintah', *Merdeka*, 15 September 1986.

102. See 'CBTI Di Muka DPR', *Business News*, 29 September 1986.

103. SEKBERTAL letter no. 020/SEKBER/X/1986, 14 October 1986. While not directly referring to this letter, the same material is quoted in reports from the ensuing press conference. See fn. 104 immediately below.

104. 'SEKBERTAL Tidak Keberatan Pungutan Asal Dilakukan Oleh Pemerintah', *Pelita*, 18 October 1986.

105. Interview, Husein Aminuddin 28 April 1987. The advertisement appeared in Pelita twice, on 18 and 20 October 1986.
106. 'Pemerintah Akan Cabut 44 SK Tata Niaga Bidang Impor', *Sinar Harapan*, 9 October 1986.
107. For a more detailed analysis of the 25 October package see 'Serangkaian Kebijaksanaan Tindak Lanjut Devaluasi 12 September 1986', *Business News*, 27 October 1986; or Pangestu (1987) pp. 29–36.
108. The relevant laws are Trade Minister Rachmat Saleh's Ministerial Decree no. 307/KP/X/1986, 25 October 1986; and the Director General for Foreign Trade B.M. Kuntjoro-jakti's implementing regulation, Decree no. 129/DAGLU/KP/X/86, 25 October 1986.
109. SEKBERTAL letter no. 022/SEKBER/11/1986, 3 November 1986.
110. Public references to this hearing can be found in, for example, 'Agar Diterbitkan, Pungutan Ekspor Pakaian Jadi Oleh API', *Prioritas*, 28 November 1986; as well as 'GINSI: Berapa Lama Sistem "Monopoli" Diperlakukan?' and 'Segala Bentuk Pungutan Ekspor Tekstil Diluar Ketentuan Agar Dihapuskan', *Harian Terbit*, 27 November 1986.
111. Interview with Husein Aminuddin, 18 April 1987.
112. In addition to writing to all spinners, he also wrote to the Director General for Foreign Trade, informing him of his move. [Director General for Multifarious Industries' letters nos. 1888/DJAI/XII/1986 and 1889/DJAI/XII/1986, 4 December 1986. Public reference to aspects of this matter can be found in 'Pembelian Kapas Lokal, Langsung Antara Industri Dan PTP', *Prioritas*, 9 December 1986.]
113. Director General for Foreign Trade's letter no. IMP.102/DAGLU/4070/86, 10 December 1986. For public reference see, 'CBTI Dilarang Buka L/C Serat Kapas', *Business News*, 15 December 1986; and 'CBTI Tidak Dibenarkan Buka L/C Serat Kapas', *Prioritas*, 15 December 1986.
114. For coverage of this, see 'Organisasi Tekstil Nasional Perlu Dibenahi', *Pelita*, 29 December 1986; and 'Indonesia Perlu Diwakili Dalam Federasi Tekstil ASEAN', *Prioritas*, 2 January 1987.
115. Yet in this respect SEKBERTAL itself was, as already noted, deficient, being only a joint secretariat. In order to improve its status in this regard, SEKBERTAL transformed itself into a himpunan (an association or club)—with the new title Himpunan Industri Pemintalan 'SEKBERTAL'. The by now well-recognised name 'SEKBERTAL' was deliberately retained in the title. Prior to this SEKBERTAL's only formal standing was through the letter reporting its establishment to the Jakarta regional office of KOPKAMTIB. In confronting API it would help to enhance its legitimacy by becoming a formal sectorally representative organisation. [The legal act transforming SEKBERTAL was gazetted in, Tambahan Berita Negara Republik Indonesia, no. 104, 30 December 1986. Press reference to it can be found in 'SEKBERTAL Masuk Berita Negara', *Pelita*, 6 February 1987.]
116. For general coverage of the situation, see for example 'Tekstil: Hura Buat Pengusaha', *Tempo*, 24 January 1987; and 'Kebijaksanaan

15 Januari Untuk Tingkatkan Daya Saing Industri', *Business News*, 19 January 1987. The key new regulation was Trade Minister Rachmat Saleh's Ministerial Decree no. 09/KP/I/87, 15 January 1987. The complete text of the new law is reproduced in, *Business News* 19 January 1987.

117. Interview Husein Aminuddin, 30 April 1987.

118. The Decree went on to stipulate that if local cotton supplies were exhausted, upon obtaining written proof from the grower, a spinning mill would be given special dispensation to proceed with imports, and the unfullfilled obligation to purchase the local cotton would be carried forward into the next season. Trade Minister Rachmat Saleh's Ministerial Decree no. 18/KP/I/87, 23 January 1987, and the Director General for Foreign Trade's (implementing) Decree no. 005/DAGLU/KP/I/87, 24 January 1987. These regulations are discussed in press reports such as, 'Ekspor Tekstil Yang Diatur Tata Niaga Masih 53.35 Persen', *Pelita*, 26 January 1987; and 'Tak Perlu Khawatir Ada Spekulasi Dan Monopoli Pembelian Kapas', *Pelita*, 6 February 1987.

119. As a result of fluctuations in the international market, local cotton had suddenly become somewhat cheaper than imported cotton—Rp 2,097 per kilogram as opposed to Rp 2,250–2,500 per kilogram.

120. 'Juklak Dirjen Daglu Tentang Impor Kapas Meresahkan', *Angkatan Bersenjata*, 5 February 1987; and 'Tak Perlu Khawatir Ada Spekulasi Dan Monopoli Pembelian Kapas', *Pelita*, 6 February 1987.

121. See 'API Bersedia Serap Produksi Kapas Dalam Negeri Sclama 5 Tahun', *Suara Pembaruan*, 10 February 1987.

122. Interview with Zachri Achmad (head of GINSI), 29 April 1987.

123. Indeed, two key SEKBERTAL sympathisers, Sumarlin and Hartarto, had in late 1986 appealed to Aminuddin to moderate SEKBERTAL's press campaign.

124. Interview with Husein Aminuddin, 30 April 1987.

125. 'Tidak Ada Monopoli Dalam Tata Niaga Impor Kapas', *Prioritas*, 12 February 1987.

126. 'SEKBERTAL Tolak Monopoli Kapas Dalam Negeri', Berita Yudha, 16 February 1987; and 'Memborong Kapas Dalam Negeri, Dinilai Sebagai Mengembalikan Monopoli', *Prioritas*, 16 February 1987. For reference to API's appearance before the Parliament see, 'API Usulkan Pembentukan Pusat Pakaian Jadi', *Pelita*, 10 February 1987; and 'Pungutan Wajar, Karena API Memerlukan Dana', *Prioritas*, 10 February 1987.

127. 'Disesalkan, Pencabutan Sementara ETPT Tanpa Ada Pemberitahuan Langsung', *Prioritas*, 28 February 1987; and 'Lima Pejabat Kanwil Perdagangan DKI Jakarta Ditarik Dari Jabatannya', *Kompas*, 26 February 1987.

128. 'Kalangan Tekstil Menyepakati Ide Dana Penyangga', *Bisnis Indonesia*, 11 March 1987.

129. For reference to this, and some of the critical press coverage of the idea of a cotton stockpile see, 'Tidak Ada Kesepakatan Dana Penyangga

Kapas', *Prioritas*, 14 March 1987; and 'Kehadiran Dirjen Aneka Industri Ke Dep. Perdagangan Dimanfaatkan Pihak Tertentu', *Sinar Pagi*, 16 March 1987.

130. SEKBERTAL letter no. 005/SEKBER/4/1987, 14 April 1987.
131. PIBTI was headed by Arnold Baramuli and Suwoto Sukendar, both of whom had major business activities outside the garment industry. Also both were very senior within KADIN circles, and were seen as typifying the ineffective representation associated with so many business organisations, and KADIN in particular.
132. Interviews with Wien Dewanta 28 April 1987, and Aminuddin 28 & 30 April 1987. For public reference to the formation of SEKBERPAK, see 'Pengusaha Pakaian Jadi Berusaha Atasi Masalah Dengan Kebersamaan', *Prioritas*, 14 April 1987. SEKBERPAK was in no sense opposed to PIBTI, indeed there was very great overlap between the two organisations. The former was merely more action-oriented than the latter.
133. For references to these various problems being faced by API and the Trade Department, see for example: 'Kemelut Landa Industri Pakaian Jadi', *Prioritas*, 7 May 1987; 'Digugat, Ketertutupan Dan Cara Pembagian Kuota Ekspor Tekstil', *Kompas*, 4 April 1987; 'Setelah Heboh Kuota Tambahan', *Tempo*, 21 March 1987; and 'Manipulasi Ekspor Tekstil Dan Kopi Pelajaran Buat Seluruh Aparat Dep. Perdagangan', *Sinar Pagi*, 18 March 1987.
134. The decision to replace the two was apparently actually taken on 2 May, at a meeting involving the President, BAPPENAS head Sumarlin, Trade Minister Rachmat Saleh and Finance Minister Radius Prawiro. [Interview with Indrawan (economics editor of *Kompas*), 8 May 1987.]
135. The business link was apparently via a palm oil plantation in Prapat, North Sumatra.
136. The decision to replace the Director Generals, as noted above, was reportedly taken on 2 May. Aminuddin had been made aware of the decision by 3 May. In addition, his sources within the Government apparently indicated to him that the strong letter SEKBERTAL had sent on 14 April had been a major factor in persuading the President to act against the Trade Department. Interview, Husein Aminuddin 1 August 1987.
137. For a summary of this conflict in departmental policy, see 'Kebijakan Perindustrian Perdagangan Tabrakan', *Prioritas*, 26 May 1987.
138. On 23 March, the Director General issued a revised list in his letter no. 366/DJAI/III/1987. For public reference to this, see 'Alokasi Serap Kapas Masa Panen Tahap II', *Prioritas*, 14 April 1987. Reference to public remarks by Hartarto can be found in, for example, 'Hartarto: SEKBERTAL Wadah Murni Penampung Aspirasi Industriawan Sejati', *Berita Yudha*, 11 April 1987; and 'Regulation 'Hampers Supply Of Cotton Raw Materials', *Jakarta Post*, 12 May 1987.
139. The clause covering procedures governing the link with banks (paragraph 2, item 4 of the agreement) was deliberately included to over-

come the uncertainty in banking circles. For public reference to the joint agreement, see 'Kesepakatan Penyerapan Serat Kaps Ditanda-tangani', *Kompas*, 15 July 1987; and 'Kesepakatan Bersama Penyera-pan Kapas Dalam Negeri', *Berita Yudha*, 15 July 1987.

140. This concern of SEKBERTAL stemmed from a belief that the API leadership had had to outlay a very large sum of money to the Trade Department in return for the granting of the initial monopoly rights. SEKBERTAL was thus worried that API was under pressure to recoup this and might try to do so at the spinning industry's expense.

141. For reference to the emergence of the KADIN issue in relation to associational status generally, see, 'Pergulatan KADIN Indonesia Dengan Asosiasi Berlangsung Hangat', *Prioritas*, 16 June 1987.

142. Interviews with Sunarto Prawirosujanto (Head of the Section for Multi-farious Industry, Small Industry and Pharmaceutical Industries, KADIN) 21 May 1987; and Alif Martadi (Secretary General of PIBTI) 22 May 1987.

143. PIBTI was put forward rather than SEKBERPAK as the latter had no associational status, and also because it was necessary that Baramuli himself have a place.

144. As mentioned earlier (see fn. 115 above) SEKBERTAL had already upgraded its status from a 'joint-secretariat' without official standing, to that of a himpunan in December 1986. In upgrading yet again (to become an asosiasi) SEKBERTAL leaders remained keen to preserve their organisation's by now well recognised name. The new institu-tion's title therefore became Asosiasi SEKBERTAL, with SEKBER-TAL now standing for Sektoral Kebersamaan Permintalan (in effect, the Joint Spinning Sector Association). The change from a himpunan to an asosiasi was made necessary by the technicality that the new law did not specifically mention the term himpunan, referring instead only to asosiasi and gabungan. See, Undang-Undang no. 1, 1987 (otherwise known as Undang-Undang KADIN), chapter 4, paragraph 1, clause 10. Interviews with Sunarto Prawirosujanto, 21 May 1987; and Husein Aminuddin, 1 August 1987.

145. See, 'SEKBERTAL Yang Mewakili 48 Perusahan Masuk KADIN', *Kompas*, 27 July 1987; and, 'KADIN Tidak Mengakui Ekistensi Aso-siasi Pertekstilan Indonesia', *Suara Pembaruan*, 27 July 1987.

146. As mentioned earlier in fn. 12 above, ASPINDO's status following the 1985 'fusion' was ambiguous. It had not dissolved itself, and had remained a member of KADIN. This meant it was sufficiently distinct from the API clique to be acceptable to Aminuddin and Baramuli.

147. See 'Asosiasi Industri Tekstil Dan Pakaian Jadi Bentuk Federasi', *Antara*, 22 August 1987; and 'Federasi Industri Tekstil Indonesia Dikukuhkan Ketua Umum KADIN Indonesia', *Berita Yudha*, 24 August 1987; and 'Industri Tekstil Bentuk Federasi', *Kompas*, 24 August 1987.

148. See, 'Menteri Hartarto Hanya Dukung Entrepreneur Sejati', *Berita Yudha*, 29 August 1987.

149. See, for example, 'Keberhasilan MPI, Cermin Kesatuan Tiga Pelaku

Ekonomi', *Pelita*, 28 September 1987; 'Musyawarah Pengusaha Indonesia Dinilai Berhasil', *Berita Yudha*, 28 September 1987; and 'Cuplikan Ekspresi-Ekspresi Kegembiraan Dari Munassus KADIN dan MPI', *Angkatan Bersenjata*, 28 September 1987.

150. At the hearing with Committee VI (13 November 1987), in addition to oral evidence FITI submitted a detailed written presentation providing copious statistical data on the commercial circumstances of the different textile sectors. In particular, it used the opportunity to further criticise API for harming both the spinning and garment industries.

151. For reports of this see, for example, 'FITI Bersuara Di Perdagangan', *Tempo*, 14 Mei 1988; 'Isi Pertemuan Menperdag Dengan FITI Sangat Menarik', Angkatan Bersenjata, 9 Mei 1988; or 'Keterbukaan Depdag Beri Angin Segar', *Merdeka*, 9 May 1988.

152. For a discussion of the decree (no. 165/Kp/VI/88, 10 June 1988), see 'Mencabut Akar Inefisiensi', *Tempo*, 25 June 1988.

153. See, 'Menghindari Antiklimaks', *Tempo*, 2 July 1988.

154. Wibisono (1987) and (1989) both offer very valuable insight in this area.

155. Interview, 24 August 1987.

5

The Pharmaceutical Industry and the Conflict over Drug Prices

In this chapter we will be looking at a policy conflict in the pharmaceutical industry. It is a case which revolves around the efforts of the pharmaceutical industry to resist various attempts by the Health Department to bring about a reduction in drug prices.

Following a long-running dispute over drug prices in Indonesia, a sudden and sharp controversy erupted in late 1986. A central feature of the case was the way in which the policy process was marked by the interaction of state and societal actors, principally the Directorate General for Drug and Food Control (a sub-section of the Department of Health) and the representative body of the pharmaceutical industry—the Pharmaceutical Association (GPF). Though the fundamental interests of these two organisations were quite divergent, they were able to form tactical alliances on key policy issues. Apart from GPF and the Directorate General, important actors included the Minister for Health, the President, Committee VIII of the Parliament, the Indonesian Doctors' Association (IDI), the Consumers' Association (YLK) and the press.

Much of the action here was taking place at the same time as the conflict in the textile industry was reaching a crescendo. There are important similarities between the cases. In both, we see a range of extra-state actors playing important political roles. In particular we again see an industry group very effectively promoting the interests of its members through involvement in the shaping of government policy. Like the spinners in SEKBERTAL, the drug manufacturers in GPF were successful in achieving their aims, but there were differences in style, GPF's approach to dealings with the state differed considerably from that of SEKBERTAL. In common with the case from the textile industry, this one reveals important aspects of

political behaviour which are at variance with existing accounts of
Indonesian politics. Again, we see societal actors forcefully projecting their interests into the policy making process.

The structure of this chapter parallels the previous one. A brief
account of the pharmaceutical industry and the interest representation structures in that sector will be provided first. Next we will
proceed to a review of the factors leading up to the mid-1986
situation. This will set the context for a detailed analysis of our main
concern, the conflict over pharmaceutical prices which peaked in late
1986 and ran into 1987. Again, the chapter concludes with a consideration of the implications of the case-study for our understanding of
Indonesian politics.

A Profile of the Pharmaceutical Industry

The pharmaceutical industry in Indonesia underwent rapid growth
after 1968. During the Sukarno period there were some thirty to forty
manufacturers, of which only a very small number were large scale
producers. Under the New Order there has been a drive towards
self-sufficiency in finished pharmaceutical products. Today there are
approximately 300 pharmaceutical manufacturers in Indonesia, of
which 40 are joint ventures with foreign firms. Among local
companies, 40 are large scale operations which were set up under the
terms of the 1968 investment laws and are characterised by modern
management and production techniques. The rest are mostly older,
small scale and often low technology family enterprises. There are
also three state-owned factories whose products are largely chan-
neled into public health projects.

Pharmaceutical production in Indonesia centres around the 'assembling' of drugs; no research or product experimentation is undertaken. Joint ventures assemble products devised by the foreign
parent company, while local companies assemble copies, or imitations of these and other drugs. Between 1971 and 1973 there was
considerable investment in Indonesia by foreign pharmaceutical
firms. This came after frequent hints by the government during
1968–69 that drug manufacturers not making direct capital investment in Indonesia would be excluded from the market. It did not
come as a surprise then, when the government did in fact prohibit the
importation of almost all assembled, or finished drugs, in April 1974.[1]
The major exceptions to this are small quantities of specialist 'life-
saving drugs' not produced in Indonesia. The raw materials for
assembling drugs are nearly all imported. In order to redress this
dependence on raw material imports and as part of the drive towards

FIGURE 5.1

Growth of the Indonesian Pharmaceutical Market
(Current Prices)

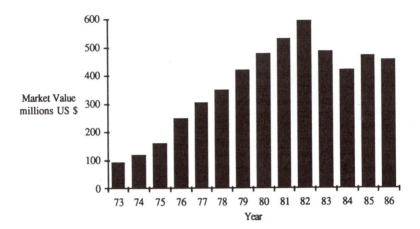

Source: Department of Health, [The figures actually originate from IMS (1987 a).]

self-sufficiency, the government requires foreign manufacturers in
joint ventures to produce at least one basic pharmaceutical substance
necessary for the production of finished drugs. Of the drugs produced
in Indonesia nearly all are consumed locally: very few are exported.
In general, the pharmaceutical industry in Indonesia, while not as
advanced as that of, for example, Brazil, Egypt, Mexico or South
Korea, is considerably more sophisticated and developed than many
other Third World countries.[2]

The value of pharmaceutical production in Indonesia is generally
agreed to be around US$500 million per annum.[3] Figure 5.1 shows
the growth of the pharmaceutical market over time. It illustrates the
steady growth in the value of the pharmaceutical market during the
1970s, and highlights the way in which the industry has suffered from
the general economic contraction that has beset Indonesia in the
1980s since the collapse in oil prices. Pharmaceutical sales have
declined with reduced consumer purchasing power.

The first thing to note about the market for pharmaceutical products in Indonesia is that it is highly fragmented. Though statistics on
the pharmaceutical industry are problematic,[4] the largest company,
Kalbe Farma Pty Ltd (a local firm), is estimated to hold only about
5–6 per cent of the total market. Between them, the five largest

companies control only about 16 per cent of the market. However, of the 300-odd producers in Indonesia, the sixty largest control over 87 per cent of the market, with the many other small firms having on average not more than .05 per cent of the total.[5] In other words, the large scale producers, both foreign and locally owned, very much dominate the market. The numerous small scale, low technology firms hold only tiny market shares. In terms of public-sector production, the state-owned manufacturers produce only about 5 per cent of the total.[6]

Product competition within the industry is at once both concentrated and fragmented. The concentration occurs around the high-demand types of drugs, with approximately 27 per cent of all drugs produced being antibiotics, 22 per cent vitamins and 12 per cent analgesics.[7] Foreign and local companies compete very intensely in these areas. However, outside this 'central' market for the most widely used drugs, there are also fragmented markets for specialised types of drugs which have only limited demand. These specialised markets tend to be dominated by various foreign companies. Generally, local companies are most active in the production of those drugs which have the largest market. This reflects the fact that local companies (except those producing under licence to a foreign company) manufacture generic drugs, while the foreign companies rely mostly on patented, or more accurately, innovative drugs. In the Indonesian context, it is meaningless to talk of 'patented' drugs as there is no patent law to protect intellectual property rights. For this reason the term 'innovative' drugs is preferred. The distinction between innovative and generic drugs is important and easily illustrated. There is, for instance, one product in Indonesia (and the world) known as Valium, a tranquilliser developed by Roche Pty Ltd. The numerous imitations of it which exist are known as generics (or colloquially, as 'me too' drugs). An example from the Indonesian market might be, Kalbrium, manufactured by Kalbe Farma Pty Ltd. An innovative drug offers some new pharmacological quality and is the product of its creator's *own* research and development efforts. Generics, then, are copies of innovative drugs. Generic products can also be divided between those which are branded—that is they carry the producer's name, such as Kalbrium—and those which are unbranded. Unbranded generics are identified simply by the active ingredient in the product.

Innovative drugs are the most expensive, though they are closely followed in Indonesia by branded generics. Unbranded generics are much cheaper and tend to be manufactured by the very small scale producers. Innovative drugs and branded generics are produced for the upper end of the market by foreign and large scale local firms.

Generic products can be produced at a fraction of the cost of an innovative product, as there are almost none of the enormous research and development costs involved. The analysis and imitation of a drug is usually a short and inexpensive process. In the absence of patent laws, the copying of an innovative product takes place very rapidly in Indonesia. Local companies are able to enjoy a direct and large windfall profit in this, as they not only do not have to bear the heavy research and development costs, but they can also import their raw materials cheaply from countries such as Italy, Spain and India which themselves do not have patent laws protecting raw material manufacture. This means the raw material import bill for local companies is very much lower than that for foreign companies, which import raw materials from their parent company—typically located in Western countries which do have patent laws. Nevertheless, there is, of course transfer pricing profits to be had by the parent company in these operations.[8] In general, Indonesia is very heavily dependent on imported chemical raw materials for the manufacture of its drugs. Ninety-five per cent of industry raw material needs are imported, with local production still being very limited.

In order to gauge the market division between foreign and local companies, it is necessary to introduce an intermediate category, to cover those local companies which manufacture products under licence to foreign companies. Table 5.1 sets out sales by these three categories of producers and their shares of the various sub-sectors of the national market. The most important of these sub-sectors is the dispensary market. Dispensaries (*apoteks*), being modern and specialised pharmaceutical retail outlets employing trained pharmacists, can be distinguished from drug stores (*toko obat*), which although also registered as drug retailers are more simple shops selling an array of medicines, both modern and traditional. After these two sub-sectors, there follows the open street market, made up of pedlars and miscellaneous shops, and the institutional market which is contract-based, mostly supplying hospitals. The plantations sub-sector is only very small.

From Table 5.1 it is evident that the overall market positions of the foreign and locally owned companies are roughly equal. Local companies operating under licence to foreign companies (not themselves present in Indonesia) make up the remainder.[9] The scope for foreign manufacturers to increase their share of the Indonesian market is limited by an array of government regulations. While both local and foreign firms complain of over-regulation, it is the latter which suffers greater restriction. Foreign companies are, for example, prohibited from launching any new products in the highly lucrative 'Over-the-Counter' (OTC) drug market, and as such are

TABLE 5.1

The Indonesian Pharmaceutical Market, 1986

MARKET SUB-SECTOR	PORTION of TOTAL MKT. per cent	FOREIGN COMPANIES mil US$ (per cent)		LICENSED MANUFACTURERS mil US$ (per cent)		LOCAL COMPANIES mil US$ (per cent)	
Dispensaries Mkt	47	116	(54)	37	(17)	62	(29)
Drug Store Mkt.	23	48	(46)	11	(10)	46	(44)
Institutions Mkt.	18	17	(20)	8	(10)	57	(70)
Street Mkt.	9	10	(25)	2	(5)	29	(70)
Plantations Mkt.	3	3	(25)	1	(10)	9	(65)
TOTAL	100	194	(43)	59	(13)	203	(44)

Source: IMS (1987 a).

forced to concentrate their energies in the other main category of drugs, namely, the ethical drug market. Ethical drugs, unlike OTC drugs, are supposed to be obtainable only upon prescription by a doctor. The significance of this is that foreign companies are unable to promote many of their products by direct advertising to the public, and must instead focus their promotional efforts on the doctors (as they determine which ethical drugs to prescribe patients). Foreign companies are not permitted to undertake new investment, except in the area of developing new material production. This obviously limits the potential for expansion by foreign firms, as investment in raw material production is regarded as a burden rather than a boon. Further, unlike local companies, they are not permitted to distribute their products to retailers themselves. Instead local distributors, or wholesalers, must be used.[10] More generally, there is a wide array of regulations governing production procedures requiring different licences, particularly with regard to the introduction of new products.

The increasing regulation of the pharmaceutical market in Indonesia marks what many company executives (especially those of foreign companies) have resignedly described as the end of the 'golden era' of the pharmaceutical industry. This is a reference to international trends that have been evident for a decade and a half in Western industrialised countries and with which Indonesia has recently been catching up. Whereas the 1950s and early 1960s had been a boom period for the industry throughout much of the world, with many new and pioneering drugs being introduced and little or no government regulation in existence, the 1970s and 1980s proved much more difficult. Two key elements in this have been the sharp

decline in the rate of development of new products, and the increasingly critical attitude of Western societies and their governments
towards the pharmaceutical industry. Following a series of scandals
(such as that over Thalidomide) governments came to demand far
tighter quality control procedures in drug manufacturing. This, in
turn, contributed to rising cost structures. At the same time, faced
with the problem of aging populations and rapidly rising national
health bills, governments have seen drug costs as one area which can
be conveniently targeted for pruning in the name of limiting overall
health care costs.[11] The tarnished reputation of the pharmaceutical
industry has contributed to its vulnerability. All of this has inclined
Western governments to adopt a tougher approach to the pharmaceutical industry, especially on the question of costs.

The trend towards greater regulation of the pharmaceutical industry spread into Indonesia (and other developing countries[12]) during
the 1970s, assisted by the fact that in Indonesia (as in other developing countries) a high proportion of the total health care bill was made
up by the cost of drugs. Whereas in Britain, for example, drugs
represent about 10 per cent of health care spending, in Indonesia the
figure is between 40 and 50 per cent.[13] Though Indonesia does not
have exactly the same problems as Western countries (for example,
an aging population), the fact that pharmaceuticals constitute such a
high percentage of the national health bill has nonetheless stimulated
the government of Jakarta to take considerable interest in the price
levels of drugs.

An important and interesting question in its own right is: Who is
'responsible' for existing pharmaceutical price levels in Indonesia and
are they unusually high? Unfortunately it is outside the parameters of
this case-study, focusing as it does on the issues of interest representation and on the way in which the pharmaceutical industry has
responded to attempts by the government to reduce prices. Nevertheless, a brief discussion of some of the factors contributing to the
high prices is instructive.

The pharmaceutical industry is just one of the links in the chain
which places drugs in the hands of consumers. Other links which have
an important role—at least in terms of influencing the prices paid by
consumers in Indonesia—include distributors, dispensaries and doctors. During the conflict over drug prices in 1986–87, it was generally
assumed that the manufacturers were the principal cause of the
problem. The basis for this assumption was not, however, clear. An
argument often heard in pharmaceutical industry circles is that the *ex
factory* prices (the prices at which manufacturers sell their products to
distributors) are no higher in Indonesia than elsewhere in the region.
Table 5.2 provides comparative data for other Southeast Asian
countries which tend to support this claim.[14] Though these figures are

TABLE 5.2

Comparison of Pharmaceutical Prices in Southeast Asia, 1986
(US$ price per capsule, tablet etc.)

PRODUCT [a]	INDONESIA	THAILAND	SINGAPORE	MALAYSIA	PHILIPPINES
1	0.18	0.17	0.27	0.23	0.19
2	0.30	0.21	0.51	0.46	0.17
3	0.33	0.23	0.66	0.58	0.37
4	0.72	0.73	-	-	0.61
5	0.07	-	0.07	0.07	0.12
6	0.80	0.70	-	-	0.59
7	0.12	0.08	0.11	0.20	0.24
8	0.26	-	0.28	0.29	0.21
9	0.42	-	-	-	-
10	0.46	0.50	0.31	0.30	0.35
11	0.07	0.05	0.05	0.04	0.11
12	0.37	-	-	-	-
13	0.46	0.25	-	-	0.29
14	0.81	0.70	1.25	1.43	0.77
15	0.13	0.17	0.26	0.23	0.25
16	0.09	0.09	0.08	0.09	0.13
17	0.33	0.35	0.39	0.35	0.27
18	0.10	0.08	0.13	0.14	0.16
AVERAGE [b]	0.26	0.23	0.36	0.37	0.27

Source: IMS (1987 b).

[a] Selected leading pharmaceutical products.

[b] The average is calculated on the basis of those products for which there was data from all five countries.

for the net price at which dispensaries purchase drugs, that is, the price at which they are sold by distributors to dispensaries, and are thus one step removed from *ex factory* prices, they do suggest that unless distribution costs in Indonesia are substantially less than elsewhere in the region (something most unlikely[15]) *ex factory* prices must compare favourably. To satisfactorily explain the fact that *retail* prices in Indonesia are higher than in most countries, it is therefore insufficient to concentrate just on the production end of the chain. Other factors that would have to be considered in a serious economic analysis of drug prices in Indonesia would include:

- problems in the system of distribution of products to retail outlets
- the reluctance of the medical profession to prescribe low-priced drugs
- the fact that price mark-up levels for distributors and retailers are artificially set at 22 per cent and 50 per cent of manufacturers' selling prices respectively

At the manufacturing end of the chain industry sources insist that profit margins are slim.[16] A key element in the cost structure of drug manufacturing in Indonesia is the dependence on imports for up to 95 per cent of raw materials. As much of this import bill is denominated

FIGURE 5.2

Per Capita Consumption of Pharmaceuticals in Selected Asian Countries, 1986

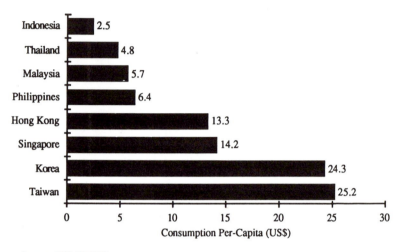

Source: IMS (1987 b).

in foreign currencies, it is subject to price fluctuations. Aside from the dependence on raw material imports, another important factor bearing on production costs is that the size of the pharmaceutical market is relatively small, thereby preventing producers from attaining economies of scale. This problem has been accentuated in a recessional environment. Despite the country's large population, it is estimated that the pharmaceutical industry supplies not more than 10 to 20 per cent of the population on a regular basis. Figure 5.2 shows *per capita* drug consumption in variety of Asian countries.

In sum, the main points to be noted about the pharmaceutical industry in Indonesia are that it has a highly competitive and fragmented market which is dominated by a small number of large scale producers. Ownership is heavily concentrated in the hands of the private sector, with foreign and local firms having roughly equal shares.

Interest Representation in the Pharmaceutical and Health Services Industries

This section provides an overview of interest representation arrangements in the pharmaceutical sector. Special attention is given to the character and dynamics of GPF, the Pharmaceutical Association, but other major actors in the case, the Department of Health, the Doctors' Association, the Consumers' Association, Committee VII of the Parliament and the press are also discussed. Noteworthy, in terms of the theoretical concerns of this study, is the diversity of extra-state actors.

GPF and the Pharmaceutical Industry

GPF is the organisation formally responsible for the representation of the interests of the pharmaceutical industry. In addition to the manufacturers, it also represents the distribution and retailing segments of the pharmaceutical sector. To this end it is divided into four constituent parts, with individual sections for the manufacturers, distributors, dispensaries and registered drug stores. The four sections are formally equal, although in practice the manufacturers are clearly dominant. For example, while each section has its own leader, the overall head of GPF has always been drawn from the ranks of the manufacturers, reflecting their greater economic importance. Indeed, GPF is commonly seen as primarily concerned with the interests of the manufacturers, rather than, for instance, with dispensaries or distributors. (Therefore, for the sake of brevity, when the abbreviation GPF is used here, it should be taken as referring only to the pharmaceutical manufacturers, and not the other sections as well, unless so indicated.) As with other state-approved business associations, GPF has a national structure with regional branches spread throughout the country.

KADIN (of which GPF is a member) also has a nominal role in facilitating interest representation in the pharmaceutical industry, in so far as it has broad responsibility for all facets of business in Indonesia. KADIN has a specific department to handle pharmaceutical affairs within its Section for Multifarious Industry, Small Industry and Pharmaceutical Industry. (This, it may be recalled, also happens to be the section handling the textile industry.) In practice KADIN is rarely used by the pharmaceutical industry, and all industry attention tends to be focused instead on GPF.

As a representative organisation, GPF exhibits a number of striking corporatist features. Formed in 1969, it was formally designated in the enabling decree issued by the Health Minister of the day as the peak association for all the pharmaceutical businesses that came within the purview of the Health Department.[17] In other words, this decree anointed GPF as the only legitimate representative organisation for the pharmaceutical industry in the eyes of the state. Since the early 1970s, moreover, membership has been compulsory for all companies, a requirement that was later extended to embrace foreign companies.[18] The requirement for foreign firms to join GPF, meant that they could no longer maintain in Indonesia a branch of the Pharmaceutical Manufacturers' Association, the international drug manufacturers' organisation based in the United States. As a result, they were restricted to just a subsection within GPF known as the IPMG (International Pharmaceutical Manufacturers' Group) which held only a minority voting position within the GPF structure (one vote in fifty).

Especially noteworthy is the informal rule that manufacturers may not approach the Department of Health independently. All approaches to state officials must be made via GPF, except on specific issues concerning individual companies. This essentially corporatist arrangement potentially restricts industry demand-making and concentrates state control over all aspects of the pharmaceutical sector. It also places great influence over industry affairs in the hands of the leadership of GPF, particularly the head of the manufacturers' section, as the great bulk of interaction between the state and industry is via GPF. As during the period of this case-study the head of the manufacturers' section and key figure within GPF was a local producer named Eddie Lembong, this interaction was largely in his hands.

A very important instrument which the Directorate of Drug and Food Control has at its disposal in dealings with the pharmaceutical industry is its regulatory power, particularly in the licensing of new products. The introduction of new drugs, regardless of whether they are genuinely innovative or simply generics, is governed by testing and licensing procedures controlled by the Director General (who during the period of interest here, was Midian Sirait). This is a crucial power, as the introduction of new products is critical to the prosperity of most manufacturers. Thus all manufacturers are, to some degree, at the mercy of the Department of Health. Foreign companies are generally seen to be in an especially weak position, however. It is commonly said by the heads of foreign firms, that whereas it might take from six to twelve months for a local company to obtain a licence for a new product, foreign companies can expect to wait for up to three years. Their situation is made still more difficult with respect to innovative drugs because of the risk that their chemical properties will be leaked directly to local manufacturers. The general sense of insecurity and weakness felt by the foreign companies is reflected by the apparent disdain in which they are held by the Directorate General of Drug and Food Control. Even though the size of the pharmaceutical market in Indonesia is still relatively small and profitable, the Directorate General correctly assumes that foreign firms are very unlikely to surrender their toe-hold in a market which they believe must assuredly expand. While the Directorate General does not want the foreign companies to leave, it has no qualms about favouring the development of local rather than foreign producers.[19]

The political weakness of the foreign companies is compounded by the requirement that lobbying activity take place through GPF channels. As will be seen, this meant that the foreign companies were forced to make use of Eddie Lembong (himself a leading local manufacturer) as their spokesman. The difficulty here was, and is, that local and foreign companies frequently have quite divergent interests.[20] While foreign companies are generally resentful of the requirement that they deal through GPF, they do concede that their interests are at least honestly and reasonably represented. Thus, although it is inevitable that GPF will tend to favour the interests of local manufacturers, there is nonetheless a working and professional relationship between the IPMG and the rest of GPF.

Three final characteristics which have a bearing on interest representation in the pharmaceutical industry are of a more sociological nature. The first concerns the fact that of all the pharmaceutical companies in Indonesia, only one is *pribumi*-owned. The overwhelmingly Chinese character of the industry is seen by many as making the task of promoting industry interests more difficult. There was some feeling in industry circles that the image of Chinese business people exploiting a 'social good' complicated the task of lobbying, especially in relation to the issue of medicine prices. Some industry leaders believed that Midian Sirait and Slamet Soesilo (respectively, the Director General and Director) were unfavourably disposed towards the industry because of its heavy Chinese dominance. It should be noted, however, that while this perception of vulnerability because of the 'Chineseness' was fairly common within the industry, Eddie Lembong (himself Chinese Indonesian) was dismissive of what he labelled this 'paranoia'. While conceding that 'Chineseness' is often an issue in Indonesian politics, he insisted that it did not inhibit GPF in promoting the pharmaceutical industry interests or interfere in his relationship with the government.[21]

If paranoia arising from ethnicity is debatable, more clear-cut are the self-doubts stemming from the broader image problems of the pharmaceutical industry. This relates to the tendency of both local and foreign drug manufacturers in Indonesia (and elsewhere) to assume that they are held in low esteem by the public. The pharmaceutical industry's sensitivity to criticism and presumption that it is almost universally distrusted, led the Director for Drug Control, Slamet Soesilo, to describe it as a 'neurotic industry'.[22] To say that the pharmaceutical industry suffers from paranoia does not mean that it does not have some real image problems. Recognising that the industry's poor image had in the past restricted its political effectiveness, Eddie Lembong was concerned to improve its public relations. This was a key factor behind, for example, GPF's introduction of a Code of Ethics to govern promotional practices by manufacturers in 1981 and similarly the donation of medicines to the victims of the Mount Galunggung disaster in West Java in 1982. By working to bolster the image of the pharmaceutical industry, GPF was hoping to make the industry less vulnerable to public criticism, and, by extension, less vulnerable to regulatory intervention from the Health Department.

A third sociological feature to be noted concerns the closely-knit nature of the pharmaceutical community. This stems from the fact that most of the heads of (local) companies are university-trained pharmacists. Moreover, of those that are, the majority were educated at a time (the 1950s) when only two institutions—the Bandung Institute of Technology and Gadjah Madah University—offered degrees in pharmacy. In consequence, many were educated together and have known each other for a long time. Significantly, this also applies to the bureaucrats. Eddie Lembong, for example, knew Midian Sirait since university days. Personal familiarity, together with the generally high level of education amongst industry leadership, contributes to a more fluent and sophisticated style of interest representation.[23]

There is a general perception within the industry (foreign and local firms alike), the Department of Health and press circles, that GPF is a very competent and professional business association. In its dealings with the government, the GPF leadership moves both at its own initiative (through anticipation of membership concerns) and also at the direct suggestion of members. If members had a grievance the usual process was to contact Eddie Lembong directly, requesting that GPF intercede on their behalf. In the case of foreign companies, the first step was usually to discuss the problem with other foreign drug companies of the same language group. Thus, in the first instance, German-speaking companies are likely to consult with each other, and Japanese with other Japanese speaking-companies. Subsequently the matter would be raised with the IPMG executive which met monthly, which would then approach Eddie Lembong. (In the event that the matter did not involve the Health Department, the IPMG executive could make an approach to the institution concerned directly, without going via the GPF leadership.) If this proved unsatisfactory, there remained the possibility of using national chambers of commerce (particularly the American Chamber of Commerce), as well as embassies.[24]

A feature of GPF's strength has been the quality of its leadership. Eddie Lembong was widely acknowledged as a shrewd operator and very successful promoter of industry interests. Previous GPF leaders had also enjoyed a high reputation as effective industry representatives. An important factor in the quality of GPF's leadership seems to have been its competitive elections for office. High standards have apparently been expected of GPF leaders. Eddie Lembong, for example, devoted approximately 90 per cent of his time to GPF affairs, relying on managers to oversee his own company.[25]

GPF's relationship with the Directorate General for Drug and Food Control has generally been smooth and amicable. Lembong emphasised that almost all major problems are handled through negotiation in private and informal meetings between himself and the relevant officials. In his view, a key element in GPF's normally successful negotiating strategy has been the avoidance of situations creating a loss of face for government officials, even if this necessitated short term sacrifices. In other words, GPF's usual approach was to adopt a low profile method of negotiation with officials on a private basis, without recourse to more public avenues.[26] As might be expected, this was also bound up with the industry's sensitivity about its public image.

The Department of Health

Drug manufacturing is one of only three industries not within the jurisdiction of the Department of Industry, the others being mining and agriculture. This is of considerable significance since the bureaucrats in the Health Department who preside over the pharmaceutical industry are trained in pharmacy, but have little or no expertise in business and industrial development. Many pharmaceutical firms believe this predisposes the Department of Health to be philosophically unsympathetic to their quest for profits, seeing drugs as social, rather than commercial goods. As one local company executive lamented: there is little controversy in Indonesia over the fact that sugar and fertilizer prices are among the most expensive in the world, but because drugs are seen primarily as a social good, their price becomes a matter of controversy.

The 'health' rather than 'business' orientation of the Directorate General of Drug and Food Control does, however, also provide the pharmaceutical industry with some advantages. As many people emphasised, the lack of economic skills among the bureaucrats tended to induce a measure of dependence on GPF for advice about business conditions in the industry. This weakness of the bureaucrats provided GPF with a valuable bargaining chip and was one of the factors underpining the tactical alliances which developed between the two sides in the shaping of key aspects of health policy.

Health policy is not an area that normally receives highest priority in Indonesia. Though certainly not a peripheral matter, it plainly ranks behind security and economic management in the government's list of priorities. Within this context, drug policy is one major aspect of Health Department activity. Because of the technical and specialised nature of pharmaceutical matters, the Directorate General for Drug and Food Control has usually acted with considerable autonomy. Health Minister Suwardjono lacked technical expertise, and did not usually involve himself in drug policy issues. Midian Sirait, the Director General, was thus the highest source of authority on most drug policy issues. Under him, Slamet Soesilo, the Director for Drug Control, had responsibility for the daily management of pharmaceutical affairs. Significantly, not only has the technical and specialised nature of drug policy issues generally discouraged involvement by the Health Minister, it has also discouraged other ministers from taking an interest. Thus, unlike the situation in the spinning industry where we saw a variety of ministers become directly or indirectly involved, in the pharmaceutical industry this very rarely happens.

Midian Sirait, the Director General, had been a member of the Indonesian Socialist Party in the early 1960s while at the Bandung Institute for Technology, but later became a member of the GOLKAR *fraksi* in the Parliament before joining the Health Department. As a member of GOLKAR, he was on the political staff of the influential General Ali Murtopo. When Sirait was appointed Director General in 1978, the pharmaceutical industry was at first quite wary of him, viewing him as being disturbingly sympathetic to anti-business attitudes. This was heightened by a pronouncement he made before the Parliament shortly after joining the Health Department to the effect that drug prices were too high and that he would ensure they were brought down by one means or another.

The Directorate General seems to have viewed the pharmaceutical industry as a force which must be reckoned with, even if it not especially liked. On many issues, and especially the question of lowering drug prices, the Directorate General had, as a matter of necessity, to take into account the likely reactions of the pharmaceutical industry. Despite an initial distrust, Midian Sirait and GPF soon established channels for the maintenance of a mutually satisfactory dialogue to handle policy matters of concern. Sirait had the authority to make policy determinations vital to the pharmaceutical industry, and GPF had the capacity to deliver valuable industry cooperation in support of government initiatives when required, as well as to offer 'guidance' on the likely commercial ramifications of different policy options. The relationship between the Directorate and the industry can probably best be described as being marked by a shifting blend of conflict and cooperation.

The Indonesian Doctors' Association

Another of the major players in this case is IDI, the Doctors' Association. The official status of doctors in Indonesia is hazy, for in some respects they are considered to be civil servants. This stems from, among other things, the requirement that all new doctors do service-time in public hospitals, and thus become members of KOR-PRI, the corporatist civil servants' organisation. In practice, however, the focus of associational loyalty for doctors is unquestionably IDI. Unlike most other existing business or professional associations, IDI was established long before the New Order. By virtue of its continued existence as the national doctors' representative organ over a long period of time, IDI has attained a considerable measure of independence and has avoided being co-opted by the government's restrictive style of corporatist management. It is not however in any sense an anti-government or even politically disruptive organisation. Though IDI has basically escaped New Order remoulding, it does exhibit a number of corporatist features. It is, for instance, the sole officially recognised voice for the whole medical profession, and membership of it is unavoidable: doctors require a letter of recommendation from IDI in order to gain registration. Further, it does serve as a conduit which regulates the flow of demands upon the state. Nevertheless, IDI has a well established tradition of autonomy from the state.[27] Apart from its long history, another factor contributing to this autonomy may be that it has members scattered in various influential positions throughout society. Not only are doctors located in the hospitals and major universities, there are also some occupying senior positions within the state apparatus. Suwardjono, the Health Minister, for instance, was a doctor. Moreover, several senior members of IDI are reportedly within the President's circle of confidants.[28]

One striking feature of IDI is its long liberal and 'civic' tradition—at least among the national leadership. It has traditionally been concerned not merely with the promotion of doctors' material interests, but also with the promotion of ethics and social justice within the health field. The head of IDI, Dr Kartono Muhammad, was very much a part of this tradition. It is much less clear, however, that the rank and file membership of IDI shares the idealism of its leaders. Indeed the high principles of the IDI leadership have at times been a source of difference within the medical profession. This tension became quite evident with the involvement of IDI leaders in the 1986–87 controversy over pharmaceutical prices and their attempts to eliminate unethical links between some pharmaceutical companies and doctors.

The Consumers' Association

An organisation with a similar civic orientation to that of IDI's leadership is the Consumers' Association, the YLK. Unlike IDI or GPF (or, for that matter, API or SEKBERTAL) which are formally classified as representative associations, the YLK is an NGO. Beyond a small number of formal associates, the YLK's constituency is in theory society-wide, as nearly all members of society are consumers. In practice, however, the principal beneficiaries of its activities are the urban middle classes—the major cost- and quality-conscious purchasers of consumer goods.

The YLK was formed in 1973, with the original aim of promoting consumption of good-quality local products. Since that time it has become more oriented towards middle-class consumer concerns. As an NGO, the YLK is very concerned to preserve its autonomy from the state. Nevertheless, approximately twenty-five per cent of its running costs are subsidised by various state agencies, including, among others, the Jakarta City government, BULOG (the powerful national logistics board) and even *Bantuan President* (official Presidential Financial Aid). Apart from these official sources of funding, the YLK generates revenues through the sale of its monthly magazine *Warta Konsumen* and its bulletin of consumer news abstracts *Sari Berita Konsumen*, as well as through organising workshops and training sessions for bureaucrats and social groups. In total, the YLK has sixteen full-time staff, of which seven are professionally qualified and receive a small salary, the remainder being volunteers.

A prominent aspect of the YLK's activities is the consumer complaints service it offers. Under this, the YLK takes up consumer grievances about faulty produce or deficient service with the company or state body concerned. The usual procedure is to allow three weeks for the offending organisation to offer reparations, after which the YLK takes the story to the media. (Table 5.3 sets out a summary of YLK activities of this sort for 1983–85) As the press is more than happy to publish these sorts of 'human interest' stories,

TABLE 5.3

Complaints Serviced by the Consumers' Association

TYPE OF COMPLAINT	1983	1984	1985
Food & Beverage	29	39	25
Drugs & Cosmetics	8	19	18
Clothing	9	6	1
Tobacco	5	3	3
Services	54	183	83
Household Utensils	7	15	6
Energy (oil & gas)	4	15	15
Housing & Environment	14	15	6
Electronics	21	37	12
Motor Vehicles	9	15	17
Construction Materials	8	70	2
Miscellaneous	12	70	23
TOTAL	180	424	201

Source: YLK statistics

the YLK thus has little trouble gaining satisfactory coverage. Indeed, the press is one of the main weapons at its disposal.

Beyond this, the YLK conducts ten to twenty product surveys each year, for which it purchases and systematically tests all products of a given kind on the market. This independent evaluation of consumer goods is evidently something valued by the government, as various departments (usually Trade, Industry or Local Goods Promotion) supply the funds to purchase the product samples to be evaluated. This introduces some scope for various state officials to influence the sorts of products tested, as they are in a position to decline to fund any YLK survey which they do not favour. While this problem has arisen in the past, it apparently does so only occasionally.[29]

The YLK has at times irritated various state officials (and certainly many business people) but so far it has not come under threat or scrutiny in the same way as, for example, the outspoken Legal Aid Institute. The YLK earned a reputation for abrasiveness as a result of the vociferous style of its previous President, Permadi. Permadi's direct and outspoken manner apparently alienated many officials. In October 1986 he was succeeded by Erna Witoelar, the former head of another NGO, the environmental organisation, WALHI.[30] While not as abrasive as Permadi, Witoelar is seen as a tough, formidable and probably more effective spokesperson for the YLK.[31]

The YLK has come into increasing contact with the Directorate for Drug and Food Control as it has widened its scope of activity. The two bodies often conduct parallel surveys of new food products, and not infrequently reach quite different verdicts. In mid-1987 the YLK conducted a major survey of powdered milk products imported from Europe following the Chernobyl nuclear disaster. The results attracted widespread media attention, and resulted in dramatic sales losses for those products which were criticised.[32] Evaluation of drugs has so far been beyond the reach of the YLK, due to the prohibitive cost involved in purchasing and testing products. The Health Department has been unwilling to fund the exercise, regarding drug analysis as its own domain. Unable to probe the pharmacological qualities of drugs, the YLK has become increasingly involved in the cost side of drugs. This reflects the considerable consumer interest in the subject which culminated in the controversy of 1986–87.

Committee VIII of the Parliament

Another actor of significance in this case is Parliamentary Committee VIII. Committee VIII is responsible for health, family planning and social affairs. Many of its members are themselves doctors, or else people with other health-related professional qualifications. The question of drug prices has been high on the list of the Committee's concerns, and it is an issue that it has pursued with considerable vigour.[33]

The main avenue by which Committee VIII has sought to involve itself in the issue of pharmaceutical prices has been through the convening of public hearings to address the matter. (This, of course, is the path adopted by any active Parliamentary Committee.) Committee VIII has held numerous public hearings on the question of drug prices to which it invited senior Health Department officials, as well as representatives from the YLK, IDI, GPF and academia. Because of the sensational nature of the issue, press coverage was always guaranteed. By this means, the Committee has provided a forum or platform for the projection of information and opinions it favoured. In particular, it has given prominence continuously to arguments in favour of lower-cost drugs. Though the Committee has not been able to compel the Health Department to undertake policy reform aimed at the lowering of drug prices, it has embarrassed key officials and drawn greater attention to the matter, thereby increasing the pressure for action on the Health Department. Aside from these public hearings, the Committee has also held regular closed-door working sessions with the Health Minister and senior officials.[34]

GPF has viewed Committee VIII, like the YLK, as being unsympathetic to pharmaceutical industry interests because of its commitment to pushing for cheaper drugs. As a result, it has rarely
attempted use the Parliament as a springboard for the promotion of
its own views.

The Press

The last of the major actors in the case-study requiring mention here
is the press. As with the Parliament, the principal reason for GPF's
reluctance to make more use of the press has been its sensitivity to
the negative light in which the pharmaceutical industry is perceived,
both within Indonesia and internationally. There has been a tendency
within the pharmaceutical industry to assume that the press is unfavourably predisposed towards it, and that any press coverage of the
industry is likely to be critical and unhelpful.

This does not mean that GPF never dealt with the media: it did.
Eddie Lembong was very accessible to journalists. The difference
between GPF and SEKBERTAL in this regard was that GPF did
not, of its own initiative, seek out the press. Within the field of health
affairs there are, according to one estimate, approximately forty
journalists at the national level.[35] Of these, two journalists stand out,
Tempo health editor, Jimmy Supangkat and *Kompas* writer Irwan
Julianto. These two enjoy senior status as the only journalists with
expertise and on-going research of particular health issues. As a
result, health stories published in either *Kompas* or *Tempo* are
usually reproduced by the journalists of other newspapers and magazines. Certainly in the 1986–87 controversy over drug prices, articles
written by Irwan Julianto acted as a catalyst in stimulating a flurry of
press activity and ultimately political action.

The Background to the Controversy Over Drug Prices

The 1986 controversy over drug prices was not, in itself, long and
complicated in the way that the conflict within the spinning industry
over CBTI was. Indeed, by comparison, it was a short and relatively
straight-forward episode. Basically, it centred on the pharmaceutical
industry's response to the sudden flare-up of latent sensitivity over
medicine prices, and the subsequent introduction by the Health
Department of a special program (the DOPB program) to address
the problem. However, while this particular conflict is comparatively
uncomplicated, it can only be understood in the context of a long-

running dispute over drug prices. Because of this, it is necessary to spend a little time rehearsing the principal elements of the case which lead up to the episode in question. To this end, the present section is devoted to introducing the main themes to the dispute and the events which lay behind it.

As seen earlier, during the 1970s and 1980s Indonesia came to follow the lead of many other countries in introducing a tighter regulatory regime to control the conditions of drug manufacturing and pricing.[36] Health authorities in Indonesia, as elsewhere, were confronted with the problem of rising drug prices in their efforts to promote national health standards. As in other developing countries pharmaceutical medication constituted the largest slice of an increasingly expensive health-care bill. Health authorities thus had a budgetary incentive to reduce the cost of drugs. More pressing still was the desire to lower drug prices so as to bring modern medication within the financial reach of the great majority of the population. High prices meant that pharmaceuticals were inaccessible to all but the affluent.

An early step to address this problem in Indonesia was the *Obat Inpres* program (medicines subsidised with special Presidential funding), commenced in the mid-1970s. Under this scheme, subsidised medicines were made available to low income people via *Puskesmas* (local level public health clinics). Health officials could be confident that these medicines were actually reaching the poorer sections of the community since well-off people were most unlikely to attend the quite rudimentary *Puskesmas* clinics. Medicines for the *Obat Inpres* program were produced by the state-owned company, Kimia Farma, as well as by private manufacturers on contract.

The scope of the *Obat Inpres* program was, inevitably, limited. As a result, the scheme had little impact on overall prices, as the great majority of drugs consumed were still being obtained via the private rather than the public health market. This meant manufacturers were still largely unrestricted with regard to the pricing of drugs. As the 1970s progressed, a momentum for state intervention aimed at limiting increases in the cost of drugs gradually developed. As noted earlier, soon after his appointment to the position of Director General for Drug and Food Control in 1978, Midian Sirait indicated publicly that he believed medicine prices were too high in Indonesia and that he would be taking action to remedy the situation. This was, of course, an attitude that the pharmaceutical industry viewed with concern.

Round One: a First Flare-up

The issue of drug prices came into sharp focus in the wake of the dramatic 15 November 1978 devaluation of the rupiah, when the prices of drugs rose steeply. The matter became politically very sensitive with the special meeting of Minister for Health Suwardjono Surjaningrat with the President on 18 November. After the meeting, Suwardjono told a press conference that the government was extremely concerned about medicine prices and that the sudden jump in prices after the devaluation was unreasonable. He went on to say that the government was considering producing essential medicines itself with a view to easing price pressure.[37] Several days later, Midian Sirait announced to the press that the Health Department would take action against any drug manufacturer who withdrew products from the market as a result of the devaluation.[38] Ultimately there was decisive government intervention, with Admiral Sudomo, the head of the security apparatus, KOPKAMTIB, summoning the leadership of GPF to a meeting, and subsequently announcing that all drug prices would return, for the time being, to their pre-devaluation levels.[39]

This sudden flare-up of controversy over medicine prices following the 1978 devaluation can be viewed as setting the pattern for state action over the next decade in the on-going conflict with the pharmaceutical industry. Drug prices had been an issue prior to the devaluation, but it was the dramatic and widespread jump in prices following the devaluation which stimulated the crisis. The Directorate General for Drug and Food Control under Sirait had two basic strategies that were established in late 1978 and came to characterise its whole approach to the problem of drug prices. On the one hand, it was strongly attracted to some form of price control: if not direct price-setting, at least indirect price limitation. On the other, it also sought to challenge the pharmaceutical industry's whole cost structure through the introduction of competition from state enterprises. It was hoped that the state-owned pharmaceutical companies could act as price leaders and force the private manufacturers to follow them in the low-cost production of generic products (especially unbranded ones) to remain competitive. In other words, if private manufacturers wished to retain their market share, they would, it was thought, lower their prices.

A general feature of the Health Department's approach in its dealings with the pharmaceutical industry over the price issue, was the way it consistently argued in the language of social needs. The pharmaceutical industry was frequently upbraided for selfishly exploiting a social good essential to the well-being of the whole community. There was constant allusion in the government's rhetoric to the need to bring medicine within the reach of all sections of society. In this respect there were striking parallels at the level of ideology to the textile case-study, with the government concerned to be seen defending the interests of low income sections of society by ensuring their access to essential goods.

In the wake of the November 1978 devaluation and KOPKAM-TIB's intervention, the Health Department took further action on the price issue. On 5 January 1979, the Minister for Health announced that, following consultations with the Trade and Cooperatives Minister, Radius Prawiro, a special committee headed by Midian Sirait would be established to examine production costs for drugs in order to identify appropriate pricing levels following the devaluation. He added that any company failing to give full and accurate information on its cost structure would have its production licence revoked.[40]

This intervention to set price limits for pharmaceuticals did not last for long, being intended only as a stabilising measure after the turmoil of the devaluation. Nevertheless, it was sufficient to induce profound concern within the pharmaceutical industry that the government was considering the introduction of systematic price controls.[41] At the same time, there was also anxiety about the other arm of the Health Department's strategy, namely the introduction of downward price competition from state-owned drug manufacturers.

Coinciding with the Health Department's introduction of direct price-fixing, senior government figures were also dropping strong hints in the media that the government might be forced to expand its own pharmaceutical production capacities to ensure a satisfactory pricing profile for drugs. Comments by Health Minister Suwardjono following his meeting with the President in late November 1978, and Midian Sirait in mid-December, indicated that the Health Department was considering the introduction of the World Health Organisation's (WHO) essential medicine concept.[42]

The idea of a list of essential medicines had been put forward in an influential WHO report published internationally in 1977.[43] The WHO report was concerned to tackle the problems of the cost of drugs and the resulting high levels of public health expenditure sustained in developing countries. Underlying the essential drugs list concept was a belief that the recent massive proliferation of near-identical generic products was central to the problem of drug prices. The compilation of a list of the most important types (as opposed to brands) of medicines would enable cost-savings for public medicine programs. Predictably, WHO's essential medicine concept, together with the whole 'basic human needs' and 'health for all' ideology was anathema to the pharmaceutical industry around the world and they strongly opposed it.

Sirait had said in December 1978 that the government would have to think seriously about making use of WHO's list of 200 essential medicines in view of the large number of drugs on the Indonesian market. This was pursued further in January 1979 when Radius Prawiro told a press conference, following a meeting with the President, that the government would encourage doctors to write only the generic names of drugs on prescription forms so that patients could negotiate with dispensaries to obtain a product which was appropriately priced. In other words, if doctors only stipulated the *type* of drug on the prescription form, patients would be given the option of choosing from among cheaper unbranded generic drugs, or more expensive branded generics and innovative products.[44] (If the doctor prescribed a specific product, dispensaries were not able to sell the patient any other.) Shortly after, Health Minister Suwardjono announced in a television interview that the state would produce essential medicines itself, and that this would set an example for private drug manufacturers by demonstrating that drugs could be produced at much lower prices. He was reported as saying that hopefully this would encourage them to fulfil their social obligations by doing likewise.[45]

If fully implemented, the concept of an essential medicines list would have severely challenged major pharmaceutical manufacturers (both in Indonesia and elsewhere) by encouraging a shift to unbranded generics with much lower profit margins than either branded generics or innovative products. However, after the furore surrounding the devaluation subsided, the issue gradually slipped from prominence. Similarly, the return to pre-devaluation prices that had been enforced by KOPKAMTIB was lifted in February 1979 by Cabinet decision, though price monitoring was nominally continued.[46] In short, the threat to the pharmaceutical industry receded.

Despite this lull in the controversy, the Health Department continued to push these issues intermittently through 1979. Midian Sirait appeared before Committee VIII of the Parliament in June, and then again in October, to restate the government's commitment, both to the introduction of an essential medicines list, and the expansion of state production of many of these products, in order to tackle the problem of the affordability of drugs. He said that the government was moving to promote unbranded generics to overcome the situation in which, for example, the anti-biotic, Tetracycline, sold for Rp. 27 per tablet as an unbranded generic, while branded generics were priced at up to Rp. 75 per tablet. He added that to this end, unbranded products would be exempted from a 2.5 per cent sales tax.[47]

The sales tax issue did not especially alarm the large producers which dominated GPF. This was because their major market lay with the urban elite, who obtained drugs from dispensaries rather than *Puskesmas*, and so were unlikely to select or be prescribed unbranded generics. The sales tax really only affected the small scale producers of unbranded generics who largely supplied the public sector institutional market anyway. While manufacturers would, of course, have preferred to avoid the tax, it was a burden they were willing to bear in view of the political sensitivity of the pricing issue. Of much greater concern at this stage, though, was the Health Department's persistence with the idea of the 'registration' of all drugs and their pricing structure. Following the experience of late 1978 and early 1979, producers viewed this as another thinly disguised attempt to institutionalise some form of price regulation. Early in 1980 Sirait notified the GPF executive that he was seeking to develop the 'registration concept', and sought their views on the matter. GPF's response was to suggest several modifications to the proposal. Typically, GPF's approach was quiet, but firm. It did not oppose Sirait's idea outright, but instead argued that *if* pricing information was to be included in the formal registration process, it should only take the form of *ex post facto* notification of the prices of products and any changes to them. In short, manufacturers should only be required to inform the Department of prices they were already charging, rather than having to justify *proposed* changes to price levels.[48]

Round Two: the C-5 and the DOEN

Late in 1980, the Health Department took two major steps in developing its two-pronged approach to the price issue. It unveiled a cluster of regulations[49] providing for new price-monitoring requirements and also the introduction of the WHO essential medicines concept. The former required drug manufacturers henceforth to register all their products and submit both pharmacological *and* pricing details for each product. This new requirement, which came to be known by the registration form number, C-5, was the first major step under the New Order towards the long term and systematic monitoring of prices. While Sirait and others went to considerable lengths to argue that this did not constitute a form of price control (which, indeed, it did not), it is quite clear that the C-5 requirement was intended to act as a direct retardant to further price rises by manufacturers. Henceforth, manufacturers would have to explain how they determined their selling prices.

The second prong of the strategy was the formal introduction of an essential medicines list; the DOEN as it became known. This provided for the production of 330 of the most important types of drugs as unbranded generics. The Health Department reactivated a disused state-owned pharmaceutical plant in Jakarta to produce many of these drugs. In many ways this represented an extension of the *Obat Inpres* scheme via the *Puskesmas*, in that it aimed at promoting the use of unbranded generics (especially those manufactured by the state) to help meet the needs of the poor.

This double-fronted approach by the Health Department was its response to the very considerable political pressure that had built up over the issue of drug prices. Both prongs of the strategy, the DOEN and the C-5, had the potential to present serious long term challenges to the pharmaceutical industry. Ultimately, however, neither did. As 1981 and 1982 progressed it became clear that both the government's DOEN and C-5 initiatives were failing to achieve their stated objectives. Both were strongly opposed by GPF. As it turned out, the DOEN faltered because of fundamental design flaws. Little action was needed by GPF apart from a quiet and continual nagging of the Health Department. By contrast, GPF was closely involved in the emasculation of the C-5 initiative.

The problems faced by the DOEN policy were twofold. It was failing to reach most low income people (other than the existing users of public health institutions); and it was also failing to have any effect as a 'price leader' in inducing downward price pressure on private drug manufacturers. The first of these failings, inability to reach the broader public, was in large measure due to the Health Department's failure to account for the role of doctors in their calculations. In focusing on the manufacturers as the source of the problem they had overlooked the fact that doctors—the principal intermediary between producers and consumers of drugs—play a vital part in determining consumption patterns. While the Health Department had drawn up and publicised the DOEN and cheap generic drugs were indeed being produced, the awkward fact remained that doctors were simply not prescribing them to patients. It was quite evident that the great majority of doctors preferred to prescribe branded products rather than the unbranded generics produced under the DOEN scheme, as the Director General for Health Services, Dr. Brata Ranuh, conceded to the press. This, he said, was happening despite the fact that the DOEN drugs were up to one-tenth the price and of guaranteed quality.[50]

The second problem for the DOEN scheme was its failure to generate any downward pressure on the pricing policies of private drug producers, a central aim of the whole DOEN strategy. In part, the inability to induce downward price movement was linked to the fact that there was only limited support for the DOEN and thus the scope of the operation was not great. More important, though, was that 90 to 95 per cent of all the essential medicines were being produced by the private sector, as Health Minister Suwardjono acknowledged in August 1982.[51] Even though state firms were indeed producing cheap drugs for the DOEN and other public health projects, the fundamental problem remained that the vast majority of drugs in circulation were being manufactured by the private sector. The state-owned factories were incapable of acting as price leaders because their market share was too small. Furthermore, such consumption of the unbranded DOEN generics as there was took place almost exclusively via public health institutions such as *puskesmas*, public hospitals and health schemes for civil servants. The DOEN was thus little more than an extension of the *Obat Inpres* program, which also supplied unbranded generics to public health institutions. As the pharmaceutical industry soon realised, the DOEN scheme would not become the threat that it might have been.[52]

If the DOEN scheme failed to have any substantial impact on the problem of making medicines more affordable, the other arm of the Health Department's strategy, the policy of price monitoring via the C-5 registration form was equally ineffectual. Although manufacturers were indeed very concerned by the C-5 system when it was introduced, persistent negotiations by GPF with the Health Department ensured that it did not become a constraint on price-setting. GPF's argument that it should be an *ex post facto* record of price movements was accepted. Once the Health Department agreed to this, it was clear that the C-5 would 'have no teeth' and become little more than a formality. Certainly, it had no significant impact in halting price rises.[53]

Round Three: C-5 Becomes IHO

As if in acknowledgment of the failure of the C-5 system to retard price increases, the Health Department moved to expand and strengthen the registration system. Appearing before Committee VIII of the Parliament in June 1983, Midian Sirait, announced that the Health Department would be publishing a complete list of all medicines, and their prices, to be distributed to every doctor in the country. He said that previously doctors had not been fully aware of the price differentials amongst drugs, and that this new publication, known as the IHO (Drug Price Information) manual would be used as a point of reference by doctors to write prescriptions which were in accordance with the purchasing power of patients. It was thus assumed that upon digestion of the IHO manual, doctors would respond to market forces and direct patients to unbranded generic products. This in turn would lead to price competition, it was hoped, and a downward spiral in drug prices.[54]

Under the new regulations, manufacturers were still required to submit the C-5 registration form detailing prices for each drug. A vital modification to the C-5 system, however, was that manufacturers would not be permitted to alter these prices for a period of six months, after which time a new round of C-5s would be submitted, and a new IHO manual published and distributed to doctors. Thus each IHO manual would remain in force for six months, during which time prices could not be adjusted. The only opportunity for price change came with the preparation of the next IHO, at which time producers could submit detailed pricing information to justify any proposed increases.

This was a much more serious attempt to restrict price rises. The Health Department was seeking to induce prior competition by the publication of the prices of all drugs, as well as attempting to delay any price rises by requiring adherence to those registered in the C-5 and published in the current IHO manual.

While the introduction of the IHO manual certainly threw the manufacturers into a panic, it failed absolutely to induce downward price competition. Indeed, the result was precisely the opposite. Prices rose faster than ever, for the simple reason that, fearing the loss of freedom to adjust prices for six month intervals, producers inflated their prices in advance and at an exaggerated rate. By this means they sought to guard against the possibility of the six-month price moratorium being extended or of losses resulting from, for instance, unforeseen currency fluctuations. Another major factor underlying IHO's lack of success was that, like the DOEN scheme, it relied on doctors choosing to prescribe the less expensive products. As with DOEN, doctors seem simply to have not behaved in the manner expected by the Health Department.

Once again flawed policy-design had played a hand. But as with the earlier C-5 initiative, GPF also played an important part in speeding the demise of the IHO system. The pharmaceutical industry had been very unhappy with IHO, regarding it as an administrative nightmare which cut their pricing flexibility.[55] As such, they were anxious that it be 'reviewed'. GPF therefore pursued an active, but low profile campaign to dissuade the Directorate General for Drug and Food Control from its chosen path. Emphasis was placed on the failure of IHO as a policy instrument. After much negotiation, GPF succeeded in having the policy very substantially modified.[56]

Ultimately, the IHO manual was published only three times. During 1984, Eddie Lembong succeeded in persuading Midian Sirait that it should be put out only once yearly, rather than twice, and that manufacturers be permitted to adjust their prices whenever they wished, provided they registered this price change with the Health Department. Such price changes would be published periodically in an IHO Supplement. These changes represented a major dilution of the original IHO policy as they eliminated the moratorium on price increases. With a view to scuttling IHO completely, GPF offered to 'assist' the Health Department's drive to lower drug prices by (magnanimously) undertaking the responsibility for the publication of the IHO Supplement in its magazine *Varia Farmasi*. By this means, GPF in effect gained control of IHO. The Health Department was happy to unload the administrative cost of compiling, publishing and distributing the IHO pricing information (which had become something of an embarrassment); and GPF was more than happy to bear this cost in the short term. After a period GPF simply informed the Health Department that it could no longer 'afford' to provide the service and that it would have to lapse unless the Department again assumed responsibility for it. In short, GPF ensured that the whole scheme quietly wound to a halt. Eventually, after having fallen from view, the IHO policy was officially abandoned (in early 1987). In order to save Sirait himself from having to make the somewhat embarrassing announcement that the IHO scheme had been dropped, GPF undertook to write to all its members informing them that it had been discontinued.[57] Once again, this was typical of the low profile and non-confrontational lobbying of GPF which continued to return good dividends for the pharmaceutical industry. Put simply, GPF had persuaded the Health Department to abandon a policy opposed by the pharmaceutical industry.

The complete abolition of the IHO scheme was a slow process. The immediate victory for GPF and the pharmaceutical industry in 1984 was the rescheduling of the IHO manual's publication and, more importantly, the cessation of the six month price increase moratorium. These were significant achievements. They were, however, set against a backdrop of increasing, if undefined, hostility towards the whole health services sector over the price of medical treatment. While the pharmaceutical industry was not seen as the only 'villain'—it was widely recognised that doctors, wholesalers and retailers all had a major role—there was a tendency to single out manufacturers. This seems to have been in large measure a product of the internationally poor image of the pharmaceutical industry, and the widespread view of it as singularly unscrupulous. Yet it is difficult to identify precisely where hostility to medicine prices emanated from. Much of the criticism was carried in the press, or in some cases was initiated by the press itself. State officials, especially those from the Health Department, as well as Parliamentarians and the YLK (the Consumers' Association) often decried the cost of drugs. And yet, that section of the population seen as being the chief victim of high drug prices, the vast low-income tier of Indonesian society, was in effect silent. In part, this no doubt reflected the fact that the scope for interest articulation by the mass of the population was limited: this, after all, had been an aim of all the corporatist restructuring described in Chapter 3. More fundamentally though, it pointed to the fact that the issue of drug prices was really an urban middle class concern. They, it must be remembered, were the main consumers of drugs.

Round Four: Another Scandal, Another Policy

In August 1984, the political sensitivity of the drug price issue was again inflamed by a major exposé in the weekly magazine, *Tempo*.[58] The article reported that enquiries by the Legal Aid Institute had led to the investigation of four doctors for malpractice. The doctors were alleged to have accepted extensive bribes from drug manufacturers in return for prescribing their products. The article argued that the practice of pharmaceutical companies offering commissions and various other material incentives to doctors was widespread. This story, in turn, generated considerable critical media interest in the question of drug prices. The GOLKAR-linked newspaper, *Suara Karya*, for example, ran an extensive feature series examining factors underlying the price of drugs in Indonesia.[59] The series, which was spread over five consecutive days, served to heighten further the prominence of the issue and the negative attention being paid to the pharmaceutical industry.

Despite the various initiatives that had been launched by the Health Department to prevent continued price spiraling, little real progress had been achieved. In this situation, there was clearly mounting pressure for some palliative action. Critical media attention served to increase the political pressure on the Health Department quite directly. In early December, Midian Sirait appeared again before Committee VIII of the Parliament to answer questions on the price issue.[60]

No doubt in response to the controversy of late 1984, in April 1985 Sirait announced yet another policy initiative designed to tackle the problem. The new scheme was in some respects a reformulation of earlier initiatives. The gist of it was that the Health Department would undertake the production of thirty-four of the most essential medicines, and the launching of them into the open market (as distinct from the public health market). These products would be designed as direct competitors to other privately manufactured equivalents and would, if necessary, be promoted by professional detailers (pharmaceutical sales representatives) to ensure marketing success. Sirait told the press that this project would be undertaken by the state-owned factory, Indofarma, in joint venture with any private firms which chose to participate. He said that he expected that this venture would operate in the same way as BULOG (the state logistics board which controls rice marketing) and that in this way it would be able to act as a price leader and achieve price stability for these products at much lower levels.[61]

This move can be seen as an attempt to increase the government's capacity to influence drug prices via expanded public sector production. That it was a direct campaign to compete with and erode private sector control of the drug market is revealed in Sirait's statement to the press that it was the responsibility of journalists to encourage doctors to choose the less expensive drugs for their patients (in other words, those manufactured by state enterprises).

Sirait discussed this initiative in advance at a meeting with the heads of Kimia Farma and Indofarma (the two large state manufacturers) and Eddie Lembong on behalf of GPF. None of the three industry figures opposed Sirait's proposal, although all three viewed it as being fraught with difficulties. Though initially silent, GPF subsequently made its strong reservations clear to Sirait. The proposed new products were supposed to enter the market by September 1985. If implemented, the plan could have been very threatening to the pharmaceutical industry. It seems that after several months a combination of scepticism on the part of the state-owned manufacturers about the viability of the project, together with the persistent lobbying of GPF, was sufficient to deter Sirait, and the entire plan was quietly aborted and sank from view without remark.[62] Yet another initiative thus fell by the wayside, and yet again, the pharmaceutical industry breathed a collective sigh of relief.

The issue of drug prices remained politically sensitive, however, though it began to recede from media prominence as 1985 progressed. Evidence of its continuing sensitivity can be found in the persistent interest of Committee VIII of the Parliament in the subject. Although the Committee lacked the authority to demand executive action from the Health Department, it did have the capacity to embarrass the officials by attracting unwanted critical attention from senior echelons within the government through press coverage. Certainly the Health Department officials did not treat appearances before the Committee lightly.[63]

In late May the YLK (the Consumers' Association) appeared before the Committee and called on the Parliament to take action to overcome the drug price problem.[64] Several days later Midian Sirait was before the Committee, this time declaring that the Health Department would commence the direct importing of drugs if prices became too high.[65] This seems to have been primarily a piece of political posturing intended to threaten manufacturers and impress the Parliament, rather than a seriously considered policy proposal. In mid-September, Sirait again appeared before the Committee, this time together with the Secretary General of the Health Department, Soekaryo. On this occasion Sirait reiterated his appeal for low-income people to use generic medicines and save money.[66] A month later, the executive of GPF came before Committee VIII to respond to criticism about prices, and argued that the responsibility did not lie with the manufacturers, but was widely dispersed.[67]

This stop-start scrutiny of the issues of drug prices characterised the lead-up to the heated 1986 dispute. The purpose of this review of the backdrop to the 1986 dispute has been to highlight the recurrent themes in the debate over pharmaceutical prices in Indonesia and to underscore the fact that the issue has a lengthy past. To recapitulate, there was a widespread perception that drug prices in Indonesia were too high and that this could be overcome by state intervention—thereby bringing modern medication within the reach of the bulk of the people. The Directorate General for Drug and Food Control was committed to somehow tackling this problem, something made plain by its persistent efforts in the four bouts reviewed here. And yet with each attempt it was unsuccessful. In part, these failures can be explained by the inherently difficult nature of the socio-economic engineering it was contemplating and the associated problems of policy design. But another consistent feature was the unremitting opposition of the pharmaceutical industry. The pharmaceutical industry, represented by GPF, quietly, but effectively, resisted all attempts by the government to restrict upward price mobility. Although GPF did not score high profile, knock-out victories, by the end of each round the government's policy initiatives had faltered and the pharmaceutical industry had managed to secure the minimum conditions it sought.

By 1986, then, the question of medicine prices was a familiar and well established item on the political agenda. Apart from the continued circling of the Health Department and GPF, other players to become increasingly involved were the press, Committee VIII of the Parliament and the YLK. Their involvement served to raise the profile of the issue, and thus increased the pressure on the Health Department to somehow cut through the problem and deliver 'health for all'. But the more pressure that was applied to the Directorate

General to 'resolve' the matter, the harder GPF struggled to preserve
what it saw as the pharmaceutical industry's essential interests.

The 1986 Conflict Over Drug Prices

The repeated frustration of the Directorate General for Drug and
Control's various policy initiatives, aimed at forcing down drug
prices, had not by 1986 dulled Midian Sirait's enthusiasm. He remained committed to the idea of expanding the state's ability to
induce downward pressure on prices via an increased public sector
presence in the market. For Sirait, the key to inducing downward
price movement lay in bringing market pressure to bear on private
drug manufacturers. From late 1985 through the first half of 1986 he
periodically discussed the general problem of prices with Eddie
Lembong on an informal consultative basis. Lembong was concerned
to retain the ear of Sirait, and so went to considerable lengths to play
down the impression that a 'zero-sum-game' situation governed
relations between the Health Department and the pharmaceutical
industry on the price question. He sought to promote GPF as an
organisation willing to cooperate and, moreover, be of assistance to
the Health Department in any way it could. For as both sides
realised, despite their fundamentally different perspectives, they had
a common interest centring on how best to deal with the political
pressure for lower drug prices.

On the occasions during 1986 when Sirait aired his concerns to
Lembong and talked of his desire to boost the public sector presence
in the pharmaceutical market, Lembong would respond by saying
that any attempt to bring down drug prices by merely focusing on the
manufacturers was doomed to failure. He repeatedly argued that the
support of the doctors needed to be enlisted.[68] His advice to Sirait
was that any new initiative should be predicated on a cooperative
effort by the various state and non-state actors involved in the
pharmaceutical and health services area. In stressing (accurately) the
complexities involved, Lembong was seeking to deflect exclusive
scrutiny of his constituency, while at the same time perhaps discour-
aging Sirait from taking action.

Controversy Erupts

After simmering for a number of months, the question of drug prices
again came rapidly to the boil in July–August 1986. Following a
meeting between Health Minister Suwardjono and the President on

10 July, Suwardjono told the press that Suharto had instructed him to arrange an investigation into the factors causing the high price levels of drugs.[69] This, together with extraordinary public statements by both the Secretary General of the Health Department, Soekaryo, and the head of IDI (the Indonesian Doctors' Association), Dr Kartono Muhammad, to the effect that Indonesia had the third most expensive medicine prices in the world (after Switzerland and West Germany), signalled the onset of yet another round of the drug price battle and saw a rapid build-up of political pressure on the price issue.[70] When Suwardjono, after a further meeting with the President on 13 August, again spoke to the press, it was apparent that something of a political crisis was erupting in the health services world.[71] Suharto apparently found the idea that the majority of people could not afford medicine unpalatable. Furthermore, he was reportedly disturbed that this should be an issue in the period leading up to the 1987 general election. Apparently Suharto indicated that he wished the problem 'solved' forthwith.[72] Interestingly, this intervention by Suharto was taking place at exactly the same time as he was becoming directly involved in the dispute in the textile industry. In neither case did he give detailed instructions as to how the problem was to be resolved, and instead simply (but emphatically) directed it be done.

Confronted with these extraordinary public pronouncements on drug prices by leading figures and highly critical press coverage, Sirait was under intense political pressure to provide a solution. Ministerial and, moreover, Presidential intervention were sure signs of top-level political disquiet. Undoubtedly, the controversy was far more acute in this round than in the earlier ones. The Directorate General was left in no doubt as to the urgency of the matter, or that it was being held responsible for the situation.[73] Anxious to take constructive steps, Sirait convened a marathon meeting in late August with representatives from GPF, IDI (the Doctors' Association) and ISFI (the Pharmacy Graduates' Association) to discuss possible measures to tackle the problem.

The pharmaceutical industry was extremely worried that a restrictive package of regulations, possibly including price controls, was about to be introduced. Industry anxiety was compounded by the fact that Eddie Lembong had been overseas throughout August—a coincidence which had the effect of robbing the manufacturers of their usual cohesiveness and sense of direction. By all accounts, the meeting called by Sirait was a traumatic affair.[74] Sirait apparently demanded actual price reductions from the manufacturers in order to alleviate the political crisis. Failure by industry to make some concessions would result in the Health Department having to take firm (and by implication draconian) measures itself, he reportedly

·threatened. This created panic in the industry and precipitated a period of open and mutual recrimination among the various groups involved. There was thus the spectacle of local and foreign manufacturers, doctors, distributors and retailers all blaming each other through the pages of the press for the high price of drugs.[75]

The highly political nature of the turmoil in the pharmaceutical sector was laid open in an important article in the leading daily *Kompas*.[76] The article, by *Kompas* journalist, Irwan Julianto, had the pointed title 'Medicine Prices—A Hot Issue' and was widely seen as marking a watershed in the conflict. Coming as it did in the wake of a substantial press build up, it had the effect of laying the issues bare for all to see.

Sirait's first step in addressing the crisis was to announce to the press on 3 September that he had established a special committee to identify any 'irrational' factors contributing to high drug costs. The committee known as the Committee of Inquiry into Rational Drug Usage and Prices, or, PPKPHO, consisted of representatives from professional associations in the pharmaceutical sector such as GPF, IDI, ISFI as well as the Dentists' Association, PDGI, and was headed by Slamet Soesilo, the Director for Drug Control together with Amir Basir, the formal chairman of GPF. Sirait emphasised that the government needed more complete information on the underlying causes of the problem before it could take action. Significantly, he specifically requested the press to allow the government two months grace in which to work on the problem without having it inflamed by the media.[77] In his comments to the press, Amir Basir argued that in order to reduce the price of drugs it was necessary to improve marketing channels, rather than to just focus on issues such as production and raw material costs. His remarks were obviously aimed at diverting attention from the drug manufacturers, and were juxtaposed in the press with those of others such as IDI head, Dr Kartono Muhamad, who tended to emphasise the central role of industry.[78]

The PPKPHO Committee seems to have been set up in direct response to the intervention by the President and Health Minister Suwardjono's assertion of the need for more complete information on the price problem to guide policy. It appears that it was established as a demonstrative suggestion of coordinated action by the Directorate General for Drug and Food Control.

The pharmaceutical industry had still to determine how it would approach this inflamed situation and to try to defuse the very real risk of the Health Department introducing new regulations which might threaten its *modus operandi*. Despite being overseas during this period, Eddie Lembong had been in contact with Sirait urging him to avoid taking any drastic measures. Lembong also communicated with industry figures, strongly advising them to hold fast and not be panicked into conceding voluntary price reductions.

When Lembong returned to Jakarta early in September, his first priority was to regain the initiative for GPF in dealings with not only the government, but also the other professional associations in the health services sector and, importantly, the press. For well over a month the pharmaceutical industry had been the subject of consistently critical coverage in the press, and held responsible for the medicine price controversy. This of course rendered the pharmaceutical industry the easiest target for unilateral reform action by the Health Department. The industry would have few supporters if the Department moved strongly against it.

An opportunity emerged for GPF to regain some initiative only a matter of days after Lembong's return. On 12 September the government announced a surprise devaluation of the rupiah, nominally by 45 per cent. The normal follow-on from this would have been for the pharmaceutical industry, like other industries reliant on imports, to raise the price of its goods by a corresponding amount. At Lembong's instigation, the GPF executive decided that as a public relations manoeuvre, it would seek a price rise of only 15 per cent. This was a very modest increase. Following executive endorsement of this scheme, the GPF leadership contacted Midian Sirait at his home on the evening of 13 September. Sirait greatly appreciated the proposal and was happy to give it his approval, since if the industry had sought to increase prices by the full 45 per cent, his problems would have only further compounded, for the outcry over medicine price-hikes would have been unrestrained.[79]

By this move GPF earned 'kudos' of two sorts. On one hand, it was seen as a bold gesture in that it grasped the price nettle firmly. (Price increase proposals were always very sensitive for any industry in the wake of a devaluation.) By its daring, the move thus enhanced GPF's reputation as a wily and professional association. But on the other hand, and more importantly, the move was also widely seen as a gesture of restraint—something which helped to redress the pharmaceutical industry's image of profiting from the misfortune of others. That the post-devaluation price restraint went some way to at least temporarily improving the industry's tarnished reputation was illustrated by the fact that the level of press criticism began to fall away immediately.

By this ploy, the industry managed to retrieve some tactical initiative and earn Sirait's gratitude, at very little cost to itself. Pharmaceutical manufacturers normally had a stockpile of most of the imported raw materials needed for drug assembly. As these would have been purchased at pre-devaluation prices, producers were suffering no loss at all in offering to sell their post-devaluation produce at prices increased by only 15 per cent. In reality, the industry was merely foregoing a greater margin of windfall profit—and only for a limited time, as the price restraint was just a temporary measure. At the meeting with Sirait on 13 September, Lembong took the opportunity to discuss more than his post-devaluation price restraint proposal. He recognised the inevitability of Sirait having to adopt some concrete reform measures both to appease his superiors, and dampen the criticism from the press. (By this stage some press items had begun to present Sirait's stewardship in a critical light.[80]) In this situation Lembong was anxious to ensure that any policy changes which did ensue were not inimical to the interests of the pharmaceutical industry. To this end, he suggested to Sirait, in private, that this might be the ideal moment to unveil a reformulation of his aborted April 1985 scheme—in other words, state manufacture of generic drugs to be sold on the open market and targeted at low income people. Lembong's reasoning was that the politically charged atmosphere made it certain that Sirait would take action of some form, and that a modified version of the April 1985 scheme was a less bad outcome than others readily imaginable—such as outright price regulation.[81]

This was a risky manoeuvre. In encouraging Sirait to revive a version of his earlier project, Lembong was gambling that the new scheme would not be too harmful to industry interests. There seems to have been an implicit bargain involved: GPF would support Sirait in a new policy initiative addressing the price problem, and in return, the policy would be tailored in a way not overly injurious to the pharmaceutical industry.

The DOPB Scheme

While Lembong and Sirait had discussed the latter's lingering determination to reintroduce some form of public sector competition for private manufacturers over a period of months, it seems evident that Lembong's sudden endorsement and offer of support for the idea had a critical bearing on Sirait's thinking. A mere two days later, on 15 September, Sirait unveiled the rough outlines of the new policy initiative while appearing again before Committee VIII of the Parliament to answer questions (in a session which lasted for five hours) on the price controversy. Though the new initiative had not been finalised, Sirait's statement indicated that it would basically involve a revival of his old scheme, plus the incorporation of Eddie Lembong's idea for the enlistment of the doctors' cooperation. Sirait told the Committee that the government would control the prices of eighty of the essential drugs most widely used by the people, and that the Health Department would finalise the list with the cooperation of representatives of the pharmaceutical and medical associations. He emphasised that this list of eighty drugs would be made up of unbranded generics which would be produced mostly by the public sector and would have their prices set at very low levels. In particular, he said that the project was aimed at helping low income people who could not conveniently attend the *puskesmas* (public health clinics) and who had heretofore been forced to obtain their medicines via private doctors and dispensaries. (*Puskesmas* clinics are only open during office hours, and are thus inaccessible to many workers.) He explained that under the new scheme doctors would be able to write special prescription forms for low income patients whom dispensaries would then be required to supply with one of the low cost drugs from the new list.[82]

A press conference was held several days later to launch the new scheme, which now bore the acronym, DOPB (Joint Program Medicine List). The press conference was attended by Health Department officials and the leaders of the professional associations already involved in the PPKPHO Committee (GPF, IDI, ISFI and PDGI) who were presented as the co-sponsors of the program. It was announced that a pilot project of the DOPB scheme would be launched in Jakarta as of 1 October 1986, and that if successful, the program would be extended to the rest of Indonesia.[83]

The political significance of these developments was well illustrated several days later when Health Minister Suwardjono reported again to the President, and spoke afterwards to the press. For a minister (especially one responsible for a portfolio outside critical security and economic management areas) to see the President for three special and publicised meetings within a relatively short period was quite unusual, and pointed to the fact that the issue had now assumed such a level of prominence as to involve the President on a continuing basis. After emerging from his meeting with the President, Suwardjono told reporters that for too long low-cost medicines had suffered from a lack of promotion, and thus lost out in competition with heavily promoted high-cost products of almost identical pharmacological specifications. He then went on to accuse drug producers of engaging in unreasonable promotion practices and of paying doctors commissions on the basis of the number of prescriptions for their products made out by the doctor.[84]

Sirait and Suwardjono were plainly very pleased with the DOPB scheme, as it promised to advance a favoured policy objective (cheap medicine) as well as provide them with a panacea for their political predicament. The general perception was that the DOPB scheme had been imposed on the pharmaceutical industry and was decidedly injurious to its interests. For the first time, cheap, publicly produced drugs were to be launched on to the private market. Indeed, many members of the pharmaceutical industry itself seem to have believed that they had just been dealt a major blow by the Health Department, and that state-produced DOPB drugs would cut into their market shares. An indication of the extent of concern within the industry can be gleaned from the fact that when GPF convened a meeting to discuss the issue with members, over 120 company representatives attended a gathering at which seating had been provided for only seventy five.[85]

This initial alarm within pharmaceutical industry circles was quite misplaced, however. The GPF executive's support of the DOPB scheme had been a calculated risk, based on the assumption that, despite appearances, the DOPB was unlikely to ever exert significant downward pressure on drug prices. In the short term, as had been the case with the post-devaluation price restraint, GPF's support for the DOPB scheme was very helpful in stemming the tide of criticism of producers over drug prices. The image of drug manufacturers actively participating in a campaign directly assisting the poor held great public relations value. In late September, for example, Eddie Lembong was able to tell the press how GPF (as distinct from the Health Department) had been voluntarily conducting deliveries of the DOPB medicines to dispensaries around Jakarta to assist the pilot project. Further, several prominent pharmaceutical companies were publicly thanked by IDI head Dr Kartono Muhamad for having helped to ensure the success of the DOPB program by arranging for their sales representatives to assist in the delivery of the special DOPB prescription booklets and price lists to some 4,000 doctors around Jakarta.[86] This was precisely the sort of publicity the pharmaceutical industry urgently needed.

Not only did the DOPB scheme bring valuable public relations benefits, of greater long term importance to the pharmaceutical industry was the fact that the likelihood of serious state intervention in drug pricing had again been averted. Concerns that DOPB drugs would take sales from private sector products were quite unfounded—as the GPF leadership foresaw. The market for drugs for low income groups, the stated target of DOPB, was in effect a separate market from that of most private drug manufacturers. The target group for their products were the more affluent sections of society who could afford the higher prices of branded products. Certainly there would be some overlap if people of relatively limited means who would otherwise have managed to afford expensive branded drugs were instead prescribed a DOPB drug by their doctor. But here GPF was able to assume confidently that the scope of DOPB would, inevitably, remain limited. This was because it was highly unlikely that the other principal actors in the pharmaceutical chain would support the DOPB either. Doctors and dispensaries were likely to be unsympathetic to the scheme, and any enthusiasm on the part of the state-owned companies manufacturing the DOPB drugs was likely to wane rapidly once it became clear that profit levels would be low.

To take the case of the doctors first, there were at least three grounds for believing that they would be unlikely to offer much support to the DOPB program. To begin with, many doctors would be genuinely reluctant to place their trust in the pharmacological qualities of unfamiliar and unbranded generics, preferring instead the more familiar and 'reliable' branded drugs. This was in part the result of a common perception that some unbranded generics were under-dosed and thus not efficacious. A second reason for lack of enthusiasm by doctors was one identified publicly by IDI head, Kartono Muhamad. This concerned practical difficulties which the DOPB scheme was likely to create for doctor-patient relations. How, for instance, were doctors to ascertain which patients should be given the 'poor peoples' medicine' or *not*. No doubt many patients would feel embarrassed to request the DOPB products, and many doctors would be reluctant to risk insulting patients by offering to prescribe cheap, as opposed to normal medicine for them.[87] The third potential problem with DOPB in the eyes of doctors, or at least those who had been receiving commissions of any sort from private drug manufacturers, was that there would of course be a material disincentive to prescribe DOPB drugs. If a doctor received commissions—in effect, bribes—from a pharmaceutical company and was keen to maintain the flow of illicit benefits, he or she would not be attracted to the idea of promoting DOPB drugs.[88]

Whereas there were several reasons likely to discourage doctor support of the DOPB, for dispensaries there was only one. It was nonetheless very powerful. DOPB drugs—with their prices set by the Health Department—carried a much lower profit margin for retailers than ordinary drugs. This meant that dispensaries were decidedly unenthusiastic about the whole scheme. As an illustration of antipathy towards the program by dispensaries and their willingness to circumvent it, one pharmaceutical company executive cited an anecdote from his own experience. Shortly after the commencement of the DOPB scheme one of his household servants fell ill. The executive, not wanting to outlay more money than was necessary on the servant's medical bill, instructed her to request a prescription for a DOPB drug from the doctor—which she did. However, upon proceeding to the dispensary to purchase the actual DOPB drug, the servant was told by the proprietor that, alas, they had just run out of that particular DOPB drug. He was however quite happy to sell her an equivalent (but much more expensive) non-DOPB product! The attitude of the state enterprises manufacturing the DOPB drugs also seems to have been ambivalent at best. Like the dispensaries, their major qualm was that there was little profit in it for them. The DOPB venture was not too onerous to begin with as they were able to produce the required drugs using raw materials which had been imported prior to the 13 September devaluation. Once this limited stockpile of cheap raw materials was exhausted their support for the scheme would, as GPF foresaw, be severely tested.

In short, there was a surfeit of major players on the scene who were either unenthusiastic, or totally opposed to DOPB. In this context, GPF did not need to oppose the policy with any vigour, it could leave that task to the others. GPF could thus proceed to support fully the implementation of DOPB in the knowledge that its chances of survival were limited. The irony was exquisite.

From GPF's point of view, the DOPB scheme, while potentially threatening if implemented on a thorough-going basis (something most unlikely), was thus really a low-cost, high-return public relations exercise. What seemed to be a great set-back and threat to the pharmaceutical industry had in fact been turned to its advantage. There were two general indicators of the success of GPF's strategy. The first, already mentioned, was the fact that the level of overtly critical press coverage of the pharmaceutical industry receded. The second was more unusual, involving a signal that the government, and more importantly the President, viewed with favour GPF's backing of DOPB. This emerged obliquely when Eddie Lembong had the opportunity in late October to speak, albeit briefly, with Suharto. Lembong was in a reception line with a group of dignitaries (unrelated to the pharmaceutical industry) greeting Suharto at an official function. When Lembong's turn to shake the President's hand came, he decided to take the opportunity to speak to Suharto about the drug price question. He therefore introduced himself to Suharto as a leader of GPF, which he emphasised, was an enthusiastic sponsor of DOPB. To Lembong's surprise, Suharto's face lit up with recognition, and he proceeded to convey his approval and appreciation of GPF's involvement.[89]

This may seem a trivial and fleeting incident. However given that access to the President is a very scarce commodity, for Eddie Lembong this presented an invaluable opportunity to gauge Suharto's feelings on the drug price issue. While Suharto was, of course, well aware that controversy existed over medicine prices—he could scarcely avoid it—it was less certain that he would have continued to monitor a health policy matter. Under normal circumstances, his indications of concern to Health Minister Suwardjono would have been sufficient to ensure a shake-up of departmental policy. It was for this reason that Lembong was surprised to discover that Suharto recognised and understood the term DOPB: he had clearly continued to follow the issue. More significant for Lembong though, was that the President was evidently pleased by GPF's association with it. To Lembong, this signalled that the pharmaceutical industry was not dangerously out of favour. That medicine prices were not actually falling did not seem to matter. The important point was that a cooperative effort was seen to be made to assist the poor, even if only in a very small way.

Actors and Interests

One need not be excessively cynical about the motives of the various players in the DOPB saga. Eddie Lembong and GPF did derive sincere pride from the pharmaceutical industry's support for the DOPB. They were not insensitive to the humanitarian aims of the scheme. As business people, however, their chief interest in DOPB lay in what it might mean for their industry. Midian Sirait and Slamet Soesilo at the Directorate of Drug and Food Control also had a genuine and long standing commitment to the idea of making medicine more affordable both for humanitarian reasons and for reasons relating to the management of the national health bill. However, the state officials also had the overriding need to respond rapidly and demonstratively to the political pressure which was being applied to them from the press, the Health Minister and indeed the President.

The situation with regard to IDI was somewhat more involved. This was primarily because the national head of IDI, Dr Kartono, held a decidedly more progressive view on the subject of the cost of health services than many of his constituents. Many doctors in private practice did not take kindly to efforts to sever their symbiotic links with the sales representatives of drug companies. To this extent, there was a perception that Kartono was in danger of being too far ahead of a significant number of his colleagues. In spite of this, he was a very active campaigner for greater social justice in the provision of health services. His public statements on the subject of medicine prices played an important part in raising the level of political debate to the point where the Health Department was forced to act. He saw the DOPB program as an instrument for achieving genuine reform. Being something of an idealist, he was apparently less conscious of the machinations that had taken place between GPF and the Health Department behind the scenes to bring DOPB into existence—for what were primarily ulterior motives.

The other groups which were both members of PPKPHO committee and joint sponsors of the DOPB program were the dispensaries, the pharmacists and the dentists. The dentists played a very minor role in the whole affair and can be set aside. The pharmacists, or rather the pharmacy graduates' association, ISFI, also played a largely formalistic role in the discussions over DOPB. This was in large part because pharmacy graduates did not have any common set of material interests. There were, after all, pharmacy graduates scattered right throughout the health services sector. Lacking a central focus, ISFI was not a decisive political body. The position of the dispensaries in the DOPB was, however, somewhat more enigmatic. They had a clear and very considerable interest in the DOPB saga. Quite simply, every DOPB drug that they sold represented lost revenue. So, they were the group who stood to lose the most from DOPB, and yet they did relatively little about it. For an explanation of this one must look to the standing of the dispensaries in terms of interest articulation. In this, their principal problem was that as one of the sub-sectors within GPF, their interests were to a very large degree overshadowed. The manufacturers dominated GPF, which was widely seen as an instrument primarily representing their interests, and only secondarily those of wholesalers and retailers.

One actor that did not come to the centre of the political stage on the DOPB issue until late in the scene was the Consumers' Association, the YLK. Along with Dr Kartono, the YLK shared what was essentially an altruistic interest in the question of the price of drugs. The YLK was seen as one of the most trenchant critics of the pharmaceutical industry, particularly under the leadership of Permadi. It was not only the pharmaceutical industry that was uncomfortable with the YLK under Permadi; the Health Department was also very wary of him because of charges he had made about corruption among Health officials. Indeed, when it was proposed by journalists to Midian Sirait at a press conference in late September that the YLK be included in the membership of the PPKPHO committee along with the other professional representative bodies, one Health Department official was quoted as responding with a pointed question as to whether or not Permadi was still leader of the YLK.[90] Under Permadi, the YLK did nonetheless attempt to involve itself in the drug price issue. In late September, for instance, he appeared before Committee X of the Parliament, and declared that a major cause of the high prices was that the government was not sufficiently brave to set the prices of pharmaceutical raw materials.[91] While it must be acknowledged that Permadi's highly outspoken style was a major factor in the YLK's not having been included in the deliberations on the question of drug prices, it nonetheless remains a striking fact that the bodies which were invited to participate in negotiations were all involved in the production or delivery of drugs and health services rather than their consumption. In other words, there was no formal mechanism for the articulation of consumer interests into the policy formation process beyond the *de facto* role of the media in acting as a conduit for the expression of these sorts of interests.

The scope for participation by the YLK increased in October 1986 when Permadi was succeeded as head by Erna Witoelar. While not as abrasive as Permadi, she nonetheless had a reputation for being a strong figure in non-governmental organisation circles. It was hoped that with the replacement of Permadi by Witoelar, the YLK might achieve greater political access as a result of her sophisticated approach to government. This expectation was ultimately borne out with the invitation in early November for the YLK to join the PPKPHO and participate as a panelist in a special forum on drug prices on 10 November.[92]

Here again, however, the potential for policy inputs by the YLK on the drug price issue was severely circumscribed. As was noted in the press at the time, YLK's inclusion was not likely to have any real bearing on policy recommendations by the PPKPHO, as these had been already determined. YLK Secretary, Tini Hadad, was quoted as saying that it seemed that their inclusion was merely a formality, intended only to promote the impression that consumer interests were in fact being represented. She went on to complain that the YLK should have been included from the beginning, and in passing, also offered thinly veiled criticism of GPF in noting that it had appeared to be continuously on the defensive over the price issue.[93]

In a telling revelation quoted in the press, Drug Control Director, Slamet Soesilo, who headed the PPKPHO, said that had the YLK been included any earlier in the consultative process it would have simply sidetracked discussions by talking nonsense. He went on to suggest that while the PPKPHO had already finalised its position, there was still scope for the YLK to contribute at the 10 November forum.[94]

Clearly then, the YLK's ability to make positive inputs into policy formation on the drug issue was limited. In spite of this, it was able to contribute, via the press, to an increase in the clamour for serious attention to be given to the matter. This was not insignificant, as indeed was suggested by the wariness of the major actors towards the YLK. Nevertheless, the fact remains that its influence was only indirect. Furthermore, it should not be forgotten that the YLK's eleventh hour inclusion in the PPKPHO seems to have been largely the result of a journalist having pressed Midian Sirait on the matter at a public press conference, and then subsequently reporting Sirait's ambivalence.[95] The press, or more accurately the few key journalists who set the agenda, were the most important countervailing force (apart from the pressure from the President and Health Minister) with which GPF and the Directorate General for Drug and Food Control had to contend. Midian Sirait acknowledged this indirectly when he publicly thanked the press for its role in the drug price issue and for supporting societal aspirations to have medicines made more affordable.[96]

All the various organised interests that were involved in the drug issue came together under one roof at the 10 November forum organised by the PPKPHO. The Health Department, GPF, IDI, PDGI, ISFI, YLK and even the press (represented by *Kompas*'s Irwan Julianto) participated in the open panel. As already hinted though, the event was mostly a formality. The forum represented the culmination of the PPKPHO Committee's meetings over the period since its formation in August. The Committee produced a list of broad suggestions for the Health Department on how the price problem might be tackled. There was, however, no coherence in this as each of the different groups put forward ideas that were consistent with its own interests and placed the onus for reform on the other groups. The meeting did not result in any changes being made to the DOPB program.

GPF was, not surprisingly, pleased with the way in which it had managed to turn a potentially disastrous situation for the pharmaceutical industry into a minor victory. While the political pressure for action on drug prices abated somewhat from its peak in August–September, it continued to receive steady media attention into 1987—the basic problem, after all, still remained. In April the DOBP program was expanded from the original Jakarta area pilot project to embrace the capital cities of all provinces in Indonesia. But as GPF had expected, the extent to which the DOPB drugs were actually used was not great. A survey conducted by the government-controlled news agency Antara suggested that in Jakarta, at least, dispensaries were receiving on average merely ten to fifteen prescriptions for DOPB drugs per month.[97] At that rate the pharmaceutical industry clearly had nothing to fear. Despite the persistence of a poor public relations image, prospects for the industry had begun to improve considerably with the receding of the immediate threat of price regulatory measures. It was at this time also, it may be recalled, that GPF was able to announce to its membership that the IHO system of publishing price levels had finally been abandoned by the Health Department.

A Sting in the Tail

What was for the pharmaceutical industry a generally more benign situation was dramatically interrupted in June, however, when, to the complete amazement of virtually everyone in the health services sector, Health Minister Suwardjono unilaterally decreed that henceforth pharmaceutical companies would be prohibited from producing the drug samples traditionally provided to doctors.[98] Indonesia thus became one of the very few countries in the world where drug samples were not permitted. The decree seems to have been intended to be another step towards inducing downwards pressure on medicine prices. This reflected the perception in some quarters that promotional costs by drug companies were one of the factors underlying high prices which could be reduced.[99] In addition to the belief that samples contributed unnecessarily to high prices, there was also a widely held view that they were representative of unethical promotional practices by pharmaceutical companies. This was because the samples provided to doctors—ostensibly to introduce new products to them—were in fact a form of material incentive, as apparently doctors frequently sold them to patients or drug sellers on the open market, thereby receiving a substantial windfall gain. In announcing the decree, Suwardjono said that samples had diverged too far from their original purpose, and that in future pharmaceutical companies could promote their products by distributing brochures or convening seminars to outline the chemical properties of their new products.[100]

It seems clear that this decision emanated not from Midian Sirait and the Directorate General for Drug and Food Control, but from the very top of the health bureaucracy, the Minister himself. It appears that there was little consultation with Sirait on the matter, if only because the measure was extremely unlikely to achieve its intended aims and because the pharmaceutical industry was strongly opposed to it. It is likely that had the idea been Sirait's initiative, there would have been some prior discussion with GPF on the matter. As drug manufacturers argued in the press (and in interviews) it was ridiculous to believe that eliminating samples would bring down prices. Promotional activity was inevitable in a competitive market, and samples were in fact one of the cheapest forms.

Other forms of information dissemination (and material incentives for doctors) would just be more expensive. That promotional activity would nevertheless continue, was certain. In terms of eliminating unethical practices, the move was a complete failure. According to industry sources, the use of material incentives *worsened* after the banning of samples. The move was further regarded as ill-conceived because the chief losers from it would be not so much the pharmaceutical companies (they would inevitably find other promotional avenues and pass on the cost to consumers), but the armies of detailmen, or sales representatives, that they employed. These were the people who visited doctors on a regular basis seeking to promote their companies' products by providing information, samples and other inducements. The Health Minister's decree placed their jobs in immediate jeopardy.[101] Indeed, discontent among the sales representative personnel, estimated at some 3,000 in Jakarta alone, was so high that they contemplated industrial action by convening a mass meeting to consider their plight in the wake of the new regulation.[102]

While pharmaceutical companies, and particularly their sales representatives, opposed the move, the YLK and the leadership of IDI openly applauded. It is less clear, however, that the sanguine attitude of Dr Kartono and the IDI leadership was shared by the rank and file of doctors, a significant proportion of whom would presumably lose special supplements to their incomes.

It is unclear what Health Minister Suwardjono hoped to achieve by this move. Some speculated that the action was stimulated by a desire to demonstrate (not least to the President) that he was capable of taking decisive action to address a problem. Whatever his motives, his timing certainly left everyone perplexed, for the intense controversy of late 1986 had abated. Almost as if to underline the inability of Suwardjono's initiative to lower price, prices of many drugs rose by up to fifteen per cent very soon after. The reasons for the increase, were in fact, more complex, but they served to discredit the banning of samples. When questioned on this by reporters after he emerged from a meeting with the President in July, Suwardjono would only say that the DOPB program needed to be promoted further, and that doctors and dispensaries needed to be 'encouraged' to support it.[103]

For present purposes, the significance of the banning of drug samples was that it showed that while GPF was often able to achieve much of what it wanted by careful lobbying and bargaining with the Directorate General for Drug and Food Control, there was little it could do, at least in the short term, if senior government figures moved decisively. Access to one part of the state-apparatus did not ensure access to another, even though closely linked. As an aside, it nicely illustrates the diversity of interests which operate even within this relatively narrow area of the state: Suwardjono was quite pre-pared to intervene in pharmaceutical affairs, over the top of Sirait, to satisfy his own purposes.

It is interesting to note that in July, in the wake of the prohibition of samples, GPF, apparently not content with its normal low profile approach to the task of persuading policy-makers, took the unusually bold step of sending Cabinet Secretary, Murdiono, an unsolicited submission for the 1988 State Policy Guidelines document (the earlier mentioned GBHN).[104] The letter was a detailed argument concerning the conditions necessary for the future prosperity of the pharmaceutical industry in particular, and the Indonesian economy in general. The outstanding feature of the letter was a sentence in its conclusion to the effect that it was essential for the government to recognise that apart from having 'social dimensions', the pharma-ceutical industry was an enterprise which was governed ineluctablely by the laws of economics. Registered copies of this letter were also sent to, among others, the head of BAPPENAS, the Coordinating Minister for Economic Affairs, the State Secretary, the Minister for Research and Technology, the Minister for Industry, and the Minis-ter for Health.

GPF's letter was a very conspicuous statement of dissatisfaction with the ideological orientation of the Health Department towards the pharmaceutical industry. It was a clear assertion of an argument for the minimisation of state intervention in business affairs. But beyond this, the remarkable thing about the exercise was that it stepped outside the normal channels of communication between Eddie Lembong and Midian Sirait and went instead right over the top of the Health Department's head to the Cabinet Secretary. Following Health Minister Suwardjono's intervention, stronger tactics were needed. This was an extraordinary move and seems to suggest an increased willingness on the part of GPF to push much harder to bring about a policy environment more compatible with industry interests.

Conclusion

What significance does this case-study have for our broader theoreti-cal concerns? Let us start by looking at the main elements in the story. By mid-1986, the beginning of our episode, there was already a long-standing debate over the price of drugs in Indonesia. In the immediately preceding years, the Directorate General for Drug and Food Control had on a number of occasions introduced measures attempting to reduce pharmaceutical prices. None, however, had succeeded more than temporarily. In August 1986 there was a sudden flare-up of the controversy which was fanned vigorously by the press. The controversy became so intense that not only was the Minister involved, but also on a number of occasions, the President, who was reportedly disturbed by the broader implications of any popular resentment that might arise over drug prices in the period leading up to a general election. The Director General, Midian Sirait, came under intense pressure to do something to resolve the problem. Correspondingly, there was extreme concern within the pharmaceutical industry that some form of price control might be introduced as Sirait cast about for a rapid solution. In a bid to avoid such an outcome, GPF encouraged Sirait to move down a policy avenue that adequately met both his minimum needs and those of the pharmaceutical industry. Thus it was that the DOPB scheme was born, and was subsequently presented as an innovative cooperative venture designed to make cheap medicine readily available. In reality, though, DOPB was never likely to have more than a temporary and sporadic effect on the price of drugs. It did, however, succeed admirably in resolving the immediate problems of both the Health Department and the pharmaceutical industry.

As in the textile case, we again see the press playing a very important role. The impact of the press was so clear that senior officials appealed explicitly for a minimisation of critical press coverage. The press thus served as something of a countervailing influence to that of the two other major players, the Health Department and the pharmaceutical industry. Interestingly, we see the press and Committee VIII of the Parliament functioning not just as mouthpieces for other interests, but also as independent participants. *Kompas* journalist, Irwan Julianto, consciously pushed the question of drug prices to a position high on the political agenda in August –September 1986.[105] The Parliament was a less influential force than the media, serving largely as a forum of the weak. Yet its activities were not without significance; pronouncements in the Parliament were noticed. Also very definitely noticed were the pronouncements of the IDI leadership. The status of IDI as a respected professional association ensured that it would be heard. Interestingly, however, although IDI was successful in helping to promote arguments for attention to high drug prices, this was not a cause which all of its membership would have supported. The YLK although largely excluded from formal participation in the development of the DOPB, also contributed in a manner similar to IDI. The irony of this case is that, with all these various actors participating in some form or other in the debate about drug prices, the poor, in whose interests the whole issue was ostensibly being debated, were almost wholly uninvolved. They participated, if at all, only vicariously through the indirect utterances and actions of self-appointed spokespeople such as the Health Department, the press, the Parliament, IDI and the YLK. Contained in almost all of the rhetoric was the notion that the well-being of the poor was of paramount concern. This is the sort of phenomenon that Liddle had in mind when he argued that the interests of the weak in Indonesia are sometimes taken up in policy deliberations without their direct involvement.

One of the aims of this chapter has been to cast light upon the processes of interest representation and policy formation in a particular issue area. The case-study has shown a part of the state apparatus, the Directorate General for Drug and Food Control, and a section of industry, the drug manufacturers, cooperating to deal with an immediate and pressing political problem, even though their underlying interests were almost diametrically opposed. Despite their differences, the two came together in a tactical alliance which had a crucial bearing on the policy process. As in the study on the textile industry, then, we again see that policy formation is not monopolised by the state; the reality is more subtle, involving a blend of conflict and cooperation between both state and societal actors. In addition to the major players, the press had a significant impact upon the conflict, and institutions such as the Parliament, IDI and the YLK all contributed to the public debate on medicine prices. In short, the picture which emerges here suggests that policy formation is considerably more complex than the conventional state-centred interpretations of Indonesian politics would indicate.

Particular consideration must also be given to the role and character of GPF. One notable feature of GPF's operations were the 'behind-the-scenes' personal links between Eddie Lembong and Midian Sirait. However, to present this case as just another example of patrimonialism would be to abuse an otherwise valuable concept. Their relationship was not patrimonial: the two men had roughly equal standing. More generally, one of the most important aspects of GPF's behaviour is that, as with SEKBERTAL, it was group-based. It was an organisation striving for collective rather than particularistic benefits.

But if GPF does not appear to be an essentially patrimonialist phenomenon, it certainly does display a number of characteristic corporatist features. Membership is compulsory, it is the sole recognised representative body for the pharmaceutical sector, and it is the conduit for almost all communication between industry and the state. And yet, the pharmaceutical industry has carved out much more independence of operation for itself than one might expect. Like SEKBERTAL and FITI, GPF has a relationship with the state which sets it apart from the prevailing pattern of corporatist arrangements in Indonesia. Rather than functioning to limit or obstruct political participation by drug producers as might normally be expected, GPF has in fact continually struggled to ensure that industry interests are effectively projected into the policy process. One respect in which the situation in the pharmaceutical industry differs from that in the textile industry, is that whereas the spinners were forced to break away from API in a dramatic way in order to achieve better political representation, drug manufacturers have worked in a more incremental way, gradually turning GPF to serve their interests rather than those of the state.

The argument that GPF is a vigorous and effective representational organ requires some qualification, however, for GPF does not serve all of its industry constituents equally well. Local manufacturers, for example, appear to benefit more from GPF than do foreign companies. While foreign producers do derive considerable benefit from GPF representation (as, indeed, this very case illustrates), they tend to suffer when their interests diverge far from those of local manufacturers. Similarly, GPF as a whole seems to operate rather more effectively for manufacturers in general, than it does for the smaller sections within the organisation, the distributors, dispensaries and drug stores. Thus, it should be acknowledged that the corporatist framework that exists in the pharmaceutical field does operate to limit the potential for interest articulation by these weaker groups. In sum, it seems that the pharmaceutical producers (especially local ones), being large, well organised and determined, have been able to twist the corporatist representational structure to their advantage, while the smaller business interests in the other sections of GPF, and perhaps the foreign drug manufacturers, have been more restricted.

The very effective representation afforded the pharmaceutical industry by GPF is one of the outstanding features of this case. For this reason, it is worth pausing to consider why this section of the business community should be so well endowed in political terms. A number of factors can be adduced to account for this. First, the pharmaceutical industry is fairly cohesive. This cohesiveness has several sources. One is the fact that many of the heads of the local drug companies have known each other for many years. Another is the high degree of geographical concentration of pharmaceutical plants in Java, and especially around Jakarta. Both of these factors lead to a relatively high level of intra-industry interaction. More generally, a factor which applies to foreign and local companies alike, is the indefinable sense of neurosis or even paranoia of the pharmaceutical industry, which somehow seems to incline drug manufacturers to band together for common protection. Put differently, there appears to be a sense of common vulnerability which inclines the pharmaceutical industry to operate in concert on matters of shared concern.[106] Arguably, the fact that all but one of the local producers are Chinese reinforces this tendency. These various elements all combine to constitute an unusually cohesive industry in so far as self-preservation is concerned.[107]

A second factor contributing to GPF's success, is the comparatively sophisticated and educated nature of the industry's leadership, with a great many company heads being university trained. It seems reasonable to assume that this enhanced the pharmaceutical industry's capacity to promote its collective interests. A third factor, and one of special importance, is the overwhelming preponderance of private ownership within the pharmaceutical industry. Unlike many other industries in Indonesia, the market-share of state-controlled enterprises is not great in drug manufacturing. Widespread private ownership appears to have inclined the industry to be more active and determined in asserting its interests. It was apparent, for example, that the state-controlled firms, even though members of GPF, were less willing to push the Health Department (to which, it must be remembered, they were answerable). Closely linked with this ownership factor is a fourth—the intensely competitive nature of the pharmaceutical industry. The fact that the industry was so highly competitive and individual market shares so small—particularly in a time of economic contraction—served to further promote industry assertiveness. Threats to industry profitability became a driving motive.

A direct product of this amalgam of factors—cohesiveness, educated leadership, predominance of private ownership and intense competition—was that the pharmaceutical industry demanded high standards of leadership from its representative organisation. Hence Eddie Lembong's position was far from a merely formal one. Most of his time was devoted to GPF affairs, rather than those of his own company. He was accountable to his membership, and could readily be replaced via the regular leadership ballots. All of this served to make GPF an organisation that was finely attuned to the interests of its constituency, and vigorous in pursuing these in dealings with the state. GPF is certainly not always successful in winning the concessions it seeks from the government, however, when its considerable organisational resources are combined with an industry-wide sense of urgency, or determination on a particular issue, it can be a formidable force.

Much emphasis has been given to GPF's tendency to adopt a low profile, non-confrontational approach in its political activities. While this has certainly been the case in recent years, there are signs that it is coming to adopt a more assertive and self-confident style. A striking example of this was GPF's decision in July 1987 to send a submission for the State Policy Guidelines document (the GBHN) to the Cabinet Secretary. More generally, it is clear that Eddie Lembong was actively committed to improving the pharmaceutical industry's poor public image, and to promoting a greater understanding of the particular problems and constraints confronting it. In pursuing these objectives, Lembong planned to make greater use of the press and the Parliament to better promote pharmaceutical industry interests.[108]

Several reasons can be offered to explain this possible trend towards greater assertiveness by GPF. One conspicuous factor is the harsher economic environment of the mid-1980s. Declining sales and profit margins have forced the industry to become more assertive. As will be discussed later, intertwined with the economic down-turn has been a greater receptivity to calls for economic liberalisation and promotion of business needs. Calls for the granting of more leeway to the private sector are increasingly common. A factor encouraging greater assertiveness by GPF is what Eddie Lembong refers to as the demands of the new generation of company heads within the pharmaceutical industry.[109] Younger proprietors and managers are apparently impatient with the low profile approach to interest representation which has characterised GPF's activities in the past.

The pharmaceutical industry's self-doubts will not recede quickly. GPF is unlikely in the foreseeable future to adopt the strident approach of SEKBERTAL. Nevertheless, it does seem that GPF— already a remarkably successful business association—is likely to become more open in its efforts to secure what it regards as a satisfactory policy environment.

1. Trythall (1977) p. 38.
2. For details on the relative sophistication of national pharmaceutical industries, see United Nations Centre on Transnational Corporations (1984).
3. Though this study is concerned only with the modern pharmaceutical industry, it should be noted that there is also a growing 'traditional' medicine industry. In recent years some producers of traditional medicines have established large and modern mass-production facilities. Between 1971 and 1986, the value of traditional medicine production grew from Rp. 3.1 billion (US$ 7.4 million) to Rp. 43.8 billion (US$ 34.1 million), with the number of producers rising from 176 to 343. For

further details, see 'Obat Tradisional Berpeluang Menjadi Alternatif Pengobatan', *Kompas*, 5 July 1988.

4. Statistics for the pharmaceutical industry are notoriously difficult to obtain. The Department of Health has no systematic data covering the whole industry, and the estimates normally used are those produced annually by a Singapore-based consultancy company which regularly surveys drug manufacturers and retailers. The company, IMS (Index of Medical Specialties) Pty Ltd, compiles a variety of publications, the most important of which, for present purposes, is the *Indonesian Pharmaceutical Audit*. The information contained in it is guarded very carefully, as the publication is extremely expensive and affordable to only the largest companies. It is thought that all these statistics have an error margin of at least ± 10 per cent. One conspicuous factor mitigating against reliable statistics is that the data on the activities and production patterns of the numerous small scale producers is almost non-existent.

5. These figures are drawn from an address by the Vice-Chairman of GPF & President Director of Pharos Indonesia Pty Ltd, Eddie Lembong (1987).

6. See Wanandi (1987) p. 24; and the report, 'Pelaksanaan Pengadaan dan Produksi Obat s/d Tahun Keempat Pelita III', *Varia Farmasi*, (Jakarta), vol. 46, no. 5 1983, p. 8. The precise value of production by the few state-owned plants is not certain. The figure usually cited is 5 per cent, though it may reach up to almost 10 per cent.

7. Interview with Hanz Rivai (former Sales Director of Wigo Pty Ltd), 12 August 1987.

8. Basically, transfer pricing involves the repatriation of profit from the subsidiary of a transnational corporation back to the parent company. This is done to avoid payment of taxation and other royalties in the subsidiary's host country. So, for example, a subsidiary might buy raw materials for drug manufacture from its parent company at inflated prices as a means of transferring revenue out of the host country. For a more detailed consideration of the issue of transfer pricing by transnational drug manufacturers operating in developing countries, see the valuable study by Gereffi (1983), especially pp. 193–8.

9. The term 'foreign company' is used instead of 'joint venture' in this chapter so as to avoid possible confusion with licensed manufacturers.

10. Interviews with David Ojerholm (General Manager of Boehringer Ingelheim Pty Ltd & Vice Chairman of the International Pharmaceutical Manufacturers' Group—IPMG) 12 August 1987; and Ron Young (Managing Director of Burroughs Wellcome Pty Ltd & Chairman of the IPMG) 7 September 1987. Both of these restrictions were very unpopular with foreign companies. The former because the development of raw materials for drug manufacture is very costly and unrewarding in Indonesia (they much preferred to import all ingredients), and the latter because distribution was a large factor in a drug's price structure. For discussion of the problems associated with the requirement to produce a raw material see Trythall (1977) p. 40.

11. For a very useful summary of the overall situation in the pharmaceutical industry internationally, see Wyke A., 'Pharmaceuticals: Harder Going' (special survey), *The Economist*, 7 February 1987 pp. 3–18.

12. For a broader consideration of the problem of drug costs in developing countries see, Gereffi (1983), and the United Nations Centre on Transnational Corporations (1984).

13. For further details, see the address by the Special Adviser to the Health Minister, Biantoro Wanandi (1987) p. 22.

14. Questions will, naturally, arise about the source of this data, but given that it was compiled, not by the industry itself, but by the Singapore Regional Office of IMS (Index of Medical Specialties Pty Ltd) it can be treated as an independent assessment. (IMS operates throughout Southeast Asia and Australia, and is thus not tied just to Indonesia.)

15. The distribution, or wholesale network in Indonesia is generally regarded as very inefficient because of the massive number of drug distributors (over 900) which must share the market. This has meant that economies of scale have remained elusive. (In the Philippines, for example, there are only about half a dozen distributors). One reason for the huge number of distributors is that in the past many licences were granted to retiring military figures to provide them with a source of income. This has made rationalisation of the industry difficult. Interview with Biantoro Wanandi (Special Adviser to the Health Minister & President Director of Anugerah Pharmindo Lestari Pty Ltd—a major drug distributor) 24 August 1987.

16. In the absense of systematic microeconomic analysis, this assertion can only be supported with circumstantial evidence. Certainly, for instance, declining profit margins were a constant refrain in producer circles. More pointedly, the highly competitive and fragmented nature of the pharmaceutical market, together with the fact that none of the major business groups associated with 'rent-taking' practices in Indonesia have so far been attracted to the pharmaceutical industry, all seem to point in the direction of profitability not being especially high. By contrast, some of the support industries linked to drug manufacturing, such as capsule production, are marked by monopolistic trade regulations and do seem to be very profitable. This is reflected in the fact that Bambang Trihatmodjo has entered into partnership with Wim Kalona via Kapsulindo Pty Ltd. Similar operations are Liem Soe Liong's Gelatino Pty Ltd and General (Ret.) Sumitro's Ria Sima Pty Ltd.

17. For background on this, see Marsyaid Yushar (1981) p. 9.

18. Compulsory membership was first introduced by the former Director General for Drug and Food Control, Sunarto Prawirosujanto (who is now head for KADIN's Multifarious Industry, Small Industry and Pharmaceutical Industry Section). Interview, 5 September 1987. The extension of this to include foreign firms was introduced by his successor, Midian Sirait.

19. Interviews with Ron Young (Managing Director of Burroughs Wellcome

Pty Ltd & Chairman of the IPMG) & 7 September 1987; David Ojerholm (Managing Director Boehringer Ingelheim Pty Ltd & Vice Chairman of the IPMG) 12 August 1987; J.W. Sudomo (President Director of Squibb Pty Ltd & member of IPMG Executive) 10 August 1987; Slamet Soesilo (Director for Drug Control, Department of Health) 7 September 1987; and Soekaryo (Secretary General, Department of Health) 4 September 1987.

20. This problem was highlighted with the recent move to introduce a legislative basis for intellectual property rights protection in Indonesia. Foreign drug companies were extremely anxious that such a law cover the pharmaceutical industry (and not just, for example, the music industry) as they were the ones who developed the new drugs. Local companies were naturally opposed to this, and supported by the Department of Health, they succeeded in ensuring that the new law (of June 1988) did not embrace pharmaceutical products.

21. Interviews with Eddie Lembong, 31 July, 21 August and 9 September 1987. It should be noted in this context that Eddie Lembong comes from North Sulawesi where, by his own admission, the status of Chinese Indonesians is considerably better than in other parts of Indonesia. This may be an important ingredient in his cultural self-confidence and out-spokeness. Also to be noted here is that, although Eddie Lembong was the Head of the Manufacturing Section, the Deputy Chairman of all GPF and the driving force behind the organisation, the actual Chairman and formal head of GPF, Amir Basir (head of the state-owned Indofarma) was a *pribumi*.

22. Interview with Slamet Soesilo (Director of Drug Control, Department of Health) 7 September 1987.

23. Interviews with, for example, Eddie Lembong, 9 September 1987 and Wim Kalona (President Director of Wigo Pty Ltd) 2 September 1987.

24. Interview with David Ojerholm (Managing Director of Boehringer Ingelheim Pty Ltd & Vice Chairman of IPMG) 12 August 1987.

25. Interview with Eddie Lembong, 21 August 1987.

26. Interviews with Eddie Lembong, 31 July 1987, and 21 August 1987.

27. More recently, this has come under pressure with the Health Department apparently giving consideration to the possibility of taking over the administration of all doctor registration requirements. See 'IDI-Depkes: Retak Berat?', *Tempo*, 24 October 1987.

28. Interviews with Dr Kartono Muhammad (Head of IDI), 28 July 1987; and Jimmy Supangkat (Health Editor of *Tempo*), 29 July 1987.

29. Interviews with Erna Witoelar (President of the YLK) 15 August 1987; and Tini Hadad (Secretary of the YLK) 18 August 1987.

30. Interviews with Permadi (former President of the YLK) 24 May 1986; Erna Witoelar (current President of the YLK) 15 August 1987; and Aswab Mahasin (Director of the LP3ES) 14 February 1988.

31. Erna Witoelar's husband, Rachmat Witoelar, is a very senior GOLKAR figure. She was in the same Socialist Party circles as Midian Sirait in Bandung in the early 1960s.

32. See for example, 'Menguji Cemaran Radioaktif Pada Susu Bubuk Di Indonesia', *Kompas*, 28 June 1987; and, 'Pengusaha Berhati-hatilah', *Kompas*, 16 July 1987.
33. Interview with Mrs. Legowo (Committee VIII leadership, GOLKAR *fraksi*) 31 August 1987.
34. Interviews with Mrs. Legowo (Committee VIII leadership, GOLKAR *fraksi*) 31 August 1987; Djoko Sudjatmiko (Committee VI leadership, GOLKAR *fraksi*) 6 June 1987; and Slamet Soesilo (Director for Drug Control) 7 September 1987.
35. Interview with Dr Frans Tshai (Director of Pharmaceutical Policy & Public Affairs, Ciba-Geigy Pty Ltd), 13 August 1987.
36. For an interesting study of the same basic problem in a European setting, see Sargent (1985); while for a useful general overview of the main themes on this subject see the special issue 'Another Development in Pharmaceuticals', *Development Dialogue*, (Uppsala, Sweden) vol. 2, 1985.
37. 'Obat-Obatan Murah Dibuat Oleh Pabrik-Pabrik Milik Depkes', *Berita Yudha*, 20 November 1978.
38. 'Jangan Coba-Coba Menghilangkan Obat-Obatan Dari Pasaran', *Antara*, 23 November 1978.
39. 'Harga Obat-Obatan Diturunkan Seperti Sebelum Kebijaksanaan 15 November', *Sinar Harapan*, 27 November 1978.
40. 'Pemerintah Akan Mencabut Ijin Produksi Obatnya', *Berita Buana*, 6 January 1979, and 'Mungkin Dilarang, Jika Produsen Obat Tidak Serahkan Kalkulasi Harga', *Kompas*, 19 January 1979. As well as drug costs, the committee also looked into the prices of medical instruments.
41. Interview with J.W. Sudomo (President Director of Squibb Pty Ltd & member of the IPMG Executive), 10 August 1987.
42. 'Diturunkan Harga Obat "Kimia Farma"', *Kompas*, 22 November 1978, and 'Depkes Akan Tentukan Bahan-Baku Obat Yang Boleh Diproduksi', *Kompas*, 18 December 1978.
43. WHO (1977) and (1979).
44. 'Mungkin Dilarang, Jika Produsen Obat Tidak Serahkan Kalkulasi Harga', *Kompas*, 19 January 1979.
45. 'Pemerintah Akan Memproduksi Obat Pokok', *Kompas*, 30 January 1979.
46. For a summary of this see The GPF Executive's *Laporan Umum* for 1978–81 p. 4.
47. 'Pemerintah Sedang Kampanyekan Penyebutan Generik Saja Dalam Penjualan Obat-Obat Di Apotik-Apotik', *Antara*, 5 October 1979.
48. See the GPF Executive's *Laporan Umum* for 1978–81, p. 18.
49. The key elements were Health Minister Suwardjono's Ministerial Instructions no. 389/Men.Kes/Per/X/80 (9 October 1980) & no. 394/Men.Kes/X/80 (11 October 1980), together with his Ministerial Decree no. 3433/A/SK/80 (11 November 1980) and Governmental Regulation PP no. 25/1980.
50. 'Para Dokter Lebih Suka Menulis Resep Obat Merek Tertentu', *Antara*, 14 January 1982.

51. '95 per cent Pengadaan Obat Dikuasai Usaha Swasta', *Antara*, 8 August 1982.
52. Interview with Professor Iwan Darmansyah (Professor of Pharmacy at the University of Indonesia, and adviser to the Health Department on the DOEN), 28 July 1987; and Dr Kartono Muhamad (Chairman of the Indonesian Doctors Association—IDI), 28 July 1987.
53. Interviews with, for example, Eddie Lembong, 31 July 1987; J.W. Sudomo (President Director of Squibb Pty Ltd & member of the IPMG Executive) 10 August 1987; Dr Frans Tshai (Director of Pharmaceutical Policy & Public Affairs for Ciba Geigy Pty Ltd) 13 August 1987; and Irwan Julianto (health reporter for *Kompas*) 8 August 1987.
54. 'Semua Dokter Akan Peroleh Buku Informasi Harga Obat', *Suara Karya*, 22 June 1983.
55. See, 'Daftar Kenaikan Harga Obat', *Kompas*, 19 January 1984.
56. Interviews with J.W. Sudomo (President Director of Squibb Pty Ltd & member of the IPMG Executive) 10 August 1987 and Eddie Lembong, 9 September 1987. The details of the regulatory change can be located in the circular letter of 5 February 1985 from the GPF executive to all members published in *Varia Farmasi*, no. 57, January–February 1985, p. 37.
57. GPF letter no. 03.001/PP.APT/1987, 12 March 1987.
58. 'Daftar Hitam Di Tengah Banjir Obat Dan Komisi', *Tempo*, 4 August 1984, pp. 63–7.
59. 'Segitiga Emas Obat Muncul Di Indonesia', *Suara Karya*, 26–30 November 1984. The series actually provides a very useful overview of the whole issue of drug prices.
60. 'Mahalnya Harga Obat Mendapat Sorotan DPR', *Suara Karya*, 6 December 1984.
61. 'Depkes Akan Produksi 34 Macam Obat Amat Esensial Tahun Ini', *Kompas*, 25 April 1985.
62. Interviews with various pharmaceutical industry figures who requested anonymity.
63. Interviews with Soekaryo (Secretary General of the Health Department) 4 September 1987; Slamet Soesilo (Director for Drug Control in the Health Department) 7 September 1987; and Mrs Lewogo (Committee VIII leadership, GOLKAR *fraksi*) 31 August 1987.
64. 'DPR Diminta Jembatani Tingginya Harga Obat', *Merdeka*, 21 May 1985.
65. 'Pemerintah Akan Impor Obat Apabila Harga Obat Produksi Dalam Negeri Lebih Mahal', *Antara*, 29 May 1985.
66. 'Obat Paten Dan Generik, Khasiat Sama Harga Jauh Berbeda', *Antara*, 15 November 1985.
67. 'Low Domestic Consumption Causes High Drug Prices', *Jakarta Post*, 10 December 1985.
68. Interviews with Eddie Lembong, 21 August & 9 September 1987; and Slamet Soesilo (Director for Drug Control) 7 September 1987.
69. 'Presiden Instruksikan Agar Depkes Meneliti Harga Obat', *Suara Karya*, 11 July 1986.
70. For reference to the remarks by Dr Kartono Muhamad and Soekaryo see

'Harga Obat-Obat Di Indonesia Terkenal Paling Mahal Di Dunia', *Berita Buana*, 25 August 1986, and 'Hangat, Masalah Harga Obat', *Kompas*, 30 August 1986.

71. 'Menkes Imbau Masyarakat Agar Tidak Terkecoh Dengan Merek Obat', *Pelita*, 14 August 1986.

72. Interviews with Sunarto Prawirosujanto (former Director General for Drug and Food Control, Special Adviser to the the Health Minister, and head of the KADIN Sections for Multifarious Industry, Small Industry and Pharmaceutical Industry) 21 May 1987.

73. Interview with Slamet Soesilo (Director for Drug Control) 7 September 1987.

74. Interviews with, for example, Anton Sunaryo (Vice-President of Kenrose Pty Ltd) 7 September 1987; and Sigit Nugraha (Director of Bintang Toedjoe Pty Ltd) 2 September 1987.

75. See, for example, 'Ekonomi Biaya Tinggi Biang Mahalnya Harga Obat', *Kompas*, 2 September 1986; 'Ketua IDI Tentang Harga Obat: Pemerintah Perlu Atur Batas Keuntungan Jalur Distribusi', *Kompas*, 3 September 1986; and 'Biaya Pemasaran Dominasi Harga Obat', *Merdeka*, 4 September 1986.

76. 'Hangat, Masalah Harga Obat', *Kompas*, 30 August 1986.

77. 'Depkes Bentuk Panitia Untuk Teliti Harga Obat', *Kompas*, 4 September 1986. There was some confusion surrounding the precise name of PPKPHO Committee, with several different combinations of initials circulating.

78. See, for example, 'Biaya Pemasaran Dominasi Harga Obat', *Merdeka*, 4 September 1986.

79. Interviews with Eddie Lembong, 31 July, 21 August & 9 September 1987.

80. See, for example, the editorial 'Tingginya Harga Obat', *Sinar Harapan*, 1 September 1986; and, 'Depkes Bentuk Panitia Untuk Teliti Harga Obat', *Kompas*, 4 September 1986.

81. Interviews with Eddie Lembong 31 July and 9 September 1987.

82. 'Harga 80 Jenis Obat Esensial Akan Dikontrol Pemerintah', *Kompas*, 16 September 1986.

83. 'Mulai 1 Oktober Berlaku Resep Murah Di Dokter Praktek Jakarta', *Suara Karya*, 22 September 1986.

84. 'Bangsa Indonesia Terlalu Dicekoki Promosi Obat', *Kompas*, 26 September 1986.

85. This general initial anxiety among the rank and file of the pharmaceutical industry was mentioned in interviews by numerous producers. For instance, interviews with Sigit Nugraha (Director of Bintang Toedjoe Pty Ltd) 2 September 1987; Con Sradaputta (Marketing Director of Ciba-Geigy Pty Ltd) 19 August 1987; and Anton Sunaryo (Executive Vice-President of Kenrose Pty Ltd) 7 September 1987.

86. See, 'Masyarakat Dilayani "Resep Khusus" Untuk Bisa Memperoleh Obat Murat', *Pelita*, 30 September 1986; and, 'Program Bersama Obat Murah Bermutu Dimulai', *Kompas*, 1 October 1986.

87. For reference to Dr Kartono's querying of this, see 'Harga 80 Jenis Obat

Esensial Akan Dikontrol Pemerintah', *Kompas*, 16 September 1986.
88. For discussion of these points, I am grateful to Dr Kartono Muhamad (Head of IDI) 28 July 1987; Jim Supangkat (*Tempo* health editor) 29 July 1987) and Irwan Julianto (*Kompas* health writer) 23 July 1987.
89. Interview with Eddie Lembong, 21 August 1987.
90. See, 'Konsumen Akan Masuk Panitia Pengkajian Penggunaan Obat', *Kompas*, 22 September 1986.
91. 'Pemerintah Tak Berani Tetapkan Harga Bahan Baku Obat', *Berita Buana*, 27 September 1986.
92. Interviews with Permadi (24 May 1986) and Erna Witoelar (15 August 1986).
93. 'YLK Diundang Setelah Rumusan Rampung', *Kompas*, 4 November 1986.
94. 'YLK Diundang Setelah Rumusan Rampung', *Kompas*, 4 November 1986.
95. 'Konsumen Akan Masuk Panitia Pengkajian Penggunaan Obat', *Kompas* 22 September 1986.
96. See, 'Dirjen POM Terima Kasih Kepada Pers', *Prioritas*, 13 October 1986.
97. 'Pelayanan Obat Murah Di Apotik Belum Banyak Peminatnya', *Antara*, 1 July 1987.
98. Ministerial Decree no. 437/Menkes/SK/VI/1987, 11 June 1987.
99. See 'Menkes: Obat Murah Terpojok Karena Tak Didukung Promosi', *Sinar Harapan*, 25 September 1986; and 'SK Menkes Diharapkan Turunkan Harga Obat, "Detailmen" Kaget', *Suara Karya*, 13 June 1987.
100. 'Menkes Larang Produksi Contoh Obat', *Kompas*, 12 June 1987.
101. '"Sample" Hilang, Komisi Tetap Terbilang', *Kompas*, 17 June 1987.
102. See, 'Pancaroba Moral Dan Mental Masih Pengaruhi "Detailer"', *Kompas*, 27 July 1987; and, 'Pedagang Besar Farmasi Dan Apotik Yang Harus Ditertibkan', *Suara Pembaruan*, 28 July 1987.
103. 'Menkes Serukan Para Dokter Dan Apotik Turut Manfaatkan DOPB', *Antara*, 22 July 1987.
104. GPF letter no. 07.021/PP.UM/1987, of 23 July 1987.
105. Interview with Irwan Julianto, 23 July 1987.
106. The world-wide peak association for drug manufacturers—the Pharmaceutical Manufacturers' Association—based in Washington is merely a larger manifestation of this phenomenon.
107. This is not to suggest that the pharmaceutical industry is always harmoniously united around a common purpose; naturally there are issues which give rise to internal division. What is striking about the industry, however, is the extent to which it is able to cooperate when the occasion requires. Otherwise existing cleavages were completely overridden in responding to the threat of price limitation.
108. Interviews with Eddie Lembong, 21 August & 9 September 1987.
109. Interview with Eddie Lembong, 9 September 1987.

6

The Insurance Industry and the Campaign for Legal Reform

This chapter presents a case-study centring around the policy struggle over the introduction of an insurance law. Insurance companies in Indonesia have long sought a clear legislative basis for their industry because the existing legal framework is seen as outdated, unclear and readily subject to change by administrative fiat. The lack of a clear legal framework has been a source of considerable uncertainty within the industry. Reform-minded leaders of the insurance industry have argued for the introduction of a general insurance law to overcome the existing *ad hoc* regulatory environment in the hope that this would allow greater predictability and long term planning, and lay the broad foundations for the future development of the industry. To date, however, they have had little success in their efforts to persuade the government to introduce such a law to the Parliament.

Unlike the two previous case-studies, then, in this instance the industry does not 'win'. Also unlike the other two cases, the issue at stake here was not as dramatic and the conflict not as heated. Instead, this case is a more commonplace example of the mechanisms of interaction between business and the state. It deals with a more routine set of grievances, and thus provides a useful contrast with the two earlier case-studies. And yet, despite its seemingly unremarkable character, it is nonetheless very illuminating and throws up interesting material for debate about the nature of the Indonesian polity. At the centre of this case-study, as in the previous two, we see an industry association behaving in ways which raise questions about the validity of the prevailing heavily state-centred approaches to interpreting Indonesian politics.

The focus of our attention are the years 1985–86, when the idea of an insurance law was most vigorously promoted by the industry. One

202

FIGURE 6.1

Structural Overview of the Insurance Industry

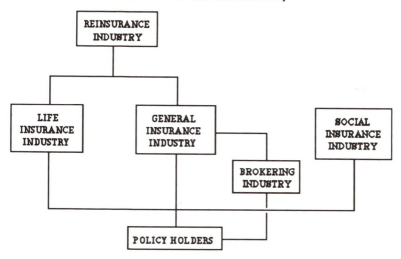

of the main features is the way in which sections of the insurance industry and its representative organisation, the Indonesian Insurance Council (the DAI), sought to induce the law by lobbying, in particular, the Department of Finance and the Parliament. The format of this chapter follows that established in the preceding two. An introductory profile of the insurance industry, together with an overview of interest representation arrangements in this section of the Indonesian business world, will be provided prior to addressing the details of the case itself. As before, the chapter closes with a consideration of the implications of the material under examination for the broader questions with which this study is concerned.

A Profile of the Insurance Industry

The insurance industry can be described on a functional basis and divided into a number of distinct sub-sectors. These are set out in graphic form in Figure 6.1. The first component in the diagram is the reinsurance sector. Reinsurance companies are, in effect, the insurers of the insurance industry itself. They underwrite the risks accepted by the life insurance and general insurance sectors. The life insurance industry, as its name suggests, sells life insurance policies. The general insurance sector (alternatively known as the non-life, or loss insurance) sells insurance policies to cover risks in areas such as fire, theft, marine and commercial insurance.

The life and general insurance sectors are strictly separated; life insurance firms do not sell general insurance, and *vice versa*. Business people wishing to operate in both the sectors must set up separate companies in each. This has led to considerable criss-crossing of ownership networks across sectoral borders. Social insurance is a special segment of the market in Indonesia which is wholly monopolised by the state. It covers such areas as civil service pensions, civil service health insurance and workers compensation. The life, general and social insurance industries all deal directly with individual and corporate consumers. In the case of the general insurance sector, however, there is also a brokering industry which acts as an independent intermediary between interested consumers and the general insurance firms, tailoring policies and seeking competitive prices.

In 1949 there were no locally incorporated insurance firms in Indonesia; all were foreign owned. In 1955, of the 135 companies in operation, twenty were local. By 1985 the total number of companies was down to eighty-nine, but the number locally-owned had risen to seventy-seven. Much of this change took place during the late 1950s and early 1960s, the years of Sukarno's Guided Democracy, when many of the foreign companies were either nationalised, or ceased operating in Indonesia. At the same time the viability of the life insurance industry was seriously threatened by the high inflation levels and political turbulence of this period.[1] During this period the insurance industry came increasingly under the control of state enterprises.

As with most other areas of business in Indonesia, the insurance industry underwent rapid growth following the transition to the New Order government. At the beginning of the New Order, state-owned insurance firms massively dominated the market. In a bid to revive the private sector, the government introduced a series of regulatory changes. A key element was Decree no. 422 of the Minister of Finance in 1968, which declared that in order to rehabilitate the national insurance industry, equal opportunity must be afforded to private and state firms alike.[2] The purpose of this decree was to assist the privately owned firms by scaling down the complete domination of the insurance market in the public and private sector. This was significant because of its implication that henceforth no objects for life or general insurance, regardless of whether located in the public or private sector, were to be the sole preserve of state-controlled firms. The 1986 ruling was a landmark which helped greatly to boost the prospects of privately owned insurance firms. However, despite the implication that private firms were now able to sell insurance to institutions in the public sector, the practice has been for most of that business to remain in the hands of state insurance firms. In other

FIGURE 6.2

Growth of the Indonesian Insurance Industry
(constant prices)

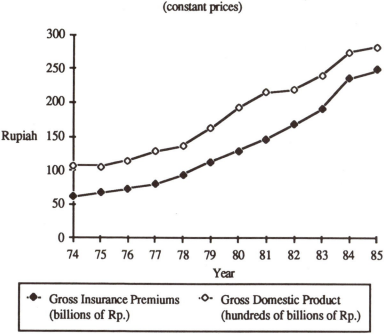

Source: Department of Finance (1986) p. 2.

words, despite the introduction of this regulation, state institutions continued to buy most of their insurance from state insurance firms, rather than turning to private insurance firms as an alternative.

Further legislative reform of the insurance industry came in 1969 with Presidential Decree no. 65. This had two main aspects: it permitted foreign firms to transact general insurance business in Indonesia, and it required that local reinsurance possibilities be exhausted before insurance firms sought reinsurance outside Indonesia. This latter element was designed to protect the small local reinsurance industry. The Presidential Decree was later reinforced by an implementing Decree of the Minister of Finance (no. 578, 1969) which gave explicit emphasis to the principle of free choice of insurer, taking this beyond the previously established freedom of choice between public and private firms, to embrace foreign firms as well.

In this more attractive environment, investment again began to flow into the insurance industry, from both foreign and local sources. Figure 6.2 lays out the growth of the insurance industry (measured in

FIGURE 6.3

Total Assets of Insurance Industry by Sector, 1985
(billions of Rupiah)

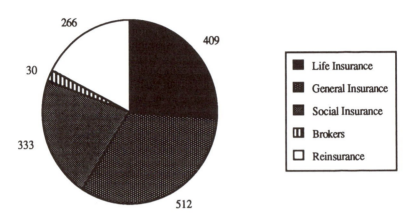

Source: Department of Finance (1986) pp. 3, 14, 74 & 78.

terms of total gross premiums) and shows the way in which this growth has paralleled the growth in the Indonesian economy.

The relative size of the different sectors of the insurance industry in terms of assets[3] can be seen in Figure 6.3. The life and general sectors are considerably larger than the social and reinsurance sectors. Because the different sectors are largely independent of each other, some brief consideration must be given to each, although greater emphasis will be given to the life and general insurance sectors, which are the two most important for the purposes of this study.

Life Insurance

The first point to be made here is that Indonesia is substantially 'underinsured' for life insurance on a *per capita* basis. A crude method for comparing the reach of the life insurance industry in different countries is to examine the value of total volume of insurance premiums earned. This gauges the absolute value of industry earnings, but does not take account of population differences. In order to measure 'insurance density' in different countries it is necessary to compare average *per capita* premium volume. To highlight the low level of life insurance in Indonesia, Table 6.1 lists both the

TABLE 6.1

International Ranking of the Life Insurance Industries of Selected Countries, 1985

	TOTAL PREMIUMS (millions US $)	INTERNATIONAL RANKING	TOTAL PREMIUMS PER-CAPITA (US $)	INTERNATIONAL RANKING
Indonesia	141	34th	0.8	52nd
Mexico	291	25th	3.7	38th
Philippines	243	26th	4.5	37th
Thailand	233	27th	4.6	36th
Malaysia	345	24th	22.2	26th
Singapore	172	29th	67.2	21st
USA	114,026	1st	476.6	2nd

Source: Swiss Re.(1987) pp. 14-15.

TABLE 6.2

Life Insurance Policy-holders Relative To Population in Indonesia

	POLICY-HOLDERS (A)	POPULATION (B)	A/B per cent
1976	1,325,493	135,190,000	0.98 per cent
1985	2,739,303	165,153,000	1.66 per cent

Source: Department of Finance (1986) p. 5.

absolute value of total life insurance premiums and the relative *per capita* measure for a selection of countries. It also lists Indonesia's ranking on an international basis for both measures. It will be noted that on the more telling *per capita* measure Indonesia's ranking slips from 34th to 52nd.

Having a small average *per capita* income and large population, Indonesia's ratio of life insurance policy-holders to population, while gradually increasing, still remains very low. Table 6.2 compares the level of insurance in 1976 with that in 1985.

Among the factors underlying the low level of investment in life insurance, four stand out. First, and most obviously, only a small percentage of the overall population has money incomes sufficiently high to consider a life insurance policy. Second, the small number of potential policy-holders is whittled down further by regulatory re-strictions. Investment in life insurance, unlike bank 'time-deposits', is subject to tax—thus reducing its attraction as a savings instrument. Similarly, the requirement that life insurance policies be denomi-nated only in rupiah has also been a disincentive to use them as a savings instrument because of the continued depreciation of the rupiah.[4] Third, the existence of the state pension savings funds in the

TABLE 6.3

Profile of the Life Insurance Industry, 1985

(millions of Rupiah)

COMPANY	ASSETS	NEW BUSINESS [a]	OWNERSHIP	ETHNICITY
Jiwasraya	167,097	336,797	state	-
Bumiputera 1912	156,648	349,457	private	pribumi
Panin Putra	29,328	7,426	private	Chinese
Bumi Asih Jaya	18,559	30,659	private	pribumi
Ikrar Abadi	7,680	35,233	joint venture [b]	pribumi
Bumiputera 1974	6,949	22,230	private [c]	pribumi
Central Asia Raya	6,723	15,051	private	Chinese
Buana Putra	4,155	8,622	private	pribumi
Koperasi Asuransi Indon.	1,915	154	cooperative	-
Purnamala Intrnl. Indon.	1,653	816	private	Chinese
Aken Life	1,255	8,622	private	pribumi
Bumi Arta Reksatama	1,364	368	private	Chinese
Century Lifindo Perdana	1,511	-	private	pribumi
Universal Life Indo	1,399	983	private	Chinese
Lippo Life	1,350	14,306	private	Chinese
Pertanggungan Jaminan	1,049	3,852	private	mixed
Dharmala Manulife	-	2,479	joint venture [b]	Chinese
Iman Adi	-	-	private	Chinese
Mahkota Sahid	-	-	private	pribumi
Pura Nusantara	-	-	private	pribumi
TOTAL	408,635	837,055		

Source: Department of Finance (1986) pp. 71 & 91.
Note: For some firms there is no data entry. This is because they failed to submit the relevant information to the Department of Finance by the required time.
[a]   Measured in terms of the total value of the sums assured.
[b]   These firms are listed here as joint ventures although it must be noted that in 1985 joint ventures had not yet been approved.
[c]   Bumiputera 1974 has an unofficial arrangement with a large American mutual firm, John Hancock, which may be a precursor to a formal joint venture.

social insurance sector not only reduces the disposable incomes of public sector employees, but also acts as a disincentive for them to purchase an independent life insurance policy.[5] Fourth, the insurance industry generally suffers from a tarnished reputation in terms of dependability. Occasional company failure or insolvency has helped to create an image of questionable reliability.[6]

In all, there are twenty-one firms in the life insurance sector, the oldest being the state owned firm Jiwasraya, which was established in 1859 as the Dutch firm Nillmij, and subsequently nationalised in 1957. Bumiputera 1912, as its name suggests, has been in continuous operation as a 'mutual society' (as distinct from a limited liability company) since 1912. It is the only mutual insurance society in Indonesia, although there is also a small cooperative life insurance company in Koperasi Asuransi Indonesia.[7]

Table 6.3 sets out a profile of the life insurance industry on a firm-by-firm basis. It highlights the total assets of each firm, the

TABLE 6.4

International Ranking of the General Insurance Industries of Selected Countries, 1985

	TOTAL PREMIUMS PER-CAPITA (US$)	INTERNATIONAL RANKING
Indonesia	3.0	53rd
Philippines	3.6	52nd
Thailand	4.2	51st
Mexico	11.2	39th
Malaysia	30.8	31st
Singapore	103.1	22nd
USA	780.2	1st

Source: Swiss Re. (1987) p. 15.

amount of new business it wrote that year, and also the nature and ethnicity of a firm's ownership. The amount of new business an insurance firm writes is one measure of its dynamism. It will be noted from the table that some firms, though having only small total assets, managed to sell a relatively large amount of new insurance. In the ownership category one company is listed here as being quasi-state owned. This is because the state holds a major share in it.

A striking feature of the table is the concentration of business in the hands of a very few firms. The largest single company is the state-owned Jiwasraya with 41 per cent of total industry assets. It is closely followed by the private mutual, Bumiputera 1912. Between them, they control 79 per cent of industry assets. If the next two largest firms are also included, 91 per cent of the total is accounted for. Another notable feature from the table is the unusually high level of *pribumi* involvement in the industry. There are eight *pribumi*-owned firms and seven owned by Chinese. In terms of assets, if Bumiputera 1912 is included with the other *pribumi* firms, they together control 82 per cent of the local private sector total, with the Chinese firms having only 18 per cent.[8]

General Insurance

Perhaps the first point to note here is that the level of penetration of general insurance in a country can be regarded as an indication of the country's acceptance of modern business practices over more traditional ones. By way of illustration, from Table 6.4 it can be seen that Indonesia has a very low *per capita* general insurance premium figure, compared with those of Singapore or the USA. This is indicative of the persistence of traditional commercial practices and small-scale agriculture in the economy of the former, and trade and more commercial activity in the case of the latter two.[9]

Table 6.5 sets out a profile of the general insurance sector similar to that above for the life insurance sector, the only difference being that instead of gauging company dynamism by the value of new business written, another measure is used, profit margin. Apart from the large number of individual firms in the general insurance sector, the most conspicuous feature is the heavy dominance of state and quasi-state firms. The largest company, the state-owned Jasa Indonesia, alone represents 23 per cent of the total assets in the general insurance sector. If the next three largest firms (one a state firm, another a quasi-state firm, and the third a joint venture with a state firm as the local partner) are included, 61 per cent of total assets are accounted for. In all, those firms which are either entirely state-owned or in which the state has a major holding together represent 69 per cent of assets in the general insurance industry.

Two of the quasi-state firms warrant special attention. Tugu Pratama, the second largest of all general insurance firms, has as its principal shareholders the state oil enterprise, Pertamina, and the Nusamba business grouping. Nusamba, in turn, is owned by President Suharto's oldest son, Sigit Harjojudanto, and Bob Hassan, a prominent Chinese business figure closely associated with the President. A key factor behind Tugu Pratama's great size is the fact that it enjoys a de facto monopoly over all general insurance business in the oil industry. The second important quasi-state enterprise is Timur Jauh, the fourth largest company in terms of assets. Timur Jauh is owned by the Berdikari group which, in turn, is controlled by the politically important National Logistics Agency (BULOG) headed by Bustanil Arifin. The head of Timur Jauh (during the period of this case-study) was Tantyo Sudharmono, the son of State Secretary (and later, Vice President) Sudharmono. Both Timur Jauh and Tugu Pratama benefit from enhanced reputations, as they are perceived to enjoy government backing and access to special insurance business opportunities, even though they are not officially classified as state enterprises.

Like the life insurance sector, the general insurance sector is marked by a high degree of concentration of industry assets among a small group of large firms. The top eight firms have 71 per cent of sector assets, with the remainder being shared among some sixty smaller companies. Unlike the life insurance sector, there are quite a few joint ventures. In all, however, the twelve joint ventures represent only 14 per cent of total general insurance assets. In terms of

TABLE 6.5

Profile of the General Insurance Industry in 1985
(millions of Rupiah)

COMPANY	ASSETS	PROFIT	OWNERSHIP	ETHNICITY [a]
Jasa Indonesia	115,475	21,973	state	-
Tugu Pratama	88,807	31,314	quasi-state	-
Jasa Raharja	83,879	35,225	state	-
Jayasraya	23,145	2,184	jnt vnt - state	-
Timur Jauh	15,723	2,365	quasi-state	-
Wahana Tata	14,880	3,247	private	Chinese
Central Asia	11,408	734	private	Chinese
Ramayana	11,007	773	private	pribumi
Insindo Taisho	8,581	1,673	jnt vnt-qsi state	-
Bintang	6,400	248	private	pribumi
Royal Indrapura	6,281	691	joint venture	pribumi
Union Far East	6,067	1,729	joint venture	pribumi
Pool Indonesia	6,011	106	private	Chinese
Cigna Indonesia	5,885	621	joint venture	Chinese
Jasa Tania	5,512	11,159	state	-
Indrapura	5,464	-326	private	pribumi
Antar Malayan Bali	4,798	507	joint venture	Chinese
Indon. America Baru	4,791	743	joint venture	pribumi
Indonesia (M.A.I.)	4,174	186	quasi-state	-
New Hampshire Agung	4,126	513	joint venture	pribumi
Nasuha	3,497	-1,425	joint venture	Chinese
Perusahaan Tri Pakarta	3,257	-314	quasi-state	-
Periscope	3,243	72	private	pribumi
Inda Tamporok	3,232	320	joint venture	pribumi
Pan Union	3,079	256	private	Chinese
Raya	2,952	99	quasi-state	-
Bina Darma Arta	2,863	161	private	Chinese
Multi Arta Guna	2,808	-70	private	Chinese
Independent	2,777	93	private	Chinese
Buana	2,768	5	private	Chinese
Djakarta 1945	2,721	-72	private	Chinese
Arthapala	2,661	1	private	Chinese
Lloyd Indonesia	2,605	340	private	Chinese
Sagita Sarana Raharja	2,516	66	private	pribumi
Dayin Mitra	2,457	22	private	Chinese
Laut & Kebakaran Samarang	2,173	-214	joint venture	Chinese
Parolamas	2,131	51	private	pribumi
Umum Wuwungan	2,116	94	private	pribumi
Sinar Mas Dipta	1,916	233	private	Chinese
Dharma Bangsa	1,896	-402	quasi-state	-
Sonwelis	1,813	100	private	Chinese
Harapan Aman Pratama	1,743	120	private	Chinese
Dana Aman Sejahtera	1,702	23	private	Chinese
Timur Besar	1,613	3	private	Chinese
Puri Asih	1,561	50	private	pribumi
Artarindo	1,557	127	private	Chinese
Sari Sumber Agung	1,506	134	private	mixed
Patriot	1,259	-11	private	Chinese
Marga Pusaka	1,254	71	private	Chinese
Rama Satria Wibawa	1,223	48	private	mixed
Nirbayasraya	1,215	1	private	Chinese
Pertiwi Agung Prawira	1,179	62	private	Chinese
Ikrar Lloyd	1,161	35	private	Chinese

continued on page 212

TABLE 6.5

COMPANY	ASSETS	PROFIT	OWNERSHIP	ETHNICITY [a]
Bumiputera Muda 1967	1,152	-143	private	*pribumi*
Purwanjasa	1,098	-142	private	Chinese
Nugra Pacific	1,070	11	private	*pribumi*
Tjahjana	963	-49	private	Chinese
Eka Lloyd Jaya	957	92	private	Chinese
Pelita	753	122	private	Chinese
Agung Asia Sejahtera	724	5	private	Chinese
Gajah Mada	656	-96	private	*pribumi*
Ampuh	-	-	private	Chinese
Fadent Mahkota Sahid	-	-	private	*pribumi*
Murni	-	-	quasi-state	-
Teladan	-	-	private	*pribumi*
Waringin Lloyd	-	-	private	*pribumi*
Yasudascope	-	-	joint venture	mixed
TOTAL	512,241			

Source: Department of Finance (1986) pp. 82-85.

[a]   In the case of joint ventures the ethnicity of the local partner is listed where the local partner is not a state, or quasi-state firm.

ethnicity, *pribumi* firms again have an unusually high profile. While their share of local and privately held assets is not as great as in the life insurance sector, a figure of 32 per cent is nonetheless still remarkably high.

Social Insurance

By contrast with life and general insurance, relatively little public information is available on the social insurance sector. It is made up of a small number of different institutions which variously handle pension funds for civil servants (TASPEN) and members of the armed forces (ASABRI), health insurance (ASKES), and workers compensation (ASTEK).[10] The institutions in this sector are each the sole operators in guaranteed markets. For example, ASABRI and ASKES have monopolies in their respective areas, and participation is compulsory for their client groups. Social insurance firms are thus qualitatively quite different from firms in the other sectors, as they do not have to compete on a commercial basis at all. Not surprisingly, they are seen by the rest of the insurance industry (and indeed see themselves) as occupying a quite separate sphere of business.[11] Therefore, while the social insurance sector must be mentioned here (if only because it involves very large capital reserves) in this case-study, its role is minor.

Reinsurance

The reinsurance sector, like social insurance, has very few participants. There are three local reinsurance firms, two of which are
state-owned. These two firms, Reasuransi Umum Indonesia (Indo
Re) and Asuransi Kredit Indonesia (ASKRINDO), between them
had assets totalling Rp. 263 billion in 1985. By contrast, the sole
private company, Maskapai Reasuransi Indonesia (MAREIN) had
assets of only Rp. 3 billion.[12] As noted earlier, the reinsurance
industry is protected by Presidential Decree no. 65 of 1969, which
provides that 75 per cent of all reinsurance needs should be covered
by Indonesian reinsurance firms. In practice, however, this limit of 25
per cent foreign reinsurance coverage is frequently breached, since
the local industry is unable to cover all risks, particularly high cost
ventures.

Brokering

The brokering industry is the smallest and least developed of all
sectors. Many insurance firms in Indonesia view brokers as parasites,
operating as unnecessary middlemen. At present, brokers may only
operate in the general insurance sector. Insurance brokers in Indonesia do not enjoy the well-established position that their counterparts in the West do, although this is gradually changing as some of
the larger insurance firms, especially the joint ventures, come to
make more use of them.

Overall, the main points to note about the insurance industry are
that state enterprises play a very large part in the market and that the
industry is sharply fragmented into several sectors. Table 6.6 provides a summary breakdown of each sector on the basis of assets

TABLE 6.6

Total Assets of the Insurance Industry by Sector and Ownership, 1985
(billions of Rupiah)

	LIFE	GENERAL	SOCIAL	REINSURANCE	BROKERS
STATE	167	199	333	263	5 [a]
PRIVATE	242	240	-	3	25 [a]
JOINT VENTURE	2 [b]	73	-	-	-
TOTAL	409	512	333	266	30

Source: Department of Finance (1986) pp. 3,14,71,74,78.

[a]   These figures are estimates only, as details on the state-private breakdown of total broker assets
      are not available. The estimates are based on the ratio of the number of firms in each category.
[b]   As noted in Table 6.3, in 1985 these joint ventures had not yet been approved.

and ownership. (Note, however, that the previously-mentioned quasi-state firms have not been included in the state classification here.) Taking the two most important sectors, life and general insurance, the state firms control 40 per cent of total assets. (If the assets of all the firms in which the state has a major share are included, this figure rises to 63 per cent of the combined life and general insurance total.) An overall figure for the entire industry, thus also counting the heavily state-dominated social and reinsurance sectors, shows that state firms (again, not including quasi-state firms) hold 62 per cent of all assets.

Interest Representation in the Insurance Industry

Standing at the centre of the insurance industry is the Indonesian Insurance Council, the DAI, the association responsible for articulating industry interests in dealings with the state. It covers all areas of the insurance industry except the brokers who have their own association. The DAI was established in 1957. In July 1965 it temporarily ceased operation because of the requirement of the Sukarno government (mentioned in Chapter 3) that business representative organisations form themselves into OPS (Organisations of Homogenous Enterprises) units. Under the New Order, the DAI was resurrected in July 1967. In common with many other business associations in Indonesia today, the DAI has corporatist characteristics. Most obvious is the fact that membership is virtually compulsory. Recommendation by the DAI is a prerequisite both for securing a licence from the Department of Finance to sell insurance as well as buying reinsurance. Thus no firm could operate without being a member of the DAI.

Universal membership does not, however, necessarily guarantee an energetic and effective organisation. In practice the firms which are active within the DAI's structure and seek to make the most of it tend to be the more professional and dynamic of the privately owned firms. These firms are also typically (though not always) the larger ones. One company head estimated that, at most, only 40 per cent of firms could be placed in this loose category.[13] The managements of the state-owned insurance companies are less committed to the operations of the DAI for the simple reason that coming within the control of the Department of Finance, they have their own direct channels of access to policy-makers. Moreover, they are usually reluctant to be seen taking a public position in the DAI which is at variance with that of their superiors in the Department of Finance. This is not to suggest that the state-owned firms ignore the DAI.

They do not. In fact, members of their management usually hold a number of offices within the DAI's structure. Rather, the point to be made is that they have little need to look to the DAI for the representation of their interests to the state.

Apart from the state-owned firms, the numerous very small insurance firms (many of which are marginal commercial propositions) make little use of the DAI. The managements of these firms are typically preoccupied with the day-to-day fortunes of their business and have little interest in 'macro' issues bearing on the future of the industry as a whole. The fact that little use of the DAI is made by the large state-owned firms, or by many of these small firms, has served to circumscribe its authority. Many company managers are apparently unwilling to commit the necessary time and energy to participate actively in DAI affairs. Indeed DAI meetings sometimes lapse because a quorum cannot be achieved. Hence, there tends to be relatively little competition among company representatives to fill positions within the DAI administration. Managers from the already mentioned professionally-oriented companies usually fill such positions. The one exception to this generalisation, however, is the position of chairman of the organisation, which is always hotly contested.[14] This position tends to go to a senior figure from within the state-owned firms rather than the private companies. The most frequently encountered explanation for this pattern is a perception that the leaders of the state-owned firms will be more acceptable to the Department of Finance and thus achieve a greater level of access for the DAI. From the viewpoint of the industry, one problem associated with the tendency for the DAI chairmanship to be filled by a state firm executive (and a useful reminder of the importance of patrimonialist behaviour) is their reluctance to confront or oppose the wishes of their bureaucratic superiors in the Department of Finance in the event of diverging industry and departmental interests. Usually these state firm executives serve only one term as chairman of the DAI before retiring to their company. This pattern of leadership mitigates against the emergence of a strong and long-serving leader of the calibre of Husein Aminuddin of SEKBERTAL , or Eddie Lembong of GPF.

Another important aspect of DAI operations—and interest representation generally within the insurance industry—is that the various sectors tend to operate in isolation. The two major sectors, general and life insurance, have very little to do with each other. This is not a function of rivalry or enmity, but simply reflects the fact that they are quite separate areas of business. The separation is also reflected in the DAI's structure and the way it operates. Each of the different sectors thus has its own organisational units within the

DAI's structure. Firms within each sector (or at least the active ones) tend to consult only with each other and co-ordinate their dealings with the state quite independently of the other sectors. Nevertheless, while frequently operating independently, the various sectors do all march under the DAI flag for some purposes so as to enhance their standing, and to promote the impression that they are not just speaking on behalf of only one segment of the insurance industry. In other words, DAI membership is invoked to suggest a broader-based constituency than is, in fact, usually concerned with any given issue.

In many respects the DAI is more significant to the insurance industry as a neutral adjudicator on technical matters than it is as an aggregator and articulator of interests. One of the DAI's functions in this respect is the setting of insurance tariff levels. Standard tariff levels are determined on a periodic basis by a special DAI committee, and are subsequently approved by the Department of Finance.[15] Another self-regulatory function the DAI occasionally performs is to act as arbitrator in disputes between policy-holders and insurance firms when there is a need for an out-of-court settlement.

While the focus of attention here is on the DAI, it should be remembered that there is also a separate association to represent the brokering industry, the Insurance Brokers' Association of Indonesia. Reflecting the recent development of that industry, the Brokers' Association was only founded in 1978. Membership of the Association is not compulsory, although nearly all brokering firms have joined. To an even greater extent than the DAI, the Brokers' Association suffers from the problem that only the more professional and forward-looking firms have any real commitment to its activities. Beside the DAI, the Brokers' Association appears as a very small organisation. Because the brokering industry provides what is really an inessential, or dispensable service, the Brokers' Association is not regarded as an especially important or influential body.[16] Our concern here is more with the DAI than the Brokers' Association. Nevertheless, much of what is said in relation to the DAI, applies also to the Brokers' Association.

As with other areas of business in Indonesia, the insurance industry has three basic channels available to it, should it seek to influence government policy. The first is to deal directly with the Department of Finance; the second, to approach the Parliament; and the third is to attempt to use the press. As with the other case-studies, this chapter exhibits all three techniques for attempting to bring pressure to bear on policy-makers. Approaches to these various institutions might take place either via the DAI (and Brokers' Association), or else on an individual and *ad hoc* basis. Brief comment will be made about each.

Of the three, the Directorate for Financial Institutions within the Department of Finance is definitely the main focus of industry attention in terms of influencing government policy. It is the source of most key policy decisions affecting the insurance industry. On the whole the DAI and the insurance industry generally enjoy good relations with the Directorate. Marzuki Usman, the Director (during the period under examination) was seen as being both reasonable and sympathetic, as well as accessible. The DAI has institutionalised meetings at an executive level with the Directorate several times each year. In addition, the life and general insurance sections within the DAI have their own regular meetings with the Director, on a less formal basis, every few months. Further, individual firms are free to approach the Directorate at any stage, outside the auspices of the DAI. The DAI thus does not monopolise access to the Department of Finance to the extent that GPF does in the case of the Health Department. By the same token, the Department of Finance does not seem concerned to limit deliberately access by individuals from the insurance industry. In short, arrangements are rather more open and less structured.

The major problem the industry has to contend with in seeking to gain a favourable hearing on an issue with the Directorate for Financial Institutions is that the Directorate is a small body and is responsible for the entire range of the non-bank financial services sector. As a result, in seeking Marzuki's attention, the various sub-sectors of the insurance industry must compete with not only each other, but also with the pension funds and leasing industry. The situation is compounded by the fact that there is a shortage of technically competent officials within the Directorate, which serves to increase the demands made upon the time of the Director and the small number of key assistants surrounding him.

In situations in which the DAI or sub-sections of the insurance industry are unable to gain satisfaction from the Department of Finance, Committee VII of the Parliament is sometimes used as an alternative point of access. Committee VII is the Parliamentary Committee responsible for such matters as finance, the Central Bank and trade. Key figures within the leadership of the GOLKAR and ABRI factions of the Committee have been readily available to approaches by industry representatives to discuss matters of concern. Importantly, not only were these few Committee leaders generally sympathetic to the insurance industry, they also possessed a working knowledge of some of its technicalities. Moreover, they represented the two main factions within the Parliament. Meetings with these Committee faction leaders (principally Beren Ginting of GOLKAR and Benny Moerdeko of ABRI) usually took place on an informal and consultative basis. They were, though, willing to convene formal and public Committee hearings into a specific issue if it was of sufficient importance. Of special relevance here is that they were sympathetic to the industry's arguments about the importance of the rapid introduction of an insurance law to provide greater predictability and stability for industry planning.

The third possible target for representational activity by insurance firms and the DAI when seeking to influence policy is the press. On this front, however, the industry suffers from something of a handicap, for insurance affairs are usually of little interest to circulation-conscious newspaper editors. Because much of the stuff of the insurance industry is of a detailed and technical nature it is often considered to be too dull. This problem of perceived lack of 'newsworthiness' is compounded by the fact that the insurance industry is not seen as a central facet of the economy. Because it is relatively insignificant in terms of capital mobilisation (in contrast with the banks), it tends to be overlooked in the financial sections of the press. The conspicuous, and unwelcomed, exceptions to the tendency for limited press coverage are the occasional dramatic closures of insurance firms or controversial disputes between an insurer and policy-holder.

This is not to say that the press is, in effect, closed as a potential channel by which the insurance industry can lobby policy-makers. Rather, the point is that the insurance industry finds it more difficult than some others (certainly far more difficult than, say, SEKBER-TAL) to attract press attention. This public relations difficulty is not made easier by a lack of journalists with the technical competence to cover insurance affairs adequately. At least part of the blame for this situation lies, however, with the insurance industry itself, because it has to date failed to pursue and cultivate press links as vigorously as it might.[17]

The Background to the Insurance Law Issue

The issue of the need for formal legislation, rather than merely administrative regulation, to govern the operations of the insurance industry is not a new one. At least as early as 1963 the Department of Finance had been giving consideration to a bill for presentation to the Parliament.[18] The impetus for the introduction of a formal insurance law has come from both the industry itself as well as the state, or more accurately, the Directorate for Financial Institutions.[19]

In very broad terms, the DAI, and the insurance industry generally, saw an insurance law as a means for providing a more stable environment in which long-term industry planning could take place. Unlike administrative regulations or ministerial and presidential decrees, laws promulgated by the Parliament are far less readily altered. There are over seventy decrees regulating the insurance industry, any of which can be superseded or revoked by the government at will. A law passed by the Parliament can only be revoked by another act of Parliament, a much more cumbersome process than executive fiat. With a firm legal basis setting out the relationship between the state and business, the insurance industry hoped to secure greater freedom from unwanted state intervention by administrative ruling.

Beyond reducing the scope for arbitrary state intervention, the insurance industry sought a clearer set of regulatory guidelines to guard against dubious business practices by some of its own members—practices which risk bringing the whole industry into further disrepute.[20] An example of this would be clarification of procedures governing bankruptcy situations. Because the insurance industry has an image or credibility problem in Indonesia, instances of company failure are viewed with grave concern by most firms. This concern prompted a desire among the better managed and more professional insurance companies to see stricter solvency margins and reserve deposits introduced, as well as clear procedures set down in law to provide for consumer compensation. Thus, by seeking to have the Department of Finance introduce stricter requirements for the operation of insurance businesses, the industry as a whole hoped to benefit from improved public standing.

If then, in broad terms, these have been the main interests of the insurance industry in pushing for the introduction of an insurance law, what have been the main concerns of the Department of Finance? To begin with, it should be noted that the introduction of an insurance law was part of a broader project of the Department to rationalise legal arrangements throughout the whole financial services sector. To this end it was drafting a set of three laws for submission to Parliament; one covering insurance, and the others being for banking and pension funds. Of the three, the insurance law was the one which stimulated greatest industry interest, and was generally considered to be the most pressing.[21]

In some respects the interests of Department of Finance in the proposed insurance law coincided with those of the industry, while in others they were quite divergent. In common with the industry, the Department has consistently viewed a formalisation and rationalisation of the legal ground-rules of the insurance business as integral to its further development. As one of the key players in the macroeconomic policy arena, the Department of Finance has been anxious to stimulate the expansion of the insurance industry so that it might play a larger role in the generation and mobilisation of capital for the broader purpose of economic development. Unlike the situation in most Western countries, the insurance industry in Indonesia has played a relatively small role as a mobiliser of capital. In Indonesia, the leading role has been played by the banks. In addition to stimulating the insurance industry to assume a larger role in national development, the Department of Finance has also been concerned to protect consumer interests and guard against the public resentment and political sensitivity associated with malpractice and company failure. In this context, the Department has viewed the idea of an insurance law as a means to clarify and enhance its authority to intervene and take action against failing insurance firms before they actually collapse. In the past the Directorate for Financial Institutions has had some hesitancy about doing this.[22]

To this extent, the interests of the Department of Finance and the insurance industry have largely coincided. Differences exist, however, over the extent to which the Department should refrain from intervening in industry affairs. The industry has generally taken the view that an insurance law should specify in detail the circumstances under which the Department of Finance is able to intervene, and that beyond this a *laissez-faire* attitude should be adopted. In short, the insurance industry took the view that state-intervention in the market should be strictly limited to certain necessary tasks. Predictably, though, the Department of Finance (in keeping with the Indonesian state's strong tradition of economic interventionism) has been reluctant to surrender its authority and capacity to intervene in industry affairs on matters it deems appropriate. This is in part because in some respects it does not yet have full confidence in the 'maturity' of some elements in the industry, but also because, as a political creature, the Department of Finance (and more broadly, the state as a whole) is inevitably reluctant to limit its own powers.

The gap between the views of the insurance industry and the Department of Finance on this issue has not, however, been enormous, as both sides agree on the need for a significant level of state intervention. The difference is that the industry has wanted this to be limited to matters which the DAI is unable or unwilling to handle (such as malpractice by individual firms) whereas the Department of Finance has wanted to retain the maximum degree of flexibility for itself. The difference of perspective is reflected in the form which the two sides have wanted the proposed insurance law to take. Generally speaking, the insurance industry has favoured a more detailed law which specifies precisely the roles and powers of the state *vis-à-vis* the industry, whereas the Department of Finance has wanted to preserve maximum flexibility and authority for itself.

In broad terms, these have been the parameters of the debate about preparation of an insurance law which has been continuing on a sustained basis since 1979, and intermittently as far back as 1963. While some of the details have changed over this period, the core issues remained the same. The main variable which has fluctuated over the years has been the *determination* of the key actors to see a draft law finally submitted to the Parliament for enactment. In 1967, the Department of Finance apparently got as far as approaching the Parliament over the possible submission of a bill for consideration, though the proposal was subsequently withdrawn.[23]

In the late 1970s, pressure for the introduction of an insurance law became more serious. In 1979, in a bid to accelerate the process, the DAI submitted its own complete and detailed draft proposal for an insurance law to the Directorate for Financial Institutions. The draft put forward by the DAI was modelled on the insurance legislation in other ASEAN countries, and particularly that of Malaysia. However, the proposal was apparently too specific for the Directorate of Financial Institution's liking in that it delineated the role of the Department of Finance too precisely, thereby restricting its freedom for action.[24] The DAI then submitted a second draft proposal for the law, which was a diluted form of the previous one, in the hope that it would be acceptable. Again, however, the Department was unhappy with the submission.

In mid-1980 a series of detailed press articles appeared that were sympathetic to the needs of the insurance industry, arguing strongly, often in a polemical manner, for the immediate introduction of an insurance law to facilitate the industry's development.[25] However, rather than accept the DAI's detailed draft law as a basis from which to work, the Directorate for Financial Institutions in 1980 appointed a team of officials to examine the subject and produce a more flexible draft. Although there were no industry representatives on the special team set up by the Department, there was consultation with the DAI to ascertain industry views. Despite the fact that this team had been set up by the Department of Finance itself, the draft law it ultimately produced, like those of the DAI, failed to gain the approval of the Department's leadership. Again the stumbling block appears to have been that the proposals were too detailed and constrictive.

In addition to this general problem, there were also some specific issues over which there was controversy. One concerned the fear of the insurance industry that the banks were encroaching on their territory. Though banks were prohibited from selling insurance directly, there was growing concern among some sections of the insurance industry about banks achieving indirect influence in the market. Concern focused on bank pension funds (separate legal bodies) either owning or acquiring a major share in insurance and insurance brokering firms. This was seen as unhealthy by those insurance firms (at that stage a majority) which did not have special links with a particular bank. The nub of such worries was the possibility of banks encouraging their investors to buy insurance policies from the insurance firm in which that bank had an interest. Because the number of investors with banks far outweighed the number of insurance policy-holders this was seen as potentially providing an unfair advantage to insurance firms which had links with a major bank. The Department of Finance was, however, reluctant to move decisively on this issue. Apart from the practical difficulties involved in eliminating the scope for this sort of activity by legislative means, the Department was, inevitably, sensitive to possible political problems arising from any such attempt, as one of the most conspicuous cases of a bank owning or controlling an insurance company was that of the Liem Soe Liong business grouping—a huge corporate empire with very close connections to President Suharto.[26]

Aside from the question of the involvement of banks in the insurance industry, another specific issue of controversy pertaining to proposals for an insurance law was the status of the so-called social insurance sector. Private and state firms alike in the life and general insurance sectors viewed with concern the prospect of an ever-expanding social insurance sector. Concern centred on the fact that the state enterprises in the social insurance sector all had effective monopolies in their respective product areas, and thus did not have to operate on a commercial basis. Worried about their continued expansion, the life and general insurance sectors sought a clear delineation of the limits to the territory set aside for the social sector. Furthermore, the life insurance industry was anxious to be able to expand into health insurance, which for historical reasons had hitherto been within the domain of social insurance.

In 1981, in a bid to push the case for the rapid introduction of an insurance law more quickly, the then head of the DAI, Doeriat, gave a number of these matters a public airing at an open insurance conference attended by the Director for Financial Institutions, Marzuki Usman.[27] But by this stage, following repeated failure, the momentum required to push the matter was beginning to flag. Throughout 1981 the issue lay dormant. Then, in 1982, the Directorate for Financial Institutions decided to produce a private draft of its own. This was done with assistance from a small group of consultants from the Harvard Institute for International Development.

During 1982–83 a very broad and general draft was developed, but was not shown to the industry. This came to form the basis of the Department's position in all future discussions of the issue.

Though its part in this case is only small, the Brokers' Association also had an interest in the introduction of an insurance law. The biggest problem faced by the brokering industry was that its role was not wholly accepted by the insurance industry. Many insurance firms would have preferred to see the brokering industry wither. For this reason the Brokers' Association was very anxious that any insurance law introduced should give explicit recognition to the existence and significance of the brokering sector. In 1981 the Association had made a major submission to Marzuki on this issue and had pursued it intermittently since. Their voice in the insurance world was, however, only a small one.[28]

The Campaign for the Introduction of an Insurance Law

By 1984 something of a stand-off had developed on the issue of the insurance law. The Department of Finance had, as just seen, already developed a draft law of its own, but had not revealed the contents of it to the industry. In this situation it was difficult for industry activists to lobby for or against the inclusion of particular aspects, as they simply did not know whether or not the Department's draft took account of their concerns.

The industry had not been wholly united on the idea of pushing for the introduction of an insurance law. Some of the very small private firms which had only limited capital assets behind them were, predictably enough, wary of the prospect of a more stringent set of legal parameters governing the operation of their businesses. The question of higher solvency margins was the most obvious issue to concern such companies. These companies tended, however, to be only marginally involved with the management and consideration of industry-wide interests. They had little to do with the DAI and tended to focus only on the day-to-day concerns of their businesses. Apart from these small firms, joint ventures or, more accurately, the foreign partners in the joint venture companies, also took little interest in the subject. While they were happy to see an insurance law introduced, it was not a cause in which they were willing to invest significant time or resources. As the foreign partners had to reduce their maximum permitted share holding from 70 per cent to 40 per cent after ten years, and then to not more than 30 per cent after twenty years, they did not have the same incentive or long term commitment to the Indonesian insurance industry that local firms had.[29]

Among the firms that did take an interest in the future development of the insurance industry and participate in DAI affairs (a number of which were also small, though nevertheless outward-looking and expanding) there was some division between those which sought a detailed and specific insurance law, and those which favoured only a broad and general law. Here the division was between state-owned and private firms. The latter were anxious to see a detailed insurance law so that the role of the Department of Finance was more clearly delineated and, preferably, circumscribed. The heads of the state firms, on the other hand, were opposed to this idea both because it would not really advantage their enterprise, and also because it was the clear preference of their superiors within the Department of Finance that a 'too-specific' law should be avoided. In this latter respect they were merely reflecting departmental policy.

In assessing overall industry attitudes, the concerns of those small firms which felt threatened by the prospect of the introduction of an insurance law, and particularly a rigorous and far reaching one, can largely be set aside. This is because their number was not great and their political significance even less. Indeed it was the questionable business practices of precisely these sorts of less professional firms that both the DAI and the Department of Finance sought to eliminate. Of more significance was the attitude of the state-owned firms. However, their unwillingness to support strongly the arguments for a detailed law did not amount to outright opposition or violent hostility to the idea. Indeed many state-owned insurance firm managers no doubt saw an insurance law as being quite beneficial to the industry's long term future, but because their superiors in the Department were opposed to the idea of a very detailed law, they were likely to indicate only luke-warm support for it. After all, an insurance law was not something of great significance to the state firms, for regardless of the sector they were in, their foreseeable futures were assured by virtue of their operations' enormous assets and the fact of their being guaranteed by the government. Thus even the commercial state-owned firms (those operating in the life, general and reinsurance sectors) which had to compete with other firms were not dependent on an insurance law to brighten their futures.[30]

By contrast, there was a very strong commitment to the introduction of a thoroughgoing insurance law among the more professionally oriented and progressive private firms. Unlike the state-owned firms, which did not really care about the issue, and the small private marginal firms which felt vaguely threatened by it, the active and expanding private firms saw great advantage in a law which on the one hand delineated the role of the government in the industry, and on the other served to rationalise business practices. They saw an appropriately constructed law as laying the foundations necessary for the further growth and development of a healthy insurance industry. This commitment to the introduction of an insurance law among those more dynamic companies stretched uniformly across sector boundaries. Thus, there were life, general and reinsurance firms all anxious to see a law promulgated as soon as possible. It was companies of this sort which were most active within the DAI in pushing for a vigorous promotion of the case for the rapid introduction of a detailed law. As one company president and former DAI head put it, the whole issue of the need for an insurance law was intimately bound up with the push to make the entire insurance industry more professional and sophisticated.[31] It was for this reason that companies with an eye to the future were committed to the idea.

Apart from the general desire to encourage the development and rationalisation of the insurance industry, many people also saw the introduction of an insurance law and the campaign for it, as an important step in promoting the industry's status and profile. The tendency for the insurance industry to be viewed as the poor cousin of the banking industry was much resented in insurance circles. The achievement of a law was seen as a means for overcoming this status problem at the same time as boosting the industry's image with the general public.[32] Significantly, this was an aim with which *all* insurance firms could identify, and over time those state-owned and small private firms which had initially been ambivalent about the proposed law, gradually moved into line behind the activists. While the active proponents of an insurance law were limited to the more professionally oriented firms, they came to be seen as representing (if still vicariously) the interests of all members of the insurance industry.

Paralleling this apparent *de facto* convergence of industry ranks was a decline in debate over the details of the law. Many of the specific issues proposed for inclusion in the law which had been the subject of controversy, gradually fell by the wayside. This was in part because it was clear that if any bill at all was to be put to Parliament by the government, it would be only very general and flexible. Thus many of the questions of detail would simply not arise. At the same time, some of the specific issues, such as the question of the covert involvement of banks in the insurance industry, were simply overtaken by events. By the mid-1980s almost all major insurance firms had established direct links with a particular bank. This either took the form of the bank having an indirect shareholding in the insurance firm via a third corporate entity such as a pension fund, or else a bank and an insurance firm simply establishing an informal symbiotic relationship. As bank involvement in the insurance industry became increasingly common, so the controversy over the matter dissipated.

By 1984 the industry was well aware that the Directorate for Financial Institutions had completed work on its preferred draft bill. In this situation, clamouring from industry circles receded in the expectation that introduction of a law was imminent. There was still some prompting, such as, for example, when Tantyo Sudharmono, the Executive Director of the large general insurance company Timur Jauh, appeared before Committee VII of the Parliament and called for an expeditious introduction of the law. Being an active figure within the DAI and the son of the powerful State Secretary Sudharmono, Tantyo Sudharmono's urgings inevitably received press attention.[33] Generally speaking, however, the industry was relatively quiet during 1984. There were several reasons for this. In part it was because the initiative had been removed from their hands following the failure of their two earlier submissions to win acceptance. Carriage of the matter thus lay exclusively in the hands of the Department of Finance. In this situation there was a feeling that industry interests would be better served by refraining from making demands about the type of law desired, as this might jeopardise or delay the introduction of any law at all. It was, though, not simply a case of the industry having been 'frozen-out' of deliberations. There was considerable optimism that the Director for Financial Institutions, Marzuki Usman, was sympathetic to the future needs of the insurance industry and would thus attempt to expedite the submission of a bill to the Parliament. Certainly there were plenty of official hints during 1984 that the submission of an insurance bill to the Parliament was imminent. Public statements by the Director General for Domestic Monetary Affairs in the Department of Finance, Oskar Surjaatmadja, in January and again in August, as well as by Committee VII leader, Beren Ginting, and Minister of Finance, Radius Prawiro, in March, all seemed to herald a quick climax to the matter.[34]

Expectations were to be disappointed however. Feeling little real urgency of pressure, senior figures within the Department of Finance did not push the insurance bill as a priority item on the government's legislative agenda. As a result, no bill was submitted to the Parliament. This was to shake the industry from its lethargy and stimulate a change of mood during 1985–86.

A Heightened Industry Effort

The failure of the government to submit a bill to the Parliament led industry activists in the DAI to become impatient. During 1985–86 industry attempts to pressure the Department of Finance on the introduction of an insurance law were rekindled and reached their peak. Apart from impatience with the Department, the other key stimulus for industry action was the financial instability resulting from the severe buffeting the industry was experiencing during the economic downturn. Not only was profitability being pressured across the industry, some smaller firms were faced with insolvency.[35] In this context, the introduction of an insurance law came to be seen as offering almost a panacea for industry woes.

Industry attempts to accelerate the introduction of the law took a number of forms. At the most formal level the DAI executive held regular and institutionalised discussions with the Directorate for Financial Institutions at which the matter was pushed in discussion with Marzuki and other officials. As well as being the most formal channel for communications between the industry and the Department of Finance, this was also perhaps the least significant. Because it was such an official occasion the scope for frank exchanges between the two sides was limited. While the DAI continued to make formal representations of this sort, a number of the more active insurance leaders felt that more needed to be done to stimulate the Department of Finance into action. Industry activists believed that the DAI was not likely to push the case for the introduction of an insurance law as vigorously as might be hoped, because it was headed by the chief officer of a state-owned firm.

With the formal meetings between the DAI executive and the Department proving an inadequate channel, the focus shifted down to the sectoral level. Like-minded activists within each sectoral grouping sought to use the valuable opportunity for forthright exchange, provided by the less formal monthly meetings with Marzuki, to raise the question of the progress of the draft law and the likely length of time before its submission to the Parliament.[36] Though the three sectors continued to operate independently of each other, there was some attempt by the leaders to orchestrate their separate efforts. Anxious to see the insurance law brought into being as soon as possible, industry activists no longer sought to introduce new variables into the equation. They therefore abandoned attempts to pressure Departmental officials about the details of the proposed law and concentrated their energies on urging them to submit the still unrevealed draft to the Parliament for ratification without further delay.

In addition to these initiatives taken by the sectoral units within the DAI, parallel informal efforts were made outside DAI channels. Typically, this took the form of loosely organised lobbying of Department of Finance officials on a personal basis by individual company heads. Thus, for example, concerned leaders of the life insurance industry would agree informally to push the question of an insurance law at every opportunity provided by private encounters with state officials. Though this was an *ad hoc* approach to the issue, many company heads viewed it as being of at least as much use as the periodic promptings which came from the DAI. These informal, individual approaches to the Department were not in any way opposed to, or even distinguished from, those of the DAI. Indeed, many of the company leaders who pushed for the introduction of a law outside the DAI's channels, were also the same people pushing from inside the DAI. This was not surprising, as a company leader who was concerned about the future direction of the industry to the extent of being willing to lobby senior officials over the matter, was also highly likely to be an active member of the industry's professional association. The significant point, however, is that many of these people felt that the DAI was not a sufficiently forceful vehicle for the delivery of their message, and that supplementary efforts were needed.

The insurance industry's efforts—both from DAI and individual channels—were not confined solely to the Department of Finance. Committee VII of the Parliament was also a focus for attention. The leaders of the GOLKAR and ABRI factions of the Committee viewed favourably the industry's arguments for the need of a rapid introduction of an insurance law in order to provide greater predictability and stability for industry planning. Meetings with the leaders of Committee VII, as with the Department of Finance, took place on both a formal and informal level. The Brokers' Association followed the DAI's lead in this and also lobbied Committee VII.

Key figures within Committee VII sought to assist the insurance industry by speaking both publicly and privately on their behalf. Apart from arranging official Committee hearings on developments within the insurance industry and the specific question of an insurance law, they were also active in openly speaking in favour of the early introduction of a law at various public meetings.[37] In addition, they also decided to push the matter in private discussions with senior officials in the Directorate of Financial Institutions.[38]

By these several means the insurance industry approached a variety of facets of the state structure, both in a formal and unified manner, as well as informally on an *ad hoc* basis, in an effort to expedite the introduction of the law. Apart from the already mentioned Department of Finance and the Parliament, other areas to be targeted were the State Secretariat, BAPPENAS, the Department of Industry, the National Investment Board and even the Co-ordinating Minister for Social Welfare.[39] At times the campaign to promote the law was conducted in a very vigorous manner. For example, at one public seminar organised to address the issue, one of the speakers,

Tantyo Sudharmono, spoke in strident terms about the failure of the government to assist the development of the insurance industry and the lack of facilities it received by comparison with other parts of the financial services sector, such as banking.[40]

The quest for an insurance law came to be regarded as somehow symbolising, or encapsulating almost all of the insurance industry's grievances. Indeed, in some quarters there were quite exaggerated and near-messianic expectations that somehow the attainment of an insurance law would be the panacea for all the industry's problems.[41]

Bumiputera 1912 and the Insurance Law

While there was a broad interest in the question of an insurance law within the industry, we have seen that some companies were far more active in promoting the idea than others. One firm, in particular, stood out. Bumiputera 1912 had a unique interest in the whole issue of an insurance law. Bumiputera 1912 was the only firm structured as a mutual society, as distinct from a limited liability company. While this form of enterprise is not uncommon in the insurance industries of the West, it is unique in Indonesia. This only became significant after it emerged that the Department of Finance, following consultations with the Harvard Institute for International Development advisory team, was contemplating the insertion of a requirement in the new law that all insurance firms be structured as limited liability companies.[42]

Bumiputera had an interest in the proposal for an insurance law on two levels. First, as one of the most prosperous and well established firms it had a strong interest in the introduction of a law to help strengthen the industry's future. At a deeper level, though, it had a more immediate and urgent interest in it, centring around the very future of the firm.[43] The possibility that Bumiputera might be forced to restructure itself as a limited liability company was viewed with horror by the firm's management. The management's position was made more difficult by the fact that it was somewhat isolated on the issue, with no obvious source of support. Indeed, it might reasonably have been presumed that some of Bumiputera's competitors in the life insurance sector would welcome the prospect of the firm having to transform itself and cope with all the ensuing administrative and commercial headaches. In this situation, Bumiputera sought to have the proposal for the elimination of mutuals erased from the—still unseen—draft law which the Department of Finance had before it.

The main strategic asset the firm's management had in their battle was that Bumiputera was one of the two giants of the life insurance industry. Furthermore, it had been in operation for a very long time, with a proven commercial track-record, and was generally regarded as a good example of what local enterprise could achieve. Bumiputera thus argued that the Department of Finance would be foolish to contemplate radically disturbing what was, after all, an Indonesian and, more pointedly, *pribumi* success story.

The first hurdle the Bumiputera management faced in seeking to promote this view was that the people they most needed to convince, Marzuki Usman and the Directorate of Financial Institutions, were seen as sceptical of their position. The Department of Finance, far from being a neutral broker on the matter, was the source of the opposing viewpoint. Bumiputera was therefore forced to seek other routes to bring pressure to bear on the Department of Finance to have it reconsider its position. Attention was thus shifted to the Parliament and, to a lesser extent, the press. The Bumiputera management approached the leadership of Committee VII on an informal basis to sound them out on the question of mutuals and the proposed insurance law. Like the DAI, Bumiputera executives focused their attention on leading figures within the GOLKAR and ABRI factions of the Committee.

Bumiputera argued its case on two main grounds. First, it insisted that a highly reputable and well-established firm should not be placed in jeopardy because of an organisational technicality. Drawing on useful technical data from the United States (supplied to the Bumiputera management by a joint venture partner)[44] it argued that mutual societies were in no sense inferior to limited liability companies. Second, and more tellingly, it argued strongly that the mutual society should, in principle, be defended as a form of business enterprise, as it was in effect sanctioned in the Indonesian Constitution. This was a very skillful appeal on the basis of Section 33 of the Constitution which embodies the rhetorically much vaunted 'family principle' (discussed in Chapter 3). The family principle—with its emphasis on cooperation and sharing—is a central tenet of the official thinking. Bumiputera was able to strike a resonant chord with key members of Committee VII at both this subjective ideological level, and at the more concrete level that the firm was a great success and should not be threatened.

After a series of informal meetings with the leaders of Committee VII had revealed that they were sympathetic to Bumiputera's plight, it was agreed that the Committee would convene a formal and public hearing on the issue. The discussion would then be re-run in a public setting so that Bumiputera's arguments would attract press attention, and also draw the attention of senior echelons of the Department of Finance and other sections of the state elite. In September 1986, the

Committee conducted a special hearing into the question of the proposed new insurance law, at which the Executive Director of Bumiputera made a high profile appearance. Responding to questions from the Committee he argued that the proposed insurance law must be guided by the ideas embodied in Section 33 of the Constitution, and provide for the three forms of economic enterprise recognised as legitimate—cooperatives, mutual societies and limited liability companies. Bumiputera also made a point of inviting journalists to observe the session.[45] Publicity of this sort, and the linking of mutuals to cooperatives served to make it considerably more difficult for the Department of Finance to eliminate mutuals. Bumiputera had therefore skillfully adapted constitutional niceties and official rhetoric to its own ends, for it was widely recognised that the government, and particularly the President, had a long-standing commitment to economic cooperatives as a form of enterprise which supposedly promoted equality.

Bumiputera thus made extensive use of Committee VII's commitment not only to the rapid introduction of an insurance law, but also to the preservation of mutuals. Beyond this, other measures used to promote both Bumiputera's profile and wider awareness of the important position it held within the life insurance industry, included the convening of a special seminar on insurance industry affairs to which leading figures from industry, government and Parliament, as well as journalists, were invited. This opportunity, together with a similar one provided by celebrations to mark the firm's seventy-fifth anniversary, were used to promote the case for the rapid introduction of an insurance law in tandem with the case for the preservation of mutuals.[46] Significantly, in all of its efforts, Bumiputera sought to downplay its own narrow self-preservation interest in the mutual issue, emphasising instead its broad commitment to the introduction of an insurance law. Other small ways in which it sought to disguise its particular interest were to use those of its executives who were also office holders within the DAI as public spokesmen, as well as using DAI stationery for letter writing, thus promoting the impression that the DAI (and by extension, the whole insurance industry) endorsed their arguments.

The Department of Finance and the Proposed Insurance Law

Thus far, emphasis has been given to the active role of industry in promoting an insurance law during 1985–86. It is important to recall, however, that much of the initiative lay with the Directorate for Financial Institutions. The Directorate was, after all, also keen to see the law finally promulgated. This was something which industry advocates occasionally overlooked. By 1985–86, as we have seen, the only real issue in question was not whether in fact an insurance law should be introduced, or what form it should take, but simply when it should happen. Marzuki Usman also had a major interest in seeing the law introduced as soon as possible. He was widely seen as having a personal commitment to the realisation of an insurance law, as well as the other two proposed financial services sector laws (banking and pension funds). The introduction of the laws would represent one of the most important achievements of his stewardship.

In a bid to advance the progress of the issue, Marzuki during 1985 arranged a series of informal meetings with various figures within the insurance industry to ascertain for himself 'grass-roots' industry attitudes. These meetings were intended to act as a supplement to the various talks held with the DAI.[47] At the same time, he convened discussions with the key members of Committee VII so as to 'sound out' possible Parliamentary objections in advance of the draft law actually being submitted as a bill for consideration. This was the principal opportunity for the activist committee members to have an input to the policy-formation process. The Department of Finance would, as a matter of course, seek to take account of possible Parliamentary reservations at this preliminary stage, long before the issue came before the Parliament formally. During these discussions, committee members were able to air matters of concern of their own about the proposed law, as well as those which had been thrown up by their negotiations with industry figures.[48]

Following the finalising of the draft by the Directorate for Financial Institutions, it was passed upwards through the Department of Finance for approval, and thence on to the State Secretariat, which checks all legislation before submission to the Parliament. At the time of writing, the bill has not emerged from the State Secretariat and industry still remains largely ignorant of its contents. The only significant exception to this is that there were suggestions that Bumiputera has been successful in its bid to lobby against the inclusion of a clause for the elimination of mutuals.

Conclusion

In 1984 the insurance industry was given clear indications by officials as senior as the Minister of Finance that an insurance law would be submitted to the Parliament in a very short time. In 1985 the DAI was given a firm assurance that a bill would be submitted to Parliament by early 1986 at the latest. As 1986 progressed, the date was again pushed back, this time to before the general election of 1987. When, in turn, this deadline came and went, they were told not to despair as it would definitely be out by the time of the confirmation of the positions of President Suharto and his Vice President in March 1988.

Why was it that the insurance law on several occasions came very close to being submitted to the Parliament, but did not actually get there? As we have seen, not only the insurance industry, but also the Directorate of Financial Institutions was very much in favour of the introduction of such a law. An important part of the answer seems to have been that the introduction of an insurance law simply was not a priority issue on the government's overall legislative agenda. Under the Indonesian Constitution, both the government and members of the Parliament are able to introduce legislation for consideration. As emphasised in Chapter 2, the practice of the New Order period has, however, been for all bills to be initiated by the executive, with the Parliament playing a more passive role. In this situation, it has been the State Secretariat which has had primary responsibility for co-ordinating with other departments and setting the legislative agenda, thereby determining which proposals are processed into laws. The problem the insurance law proposal has faced has been competition both with other issues requiring legislative attention within the pur-view of the Finance Department, and also at a higher level, with all the many priorities of the numerous areas of government activity that are inevitably channelled via the State Secretariat. Other issues which have in the past been given precedence over the insurance law include taxation law, the KADIN law, the intellectual property rights law and state protocol law. Thus the fact that the Directorate for Financial Institutions supported the submission of a bill to the Parliament, was of itself, insufficient. The matter also needed the full support of both the Minister of Finance and the State Secretariat—a set of conditions which has to date not existed.

Why has the insurance law been unable to secure a high ranking in the government's priorities? A number of factors stand out. First and foremost, there has been no acute crisis in the insurance industry which has demanded urgent government attention. While there was some concern in late 1985 about the closure of insurance firms—which did at the time, it should be noted, generate increased activity by the Department of Finance—there has not been a high profile crisis or controversy in the industry. Ironically, had the insurance industry been obviously in dire circumstances, its chances of having the insurance law introduced promptly would have been very much greater. In the absence of controversy (such as existed in the textile and pharmaceutical case-studies) it has been much more difficult for the case for an insurance law to win a priority ranking. In Indonesia, as elsewhere, management of 'crises' consumes much of the time and energy of political leaders and, as such, problems that are not acute do not quickly come to the attention of government.

A second factor, which is closely linked to the first, is that the insurance industry is not a pivotal industry. It does not occupy a strategic position in the national economy such as that of rice or oil production, or the banking industry. Similarly, it is not an important export revenue earner—a key criterion since the slump in oil prices. Nor does it perform a socially and politically sensitive function in the way that, for instance, the pharmaceutical industry does. (Widespread company failure in the insurance industry would, however, presumably be an emotive issue, with people losing long term savings and investment.) A third factor is that despite the exaggerated expectations of some sections of the industry as to the benefits an insurance law might bring, it was not crucial to the industry's survival. The introduction of an insurance law—while definitely desirable—was not critical. The industry would, and did, continue to operate and grow without it. The Department of Finance was clearly cognisant of this, and thus not susceptible to being overwhelmed by industry rhetoric.

A final factor is that the political clout of the insurance industry (which, as already noted, was not great)[49] was diminished further by the fact that although during 1985–86 no one opposed the idea of the law, it was quite evident that only a portion of all firms were strongly committed to pushing for it. Many of the numerous small insurance firms were preoccupied with short term survival rather than the long term future of the industry and a substantial number of joint ventures were not particularly interested in the issue. But more importantly than this, the state-controlled firms have not been avid supporters of the law. This is especially significant in the insurance industry where—unlike the spinning or pharmaceutical industries—state enterprises loom very large. Being so dominated by the state-controlled firms, the concerns of the activist private sector firms have tended to be overshadowed in the insurance industry.

All of these various factors have so far combined to deny the industry activists their prize. In the meantime, the Department of Finance has continued to make adjustments to the existing regulatory framework.[50] Sooner or later the government will introduce a broad-based insurance law—it has no reason not to.[51] Too much time and money have been invested in preparing a draft and steering it to the stage of being 'on-hold' in the State Secretariat. This investment will not lightly be discarded.

What does this case-study have to offer in terms of the theoretical debates about the nature of the Indonesian polity? Certainly the DAI's story is less dramatic than those of either SEKBERTAL or GPF. Not only did the insurance industry not 'win', it also did not organise itself in an especially remarkable way. Furthermore, this has not been a case in which the industry was the 'initiator' of a policy change. Unlike the spinning or pharmaceutical cases, where much of the initiative lay with the industry group, in this case it cannot be claimed that the Department of Finance was primarily responding to an industry stimulus. Though the Department of Finance was not insensitive to industry wishes, carriage of the matter remained very much in its hands. Indeed, an adequate account of the insurance law could be given with far less reference to industry activities than in the two previous case-studies. And yet, in many respects this is precisely what makes this such a useful case, for it provides us with a more typical illustration of the dynamics of relations between business and the state in Indonesia. After all, it is not everyday that an industry is locked into an intractable dispute with the government such as that concerning CBTI in the textile industry.

But here it must be recalled that even though the bargaining position of the DAI vis-a-vis the Department of Finance was decidedly weaker than that of either SEKBERTAL or GPF and their bureaucratic counterparts, it is evident that activist elements within the organisation took a variety of initiatives to promote their demands for the introduction of an insurance law. For example, industry representatives deliberately sought to take advantage of the differences between Committee VII of the Parliament and the Department of Finance by playing them off against one another. Similarly in terms of appeals on the basis of the family principle (section 33 of the Constitution), what is noteworthy is the way in which industry deliberately attempted to exploit this pervasive set of ideas in order to constrain state officials. Though not decisive in its impact, the insurance industry was nonetheless active in seeking to push for preferred policy outcomes. While less striking than in the two previous cases, we again see loose partnerships and tactical alliances being formed between industry leaders and various figures within the state structure in a bid to influence a policy outcome.

The individual, or personal approaches to the Department of Finance, were part of a broader, albeit loosely coordinated, effort towards a *collective* goal. In using personal relationships to advance the case for an insurance law, the industry activists were not just seeking a private benefit for themselves, they were promoting a collective industry goal. As such, the phenomenon should not be described as patrimonialist. Furthermore, the recourse to the Parliament by the DAI was an at least gentle attempt to openly pressure the government to move on the issue. Most notable, though, in this respect were the efforts of Bumiputera, both to expedite the law, and ensure that it did not preclude mutual insurance firms. With greater organisational coherence and a more immediate interest in the matter than the rest of the DAI, Bumiputera was able to wage a vigorous and open campaign in a bid to influence the policy outcome.

With regard to questions about corporatism and state-society relations, the DAI presents a more subtle case than either SEKBERTAL or GPF. The fact that membership of the DAI was, in effect, compulsory and that it therefore served to herd all companies into one group, together with the tendency for the DAI chairmanship to be filled by the heads of state enterprises who have typically been reluctant to challenge the Department of Finance with any vigour, suggest a picture which seems quite in keeping with ideas about restrictive and exclusionary corporatist structures in New Order Indonesia. But here it must be recalled that to the extent activists within the industry were dissatisfied with the DAI's performance, they simply took matters into their own hands. Certainly the Department of Finance does not appear to have attempted to confine representational activity to the DAI. Thus, if the DAI was a corporatist pen erected by the state, the fences were not high.

While the action of a section of the insurance industry to take charge of promoting the law itself was not on a scale comparable to the SEKBERTAL movement, it was nonetheless indicative of the ability of the industry to pursue alternative channels for interest representation, to the extent that it was so motivated. In this respect it is salutary to note, regardless of the immediate fate of the law, the way in which the history of this issue from 1985 onwards has paralleled an increase in the insurance industry's capacity for interest representation.

There are signs that the industry's ability to gain an effective hearing from the government is improving. This change has come on two fronts: first, the government, and more broadly the state elite, is now more willing to listen, and second, the insurance industry is refining its capacity to promote industry interests. In the case of the former, the Department of Finance appears to be following a pattern that has emerged in Indonesia during the mid-1980s for government agencies to deal with industry groups on a more sensitive and sympathetic basis. The Department has become increasingly willing to pay attention (even if not necessarily act upon) insurance industry opinions. DAI leaders have been obtaining far better access at higher levels within the Department. Whereas, traditionally, access above the level of Director for Financial Institutions has been very limited, industry representatives have recently been gaining reasonable access at the much more powerful Director General level. Symbolic evidence of the greater attention being accorded to the industry by the Department can be found in the fact that the Minister of Finance, Radius Prawiro, officially opened the annual insurance congress in January 1987. While this may not seem important, it was the first time that a Minister had done so, and moreover it was a gesture from which industry leaders drew considerable satisfaction.[52] More concretely, there were suggestions in 1987 that the Sub-Directorates handling insurance (within the Directorate for Financial Institutions) would be strengthened, or even, perhaps, that the administrative architecture of the Department of Finance would be altered, with the insurance industry being upgraded to a Directorate of its own. Changes of this sort would significantly enhance the industry's profile politically, and strengthen the Finance Department's ability to respond to industry needs.

Sections of the insurance industry have also been active in seeking to promote the professionalism and representational capabilities of the DAI. An important step in this respect was the DAI's decision to appoint a full-time and professionally qualified Secretary General to administer the organisation. In the past, apart from clerical assistance, the DAI has been dependent on company executives voluntarily giving their time outside working hours. Since the appointment of a Secretary General the organisation has been not only more efficiently run, but also better informed and equipped to represent industry interests. A second change to the industry's approach to representation has been the recognition of the value of developing working links with sections of the Parliament, and particularly the press. Experience has shown both the DAI and individual companies that these two institutions can be of value in seeking to influence policy formation. Effort has been made by the DAI, for example, to promote understanding of and interest in the insurance industry among journalists, and to cultivate links with the more professional of them.[53] The brokering industry, in a smaller way, has also been following this path, seeking to increase its capabilities to advance brokering industries.

The catalyst for these internal industry reforms of representational capabilities has been dissatisfaction with the past performance of the DAI (and the brokers' association) inspired by the more difficult conditions associated with economic down-turn. Whereas in the past the passive performance of the DAI might have been acceptable, the tighter commercial conditions of the mid-1980s generated pressure for change. The more dynamic of the privately owned firms, in particular, became increasingly dissatisfied with the performance of the DAI. If membership in the only officially sanctioned representative organisation was, in effect, compulsory, company heads wanted to see some return on their regular membership fees. While dissatisfaction led some companies to pursue their own dealings with the state independently rather than rely on the DAI, discontent has not been sufficiently acute to generate the sort of revolution that took place in the representational arrangements in the textile industry. There has been no wholesale abandonment of the DAI. Instead it has been gradually reformed. The DAI is thus quietly evolving from a tame and very largely state-dominated corporatist body, to become more active and professional in promoting member interests to policy-makers. In this respect the DAI seems to be following the gradualist reform path of GPF rather than the more cataclysmic road of SEKBERTAL.

A key factor in determining whether this process develops much further seems likely to be whether the industry continues to be dominated by placid state-owned companies. Here it is instructive to contrast the DAI with GPF for, although the overall chairman of GPF was from a state-owned firm, this did not restrict effective representation of industry interests because state enterprises did not dominate the industry. As we saw, the private pharmaceutical manufacturers managed to ensure very effective promotion of their interests. Given that state enterprises happen to control a large slice of the various sub-sectors of the insurance industry, the character of their business operations is likely to have a significant impact on the political representation the industry enjoys. If they are forced to operate on a more competitive basis or, alternatively, the private sector is able to significantly increase its share of the market, more rapid changes in representational patterns may follow.

1. McLeod (1984) p. 86; and Emery (1970) pp. 205–6.
2. I am much indebted here to Henri Gunanto's valuable paper on insurance law in Indonesia. Gunanto (1985) pp. 4–6. Also important was the Minister of Finance's Decree no. 118 of 1966.
3. It is technically difficult to compare the size of life and general insurance industries. Assets are only a rough guide, since in the life insurance industry assets are not a good measure of strength or profitability. (This is because a large portion of a life insurance firms assets are held in trust for policy holders.)
4. This requirement was eventually dropped following regulatory reforms introduced in December 1988. (See 'Lebih Leluasa Tapi Lebih Ketat', *Tempo*, 31 December 1988.) Previously, the prohibition on selling foreign policies led to an apparently sizeable 'under-the-counter' trade

in such policies. In the early 1970s life insurance firms were permitted to write policies denominated in foreign currencies.

5. Skully (1985) p. 134.
6. Interviews with Suratno (Director of Bumiputera 1912 and Head of the DAI's Life Insurance Section) 10 June 1987; and Amiril (Director of Asuransi Jiwasraya Pty Ltd) 17 June 1987.
7. Wibisono (1987) p. 23.
8. These figures are illustrative only. Several factors make them of questionable accuracy. Most importantly, because Bumiputera 1912 is a mutual firm, rather than limited liability company, its actual ownership is dispersed among all policy holders. Nevertheless, it is widely regarded as a *pribumi* controlled firm. More generally, figures are obviously not available for all the firms in the list.
9. Skully (1985) p. 136.
10. Not included here is Jasa Raharja, the state-owned passenger accident insurance firm. While Jasa Raharja is often considered a social insurance firm (it bears all the hallmarks) many Finance Department statistics treat it as a general insurance firm. For consistency, this classification will be followed. For further detail on social insurance see, McLeod (1984) p. 87–89.
11. Interview with J. Tinggi Sianipar (Director of Jasa Raharja Pty Ltd) 19 June 1987.
12. Department of Finance (1986) p. 78. A fourth reinsurance firm, Tugu Reasuransi Pty Ltd, was opening in late 1987. The firm, a subsidiary of the giant Tugu Pratama Pty Ltd in the general insurance sector, seems likely to become a dominant force in the reinsurance sector.
13. Interview with H.L. Rumamby (President Director of Asuransi Sari Sumber Agung Pty Ltd and member of the DAI executive) 7 August 1987.
14. A nice illustration of this was the competition and controversy surrounding the selection of the chairman for the 1987–89 period. It was widely expected that Tantyo Sudharmono, the very young head of the large (quasi-state) Timur Jauh company and son of State Secretary Sudharmono would get the position. In a surprise outcome it went instead to the head of Reasuransi Umum Indonesia, the state-owned reinsurance firm, following considerable lobbying to and fro. For a lively account of this see 'Purwanto, Ketua Baru Asuransi', *Prioritas*, 8 December 1986.
15. In the case of fire insurance tariffs—an area of some controversy—the committee is chaired by a representative of the Department of Finance.
16. Interviews with Tanto Sudiro (Chairman of the Brokers' Association) 23 June 1987; and Djonny Wiguna (President Director of Indosurance Broker Pty Ltd) 1 July 1987.
17. It should be noted, though, that this is a problem for insurance industries the world-over; the highly technical nature of the business has often deterred media interest.
18. Interview with Sri Muardjo Srimardji (PresidentDirector of Lippo Life

Pty Ltd), who was an official with the Department of Finance in the early 1960s, 26 June 1987.
19. In the early 1960s there had been a Department of Insurance, and then a Directorate of Insurance before insurance industry affairs were brought under the ambit of the Department of Finance in 1969. Interview with Wibowo Wirosudiro (Head of the Sub-Directorate for General Insurance, in the Directorate for Financial Institutions) 14 July 1987.
20. The emphasis here is very much on the relationship between the insurance industry and the state, rather than the industry and the consumer. The latter relationship—between the insurer and the insured—is the subject of contract law, technically a part of private law rather than public law. Our concern here is primarily with the public law side. At present the private law governing commercial contracts is embodied in the *Kitab Undang Undang Hukum Perdata* and the *Kitab Undang Undang Hukum Dagang*, bodies of legal statute left over, almost as relics, from colonial times. Because the relevance of these to modern disputes over insurance contracts is so cloudy both parties to disputes have often been unable to have the matter brought before a court. In this situation it has been necessary to reach 'out-of-court' settlements, sometimes adjudicated by the DAI or possibly KADIN. Many insurance executives believe that this has necessitated financial pay-outs which would not have been required were the matter to be decided by a court. [Interviews with, for example, Djonny Wiguna (President Director of Ausransi Jiwa Central Asia Raya Pty Ltd, and DAI co-treasurer) 1 July 1987; and Gerit Hutabarat (Director Reasuransi Umum Indonesia Pty Ltd and member of the DAI Legal Section) 11 July 1987.]
Some confusion arises surrounding the distinction between public and private law. In relation to insurance, public law regulates the overall operation of insurance enterprise, while private law pertains to contract law. However, this distinction in principle is not consistent in actual practice as there is considerable blurring, with some aspects of public law governing private law. Although this case-study is concerned with the public law governing the insurance industry, it should be noted that parallel with the Department of Finance's consideration of reform to the public law governing the insurance industry, the Justice Department, in a separate exercise, is reviewing insurance contract law. It needs to be emphasised, then, that reference here to the preparation of an insurance law by the Finance Department should be understood as relating to public law. For further details on the distinction see, Gunanto (1985) pp. 2–4.
21. Interviews with Priasmoro Prawiroardjo (President Director of Bank Perkembangan Asia) 6 June 1987; and Beren Ginting (Deputy Head of Committee VII, GOLKAR *fraksi*) 13 June 1987.
22. Interview with Amiril (Director of Jiwasraya and formerly an insurance official with the Department of Finance) 17 June 1987.
23. Interview with R.G. Doeriat (Executive Director of Ramayana Pty Ltd

and former DAI Director); see 'Mengapa UU Perasuransian Perlu Diciptakan?', *Berita Buana*, 22 April 1980.

24. Interviews with Rudy Sidharta (President Director of Tugu Reasuransi Pty Ltd and former head of the DAI) 30 June 1987; Amiril (Director of Jiwasraya Pty Ltd and formerly an insurance official with the Department of Finance) 17 June 1987; and Marzuki Usman (Director for Financial Institutions) 13 July 1987.

25. See for example 'Mengapa UU Perasuransian Perlu Diciptakan?', *Berita Buana*, 22 April 1980; 'Dunia Asuransi Dikhwatirkan Jadi Penghambat Pembangunan', *Kompas*, 2 June 1980; and 'Sektor Asuransi Perlu Dibenahi', *Suara Karya*, 30 June 1980.

26. Liem Soe Liong's interest in the financial services sector of the Indonesian economy centre around Bank Central Asia (Indonesia's largest private bank). In the insurance industry he owns or has major and direct shares in Asuransi Jiwa Central Asia Raya Pty Ltd (life), Asuransi Lippo Life Pty Ltd (life), Maskapai Asuransi Djakarta 1945 Pty Ltd (general), Ausransi Central Asia Pty Ltd (general), Maskapai Asuransi Nasuha Pty Ltd (general), Maskapai Asuransi Marga Pusaka (general), Asuransi Pertiwi Agung Prawira Pty Ltd (general), Ausransi Purwanjasa Pty Ltd (general). For further details of Liem Soe Liong's business activities, see Robison (1986 a) and Harahap (1986).

27. Interview with Doeriat (President Director of Maskapai Asuransi Ramyana Pty Ltd and former head of the DAI) 9 July 1987. For public reference to this, see 'Ketua DAI: Masih Tetap Ada Perusahaan Asuransi Yang Nakal', *Kompas*, 16 February 1981.

28. Interviews with Wahjoe (President Director of Bimantara Graha Pty Ltd) 30 June 1987; and Tanto Sudiro (Chairman of the Brokers' Association) 23 June 1987.

29. Unlike many other industries in which a satisfactory return can usually be obtained within such a time frame, the insurance industry generally requires a longer period to fully realise investment potential. The relevant regulation here is article 6 of the Minister of Finance's Decree no. 292/KMK.011/1982.

30. Interviews with Henri Gunanto (Attorney at Law, Gunanto, Prasasto & Co) 14 July 1987; Amiril (Director of Jiwasraya Pty Ltd) 9 July 1987; and J. Tinggi Sianipar (Director of Jasa Rahrja Pty Ltd) 19 June 1987.

31. Interview with Rudy Sidharta (President Director of Tugu Reinsurance Pty Ltd) 30 June 1987.

32. Having a basis in law is widely seen as an affirmation of status. The explicit reference to the insurance industry in REPELITA. IV (1984), was for example, seen as an important first step in promoting the industry's standing. The quest for an actual law was thus in many respects comparable to KADIN's obsession with pursuing recognition in law.

33. See, for example, 'Perlu Dibatasi Pemberian Izin Pendirian Asuransi Baru', *Pelita*, 13 February 1984.

34. For public reference to statements presaging an imminent introduction of an insurance law see, 'RUU Tentang Pokok-Pokok Usaha Perasu-

ransian Akan Diajukan Ke DPR', *Kompas*, 5 January 1984; 'Konsep
RUU Usaha Perasuransian Tengah Disiapkan', *Business News*, 20 Au-
gust 1984; 'Baru 20–30 Persen Masyarakat Golongan Mampu Terserap
Asuransi', *Antara*, 24 March 1984; and 'Pemerintah Menyiapkan RUU
Perbankan Dan Perasuransian', *Kompas*, 2 April 1984.
35. Interviews with Rudy Wanandi (President Director of Wahana Tata Pty
Ltd and Deputy Head of the DAI) 23 July 1987; and H.L. Rumamby
(President Director of Asuransi Sari Sumber Agung Pty Ltd and DAI
executive) 7 August 1987. For reference to the forced closure of one
firm see, 'Dicabut, Izin Usaha Perusahaan Asuransi Rafelsa Raya',
Pelita, 29 June 1985.
36. Interviews with Djonny Wiguna (President Director of Asuransi Jiwa
Central Asia Raya Pty Ltd and co-Treasurer of the DAI) 1 July 1987;
and Sujono Soepeno (Director of Auransi Panin Putra Pty Ltd and
Deputy Head of the life Insurance Section of DAI) 3 July 1987.
37. For reference to public occasions on which senior Committee VII figures
have spoken openly on this, see, for instance, 'Harus Terjamin,
Kepastian Hak Pemegang Polis Asuransi', *Kompas*, 30 June 1986;
'Pengusaha Asuransi Di Indonesia Berjalan Sendiri-Sendiri', *Suara
Karya*, 11 August 1986; and 'Dana Asuransi Jiwa Bisa Gantikan Posisi
Pinjaman Luar Negeri', *Merdeka*, 27 October 1986.
38. Interviews with Beren Ginting, (Deputy of Committee VII, GOLKAR
fraksi) 13 June 1987 and 19 August 1987.
39. Interview with Tantyo Sudharmono (President Director of Timur Jauh
Pty Ltd and member of the DAI Advisory Council) 24 August 1987.
40. 'Pengusaha Asuransi Di Indonesia Berjalan Sendiri-Sendiri', *Suara
Karya*, 11 August 1986.
41. Interviews with Catherine Prime and Andrew Giffin (Harvard Institute
for International Development consultants to the Department of
Finance) 13 June 1987.
42. Two factors lay behind their preference for the limited liability company
rather than the mutual. First, there was seen to be less effective control
by 'shareholders' over the direction of firm policy in mutuals for the
simple reason that shareholders in a mutual are the thousands of
individual policy holders, as opposed to the relatively few initial capital
investors who found a limited liability company. Secondly, mutuals
were seen to be of relatively less use for the ultimate goal of assisting
national economic development (via the mobilisation of capital resources) as the firm's earnings were dispersed among policy holders
rather than accumulating as retained earnings. Interviews with Suratno
(Director of Bumiputera 1912 and Head of the DAI's Life Insurance
Section) 9 July 1987; and Wibowo Wirosudiro (Head of the Sub-
Directorate for General Insurance, Department of Finance) 14 July
1987.
43. For much of this material on Bumiputera's experience I am grateful for
interviews with, among others, Suratno (Director of Bumiputera 1912
and Head of the DAI's Life Insurance Section) 10 June 1987 & 9 July
1987; Wibowo Wirosudiro (Head of the Sub-Directorate for General

Insurance, Department of Finance) 14 July 1987 & 25 August 1987; and Beren Ginting (Deputy Head of Committee VII, GOLKAR *fraksi*) 13 June 1987 & 19 August 1987.

44. Bumiputera 1912 has an informal arrangement (which seems to be a precursor to an official joint venture) with the large US based mutual insurance firm, John Hancock, in Asuransi Pensiun Bumiputera 1974.

45. See, for example, 'Perlu Diciptakan Persaingan Antar Perusahaan Asuransi', *Berita Buana*, 23 September 1986.

46. See, 'Perasuransian Tak Punya Kekuatan Karena Belum Ada Undang-Undangnya', *Pelita*, 28 November 1986.

47. Interviews with Sonni Dwi Harsono (President Director Tugu Pratama Pty Ltd) 25 June 1987; Marzuki Usman (Director for Financial Institutions) 9 & 13 July 1987; and Wibowo Wirosudiro (Head of the Sub-Directorate for General Insurance) 14 July 1987.

48. Interviews with Beren Ginting (Deputy Head of Committee VII, GOLKAR *fraksi*) 13 June 1987; and Marzuki Usman (Director for Financial Institutions, Department of Finance) 9 & 13 July 1987.

49. It might be thought that the public commitment of Tantyo Sudharmono to the early introduction of an insurance law would have guaranteed success because of the fact that his father was the extremely influential State Secretary. While this would have afforded a nice illustration of patrimonialism, in practice the 'connection' proved unrewarding. Though in a senior position, Tantyo was a very young man. Following a minor personal scandal, he resigned from his position at Timur Jauh in early 1988.

50. See 'Lebih Leluasa Tapi Lebih Ketat', *Tempo*, 31 December 1988.

51. Noteworthy in this regard are the comments made at the meeting of the Inter-Governmental Group on Indonesia (the county's foreign financial backers) in June 1988 by the new Finance Minister, Sumarlin. Speaking after the meeting, Sumarlin told reporters that, in order to enhance the country's capability for domestic capital mobilisation, work was underway on the drafting of a set of laws on the insurance, pension and banking industries. See, 'Optimists Pour in More Money', *Far Eastern Economic Review*, 30 June 1988.

52. Interview with H.L. Rumamby (President Director of Asuransi Sari Sumber Agung Pty Ltd and DAI executive) 7 August 1987.

53. Interview with Sujono Soepono (Director of Panin Putra Pty Ltd and DAI official) 3 July 1987.

7

Business and Political Change

A central aim of this study has been to cast light on the processes of political representation, and more broadly, policy-formation, in order to understand better the system of governance in contemporary Indonesia. While the focus has been on the business sector, a range of other interests and actors have, inevitably, also drawn our attention. In this respect the three stories presented here have usefully highlighted the fact that policy formation in Indonesia is far more complex, and in particular, involves more bargaining and coalition-building among both state and societal actors than has been generally recognised.

At a general level the three stories are about the politics of policy-making. A central feature of the policy disputes associated with the various cases was the vigorous political bargaining and debate among a range of actors and institutions within the overall state structure. Not only were bureaucrats and departments involved in conflict and negotiation, but parliamentarians, ministers and even the President himself were all variously involved. Central though the involvement of these players was, undoubtedly the most remarkable aspect of the stories was the part played by the extra-state actors. Aside from the industry groups, we saw a number of other extra-state actors all playing a part in the shaping of policy outcomes. Particularly notable here was the role of the press; it proved to be very important as an articulator of interests from both in and outside the state, as well as an active player in its own right. But it is, of course, the role of the industry groups which was most salient, for at the core of each of the stories was a desire by a broad-based industry association to seek significant changes to existing government policy. In the textile and pharmaceutical cases the industry group was successful in achieving its major goals, while in the insurance case it was less clear cut.

But more important than whether or not they actually 'won', was the *way* in which each industry's interests were promoted. In this respect, although there were differences among them, the three cases all basically point in the same direction: sections of business in Indonesia today can and do organise themselves in a collective fashion and pursue group interests in an independent manner. Phenomena of this sort are very much at odds with the received wisdom about the nature of political representation and policy formation in Indonesia.

As we saw at the outset, there is a strong consensus in the scholarly literature on Indonesian politics that influence over policy is very largely limited to the state, with societal groups being almost wholly excluded from participation on any systematic basis. In the authoritarian environment of the New Order, only three types of political linkage between state and society have been seen as of any note: corporatist institutions, political 'osmosis' and patron client links. None is regarded as offering a real opportunity for input to the policy process on any sustained or systematic basis. The existing exclusionary corporatist representational structures are widely viewed as little more than state-sponsored instruments to limit rather than enhance interest representation. Political input by way of what has here been termed 'osmosis', or absorption, is seen to operate in only a very indirect and gradual manner, while clientelistic links are by their nature highly personalised and individualised. Evidence of all three was thrown up in the stories, and the reality of any of these forms of political linkage is not in question here. What *is* at issue, is the fact that the organised and group-based activities of SEKBERTAL, GPF and (even) the DAI is a phenomenon which is qualitatively different. It is evident that their behaviour was not primarily of a clientelistic nature; in pursuing their objectives these organisations were not dependent on personal patrons within the government. Equally, their behaviour does not seem to correspond to that which would not normally be associated with a 'state' (to use Schmitter's term) or restrictive authoritarian style of corporatism. In this regard, what is striking is the way in which two of the organisations, SEKBERTAL and GPF, operated quite independently of state control, and in the case of SEKBERTAL arose spontaneously. Neither of the associations was in any real sense controlled or managed by the state. They did not function to limit or exclude the demands of their membership. Precisely the opposite; they served to facilitate and enhance the capacity of their constituents to achieve vital input to the policy process. This is not to question the fact that, as we saw early on, a fundamental feature of politics in Indonesia is the government's restrictive corporatist strategy which was specifically intended to limit and reduce the capacity for independent demand-making by groups in society. As was stressed early in this study, the Indonesian political landscape is indeed dotted with state-sponsored corporatist organisations which seem to perform this restrictive role.

An important point to emerge here, then, is the idea that business groups can turn a restrictive corporatist institution to serve their own purposes, rather than those of the state's political strategists. GPF was quietly transformed to become a powerful instrument for pharmaceutical manufacturers. The DAI appears to be undergoing a slower, though comparable, transition. On the other hand, SEK-BERTAL, and more broadly FITI, sprang up as a result of extreme alienation among a critical mass of producers with existing representational arrangements across the textile industry. In this case, rather than gradual metamorphosis in the character of an existing corporatist structure, it was dramatically swept aside in an outburst of political activity as producers moved to establish a representational structure which would better serve their collective interests.

SEKBERTAL, FITI, GPF (and to a lesser extent, the DAI) present an interesting challenge, for though they have established a political identity and momentum which is autonomous of the state, they are recognisably corporatist in form. Here it is useful to recall Schmitter's basic distinction between what he termed 'state' (authoritarian) and 'societal' (liberal) patterns of corporatism. In his study of Peru, Alfred Stepan[1] takes this rudimentary division a step further by subdividing the 'state' variant of corporatism between what he labels 'inclusionary' and 'exclusionary' poles. The exclusionary end of the spectrum is characterised by a more repressive approach and a heavy reliance by the state on coercion. At the inclusionary end, while the state remains dominant, there is much greater scope for societal participation. Though functionally organised and state-designated representative organisations are common to both, in the latter they facilitate the channeling of the demands of various social sectors up to policy-makers, rather than serving primarily to obstruct or suppress interest articulation. Importantly, as Stepan himself emphasises, inclusionary patterns of corporatism should not be equated with liberal democracy or other imaginable systems of interest representation in which power is widely diffused. In the inclusionary model, though the state still largely dominates the political landscape, corporatist representational structures do provide a means by which extra-state groups can effectively transmit their concerns to decision-makers.

Indonesia seems to be in the process of evolving from an exclusionary to a more inclusionary style of corporatism. Though, unquestionably, the state remains pre-eminent in Indonesian politics, some of the corporatist structures which previously obstructed demand-making are now being turned around by their client groups. This is not to suggest that the character of the whole state-sponsored corporatist network is now leaning in a much more inclusionary direction. Many, indeed most, of the corporatist representational structures in Indonesia are still decidedly closer to Stepan's exclusionary pole than, for example, SEKBERTAL, FITI or GPF. But if the focus is shifted from this macro level down to a sectoral level, greater clarity is possible. It does seem that some sectors are beginning to develop more independent representational capabilities and are becoming better placed to project their demands into the policy process. This, however, begs the further question of which sectors are most likely to have or develop stronger political impact. Was it simply a random occurrence that it should have been the textile and pharmaceutical industries which mobilised so successfully, or are there some common variables?

At a general level it is possible to identify a number of telling factors which emerge from the three stories presented here. Some of these have been noted by analysts working in other areas. Bates,[2] working on agriculture in Africa, and Ramsay on sugar in Thailand,[3] concur on three factors affecting the propensity of producers to organise themselves on a group-basis: the level of concentration of production, the commercial scale of producers and their geographical spread. They found that producers were more likely to mobilise effectively if the farms (or firms) were relatively large, ownership was concentrated in relatively few hands and production was not too geographically dispersed. That is, it is much easier for business people to organise themselves successfully if they are fewer, larger and near to each other.

These are all sound propositions which are supported by the three cases here. It was a common-place observation in the textile industry, for example, that the weaving sector had never been well organised or represented because there were so many producers, many of them small, and they were scattered widely. The spinning sector, by contrast, had comparatively few producers and they were very largely concentrated in Bandung and nearby Jakarta. Similarly, in the pharmaceutical industry, though there were some 300 manufacturers, the salient fact was that the great majority of production was concentrated in the hands of about 80 firms which were nearly all based in Jakarta. It was these firms which were the driving force behind pharmaceutical industry representation in GPF.

Another factor (which Ramsay also notes[4]) is the importance of the quality of industry leadership. In both GPF and SEKBERTAL a striking feature of their success was the political acumen of the leadership. Related to this is the degree to which an industry, or an industry association, is riven with divisions and factional cleavages. A united and cohesive political group will always stand a better chance of success.

An additional variable suggested by the case-studies is the strategic importance of an industry within the overall national economy. An industry which produces a vital good or service, is a major employer, is a major generator of export revenue or mobiliser of capital, will find it much easier to command the sympathetic attention of policy-makers than a relatively unimportant one.

More important than any of these various factors, however, seems to be the question of ownership. Privately owned firms (especially those of medium to large scale) tended to be much more active within their industry association than state owned enterprises or cooperatives. Extrapolating, it seems probable that industries in which the private sector is dominant are more likely to organise an effective representative association to promote collective interests. This was one striking difference between the pharmaceutical and spinning industries on the one hand, and the insurance industry on the other. And yet, even in the insurance industry, though the private sector did not dominate, it was precisely the private firms which were the most active in seeking to mobilise for collective action. This proposition does not rest just on the idea that risk-taking by private capital, with its short-term profit drive, begets greater dynamism.[5] If managers of state enterprises fear their positions may suffer, they are unlikely to agitate for policy reform in a situation where this is opposed by their political masters in the bureaucracy.

These various criteria give us some idea of the sectors of industry which are more likely to be politically active. It is only a very rough guide they provide, however. Less predictable circumstantial factors will, inevitably, also be important. Most obviously, it depends on the importance of the particular issue under contention. Business people (like others) will naturally tend to mobilise more cohesively and effectively on a matter of great concern to them, than on a less pressing issue. The sense of urgency and determination is a vital ingredient. The failure of the DAI to secure an insurance law illustrated this. Possibly SEKBERTAL or GPF would have been less able to intervene effectively on matters which were not of such fundamental interest to their membership. Similarly, in a basically authoritarian setting such as Indonesia's it will obviously also be more difficult, and possibly even dangerous, to mobilise group action if it clashes with the personal interests of powerful figures within the government. With issues that are imbued with this sort of political sensitivity, the risk of provoking coercive countermeasures may outweigh the desire to pursue reform.[6]

There are, then, a range of factors or circumstances which can favour or hinder effective political mobilisation. The level of political representation is certain to vary across sectors in the community and across issues. Though drawing on sector-based situations, this study has been cast at a macro level. For the argument here about the emerging but largely overlooked political capabilities of extra-state groups to be further explored and extended, new research which has a higher degree of sector and issue specific sensitivity is needed. Moreover, in addition to information about other areas of business, there is a pressing need for research into the capacity of segments of society with fewer political resources (for instance, labour and religious organisations) to project their demands into the policy process.

It is worth pausing here to ask: why, if the basic thesis about the significance of societal groups developed here is valid, has it not been propounded before now? Why have other observers not drawn similar conclusions? Two types of explanation suggest themselves. One line of argument is that political scientists have been consistently misinterpreting, or at least overlooking, important elements of political life in Indonesia. The second possible explanation for this puzzle is that the subject of our inquiries has been changing. In other words, the politico-economic character of Indonesia is in a state of flux, and the phenomena identified in this study are indicative of these changes.

Taking the first of these explanations, the possibility of systematic misperception, it is useful to reflect for a moment on the debates which have taken place regarding Western writing, particularly American, on the Soviet Union. Writing in 1977 (and thus well before Mikhael Gorbachev and *glasnost*), the prominent Soviet specialist, Jerry Hough, argued that American political scientists had steadfastly overlooked the complexity of state-society relations in the Soviet Union.[7] He speculated about possible reasons for this, and noted, among others, the likely influence of the ideological conditioning of the Cold War. Hough went on to argue that in attempting to address the question of how responsive to societal demands or inputs one political system (the Soviet Union) is compared to another (the United States), political scientists have tended to focus primarily on the extent to which Western notions of civil rights are guaranteed in a country.[8] Comparable observations have been made in the

context of a study of Indonesia by at least one analyst, William
Liddle, who argued that the true complexity of state-society relations
is often overlooked 'because political scientists are too caught in the
search for ways to transform rightist dictatorships into regimes more
to our normative taste.'[9]

Looking back on the currents of foreign writing on Indonesian
politics, it is clear that since about the time of the Australian scholar
Herbert Feith's celebrated analysis of the decline of constitutional
democracy during the late 1950s, there has been growing moral
discomfort about the increasingly authoritarian and anti-democratic
nature of Indonesian politics. This normative vein grew markedly
after the coup attempt of 1965 and the rise of Suharto's military-
based New Order government. It is not hard to identify with the
concerns of these many writers. Be that as it may, the point to made
here is that, particularly since 1965, there has been a tendency for
academics to focus on the way in which power has become concentrated inside the state in the hands of a small number of mostly
military figures. Academics have tended to emphasise the way in
which societal interests have been increasingly excluded from political participation and policy formation. This is scarcely surprising
given the increasingly stark contrast between the style of New Order
politics and what had gone before it. However, we have now reached
a position where the literature of the last five to ten years contains
very little recognition of the possibility of significant societal inputs at
all. And it is in this respect that a comparison with studies of the
Soviet Union becomes interesting. The link, of course, is the un-
divided attention to the state. It is intriguing to note the way that,
while still remaining state-centred, corporatist and bureaucratic pluralist accounts of politics in Indonesia have been put forward, just as
they were in Soviet studies.[10] The point of raising Hough's critique of
Soviet studies is not to suggest that the Indonesian and Soviet
political systems are similar (though there are some striking parallels). Here the concern is not with the nature of the Soviet political
system, but rather with the way in which academic interpretations of
it have evolved. Students of Indonesian politics might well benefit
from a consideration of Hough's arguments, regardless of the validity
of his account of the Soviet Union.

The more familiar channels of interest representation in Indonesia
may well be almost lifeless, as indeed was argued in Chapter 3.
Certainly, the political parties in themselves are no longer a force,
and most interest associations have been herded into corporatist pens
and castrated, while more generally, the military does seem far from
sympathetic to spontaneous and organised interest representation

activities. And yet, as this study has shown, there are still signs of political life in Indonesia. It is no longer tenable, if it ever was, to argue that political influence is effectively confined to the state elite, barring individual patrimonial links. There is a danger in making this claim that it may be interpreted as an attempt to defend the New Order against charges of repression or excessive exclusion of societal actors. That is certainly not the aim of this study; rather its objective is to draw analytical attention to the fact that more is going on in Indonesian politics, even if only among economic interests, than an almost exclusively state-centred approach has allowed us to see.

There are, then, grounds for concluding that an enduring fixation by political scientists with the State and ideas of political exclusion are at least partially responsible for the failure to recognise the greater plurality and complexity of Indonesian politics. But what of the second suggested explanation, namely that rather than prolonged misperception (or perhaps, in addition to it) the problem has been one of changing reality? In short, is the Indonesia of today significantly different to the Indonesia of the early 1970s? Here the evidence is much more clear cut; there are indeed very strong reasons for believing that there have been fundamental changes to Indonesia's political economy during the mid-1980s. Changes can be identified in three broad areas: the structure of the economy, representational institutions and ideology.

Changes on the economic front have been the most obvious and dramatic. It is now clear that there has been a process of basic structural change taking place in the Indonesian economy and that the private sector is coming to overshadow the public sector. Not surprisingly, the private sector has gradually grown in size and relative importance as the economy has expanded. However, in addition to the long term processes associated with economic development, the collapse in oil prices during the mid-1980s dramatically reduced state revenue and thereby accentuated the growth of the private sector, thrusting it, as it were, into the economic limelight.

Complications in measurement techniques make it difficult to obtain a precise picture of the shifting balance between the public and private sectors. A rough indication of the approximate ratios can, however, be obtained by comparing the public and private shares of total investment. (See Table 7.1) It should be noted, though, that this measure probably understates the shift towards to the private sector.[11]

In 1986 the Australian economist, Anne Booth, drew attention to the emerging shift towards the private sector.[12]

TABLE 7.1
Sources of Investment Funds
(billions of Rupiah, at current prices)

	Public		Private	
1979-1983 (REPELITA III)	51%	(21,849)	44%	(20,986)
1984-1988 (REPELITA IV)	54%	(77,740)	46%	(67,484)
1989-1993a (REPELITA V)	45%	(107,500)	55%	(131,600)

a Official projections
Source: REPELITA III (table 2.3), REPELITA IV (table 2.3) and REPELITA IV (table 2.5).

Indonesia is now at a watershed in its post-independence economic history. Throughout much of the early independence and the Guided Democracy periods, and during the two decades of the New Order, government has, for better or worse, been the main driving force behind the economy. For a range of complex historical, ethnic and cultural reasons the private sector has been relegated to secondary importance . . . The decline in real resources available to the government over the past two years has coincided with growing sentiment in favour of deregulation and liberalization in many aspects of Indonesia's economy. For the first time in her post-independence history it now seems as if the private sector could become the engine of growth for the national economy.

Three years later, when launching the Fifth Five Year Development Plan (REPELITA V) National Planning Minister, Saleh Afiff, acknowledged that the private was now overtaking the public sector when he remarked: 'We [the state] are not the main players anymore.'[13]

The rising importance of the private sector can also be seen from a revenue angle. During the fat years of the oil boom the state was awash with funds. The great bulk of tax receipts in this period came, of course, from oil and gas earnings. This meant that the state enjoyed a high degree of fiscal autonomy—revenue from oil companies (mostly foreign) was politically painless to extract by comparison with the challenge of raising local company and personal income tax as well as indirect tax. The level of fiscal autonomy enjoyed by the state was further enhanced by the very substantial flows of official development assistance funds (foreign aid). This comfortable situation changed very rapidly with the country's economic downturn in the mid-1980s. Within a relatively short space of time, fiscal luxury turned to fiscal crisis. Suddenly non-oil tax receipts (which can be roughly equated with local tax) assumed great import-

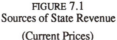

FIGURE 7.1
Sources of State Revenue
(Current Prices)

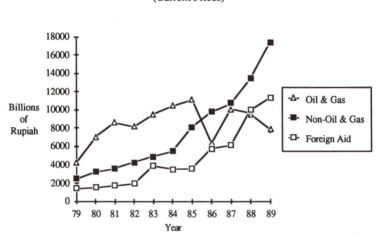

Source: Department of Finance (1989)

ance. Figure 7.1 provides an indication of the changing significance of the three principal sources of state revenue. Note, in the graph, the way in which official development assistance funding rises in the latter 1980s. While this did serve to soften the impact of falling oil and gas receipts to some extent,[14] as can be seen from the graph, it did not disguise the striking growth in the importance of local taxation (non-oil taxes).

The drift towards greater reliance on non-oil taxes in the latter 1980s has been of considerable political significance. When the state derived most of its revenue from a small number of oil companies there was little need to pay attention to, or heed, the demands of local industry. With the onset of fiscal hardship and the corresponding need to raise non-oil tax earnings, the state was forced to adjust its attitude towards the private sector; industry complaints could no longer be so readily ignored. Put simply, taxation carries a political price.

The changing relationship between government and business does not, however, simply reflect the fact that, for pecuniary reasons, the political antennae of the former have become more sensitive. The business sector has not just been a passive actor in these developments; the other side of the coin is that business has been shouting louder. Whereas during the boom years of the 1970s business was more willing to abide government policies with which it disagreed, in the leaner times of the mid-1980s this began to change. Hit hard by declining domestic demand and mounting surplus capacity, many producers were driven from their traditional political docility. The need to communicate effectively with policy-makers became more pressing. This has led to changes in the arrangements for the representation of business interests on an institutional front, in particular with the existing representation structures, headed by KADIN. As discussed in Chapter 3, the activist industry associations have long been unhappy with their lack of influence within KADIN. This, it will be recalled, centred around the fact that they did not have voting rights for the election to determine the KADIN executive. Only the regional KADIN branches, the KADINDA, held voting rights. Following the introduction of the KADIN law in January 1987 and the ensuing need to restructure the organisation and its constitution to embrace the state enterprises and cooperatives as members, the question of voting rights again became a hot issue with business activists fearing that their situation would only be worsened once public sector enterprises were included. It was indicative of the pressure for reform by the activist associations that a compromise agreement was reached whereby the associations would at least be permitted to participate in leadership elections, even if on a minority footing.[15] While certainly not a decisive victory for the activist associations, it was reflective of their growing strength and determination to achieve better representational channels.[16]

This achievement did not however assuage the fears among activists that the inclusion of the state enterprises and cooperatives in KADIN would lead to the diminution of an effective voice for private sector interests. These concerns erupted into open conflict in 1988 with the prospect of a public sector business leader (that is, one from state enterprise) securing the chairmanship of the Jakarta branch of KADIN.[17] After KADIN central, the Jakarta branch is the most important, with its membership being very heavily made up of individual industry associations (which are largely concentrated in Jakarta). This conflict provided clear evidence of both the associations' desire to enhance their representational capacities, as well as of the cleavage between them and the other elements of KADIN. Another indicator of the growing strength of activists elements within the private sector was the appointment of SEKBERTAL head, Aminuddin, to the KADIN Advisory Board in late 1987. Aminuddin's appointment to the position (previously he was not even a member of KADIN) was greeted in the press as the elevation of a champion of business interests.[18]

These developments do not mean that KADIN is about to grow,

overnight, into a dynamic institution effectively representing business interests. That still seems a remote prospect. What does appear to be happening, though, is that the voice of the associations is increasing within KADIN. This, in turn, is likely to enhance the associations' capacity to lobby policy-makers effectively themselves, quite *independently* of KADIN. Furthermore, it seems plausible that the now more conspicuous behaviour of the activist associations may set an example for those many others which have atrophied or remained docile within the corporatist network.

Perhaps the most interesting development on this institutional front, however, was the decision by business activists to form a new umbrella organisation made up exclusively of private sector enterprises. The new body, the Indonesian Business Council (DPSN) was established as a direct response to the inclusion of public sector enterprises into KADIN and the appointment of a former civil servant, Sotion Ardjanggi, as chairman of the organisation. Importantly, DPSN leaders stressed that the new organisation was not set up in opposition to KADIN (such a move would not have been permitted) but rather as an affiliated offshoot of it. Plainly, however, it was the hope of the activist leaders within the DPSN that it would become a major force before too long. While the significance of the DPSN, and indeed its very future, are as yet unclear, the important point for present purposes is that its very creation is indicative of the growing preparedness of business interests to organise on a collective basis in order to secure more effective representational channels than the restrictive state-controlled corporatist bodies have hitherto allowed.

The third area of change in recent years has been in the realm of ideas. It appears that social attitudes towards business are altering and that some of the traditional ideological stigma attaching to it is receding. Inevitably, propositions of this sort are shaky, for firm evidence of attitudinal changes is non-existent. There are, however, a number of pointers in this area. A very important one was the historic formal recognition of profit-making as something legitimate in the KADIN law of January 1987. As discussed in Chapter 3, this was truly a watershed development. Similarly, during the latter-1980s there was very lively public debate in Indonesia about the possible privatisation of state enterprises. The idea of selling state instrumentalities to the private sector would have been inconceivable ten, and probably even five, years earlier. Although the debate subsequently trailed off, it is indeed remarkable that it arose at all. An even more striking indication of shifting sentiment was the extraordinary public scramble that took place in 1989 as small investors queued to buy shares on the newly invigorated Jakarta Stock Exchange. Other more general indications of change include the mushrooming of business

magazines in recent years and the changing imagery used for advertising consumer goods. While commonplace in industrialised
countries, it is remarkable how the images of success promoted in
advertisements in Indonesia are now widely defined in terms of
successful business figures. Another pointer, though one which can at
best be considered only suggestive, was the frequency with which
interviewees would express the hope that their sons, unlike their own
generation, would go into business rather than the bureaucracy.
Finally in this vein, there is the issue of ethnicity. The fact that the
business community has been dominated by Chinese Indonesians for
so many years is one of the most basic reasons for the traditional
stigmatisation of business. While there can be no doubt that actual
ownership of capital remains largely in Chinese Indonesian hands,[19]
increasing numbers of *pribumi* Indonesians have been drawn into
management positions in recent years. Large corporations have ever
greater demands for MBA-type graduates—regardless of ethnic
background. Indeed, some of the very largest Chinese-controlled
companies are said to actively discriminate in favour of *pribumi*
Indonesians when recruiting management staff. As more and more
pribumi Indonesians enter and acquire a direct stake in the business
world, its pejorative image as an almost exclusively Chinese domain
is beginning to break down.

These various straws in the wind do not represent a conclusive
argument that a major ideological shift has occurred. Taken
together, though, they do suggest changing public attitudes towards
business. That public attitudes should become more positive and the
status attaching to business people should improve is, of course,
scarcely surprising. The immediate significance of this development is
that, in future, state officials are presumably less likely to take a
disdainful attitude towards business representatives, while, conversely, business organisations are less likely to be hesitant about
openly pursuing business causes.

Daniel Lev has located these changing attitudes towards business
in the context of a broader sea-change in middle class ideology and
values.[20] He sees this change as taking place on three fronts—greater
currency for liberal economic views, greater demand for some form
of political liberalisation, and a redefinition of religious values. Thus
for Lev, changing attitudes towards business are a part of an ethical
and ideological realignment in Indonesia: a desire for change after
more than twenty years of a regime based on political exclusion.

If we take this argument concerning ideological change and link it
with those concerning changes to the representational institutions for
business and the structural changes in the Indonesian economy, a
strong case can be made that there have indeed been important
changes in Indonesia's political economy in recent years. Some of

these changes are of a long term and evolutionary nature. They are, in short, political changes usually associated with capitalist economic development. But in addition to these more familiar forces and processes, it does seem that the sudden and sharp externally-induced shock to the Indonesian economy in the mid-1980s has served to accelerate change. Peter Gourevitch has highlighted the importance of major jolts in the international economy as a stimulus for domestic political change in the context of his impressive study of the historical responses of the United States and a number of European countries to crises in the global economy.[21] One of the main ideas he develops concerns the way in which the state's relationship with society, or more particularly certain elements of it, can change over time, especially as a result of major economic upheaval. With this in mind, it is likely that the sharp economic down-turn of the mid-1980s will come to be seen as a catalyst which accelerated the processes of political change in Indonesia. In retrospect, the mid-1980s may well appear as an important historical juncture, marking something of a turning point in the trend during the New Order years for the state to strengthen its capacities and autonomy. In other words, it was a period in which the state began to come under greater constraint from parts of the business sector in particular, and possibly societal interests more generally. In this light, it becomes somewhat less surprising that other analysts (many of whom were writing in the early 1980s, before the economic down-turn) have not drawn similar conclusions to those of this study.

To summarise, then, it seems that both of the suggested explanations for the novelty of this book's argument are illuminating. There can be little doubt that Indonesia has been going through an important period of change since the mid-1980s. However, it also seems to have been the case that the general academic concentration on the power of the state in Indonesia has resulted in a failure to recognise increasingly important political action outside the state. Societal interests can and do participate in the formation of policy. Moreover, some industry groups, at least, have done so in a manner which we are not led to expect in Indonesia. I have argued here that there are signs that the character of corporatist structures representing segments of business is undergoing an important transition and is becoming more inclusionary. Rather than restricting and containing member demands, some of these organisations have become important vehicles for their projection.

In a liberal democratic setting such propositions would be most unlikely to result in the raising of any eyebrows. In the authoritarian context of Indonesia, however, claims about direct political influence by societal groups and the importance of alliances between state and societal actors in the policy process are quite remarkable, for they bring into question the tight monopoly over policy-making the state has long been presumed to enjoy. To be sure, these events took place within a political framework which was very much state dominated. And there is no doubting that the state must continue to stand at the very centre of any understanding of Indonesian politics today. My argument, however, is that we have not gone much beyond this none-too-surprising proposition. Our analysis has been so state-centred that we have overlooked real and significant society-based political activity.

Paradoxically, these developments in Indonesia have been taking place at a time when one of the most fashionable arguments in Western political science is that the state has been neglected for too long by most writers. One of the most frequently noted studies in this vein is the volume, *Bringing the State Back In*.[22] In her introductory essay to this work Theda Skocpol argues that the American pluralists and structural-functionalists of the 1950s and 1960s, together with more recent neo-Marxists, have all been fixated with society-centred approaches and have thus not recognised the importance of the state as an independent actor in its own right. In other words, to explain policy patterns we cannot simply look to the interests and actions of sections of society, but must also look at least as much to the interests and actions of the state, or its various constituent parts. While we can probably go along with Skocpol in this with regard to scholarship on Western industrialised countries, the argument is much less persuasive in the case of many developing countries, for the state has been at the centre of much of the work on industrialisation in Latin America and Asia.[23]

In Indonesia, as we have seen, there is a very firmly established tradition of scholarship which focuses narrowly on the state, seeing it (either implicitly or explicitly) as an independent actor. While there may well be a need to 'bring the state back in' to the analysis of a good many countries (particularly those of the industrialised West), in Indonesia at least, it is some time since the state has occupied a position other than centre-stage in most analyses. Far from scholarship on Indonesia being rooted in society-centred approaches, precisely the opposite is the case. As strange as this would have sounded just ten years ago, we are fast reaching the stage when we will need to start talking about 'bringing society back in'.

Future Directions: Democratisation?

The argument running through this book has been that the 1980s have been a time of crucial change in Indonesia's political history, during which forces leading to a pluralisation and diffusion of power have begun to emerge. As the New Order state's grip on the political system has gradually been loosened, the character of the vast corporatist network created to limit political participation has begun to change and, at least in some parts of the business sector, become more inclusionary. This gives rise to the question of how far the process of political pluralisation is likely to go, and in particular whether it will lead to some form of democratisation along the lines of a growing number of countries in Asia, Latin America and Eastern Europe during the 1980s.[24]

This question received extensive consideration in Indonesia as the 1980s drew to a close and the 1990s opened. As speculation has mounted about the possibility that Suharto may step down from the Presidency when his current term expires, there has been an unusual level of open discussion about the possibility of greater political openness and democratisation in Indonesia. A series of events since 1988 has fuelled speculation that pressure for democratisation is mounting. One of the first was the unprecedented challenge to Suharto's nominee for Vice-President in March 1988 (in the past, the People's Consultative Assembly has rubber-stamped the candidacy of Suharto and his running-mate with little fuss). Though the affair ultimately came to nothing, it was quite extraordinary that such a hiccough should have occurred in what is normally a carefully stage-managed event of considerable symbolic importance. A second development which is widely seen as signalling a loosening in the government's political grip is the growing activism within the Parliament (the DPR). As mentioned in Chapter 3, this involved sections of the ABRI and GOLKAR *Fraksi* in the Parliament taking a vigorous and high profile interest in a number of major policy issues. The most celebrated of these was a free-ranging inquiry by one of the Parliamentary committees into the state of national politics, which amounted to a public call for more political openness and greater executive accountability to the legislature. A third manifestation of heightened political activity was the outbreak of a number of student demonstrations in various parts of the country which were marked by demands for fairer and more accountable government. Running parallel with these developments has been an unusually high level of open discussion in the press about the nature of the country's political system and the desirability of reform. This upsurge in debate has been fuelled by a steady stream of public statements on the country's political future by senior figures within the government; comments which continued to flow despite sometimes angry demands by the President on several occasions that such speculation cease.[25]

This remarkable stream of events, and continuing speculation about the prospect of Suharto departing the political stage, have come together to stimulate discussion about possible moves towards democratisation. Consciousness of the apparently successful experience of pro-democracy movements in bringing about reform in other countries has encouraged expectations in this direction. But is Indonesia likely to move in the direction of, say, South Korea or the Philippines?

There are several basic reasons for doubting that Indonesia will move towards democracy in a conventional sense of the word; that is, involving as minimal conditions a regularised system providing for the election of an alternative political leadership on the basis of free and competitive elections.[26]

First, the catalyst for the recent upsurge in political activity appears to stem from differences between the President and key elements in the Armed Forces about the future leadership of the country and questions of personal excess. Without these differences, there would have been little scope for open discussion about political reform nor what amounts to a questioning of Suharto's style of rule. The recent surge of Parliamentary assertiveness and student demonstrations as well as the extensive press coverage of these developments, would not have been possible without the support, or at least tolerance, of important segments of the Armed Forces' leadership. Regardless of whether these tensions between the President and key military leaders continue, it is most unlikely that the military would wilfully jeopardise its pre-eminent position in Indonesian politics. While it may suit the immediate interests of some military leaders to fan open criticism of the existing style of government, it is difficult to imagine that they or their colleagues would allow this to continue to the point of seriously questioning the pivotal role of the Armed Forces in politics. Indeed, the military appears to be actively seeking to preserve its position and ensure that it is not gradually eased from the centre of power in the way that its counterpart in Thailand has in recent years. The army has moved to bolster its influence within GOLKAR's organisational structure, apparently to obviate the 'risk' of greater civilian control.[27] Similarly, rather than simply seeking to raise embarrassing questions about Suharto's style of government, the recent assertiveness of the Armed Forces *Fraksi* within the Parliament seems likely to have been part of a deliberate strategy further to involve and integrate itself in all institutions of government.

Second, a resurgent democracy in Indonesia would be impossible without major changes to the country's political institutions. The party system in Indonesia has atrophied. Neither of the minor parties is presently capable of providing an alternative national leadership.

Indeed, Indonesia is not far from a *de facto* one-party political system. After having been dismantled with such care and thoroughness during the 1970s, is a genuinely competitive party system now to be reconstructed? Furthermore, what of the executive's massive domination of the legislature? Is the government's influence over both the Parliament and the People's Consultative Assembly, via its directly appointed representatives, likely to be slackened?

Third, there is currently no coalition of 'opposition' civilian groups which carries great weight. At present the reform-oriented civilians who are of greatest significance are the civilian leaders of GOLKAR. This group, however, faces an acute dilemma: on the one hand it seeks to boost a 'moderating' civilian influence within GOLKAR (at the expense of the military), but on the other it, and GOLKAR in general, are dependent on the support of the military to enforce a set of arrangements which ensure that GOLKAR will dominate the electoral process. While this progressive group may well be anxious to promote greater openness and accountability in government, any serious movement in the direction of genuine competitive democracy could quite possibly be at GOLKAR's—and thus their own—expense. Rather than any notions of empowering the mass of the population by means of the ballot, the priority for civilians leaders within GOLKAR is therefore likely to remain the promotion of countervailing (civilian) forces within the existing structure of government.

For the foreseeable future, Indonesia is unlikely to experience democracy. Dabbling in the area of prediction is, of course, always risky, a fact only too clearly highlighted by the staggering changes in the Soviet Union and Eastern Europe.[28] It is quite possible, for instance, that the Parliament will continue to grow in significance. Military leaders in Jakarta are very conscious of the political changes that have taken place in a number of other countries, and allowing the Parliament to become more active may indeed have appeal as a reform measure to counteract the image that all power is tightly centralised in the hands of the executive. While not to be scorned, change of this sort is of an altogether different order of magnitude than the determination of positions of executive authority by competitive elections.

But if Indonesia does not appear to be moving towards democracy, it does appear to be moving in the direction of a form of political liberalisation and a greater pluralisation of power. Rather than focusing on the possibilities of competitive elections and parties, we should be turning our attention to the gradual movement within the extensive network of corporatist institutions. This is a development which could enable a much greater level of societal involvement in the shaping of a range of policy outcomes. As the present study has shown, there has already been some movement in the direction of a less restrictive style of corporatism in the business and professional sectors. If there is to be substantive political liberalisation in the near future, this seems the most likely route. While change of this sort would be gradual and probably partial in nature, it is more plausible than the development of genuinely competitive parties and elections for the critical reason that it would not necessarily threaten what has been the fundamental feature of government in modern Indonesia— the pre-eminence of the Armed Forces in political life.

1. Stepan (1978).
2. See Bates (1981) especially chapters 5 & 7.
3. Ramsay (1987).
4. Ramsay (1987) p. 266.
5. It is of course quite possible for public enterprises to be well managed. Hal Hill has indeed argued that a number of the state-owned firms in Indonesia do fall into this category. He emphasises, though, that on the whole, the state enterprises perform very poorly, whether due to firm-level inefficiencies, or government constraints. Hill (1988) p. 139.
6. A useful illustration of this concerns the plastic industry in Indonesia. During 1986–87 there was widespread resentment among producers in the plastics industry arising from the substantial additional costs imposed upon them as a result of a raw materials import monopoly held by a company associated with one of President Suharto's sons. Though the financial drain on the producers was very costly there was a general reluctance to protest openly through fear of possible repercussions. Interestingly, one prominent business leader, who had achieved considerable success in pushing his own industry's deregulatory interests was contacted privately by plastics producers asking him to organise a lobbying campaign for the abolition of the import monopoly in their industry as well. Despite a very lucrative offer, he declined.
7. Hough (1977).
8. Hough (1977) p. 187.
9. Liddle (1987) p. 128.
10. See for example, Skilling (1966); Kelley (1976); Kelly (1980); and Ziegler (1986).
11. I am grateful to Dr. Hal Hill, of the Australian National University, for his assistance on this matter.
12. Booth (1986) p. 24. See also, for example, Simandjuntak (1989) p. 8 and Booth (1989).
13. Vatikiotis, M. 'The Private Push: Government Yields Lead in Indonesia's Development', *Far Eastern Economic Review*, 9 February 1989, pp. 48–49.

14. In practice the 'cushion' provided by official development assistance flows has been much smaller than is suggested by Figure 7.1. A large percentage of gross aid inflows is in fact used immediately to repay existing official loans. The nett aid inflow—the amount of money available to support new development spending—is substantially smaller.

15. The compromise reportedly agreed to was for a total of 60 votes to be divided into four blocks with the KADINDA having 27, and the associations, the state enterprises and the cooperatives having 11 each. Interviews with Probosutedjo (Deputy Chairman of KADIN) 8 September 1987; Ariono Abdulkadir (Head of KADIN's Mining & Energy Section) 8 September 1987; and Sjahfiri Alim (President Director of Goodyear Pty Ltd & Head of KADIN's Chemical Industries Section) 10 September 1987.

16. An indication of the frustration of the associations was a report in the state-run paper *Suara Karya* in mid September 1987, during the lead-up to a special KADIN executive conference. It was reported that KADIN had recently been severely criticised for its failure to work for its members, and the head of the Metal and Machinery Industries' Association, Suhari Sargo, was quoted as criticising the KADIN leadership for being self-serving and failing to serve members' interests. This was reproduced in the 'KADIN under Attack' in, *Jakarta Post*, 18 September 1987.

17. See, 'Pihak Swasta Keberatan Nonswasta Pimpin KADIN' in, *Suara Pembaruan*, 14 July 1988.

18. See, for example, 'Keberhasilan MPI, Cermin Kesatuan Tiga Pelaku Ekonomi', *Pelita*, 28 September 1987; 'Musyawarah Pengusaha Indonesia Dinilai Berhasil', *Berita Yudha*, 28 September 1987; or 'Cuplikan Ekspresi-Ekspresi Gembiraan Dari Munassus KADIN dan MPI', *Angkatan Bersenjata*, 28 September 1987.

19. One recent survey suggested that 163 of the top 200 companies in Indonesia are controlled by Chinese. (See Schwarz, A., 'Call For Constraints', *Far Eastern Economic Review*, 28 December 1989 p. 25). Interestingly, while this estimate does indeed confirm the dominance of Chinese Indonesians, many observers would probably be surprised that there are *as many* as 37 *pribumi* firms in the ranks of the top 200.

20. Lev (1988). See also Lev (1986).

21. Gourevitch (1986).

22. Evans, Rueschemeyer & Skocpol (1985). For other exemplars see, *inter alia*, Nordlinger (1981), Stepan (1978), Krasner (1977), Block (1980) and Skocpol (1979).

23. Regarding Latin America, this same point is in fact made by Stepan in an essay contained in the same volume as that of Skocpol. Stepan (1985) p. 317. Concerning East and Southeast Asia see, for example, Deyo (1987) and Robison, Hewison & Higgot 1987.

24. For an historically-based study of democracy in Indonesia, see Sundhausen (1989). More generally, for comparative studies of the movement towards democratisation in Latin America and other parts of

Asia, see Diamond, Linz & Lipset (1989), O'Donnell, Schmitter & Whitehead (1986) and Malloy & Selligson (1987).

25. See, for instance, Vaitikiotis, M. 'Rumbles in the Ranks: President's Warning Fails to Quell Military Critics', *Far Eastern Economic Review*, 3 August 1989, pp. 26–27.

26. For a more extensive discussion of democracy and democratisation, see, *inter alia*, Huntington (1984), the preface to Diamond, Linz & Lipset (1989) and Dahl (1971).

27. Vatikiotis, M. 'Jungle-Greening of GOLKAR Shows Military's Concern', *Far Eastern Economic Review*, 10 November 1988, pp. 28–29.

28. Guessing about possible political futures is even more problematic in the case of authoritarian political systems, for as Juan Linz has noted, unexpected change can take place rapidly since power is, by definition, concentrated in relatively few and unconstrained hands. Linz (1975) p. 355.

Bibliography

Allinson, G.D. 1987: 'Japan's Keidanren and Its New Leadership', *Pacific Affairs*, vol. 60, no. 3, (Fall).

Almond, G.A. 1987: 'The Development of Political Development' Weiner, M. & Huntington, S.P. (eds.), *Understanding Political Development*, Little, Brown & Co., Boston.

Amaludin, Ganie 1982: 'KADIN dan Sejarahnya', *Merdeka*, Jakarta, (20–22 September).

Anderson, B.R. O'G. 1972: 'The Idea of Power in Javanese Culture', in Holt, C. (ed.), *Culture and Politics in Indonesia*, Cornell University Press, Ithaca, N.Y.

—— 1978: 'Last Day's of Indonesia's Suharto', *Southeast Asia Chronicle*, no. 63.

—— 1983: 'Old State, New Society: Indonesia's New Order in Comparative Historical Perspective', *Journal of Asian Studies*, vol. XLII, no. 3, (May).

Anek Laothamatas 1987: 'Business and Politics in Thailand: New Patterns of Influence', *Asian Survey*, vol. 28, no. 4.

—— 1989: 'No Longer a Bureaucratic Polity: Business Associations and the New Political Economy of Thailand,' Ph.D. dissertation, Columbia University, New York.

Bachrach, P. & Baratz, M. 1962: 'Two Faces of Power', *American Political Science Review*, vol. 56.

Bates, R.H. 1981: *Markets and States in Tropical Africa: The Political Basis of Agricultural Policies*, University of California Press, Berkeley.

Bianchi, R. 1984: *Interest Groups and Political Development in Turkey*, Princeton University Press, Princeton, New Jersey.

—— 1986: 'Interest Group Politics in the Third World', *Third World Quarterly*, vol. 8, no. 2, (April).

Block, F. 1980: 'Beyond relative Autonomy: State Managers as Historical Subjects', in Miliband, R. & Saville, J. (eds.), *Socialist Register*, Merlin Press, London.

265

Boileau, J.M. 1983: *GOLKAR: Functional Group Politics in Indonesia*, Centre for Strategic & International Studies, Jakarta.

Booth, A. 1986: 'Survey of Recent Developments', *Bulletin of Indonesian Economic Studies*, vol. 22, no. 3 (December).

—— 1989: 'Repelita V and Indonesia's Medium Term Economic Strategy', *Bulletin of Indonesian Economic Studies*, vol. 25, no. 2 (August).

Bourchier, D. 1988: 'Behind Indonesia's Courts', *Inside Indonesia*, no. 14, (April).

Bureau of Statistics. 1987: *Sensus Ekonomi 1986: Statistik Industri Besar dan Sedang*, Jakarta.

Campbell, C.S.J. 1987: 'Administrative Politics: the State Apparatus and Political Responsiveness', *Comparative Politics*, vol. 19, no. 4, (July).

Carnoy, M. 1984: *The State and Political Theory*, Princeton University Press, Princeton.

Cawson, A. 1982: *Corporatism and Welfare*, Heinemann, London.

Chandler, D. & Ricklefs, M. (eds.) 1986: *Nineteenth and Twentieth Century Indonesia: Essays in Honour of Professor J.D. Legge*, Centre for Southeast Asian Studies, Monash University, Melbourne.

Cohen, J.L. 1982: *Class and Civil Society*, University of Massachusetts Press, Amherst.

Collier, D. (ed.) 1979: *The New Authoritarianism In Latin America*, Princeton University Press, Princeton.

Crone, D.K. 1988: 'State, Social Elites, and Government Capacity in Southeast Asia', *World Politics*, vol. XL, no. 2, (January).

Crouch, H. 1978: *The Army and Politics in Indonesia*, Cornell University Press, Ithaca N.Y.

—— 1979: 'Patrimonialism and Military Rule in Indonesia', *World Politics*, vol. 31, no. 4, (July).

—— 1980: 'The New Order: the Prospect for Political Stability', in Fox, J.J., Garnaut, R.G., McCawley, P.T. & Mackie, J.A.C. (eds.), *Indonesia: Australian Perspectives*, Research School of Pacific Studies, Australian National University, Canberra.

—— 1984: *Domestic Political Structures and Regional Economic Co-operation*, Institute of Southeast Asian Studies, Singapore.

—— 1986: 'The Missing Bourgeoisie: Approaches to Indonesia's New Order', in Chandler, D. & Ricklefs, M. (eds.), *Nineteenth and Twentieth Century Indonesia: Essays in Honour of Professor J.D. Legge*, Centre for Southeast Asian Studies, Monash University, Melbourne.

—— 1987: 'The Politics of Industrialisation in Southeast Asia', Paper presented to the Department of Political & Social Change, Research School of Pacific Studies, the Australian National University, Canberra, (8 October).

Curtis, G.L. 1975: 'Big Business and Political Influence', in Vogel, E.F., (ed.), *Japanese Organisation and Decision Making*, University of California Press, Berkeley.

Dahl, R. 1971: *Polyarchy: Participation and Opposition*, Yale University Press, New Haven.

Data Consult Inc. 1986: 'The Indonesian Textile Industry—Its Developments

and Problems', *Indonesian Commercial Newsletter*, no. 293, (12 May).
Davis, G. (ed.) 1979: *What is Modern Indonesian Culture?*, Ohio University Southeast Asia Program, Athens, Ohio.
Diamond, L., Linz, J. & Lipset, S.M. (eds.) 1989: *Democracy in Developing Countries: Asia*, (vol. 3), Lynne Reiner Publishers, Boulder, Colorado.
Department of Agriculture. 1988: *Review Program Penelitian dan Pengembangan Tanaman Industri*, Bogor, (April).
Department of Finance. 1986: *Laporan Ke-XVIII Tentang Kegiatan Usaha Perasuransian 1985*, Jakarta.
Department of Finance. 1988: *Nota Keuangan dan Rancangan Anggaran Pendapatan dan Belanja Negara 1988/1989*, Jakarta.
—— 1989: *Nota Keuangan dan Rancangan Anggara Pendapatan dan Belanja Negara 1989/90*, Jakarta.
Deyo, F.C. (ed.) 1987: *The Political Economy of the New Asian Industrialism*, Cornell University Press, Ithaca, N.Y.
Doner, R. 1988: 'Weak State—Strong Country? The Thai Automobile Case', *Third World Quarterly*, vol. 10, no. 4 (October).
Doner, R. & Wilson E.J. 1988: 'Business Interest Associations in Developing Countries', paper presented at the Annual Meeting of the International Political Science Association, Washington D.C., (September).
Eisenstadt, S.N. 1973: *Traditional Patrimonialism and Modern Neo-Patrimonialism*, Sage Publications, Beverly Hills.
Eldridge, P. 1984–85: 'The Political Role of Community Action Groups in India and Indonesia: In Search of a General Theory', *Alternatives*, vol. X, no. 3, (Winter).
Emery, R.F. 1970: *The Financial Institutions of Southeast Asia: A Country-by-Country Study*, Praeger, New York.
Emmerson, D.K. 1976: *Indonesia's Elite: Political Culture and Cultural Politics*, Cornell University Press, Ithaca, N.Y.
—— 1978: 'The Bureaucracy in Political Context: Weakness in Strength', in Jackson, K.D. & Pye, L.W. (eds.), *Political Power and Communications in Indonesia*, University of California Press, Berkeley.
—— 1983: 'Understanding the new Order: Bureaucratic Pluralism in Indonesia', *Asian Survey*, vol. XXIII, no. 11, (November).
Evans, P., Rueschemeyer, D. & Skocpol, T. (eds.) 1985: *Bringing the State Back In*, Cambridge University Press, Cambridge.
Fachry, Ali 1986: 'Refleksi Paham "Kekuasaan Jawa"', in his, *Indonesia Moderen*, Gramedia, Jakarta.
Feith, H. 1962: *The Decline of Constitutional Democracy in Indonesia*, Cornell University Press, Ithaca, N.Y.
Gereffi, G. 1983: *The Pharmaceutical Industry and Dependency in the Third World*, Princeton University Press, Princeton, N.J.
Giddens, A. 1979: *Central Problems in Social Theory*, MacMillan, London.
Girling, J.L.S. 1981: *The Bureaucratic Polity in Modernizing Societies: Similarities, Differences and Prospects in the ASEAN Region*, Occasional Paper no. 64, Institute of Southeast Asian Studies, Singapore.
—— 1984: 'Thailand in Gramscian Perspective', *Pacific Affairs*, vol. 57, no. 3, (Fall).

Goenawan Mohamad 1988: 'The Press in Indonesia', seminar in the Department of Political & Social Change, Australian National University, (23 March).

Gourevitch, P.A. 1986: *Politics in Hard Times*, Cornell University Press, Ithaca, N.Y.

Gray, C.W. 1987: 'Indonesian Public Administration: Policy Reform and the Legal Process.' Ph.D. thesis Harvard University (1986), U.M.I. Dissertation Information Service, Ann Arbor.

Grindle, M.S. (ed.) 1980: *Politics and Policy Implementation in the Third World*, Princeton University Press, Princeton.

Gunanto, H. 1985: *A Report on the Indonesian Insurance Regulations and Review of Matters of Topical Interest*, presented to the 7th Conference of the International Bar Association (Section on Business Law), Singapore, (3 October).

Hall, P.A. 1986: *Governing the Economy: the Politics of State Intervention in Britain and France*, Polity Press, Cambridge.

Handley, P. 1985: 'A Matter of Influence', *Far Eastern Economic Review*, (17 October).

Harahap, Sori M. 1986: *Reference Book on Indonesia's Major Business Groups*, Datatrust, Jakarta.

Haseman, J.B. 1986: 'The Dynamics of Change: Regeneration of the Indonesian Army', *Asian Survey*, vol. 26, no. 8.

Held, D. (ed.) 1983: *States and Societies*, New York University Press, New York.

—— 1984: 'Central Perspectives on the Modern State', in McLennan, G., Held, D. & Hall, S. (eds.), *The Idea of the State*, Open University Press, Milton Keynes.

Higgott, R. & Robison, R. (eds.) 1985: *Southeast Asia: Essays in the Political Economy of Structural Change*, Routledge & Kegan Paul, London.

Hill, H.C. 1979: 'Choice of Technique in the Indonesian Weaving Industry,' Ph.D. thesis in the Department of Economics (Research School of Pacific Studies), Australian National University.

—— 1988: *Foreign Investment and Industrialization in Indonesia*, Oxford University Press, Singapore, 1988.

Hough, J.F. 1977: *The Soviet Union and Social Science Theory*, Harvard University Press, Cambridge, Mass.

Ikvo Kume. 1988: 'Changing Relations Among the Government, Labor, and Business in Japan After the Oil Crisis', *International Organisation* vol. 42, no. 4 (Autumn).

IMS 1987 (a): (Index of Medical Specialties) *Indonesian Pharmaceutical Audit: 1986*, Singapore.

—— 1987 (b): (Index of Medical Specialties) Unpublished Consultant's Survey on the Pharmaceutical Industry in Southeast Asia, Singapore.

Jackson, K.D. 1978: 'Bureaucratic Polity: A Theoretical Framework for the Analysis of Power and Communications in Indonesia', in Jackson, K.D. & Pye, L.W. (eds), *Political Power and Communications in Indonesia*, University of California Press, Berkeley.

Jenkins, D. 1984: *Suharto and His Generals: Indonesian Military Politics 1975–1983*, Cornell Modern Indonesia Project, Ithaca.

JETRO 1987: (Japan External Trade Organisation), *Japanese Investment Projects in Indonesia*, Jakarta.

Johnson, C. 1987: 'Political Institutions and Government Performance: the Government-Business relationship in Japan, South Korea and Taiwan', in Deyo, F.C. (ed.), *The Political Economy of the New Asian Industrialism*, Cornell University Press, Ithaca, N.Y.

Jones, L.P. & Sakong, I. 1980: *Government, Business, and Entrepreneurship in Economic Development: The Korean Case*, Harvard University Press, Cambridge, Mass.

Jones, S. & Pura, R. 1986: 'Suharto-Linked Monopolies Hobble Economy', *Asian Wall Street Journal*, (24–26 November).

KADIN 1987 (a): *Buku Informasi KADIN Indonesia 1987–88*, Jakarta.

—— 1987 (b): 'Penyempurnaan AD-ART KADIN Lewat MUNAS Khusus', *Kadin*, vol. 3, no. VIII.

Kaisiepo, Manuel 1986: 'Dari Kepolitikan Birokratik Ke Korporatisme Negara: Birokrasi dan Politik di Indonesia Era Orde Baru' a Paper presented to an Indonesian Political Science Association and Indonesian Institute of Science joint seminar, Jakarta, (10 December).

Kaplan, E.J. 1972: *Japan: The Government-Business Relationship*, U.S. Department of Commerce, Washington.

Kaufman, R.R. 1977: 'Corporatism, Clientelism, and Partisan Conflict: a Study of Seven Latin American Countries', in Malloy, J.M. (ed.), *Authoritarianism and Corporatism In Latin America*, University of Pittsburgh Press, London.

Kelley, D.R. (ed.) 1980: *Soviet Politics in the Brezhnev Era*, Praeger, New York.

—— 1976: 'Environmental Policy-Making in the USSR: The Role of Industrial and Environmental Interest Groups', *Soviet Studies*, vol. XXVIII, no. 4 (October).

King, D.Y. 1977: 'Authoritarian Rule and State Corporatism in Indonesia', Paper presented at the Annual Meeting of the American Political Science Association, Washington, (1–4 September).

—— 1979: 'Defensive Modernization: the Structuring of Economic Interests in Indonesia', in Davis, G. (ed.), *What is Modern Indonesian Culture?*, Ohio University Southeast Asia Program, Athens, Ohio.

—— 1982 (a): 'Indonesia's New Order as a Bureaucratic Polity, a Neopatrimonial Regime or Bureaucratic Authoritarian Regime: What Difference Does it Make?', in Anderson, B. & Kahin, A. (eds.), *Interpreting Indonesian Politics: Thirteen Contributions to the Debate*, Cornell Modern Indonesia Project, Ithaca.

—— 1982 (b): *Interest Groups and Political Linkage in Indonesia, 1800–1965*, Center for Southeast Asian Studies, Northern Illinois University, DeKalb.

King, R. 1986: *The State in Modern Society*, MacMillan, London.

Krasner, S. 1977: *Defending the National Interest*, Princeton University Press, Princeton, N.J.

Lahur, Rufinus 1973: 'The Broad Lines of State Policy', *Indonesian Quarterly*, vol. I, no. 3, (April).

Latief, Abdul 1987: 'KADIN Untuk Mempersatukan Dunia Usaha, Sentuhan Profesionalisme dan Transparansi Bisnis di Indonesia', presented to a public forum on Professionalism and the Business Environment, Jakarta, (4 August).

Lembong, E. 1987: *Pengrauh Kelesuan Ekonomi Dunia Terhadap Kehidu-pan Kefarmasian Di Indonesia & Prospek Industri Farmasi Di Indonesia*, address to Musyawarah Nasional III ISMAFARSI, Yogyakarta (27 July).

Lesmana, Tjipta 1985: *20 Tahun KOMPAS: Profil Pers Indonesia Dewasa Ini*, Erwin-Rika Press, Jakarta.

Lev, D.S. 1986: 'Intermediate Classes and Change in Indonesia: Some Initial Reflections', Paper presented at the Conference on the Politics of the Middle Class in Indonesia, Centre for Southeast Asian Studies, Monash University, (27–29 June). [Publication forthcoming in Young, K. & Tanter, R. (eds.), *The Politics of the Middle Class in Indonesia* from Monash University.]

—— 1987: 'Legal Aid in Indonesia', *Working Paper* no. 44, Centre for Southeast Asian Studies, Monash University, (August).

—— 1988: 'Ideology and Class in the Politics of Southeast Asia', Paper presented to the Department of Political and Social Change, Research School of Pacific Studies, Australian National University (8 March).

Liddle, R.W. 1978: 'Participation and the Political Parties', in Jackson, K.D. & Pye, L.W. (eds.), *Political Power and Communications In Indonesia*, University of California Press, Berkeley.

—— 1985: 'Soeharto's Indonesia: Personal Rule and Political Institutions', *Pacific Affairs*, vol. 58, no. 1, (Spring).

—— 1987: 'The Politics of Shared Growth: Some Indonesian Cases', *Comparative Politics*, vol. 19, no. 2, (January).

Lindblom, C.E. 1977: *Politics and Markets: The World's Political-Economic Systems*, Basic Books, New York.

Linz, J. 1970: 'An Authoritarian Regime: Spain', in Allardt, E. & Rokkan, S., *Mass Politics: Studies in Political Sociology*, Free Press, New York.

—— 'Totalitarian and Authoritarian Regimes' in Greenstein, F. & Polsby, N. (eds.) *Handbook of Political Science*, Addison—Wesley, Reading, Mass.

LPEM. 1987: (University of Indonesia). *Laporan Pengkajian Dunia Usaha Menurut Undang-Undang No. 1 Tahun 1987 Tentang Kamar Dagang dan Industri Indonesia*, Jakarta (May).

Lukes, S. 1974: *Power: a Radical View*, MacMillan, London.

MacIntyre, A.J. 1989: 'Politics, Policy & Participation: Business-Government Relations in Indonesia,' Ph.D. thesis, Department of Political and Social Change, Research School of Pacific Studies, the Australian National University.

—— 1989: 'Corporatism, Control and Political Change in 'New Order' Indonesia' in, R.J. May and W.J. O'Malley (eds.), *Observing Political Change in Asia: Essays in Honour of J.A.C. Mackie*, Crawford House Press, Bathurst, N.S.W.

—— 1990: 'Rethinking State-Society Relations in 'New Order' Indonesia: Challenges from the Business Sector' in, Arief Budiman (ed.), *The State and Civil Society in Indonesia*, Centre for Southeast Asian Studies, Monash University, Melbourne (forthcoming).

—— 1990: *Business-Government Relations in Industrialising East Asia: South Korea and Thailand in Comparative Context* Centre for the Study of Australia-Asia Relations, Griffith University, Brisbane (forthcoming).

Mackie, J.A.C. 1986 (a): 'Property and Power in Indonesia', [publication forthcoming in Young, K. & Tanter, R. (eds.), *The Politics of the Middle Class in Indonesia* from Monash University.]

—— 1986 (b): 'Money and the Middle Class: Indonesia and Elsewhere', Paper presented to the conference on The Politics of the Middle Class in Indonesia, Centre for Southeast Asian Studies, Monash University, (27–29 June). [Publication forthcoming in Young, K. & Tanter, R. (eds.), *The Politics of the Middle Class in Indonesia* from Monash University.]

Macridis, R. 1977: 'Groups and Group Theory', in Macridis, R. & Brown, B. (eds.), *Comparative Politics*, Dorsey, New York.

Makarim, Nono Anwar 1978: 'The Indonesian Press: An Editor's Perspective', Jackson, K.D. & Pye, L.W. (eds.), *Political Power and Communications In Indonesia*, University of California Press, Berkeley.

Malloy, J.M. (ed.) 1977(a): *Authoritarianism And Corporatism In Latin America*, University of Pittsburgh Press, London.

—— 1977(b): 'Authoritarianism and Corporatism in Latin America: the Modal Pattern', in Malloy, J.M. (ed.), *Authoritarianism And Corporatism In Latin America*, University of Pittsburgh Press, London.

Malloy, J.M. & Selligson, M.A. (eds.) 1987: *Authoritarians and Democrats: Regime Transition in Latin America*, University of Pittsburgh Press, Pittsburgh.

Mann, M. 1986: 'The Autonomous Power of the State: Its Origins, Mechanisms and Results', in Hall, J.A., (ed.), *States in History*, Basil Blackwell, Oxford.

Marsyaid, Yushar 1981: 'Wadah Induk Perusahaan-Perusahaan Farmasi', *Varia Farmasi*, (Jakarta) no. 25.

Mas'oed, Mohtar 1989: 'The State Reorganisation of Society under the New Order', *Prisma*, no. 47, (September).

McLellan, D. 1986: *Ideology*, Open University Press, Milton Keynes.

McLennan, G. 1984: 'Capitalist State or Democratic Polity?: Recent Developments in Marxist and Pluralist Theory', in McLennan, G., Held, D. & Hall, S. (eds.), *The Idea of the Modern State*, Open University Press, Milton Keynes.

McLennan, G., Held, D. & Hall, S. (eds.) 1984: *The Idea of the State*, Open University Press, Milton Keynes.

McLeod, R. 1984: 'Financial Markets and Institutions in Indonesia', in Skully, M.T. (ed.), *Financial Institutions and Markets in Southeast Asia*, MacMillan, London.

McVey, R.T. 1982: 'The Beamtenstaat in Indonesia', in Anderson, B. & Kahin, A. (eds.), *Interpreting Indonesian Politics: Thirteen Contributions to the Debate*, Interim Report Series, no. 62, Cornell Modern Indonesia Project, Ithaca.

Migdal, J.S. 1987: 'Strong States, Weak States: Power and Accommodation' in, Weiner, M. & Huntington, S.P. (eds.), *Understanding Political Development*, Little, Brown & Co., Boston.

—— 'Policy and Power: A Framework for the Study of Comparative Policy Contexts in Third World Countries', *Public Policy*, vol. 25, no. 2, 1977.

Miliband, R. 1977: *Marxism and Politics*, Oxford University Press, London.

—— 1982: *Capitalist Democracy in Britain*, Oxford University Press, Oxford.

Milne, S. 1983: 'Corporatism in the ASEAN Countries', *Contemporary Southeast Asia*, vol. 5, no. 2, (September).

Morfit, M. 1981: 'Pancasila: the Indonesian State Ideology According to the New Order Government', *Asian Survey*, vol. XXI, no. 8, (August).

Muhaimin, Yahya 1980: 'Beberapa Segi Birokrasi di Indonesia', *Prisma*, no. 10, (October).

Nasution, A. 1983: *Financial Institutions and Policies in Indonesia*, Institute of Southeast Asian Studies, Singapore.

Nordlinger, E.A. 1981: *On the Autonomy of the Democratic State*, Harvard University Press, Cambridge, Mass.

—— 1987: 'Taking the State Seriously', in Weiner, M. & Huntington, S.P. (eds.), *Understanding Political Development*, Little, Brown & Co., Boston.

O'Donnell, G. 1977: 'Corporatism and the Question of the State', in Malloy, J.M. (ed.), *Authoritarianism And Corporatism In Latin America*, University of Pittsburgh Press, London.

—— 1978: 'Reflections on the Patterns of Change in the Bureaucratic Authoritarian State', *Latin American Research Review*, vol. XIII, no. 1.

O'Donnell, G., Schmitter, P.C. & Whitehead, L. (eds.) 1986: *Transitions from Authoritarian Rule: Prospects for Democracy*, John Hopkins University Press, Baltimore.

Offe, C. 1984: *Contradictions of the Welfare State*, Hutchinson, London.

Palmer, I. 1972: *Textiles in Indonesia: Problems of Import Substitution*, Praeger, New York.

Pangestu, M. 1987: 'Survey Of Recent Developments', *Bulletin of Indonesian Economic Studies*, vol. 23, no. 1, (April).

—— 1989: 'Managing Economic Policy Reforms in Indonesia', paper presented at the Senior Policy Seminar: *Managing Trade and Industry Reform in Asia: The Role of Policy Research*, National Centre for Development Studies, the Australian National University, Canberra (30 April–1 May).

Pierson, C. 1984: 'New Theories of State and Civil Society: Recent Developments in Post-Marxist Analysis of the State', *Sociology*, vol. 18, no. 4, (November).

Poulantzas, N. 1973: *Political Power and Social Classes*, New Left Books, London.

Pye, L.W. 1985: *Asian Power and Politics: The Cultural Dimensions of Authority*, Balknap Harvard, Cambridge, Mass.

Ramsay, A. 1986: 'Thai Domestic Politics and Foreign Policy' in, Karl Jackson, Sukhumbhand Paribatra & Soedjati Djiwandono (eds.), *ASEAN in Regional and Global Context*, Research Papers & Policy Studies, no. 18, Institute of East Asian Studies, University of California, Berkeley.

—— 1987: 'The Political Economy of Sugar in Thailand', *Pacific Affairs*, vol. 60, no. 2, (Summer).

Reeve, D. 1985: *Golkar of Indonesia: an Alternative to the Party System*, Oxford University Press, Singapore.

Rice, R.C. 1983: 'The Origins of Basic Economic Ideas and Their Impact Upon 'New Order' Policies', *Bulletin of Indonesian Economic Studies*, vol. XIX, no. 2, (August).

Rickard, D. 1983: 'The Law on Social Organisations: New Restrictions for NGOs', *Inside Indonesia*, no. 12, (October).

Riggs, F.W. 1964: *Administration in Developing Countries: the Theory of Prismatic Society*, Houghton Miflin, Boston.

—— 1966: *Thailand: The Modernization of a Bureaucratic Polity*, East-West Center Press, Honolulu.

Robison, R. 1978: 'Toward a Class Analysis of the Indonesian Military Bureaucratic State', *Indonesia*, no. 25, (April).

—— 1981: 'Culture, Politics, and the Economy in the Political History of the New Order', *Indonesia*, no. 31, (April).

—— 1982: 'The Transformation of the State in Indonesia', *Bulletin of Concerned Asian Scholars*, vol. 14, no. 1, (January–March).

—— 1985: 'Class, Capital and the State in New Order, Indonesia', in Higgott R. & Robison, R. (eds.), *Southeast Asia: Essays in the Political Economy of Structural Change*, Routledge & Kegan Paul, London.

—— 1986 (a): *Indonesia: the Rise of Capital*, Allen & Unwin, Sydney.

—— 1986 (b): 'Industrialization and the Economic and Political Development of Domestic Capital: the Case of Indonesia', Paper presented at the Social Science Research Council's conference on *Industrializing Elites in Southeast Asia*, at Sukothai, Thailand (December).

—— 1986 (c): 'The Rise of Capital', *Inside Indonesia*, no. 9 (December).

—— 1987: After the Gold Rush: the Politics of Economic Restructuring in Indonesia in the 1980s', in Robison, R., Hewison, K. & Higgott, R. (eds.), *Southeast Asia in the 1980s: the Politics of Economic Crisis*, Allen & Unwin, Sydney.

—— 1988: 'Authoritarian States, Capital-Owning Classes and the Politics of Newly Industrializing Countries: the Case of Indonesia', *World Politics*, vol. XLI, no. 1, October 1988.

Robison, R., Hewison, K. & Higgott, R. (eds.) 1987: *Southeast Asia in the 1980s: The Politics of Economic Crisis*, Allen & Unwin, Sydney.

Rodgers, P. 1980: 'The Domestic and Foreign Press in Indonesia: "Free But Responsible"?', *Research Paper* no. 18, Centre for the Study of Australian-Asian Relations, Griffith University, (February).

Roth, G. 1968: 'Personal Rulership, Patrimonialism and Empire-Building in the New States', *World Politics*, vol. XX, no. 1, (January).

Samuels, R.J. 1987: *The Business of the Japanese State: Energy Markets in Comparative and Historical Perspective*, Cornell University Press, Ithaca, N.Y.

Santoso, Amir 1986: 'Public Policy Implementation: Rice Policy at the Regional Level in Indonesia, 1970–1984', Ph.D. thesis in the Department of Political & Social Change (Research School of Pacific Studies), Australian National University.

Sarjent, J.A. 1985: 'The Politics of the Pharmaceutical Price Regulation Scheme', in Streek, W. & Schmitter, P.C. (eds.), *Private Interest Government: Beyond Market and State*, Sage Publications, London.

Schiller, J. 1986: 'State Formation in New Order Indonesia: The Powerhouse State in Jepara,' Ph.D. dissertation, Monash University Press, Melbourne.

Schmitter, P.C. 1979 (a): 'Still the Century of Corporatism?', in Schmitter,

P.C. & Lembruch, G. (eds.), *Trends Towards Corporatist Intermediation*, Sage Beverly Hills.

—— 1979 (b): 'Modes of Interest Intermediation and Models of Societal Change in Western Europe', in Schmitter, P.C. & Lembruch, G. (eds.), *Trends Towards Corporatist Intermediation*, Sage, Beverly Hills.

Simandjuntak, Djisman 1989: 'Survey of Recent Developments', *Bulletin of Indonesian Economic Studies*, vol. 25, no. 1 (April).

Sjahrir, 1987: *Kebijaksanaan Negara: Konsitensi dan Implementasi*, LP3ES, Jakarta.

Skilling, H.G. 1966: 'Interest Groups in Communist Politics' in, *World Politics*, vol. XVIII, no. 3 (April).

Skocpol, T. 1979: *States and Revolutions: A Comparative Analysis of France, Russia and China*, Cambridge University Press, Cambridge.

—— 1985: 'Bringing the State Back in: Current Research' in, Evans, P.B., Rueschemeyer, D. & Skocpol, T. (eds.), *Bringing the State Back In*, Cambridge University Press, Cambridge.

Skully, M.T. & Viksnins, G.J. 1987: *Financing East Asia's Success*, St. Martin's, New York.

Skully, M.T. 1985: *ASEAN Financial Co-operation: Developments in Banking Finance & Insurance*, St. Martin's Press, New York.

Smith, T.B. 1973: 'The Study of Policymaking in Developing Nations', *Policy Studies Journal*, vol. 1, no. 4, (Summer).

Soedjatmoko, 1983: 'Sistem Politik dan Pembangunan dalam Agenda Penelitian Asia, Sebuah Renungan' in his, *Dimensi Manusia dalam Pembangunan*, LP3ES, Jakarta.

Soesastro, M. Hadi 1989: 'The Political Economy of Deregulation in Indonesia', *Asian Survey*, vol. 29, no. 9 (September).

Stepan, A. 1978: *The State and Society: Peru in Comparative Perspective*, Princeton University Press, Princeton.

—— 1985: 'State Power and the Strength of Civil Society in the Southern Cone of Latin America', in Evans, P.B., Rueschemeyer, D. & Skocpol, T. (eds.), *Bringing the State Back In*, Cambridge University Press, Cambridge.

Streek, W. & Schmitter, P.C. (eds.) 1985: *Beyond Market and State*, Sage Publications, London.

Sundhausen, U. 1989: 'Indonesia: Past and Present Encounters With Democracy' in, Diamond, L., Linz, J. & Lipset, S.M. (eds.), *Democracy in Developing Countries: Asia*, (vol. 3), Lynne Reiner Publishers, Boulder, Colorado

Swiss Re. 1987: 'World Insurance 1985', *Sigma*, (journal of Swiss Reinsurance Pty Ltd) no. 5, (May).

Thee Kian Wie & Kunion Yoshihara 1987: 'Foreign and Domestic Capital in Indonesian Industrialization', *Journal of Southeast Asian Studies*, (Kyoto), vol. 24, no. 4 (March).

Thoolen, H. (ed.) 1987: *Indonesia and the Rule of Law: Twenty Years of 'New Order' Government*, International Commission of Jurists, Frances Pinter, London.

Tobacco and Plant Fibre Research Institute 1988: 'Program Nasional Penelitian Tanaman Serat Buah 1988–1995', Report prepared for the Department of Agriculture's *Review Program Penelitian dan Pengembangan Tanaman Industri*, Bogor (March).

Trythall, I.R. 1977: 'The Drug Industry in Indonesia', *Drug and Cosmetic Industry*, (New York) vol. 120, no. 4 (April).

United Nations Centre on Transnational Corporations 1984: *Transnational Corporations In The Pharmaceutical Industry Of Developing Countries*, United Nations, New York.

Urry, J. 1981: *The Political Economy of Capitalist Societies*, MacMillan, London.

W.H.O. 1977: *The Selection of Essential Drugs*, W.H.O. Technical Report Series (Geneva) no. 615.

—— 1979: *The Selection of Essential Drugs*, W.H.O. Technical Report Series (Geneva) no. 641.

Wanandi, Biantoro 1987: 'Dampak Resesi Ekonomi Terhadap Pengembangan Program Kesehatan Rakyat Dan Farmasi Di Indonesia', *Varia Farmasi*, (Jakarta) no. 71 (January–February).

Ward, K. 1974: *The 1971 Election in Indonesia: An East Java Case Study*, Monash Papers on Southeast Asia, no. 2, Centre for Southeast Asian Studies, Monash University, Melbourne.

Watson, C.W. 1985: *State and Society in Indonesia: Three Papers*, Occasional Paper no. 18, Centre for Southeast Asian Studies, University of Kent at Canterbury.

Weatherbee, D.E. 1985: 'Indonesia in 1984: Pancasila, Politics and Power', *Asian Survey*, vol. XXV, no. 2, (February).

Weiner, M. & Huntington, S.P. (eds.) 1987: *Understanding Political Development*, Little, Brown & Co., Boston.

Wibisono, Christianto 1987: 'Efisensi Industri Asuransi Indonesia', *Informasi*, (Pusat Data Business Indonesia) vol. 89, (July).

—— 1988: 'Siapa Raja Pers Indonesia', *Swasembada*, vol. 12, no. III, (April).

Wibisono, Makrim 1987: 'The Political Economy of the Indonesian Textile Industry Under the New Order,' Ph.D. thesis in the Graduate School of Ohio State University.

—— 1989: 'The Politics of Indonesian Textile Policy: The Interests of Government Agencies and the Private Sector', *Bulletin of Indonesian Economic Studies*, vol. 25, no. 1 (April).

Willner, A.R. 1970: 'The Neotraditional Accommodation to Political Independence: The Case of Indonesia', in Pye, L.W. (ed.), *Cases in Comparative Politics*, Little Brown & Co., Boston.

Wilson, G.K. 1981: *Interest Groups in the United States*, Oxford University Press, Oxford.

Winters, J.A. 1988: 'The Rise of Capital: a Review Essay', *Indonesia*, no. 45 (April).

World Bank. 1986: *Indonesia: Adjusting to Lower Oil Revenues*, Jakarta.

—— 1986: *Indonesia: Policies and Prospects for Non-Oil Exports*, Jakarta.

—— 1987: *Indonesia: Strategy for Economic Recovery*, Jakarta.

—— 1987: *The Indonesian Textile Industry*, Jakarta.

Wyke, A. 1987: 'Pharmaceuticals: Harder Going' (special survey), *The Economist*, London, (7 February).

Ziegler, C.E. 1986: 'Issue Creation and Interest Groups in Soviet Environmental Policy: The Applicability of the State Corporatist Model', *Comparative Politics*, vol. 18, no. 2 (January).

Zysman, J. 1983: *Governments, Markets and Growth: Financial Systems and the Politcs of Industrial Change*, Cornell University Press, Ithaca, N.Y.

Index